16.00
sch.

PS
221
F69   French,
         The twenties: fiction, poe-
         try, drama.

                    76-105

Date Due

		JUL	2000
		JUN	2004
		JUL	09
		JUL	X X 2015

PRINTED IN U.S.A.

The Twenties :
fiction, poetry, drama

The Twenties

fiction, poetry, drama

Edited by Warren French

everett / edwards, inc.
post office box 1060 / deland, florida 32720

SIGNIFICANT · EDUCATIONAL · MATERIALS ·

FIRST EDITION

Library of Congress Cataloging in Publication Data

French, Warren G   1922-
    The twenties.

    Includes index.
      1. American Literature—20th century—History and criticism—Addresses, essays, lectures.
1. Title
PS221.F69   810'.9'0052   74-24534
ISBN 0-912112-05-0

Table of Contents

About the Editor

WARREN FRENCH is a Professor of English at Indiana University, but he spends as much time as possible in a New England retreat. In what seems another life, he served as Chairman of the English Departments at the University of Missouri-Kansas City and Indiana University-Purdue University at Indianapolis, after making his way through teaching positions at the Universities of Mississippi, Kentucky, and Florida, Stetson University and Kansas State University. He has also been a summer visiting lecturer at Appalachian State College, the University of Wisconsin-Madison, the State University of New York College at New Paltz, and Dalhousie University, Halifax. *The Twenties* is the dozenth book he has written or edited. Besides others in the "decades" series — *The Thirties, The Forties* and *The Fifties,* he has written three books for the Twayne United States Authors Series, *John Steinbeck* (originally published in 1961 and completely rewritten in 1974), *Frank Norris,* and *J. D. Salinger.* His major work is *The Social Novel at the End of an Era* (1966), an intensive study of important American fiction at the end of the 1930s. He has also written *Season of Promise: Spring Fiction, 1967* and *A Filmguide to "The Grapes of Wrath"* and edited *A Companion to "The Grapes of Wrath"* and *American Winners of the Nobel Literary Prize* (with Walter Kidd). He has edited the "Current Bibliography" in *Twentieth Century Literature* and contributed review-essays since 1966 to the annual volumes of *American Literary Scholarship.* He is President of the John Steinbeck Society of America and a former director of the Midwest Modern Language Association. He has served on the editorial boards of the *Midcontinent American Studies Journal* and *College Composition and Communication,* and he is serving a four-year term on the editorial board of *American Literature.* His permanent address is Cornish Flat, New Hampshire, 03746.

xi

Introduction

Another book about the American literature of the 1920s? Many excellent studies from Frederick J. Hoffman's *The Twenties* to Malcolm Bradbury's *The American Novel of the Nineteen Twenties* already exist. Is there more to be said?

First, this book is not an entirely new survey of the rich writing of the decade that may have been one of the most significant in American literary history, but an expansion of a collection of essays on the literature of the twenties that launched this press a decade ago. The subsequent books on the literature of the next three decades are more elaborate in format. With these completed, we wished to go back and expand the book on the twenties into a comparable companion volume.

So much has been written, however, about the paradoxical age of jazz and prohibition—when the conflicting expansive and repressive elements in American culture underwent their climatic confrontation—that no collection of even the most insightful miscellaneous essays about its varied literature can serve any useful purpose. Such an investigation must shed light on the period from a particular, meaningful perspective.

Surprisingly, despite the general acclamation of T. S. Eliot's *The Waste Land* as the emblematic or keystone work of this period, we could not discover that so far there had been a comprehensive study of the acceptance or rejection of the concept of "the waste land" as a suitable and adequate description of Western culture after World War I. Had the ubiquitous lamentation and denunciation of this "waste land" served to spur reclamation efforts or simply—as such a too long unacknowledged counter-force as William Carlos Williams claimed—reduced the visionaries who should shape our cultural growth to the paralysis and despair that affirmed William Butler Yeats's observation in "The Second Coming" that "The best lack all conviction, while the worst/Are filled with passionate intensity?"

This volume was originally planned to appear in 1972 as a commemorative tribute on the fiftieth anniversary of the appearance of Eliot's epic. While this intention could not be realized, the contributors are pleased to be able to offer it as a follow-up to the publication of Valerie Eliot's edition of the original manuscripts of *The Waste Land*—embodying Ezra Pound's and Vivian Eliot's suggestions for revisions—which gives us fresh perspectives on this focal work of a period that was attempting to build a new world on the ruins of an old.

While this book follows the plan of its predecessor on the 1920s, it deviates from the subsequent volumes on the 30s, 40s and 50s, by including several essays on key authors, especially the regrettably neglected Ring Lardner, whose work provides actually a colloquial counterpart to Eliot's. This book, in fact, includes several books-within-books—the group of essays on Faulkner as a "waste land" writer and on the "anti-Eliot" poets (Crane, Williams, Jeffers) constitute substantial monographs in themselves.

The earlier "decades" books have also included only material written especially for them. This book contains some essays, like Max Haperen's "How to Read a Canto," that are revised from the earlier book on the twenties, since their relevancy appears undiminished and they contribute to the fulfillment of the present thematic design. James E. Miller, Jr.'s essay on William Faulkner's *Sanctuary* is also abridged from a longer study of this novel in *The Individual and the Community: Variations on a Theme in American Literature*, edited by Kenneth H. Baldwin and David Kirby for the Duke University Press.

Two things we have not attempted: a detailed analysis of Ezra Pound's work and influence upon Eliot during the decade and an extended history of the Harlem Renaissance. The appearance recently of Hugh Kenner's *The Pound Era* and Nathan Irvin Huggins' *The Harlem Renaissance* would render such enterprises nugatory; and these two landmark studies should be read as imperative complements to this book. Much attention, on the other hand, is devoted to our Nobel laureates—Faulkner, Hemingway, Steinbeck—as "waste land" authors, since their responses to the crises of the 1930s and 1940s have often obscured their beginnings as world-weary authors of the decade dominated by Eliot. The Harlem Renaissance, furthermore, poses a different set of problems from those investigated here. Although American Blacks in the twenties surely lived in a "waste land," they did not see it as springing from the same sources or being of the same nature as the one that tormented Eliot. We do include two essays by a perceptive Black scholar that concern two long-neglected Black works of the twenties—one, Jean Toomer's *Cane*, in the Eliot tradition (perhaps the most potent presentation of that tradition in terms of the dilemma of the American Black); the other, Langston Hughes's *Not Without Laughter* in the William Carlos Williams tradition that has begun to gain favor as Eliot's influence has declined.

Like its predecessors, this book is the work of a group of scholar-friends, who may not agree with each other, but who are willing to listen to each other sympathetically. We are pleased that this is the work of at least two generations of scholars, some of whom have been students of others, and again that at least two of our essays are by British students of American culture.

Among us we hope to have conveyed some sense of the way in which sensitive artists responded to the disillusioned concept of the United States of the 1920s as a "waste land"—the ultimate betrayal, in the words of F. Scott Fitzgerald (whose *The Great Gatsby* remains the consummate expression of the frivolous hopes and ponderous disappointments of the era), of Western man's being "compelled into an aesthetic contemplation he neither understood nor desired"— and also of the way in which visionary artists continued to insist, despite their rueful observations, that man should measure up to what Fitzgerald called "his capacity for wonder."

A final note: While this book was at the typesetter's a number of commentaries on the "making" of *The Waste Land* appeared. Only Lyndall Gordon's *"The Waste Land* Manuscript" (*American Literature,* January, 1974, pp. 557-70) seems to me to require notice. While it would have been enormously useful to have this complex and valuable analysis available as I was composing the "postscript" to my original article, I can find only that Professor Gordon's disclosures serve to confirm some of my speculations. That "Gerontion" was once contemplated as "a prelude" to *The Waste Land* seems to establish its occupying the crucial place that I assigned it in the development of Eliot's thought and art and also to explain the absence at its conclusion of the ameliorating note that would be provided by the longer poem. Professor Gordon's remark that at Lausanne "Eliot shifted the emphasis of his poem from personal case history to cultural disease" brilliantly puts into a few words the refutation I have undertaken of seeing the poem as only "a personal grouse." While I agree with Professor Gordon's conclusion that Eliot, "like many autobiographers . . . compelled attention by presenting himself as a child of the times, with the result that readers overlooked the would be saint," I think that he does push his argument too far when he finds it "crucial" to see *The Waste Land* and "indeed all of Eliot's subsequent work" in the context of the withdrawn "The Death of Saint Narcissus," the "Martyr's tale" of "an unsuccessful saint." "The Hollow Men" still strikes me as a voicing of unredeemed despair — the very reason for the existence of this poem at a time that Eliot was publishing few, as I have argued earlier, seems to have been to reflect the bottom

point of his disillusionment. *Ash Wednesday,* as its structure
suggests, seems to me not a re-assertion of faith but a return
to faith after a wandering in the void.

August, 1974

The Age of Eliot:
The Twenties as Waste Land

Warren French

The 1920s were not greeted with enthusiasm by the remaining devotees of the classical cultural tradition. "Things fall apart," William Butler Yeats observed in 1921, sensing the end of an epoch. Indeed, they did. The beast that slouched toward the New Bethlehem threatened to be "rough" indeed on cultivated sensibilities—"uncouth" would be the word for a decade during which both skirts and stock prices rose with an unwonted rapidity that a truly intricately sensitive machine would have seen portended disaster.

Before 1900, "higher education"—except in a few narrowly technical institutions—was likely to mean the study of Greek and Latin—the handing down from one fastidious torch-bearer to another of the brittle fragments of our classical heritage. This tradition had been pretty well shattered in the United States before World War I as classical studies were dethroned by the "business interests" that supported our universities and looked upon them as training grounds for a future managerial class rather than as Brahmin refuges.

The classics hung on a bit longer in Europe, but suffered a fatal blow when most of the young Universitarians who would have been the classicists of the future—displaying rare sensibility and little sense—hastened to enlist as junior officers in

World War I and were among the first battle casualties.
Reginald Pound explains in *The Lost Generation of 1914* that
in the first months of the War, England alone lost "6 peers, 16
baronets, 6 knights, 164 companions of orders of chivalry, 95
sons of peers, 82 sons of baronets, 34 sons of knights;" as a
result, Pound comments, "culture bearers of the European
tradition were being extinguished every day; lamps that could
never be lighted again....On every field of battle there were
casualties that devitalized the republics of learning and letters,
the creative arts and crafts, constructive thought, the sanity of
nations."

Their survivors were perhaps, however, even worse off than
those who died to preserve their chivalric fantasies, because
those who tried to rebuild the Western World after World War
I experienced a profound disillusionment and despair that T.
S. Eliot especially dramatized in *The Waste Land*. Ezra Pound
wrote in "E. P. Ode pour L'Election de son Sépulchre"—
bitterly lamenting the loss of influence of the classical
tradition—"The age demanded an image/Of its accelerated
grimace." Eliot's distinction rests largely upon his providing
that image.

Actually Eliot did not conjure up the single most
memorable picture of the "waste land" of the 1920s; that is
found in F. Scott Fitzgerald's *The Great Gatsby*. The narrator
describes the landscape that separates the bustling, corrupt
city from the decadent, pseudo-manorial countryside:

> About half way between West Egg and New York the motor
> road hastily joins the railroad and runs beside it for a quarter
> of a mile, so as to shrink away from a certain desolate area of
> land. This is a valley of ashes—a fantastic farm where ashes
> grow like wheat into ridges and hills and grotesque gardens;
> where ashes take the forms of houses and chimneys and rising
> smoke and, finally, with a transcendent effort, of ash-grey men
> who move dimly and already crumbling through the powdery
> air.

Fitzgerald flashes past the place on huddling cars and trains;
Eliot plunges in to provide the Baedeker.

Actually "waste land" stood for a variety of grim things during the 1920s. Most pointedly and poignantly the phrase summoned up the "no-man's-land" between the trenches of the opposing armies in World War I, devoid of life, pockmarked with craters from spent artillery shells, where indeed only corpses sprouted in the powdery air. This life-denying belt brought home to the world the meaninglessly destructive and degenerative force of mechanized warfare.

As Fitzgerald's description makes us realize, "waste land" also described those areas in and especially around our great cities where the detritus of an industrial civilization was piling up—ashes from the ovens, oil waste, decaying garbage, the vast litter of sensational newspapers and ticker-tape parades for killer heroes. The "dust piles" of Dickens' *Our Mutual Friend* now spread over acres and threatened to contaminate our air and streams and choke us all with the noxious odors that arose from the decaying or slowly burning wastes. In our frenzy to industrialize our land, electrify our cities, and make every man a millionaire, we had turned the green belts that should have surrounded and revitalized our cities into uninhabitable, even unvisitable waste lands.

Still in a physical sense, the phrase "waste land" reminds us of the ice and sand deserts that lay just beyond the last outposts of our Western civilization—waste lands that even a technology that has conquered the moon has failed to master. The Indo-European culture that originated in ancient Persia, Greece, and Rome had thrived on migration, conquest, and the domestication of hitherto wild lands. By 1890, however, restless Western man had reached in the North, South, and West the limits of the domesticable wilderness. Beyond lay the fiery deserts of the American West and Mexico, of the Sahara, the ice-barrens of Canada and Siberia. No new worlds remained to be conquered except by moving bloodily against the less technologically advanced cultures of Asia and Africa— a process that Joseph Conrad warned against at the turn of the century in *Heart of Darkness.* Western man's momentum was thus arrested by his reaching the boundaries of lands that were unassimilable wastes or that could be assimilated only by laying waste to their "savage" occupants. This arrest of physical motion induced in Western man the profound depression that triggered such theorizing as Spengler's *Decline of the West* (the German title might even more provocatively and colloquially be translated "That Evening World Goes Down")—a depression suggesting that the physical exertion had resulted from an overpowering fear of really looking inside himself and coming to know himself.

"Waste Land" also had a spiritual meaning in the 1920s. Even the world that was bounded by dust-heaps and deserts seemed to many a waste land, littered with the dead fragments of dead civilizations and the fading hopes of dying religions. Much of Europe—especially of France—was a waste land of shattered cathedrals, testaments to the incapacity of man's spiritual cravings to cope with his bloodlust. Much of England and the United States were festering tenements—rickety towers of Babel, thrown up during the optimistic twilight of the expansive Victorian age, now overcrowded with ill-fed and ill-paid people and crumbling before the eyes of landlords indifferent to everything but extracting as much profit as possible from their investments.

Wherever one turned, in short, one found waste. Even in those oases of the gilded twenties where the old and new rich lived in superficial splendor and spent the nights in revelry, the waste was appalling. Fitzgerald gives us a glimpse behind the scene in Gatsby's mansion: "Every Friday five crates of oranges and lemons arrived from a fruiterer in New York— every Monday these same oranges and lemons left his back door in a pyramid of pulpless halves. There was a machine in the kitchen which could extract the juice of two hundred oranges in half an hour if a little button was pushed two hundred times by a butler's thumb." Our technological advances had indeed produced an uncountable myriad of such buttons that could extract the juices not just from oranges, but from men, producing "pulpless halves" faster than our slow-moving bureaucracies could clear away the debris.

Throughout the whole gray or glittering world *waste* in physical, intellectual or spiritual manifestations was everywhere evident.

The uncannily exact relationship between Eliot's "Waste Land" period and the 1920s has been surprisingly little noted, despite the heaps of speculation about his work. Exactly in 1920 the poet began his public descent into the waste land; in 1930 he announced the beginning of his ascension from it. For exactly the tumultuous and troubled decade of false prosperity—marked by the triumph of chaos abroad and bigotry in the United States—Eliot made his pilgrimage through the arid land, providing the few contemplative members of a generally sensual society with the poetic metaphor that brought their own distraught vision into focus.

Eliot had already published a number of short poems before 1920, including the celebrated "The Love Song of J. Alfred Prufrock" and "Portrait of a Lady." He had also created and just about dismissed the figure of "Sweeney" as an embodiment of the grossness he deplored ("The lengthened shadow of a man/ Is history, said Emerson/ Who had not seen the silhouette/ Of Sweeney straddled in the sun"). As M. C. Bradbrook observes in her *T.S. Eliot,* "Eliot's early poetry... depicts in ironic and epigrammatic terseness the little anxieties, social embarrassments, and unacknowledged vacuity of polite society in Boston and London. The world he displays is the world of Henry James's novels...." Eliot was writing during World War I in the dandyish tradition of the turn-of-the-century decadents, preoccupied with delicate satirizations of stylized puppets like "Aunt Helen" and the readers of the *Boston Evening Transcript,* as well as the tortured exploration of the inner consciousness of finicky people like J. Alfred Prufrock, who measured out their lives in "coffee spoons." Only in the ominous "Sweeney Among the Nightingales" had Eliot broken out of the bounds of his exhausted, introverted aristocratic society to consider the larger issues of man's alienation from the natural world ("The nightingales are singing near/ The Convent of the Sacred Heart,/ And sang

within the bloody wood/ When Agamemnon cried aloud");
but this cryptic poem remains a challenge to explicators.

In 1920, however, Eliot emerged as a cultural spokesman
when he headed his second thin collection of poems (*Ara Vus
Prec*) with the only one of the group that had not been
previously published, "Gerontion," a work different from any
that had preceded it—the forerunner of *The Waste Land* and
the most darkly pessimistic of all Eliot's poems.

The speaker in this dramatic monologue is no longer a
fastidious time-server like Prufrock or a waspish ironist
surveying his provincial society with disdain, but an old man
who is unmistakably an allegorical representative of Western
culture—dried-out, dull-headed, devoid of hope—sitting in a
"decayed house" being read to by a boy. The setting is a
"waste land": "Rocks, moss, stonecrop, iron, merds." Gerontion laments the passing of the once youthful and vital
Christian tradition into alien hands ("Hakagawa, bowing
among the Titians") and the resorting to dubious spiritual
practices ("Madame de Tornquist, in the dark room/ Shifting
the candles") because of man's being out of harmony with any
kind of natural cyclical rhythm such as the transcendentalists
had praised. History, Gerontion observes, "Gives too late/
What's not believed in..../"Gives too soon/ Into weak hands,
what's thought can be dispensed with/ Till the refusal
propagates a fear." "Unnatural vices/ Are fathered by our
heroism. Virtues/ Are forced upon us by our impudent
crimes," he discovers; thus because of man's inability to
respond passionately with the appropriate acceptance or
rejection to events, "what is kept," he observes at the climax
of his meditation, "must be adulterated." The next-to-last
stanza envisions this hopelessly fragmented world that man—
with his conscious mind—has created being "whirled / Beyond
the circuit of the shuddering Bear/ in fractured atoms," while
the consciousless spider and weevil go about their timeless
operations.

Two years later Eliot followed up this hopeless portrayal
of "The Decline of the West" with *The Waste Land*.

The first section of the poem, "The Burial of the Dead" is basically a reportrayal of the world of "Gerontion," with the added ironic twist that the timeless operations of the natural world make man's self-created plight particularly hard to bear ("April is the cruellest month, breeding/ Lilacs out of the dead land...."). Again we see the fragmented society, the bleak landscape ("you know only/ A heap of broken images, where the sun beats,/ And the dead tree gives no shelter...."), and the sub-rosa resorting of the Mrs. Equitones of the fashionable world to forbidden arts ("Madame Sosostris, famous clairvoyante,/.../Is known to be the wisest woman in Europe..."). The Western city has become "unreal," site only of an unending procession of the dead—the physical victims of World War I, the intellectual victims of exhausted philosophies that had not been able to prevent this catastrophe, and the spiritual victims of the adulteration of the springtime promise of Christianity.

This first section of the poem offers a panoramic view of the Waste Land, what would be called in a film "a long shot." In the second part of the poem, "A Game of Chess," there is little forward movement; rather—to continue the cinematic comparison—the author moves his camera in for two "close-up" shots of scenes representative of the society portrayed in the first section. Eliot is actually employing a cinematic technique that intrigued many writers in the twenties and thirties (Steinbeck used it extensively in *The Grapes of Wrath*) of following a general view of a landscape (usually—in those years—blighted) with a close-up view of one small group of people living in this land. In the first half of the second section of *The Waste Land*, we see that the wealthy, aristocratic class upon whom the Western world has traditionally relied for leadership has been reduced to a languid, neurotic, game-playing group. ("'My nerves are bad to-night.'" "'What are you thinking of? What thinking? What?'" "'I think we are in rats' alley/ Where the dead men lost their bones.'") The bejeweled members of this elegant society have lost touch with the classical culture that was the source of their vitality; the "inviolable voice" of the nightingale is to them but a "'Jug

Jug"—the scenes on their walls but "withered stumps of time."
Isolated from nature, their lives have become meaningless
routines: "The hot water at ten./ And if it rains, a closed car at
four./ And we shall play a game of chess."

The scene shifts abruptly from the luxurious room with a
"coffered ceiling" to a lower-class pub, whose proprietor is
trying to get his reluctant customers to leave at closing time.
"Hurry up please its time," he cries, intimating—within the
portentous context of the poem—that more is ending than this
one sodden evening. The conversation of the pub-crawlers
indicates that there is no more life or vitality among them than
among the aristocrats. ("Well, if Albert won't leave you alone,
there it is, I said,/ What you get married for if you don't want
children?") The very act of creating life has become a burden
and a bore.

This second part of the second section of *The Waste Land*
indicates Eliot's lack of faith in some of the panaceas that
were being prescribed for social ills in the 1920s. While nearly
everyone agreed that—as Eliot indicated in the first part of "A
Game of Chess"—the old aristocractic leaders of Western
society had outlived their usefulness (few but the families
themselves lamented the fall of the Hapsburgs, Hohenzollerns,
and Romanoffs), some theorists—especially Marxists— saw
hope in a future dominated by a liberated proletariat. Eliot,
however, had no confidence in the efficacy of simply putting a
different class as exhausted and corrupt as the upper; the fault
lie in our whole society, not in a particular ruling element
(thus he implicitly rejects the frequent arguments during
World War I and II that England and its allies had no quarrel
with enemy peoples but only particular leaders.)

The third section of the poem functions in the same way
as the similarly placed fifth section of "Gerontion" that begins
with the question, "After such knowledge, what forgiveness?"
and laments man's seeming inability to use his consciousness
to direct the course of history. In *The Waste Land*, however,
instead of asking questions prosily as in "Gerontion," Eliot
presents them dramatically through a series of tableaux that

conjure up a vision of a past better than the present, comparing the resplendent Thames of the Age of Elizabeth I with the "oil and tar" sweating river of the industrial twentieth century and suggesting that the joy of the past survives only in rare enclaves where un-self-conscious people meet to celebrate life ("I can sometimes hear/ Beside a public bar in Lower Thames Street/ The pleasant whining of a mandoline/ And a clatter and a chatter from within/ Where fishmen lounge at noon.") The climactic question in "Gerontion"—Why should one struggle to keep one's passion, since "what is kept must be adulterated?" is posed again in *The Waste Land* at the climactic point at which the monologuist reveals himself as the blind prophet Tiresias through the grubby incident of the visit of "the young man carbuncular" to a typist's flat.

The difference between past and present is presented through Eliot's manipulation of one of the most adroitly used of the many allusions to "traditional" poetry in his work, a parody of a song from Oliver Goldsmith's novel *The Vicar of Wakefield.* Goldsmith's version runs: "When lovely woman stoops to folly,/ And finds too late that men betray,/ What charm can soothe her melancholy,/ What art can wash her guilt away?/ The only art her guilt to cover,/ To hide her shame from every eye,/ To give repentance to her lover,/ And wring his bosom—is to die." Eliot compresses the two quatrains into one: "When lovely woman stoops to folly and/ Paces about her room again, alone,/ She smoothes her hair with automatic hand,/ And puts a record on the gramophone." In the past there were standards of decorum; actions did have consequences. Today there are no standards and no consequences; but the result of this liberation is not that man has become happier, but that he has lost sensitivity. His life has become purely mechanical.

Curiously, we cannot be sure that the song Eliot parodies should actually be taken at face value as the expression of the philosophy of the age that produced it. The traditional society—as Goldsmith himself lamented in "The Deserted

Village" (in many ways a precursor of *The Waste Land*)— was already decaying and breaking up when he wrote. *The Vicar of Wakefield* may be read as a caution against un-self-conscious innocence as a vice rather than as a tribute to it as a virtue. Even the rendition of the original song by a girl who fancies herself to have been seduced is preceded by the author's wry observation that "melancholy which is excited by objects of pleasure or inspired by sounds of harmony soothes the heart instead of corroding it," surely suggesting the same kind of evasive self-indulgence that Eliot castigates throughout his early poems.

Considered out of context, however—as it almost always is—the poem recalls a perhaps hypothetical time when people experienced and expressed strong passions. Eliot is despondent over having lost this capacity for passion and with it the significant distinction between man and machine. Widespread fears were expressed after World War I in plays like Capek's *R.U.R.* and films like Fritz Lang's *Metropolis* that robots would indeed replace men; Eliot's *The Waste Land*, with its suggestion that man is robotizing himself, is not an isolated meditation, but part of this international movement.

I must dwell still longer on this climactic moment in the poem because it serves to illustrate also another of Eliot's principal motives and to pull together the sometimes seemingly unrelated parts of the whole. Unless one does recognize the allusion to the Goldsmith song in this passage, the ironic impact of Eliot's strategy is lost and the lines seem simply a clever, cynical thrust in the then-popular manner of Ogden Nash ("Candy is dandy, but liquor is quicker") and Dorothy Parker. If the tradition which includes the Goldsmith poem is not alive for the reader—if he does not himself experience a passion for art—the lines alluded to are simply another "withered stump of time"—all that comes across is the "jug jug" that dirty ears hear. The allusions that Eliot incorporates into his epic of a subverted consciousness are not pedantic displays of miscellaneous erudition, but are rather themselves illustrations that without a knowledge and understanding of a tradition one has no perspective for judging the present. The thesis of "The Fire Sermon"—as the third part of the poem is called—is that the burning down of the past diminishes, perhaps destroys, man's capacity for genuine passion—an argument that would have struck specially forcefully observers in the early 1920s of the burned-out landscapes of Europe that might well recall the ancient city of Carthage summoned up at the end of the "sermon."

The very short fourth section serves to provide a counter movement to correct an unbalance that has been developing in the poem. So strong has been the emphasis upon dryness (the condition, of course, that is most propitious for spontaneous conflagration) and on destruction by fire and the counter-emphasis upon water as the redeeming, rejuvenating element that an almost complete fire/water dichotomy has developed, obscuring the principle finally to be emphasized that any force is dangerous in excess. As early as the first section of the poem, Madame Sosostris has reminded her clients to "fear death by water"; in the story of Phlebas in the fourth section, Eliot succinctly reminds us that water can destroy as well as create. (The world was once virtually destroyed by flood.) There is an even more specific warning in the dead sailor's having been a Phoenician. The Phoenicians are famed as the first great traders, reputedly having even devised the alphabet as a convenience in business transactions. Living in a narrow fertile belt along the sea in a region that is chiefly desert, the Phoenicians had to take to the sea in order to advance their trade, thereby risking the death by water that the poem warns against. The commercial motives of the Phoenicians are pointed out by the dead Phlebas's having forgotten not only "the cry of gulls" (perhaps a double entendre), but also "the profit and loss." People often take dangerous chances in pursuit of financial gains. This section of the poem implores "Gentile or Jew" in the modern world to "consider" that the Phoenicians' extinction may have been the result of their avid search for profits causing them to be insufficiently respectful of such natural forces as the sea. Perhaps Eliot's injunction

12   WARREN FRENCH

even conjured up in early readers' minds charges circulating
after World War I that the vastly destructive conflict had been
promoted principally by munitions makers greedy for gain and
recalled the many "deaths by water" resulting from the
sinking of the passenger liner *Lusitania*—an event that did
much to precipitate the entry of the United States into the
war. (The Germans justified their sinking of the ship by since
verified claims that it was being used to transport contraband
munitions.)

The fifth section of the poem starts out much like the final
section of "Gerontion" that contains the self-portrait of "an
old man driven by the Trades/ To a sleepy corner." His
condition is well described by the lines in the later poem, "We
who were living are now dying/ With a little patience." Eliot
goes on to paint a quite specific picture of the "Decline of the
West" like that Archibald MacLeish would subsequently
provide in "You, Andrew Marvell": "Falling Towers/ Jerusalem Athens Alexandria/ Vienna London." This is no random
cruise conniver's itinerary for jaded tourists. That the five have
special significance is suggested by the omission of Rome,
Byzantium, and Paris, which would surely be included if the
list is simply of the most important centers of Western culture.

What the first four cities listed share is that each played
some specially important role in the intellectual and spiritual
development of Western man—in the emergence of the Western
consciousness—and each was subsequently in some fashion
destroyed. Cities that were only politically significant are
omitted. Jerusalem had been the wellspring of the Judaeo-
Christian tradition, but since the destruction of the Hebrew
temple it had been reduced to a dusty provincial town. Athens
had been the fountainhead of the great philosphy and drama
that had mingled with the theological tradition emanating
from Jerusalem to give Western culture its counter-balancing
intellectual tradition; but Athens had been reduced to rubble
and had been occupied for centuries by heathens. There had
been pooled in Alexandria's library the greatest collection
early writings in the Western world; but the library itself and

much of our classical heritage had been reduced to ashes. It had been at the siege of Vienna in 1529 that the furthest westward wave of the flowing tide of the Ottoman armies had been turned back, an event that is generally credited with preserving Western Christendom; for had the Turks occupied this central city of the traditional Holy Roman Empire, the Western world might have been irreparably fragmented. World War I had accomplished the task the Turks could not of reducing this once glorious imperial city (center of one of the largest but least homogeneous empires in pre-World War I Europe) to the shadowy capital of a prostrate and inconsequential nation.

The inclusion of London in this list shows the warp of Eliot's sympathy. As his subsequent conversion to Anglo-Catholicism suggests, he looked upon the British capital rather than Rome as the inheritor of the spiritual tradition of Jerusalem and Vienna, as well as (he is probably thinking quite specifically of the British Museum and the nearby Oxford libraries) the central repository of the intellectual tradition of Athens and Alexandria. (In the early 1920s, too, the Roman Catholic pope was still essentially a political prisoner.) Clearly, too, a warning is intended that London can go the way of its four predecessors—a warning of a catastrophe nearly realized during the fire-bombings of World War II, after which the modern equivalents of the onrushing Ottomans were at last turned back by a battle in "the violet air."

After the recital of the list of cities, the poem takes at last a different course from "Gerontion." In the earlier poem no hope is expressed that the fragmentation and dispersion of the Western tradition is not inevitable, that London will not indeed become a backwater like its predecessors. In the last lines of *The Waste Land*, however, the thunder—indicative of the coming of the storm that may bring water to the parched land—speaks at last and suggests that there may be a way out of the waste land if Western man can master the three techniques prescribed in the Hindu *Brihadaranyaka -Upanishad*—giving, sympathising, controlling. Our narrator is

not certain that recovery is possible: as the action ends
"London Bridge is falling down" (it has, in fact, lately been
put together again in a retirement colony in the desert wastes
of Arizona), and he sits among the fragments "shored against"
his ruins. Yet a promise exists in the venerable teachings of an
alien culture, and the poem ends not with the "thoughts of a
dry brain in a dry season," but with a prayer for peace.

At the moment that Eliot was composing *The Waste Land*
he served indeed as a spokesman for an entire world weary of
war and destruction. The winter of 1921-22 witnessed the
most noteworthy political effort to achieve the kind of
"control" that Eliot's poem finally commended. This was the
Limitations of Armaments Conference in Washington, D. C., as
a result of which the victorious allies of World War I agreed to
curtail naval construction and outlaw the use of poison gas and
attacks on merchant shipping.

The very month that *The Waste Land* appeared in *The
Criterion* (October, 1922), however, the alliance forged in
Washington began to break up as Mussolini's fascists seized
power in Italy. A year later the Beer Hall Putsch in Munich
launched Hitler's rise to power. The attempts to "sympathize"
and "control" had been short-lived indeed; Eliot's poetic
voicing of a promise for the world appeared at the very
moment that promise was fading.

Although the 1920s were one of Eliot's most productive
decades, he published comparatively little poetry after *The
Waste Land* until 1930. He was occupied principally with
literary criticism, and it is not my purpose to trace through his
essays the development of his intellectual, political and
religious positions that culminated in his announcement in
1928 in the preface to *For Lancelot Andrewes* that he was "a
royalist in politics, a classicist in literature, and an Anglo-Cath-
olic in religion," because my concern is with suggesting how
his relatively infrequent poetic utterances crystallized the
feelings of his age. Clearly, however, by the time that Eliot
made his famous confession of faith, he no longer was fully
representative of his era, since relatively few other intellectuals

would have accepted any of the three identifications and hardly any all of them.

During the mid-1920s, Eliot had moved steadily in a direction that turned him from functioning—probably unintentionally—as the most articulate poetic voice of first the despair and then the conscientious hope of Western society into—quite consciously—an outspoken promoter of causes that few others felt so strongly might provide solutions for the world's dilemma.

Eliot published relatively little poetry during the five years after the appearance of *The Waste Land*: only "The Hollow Men" and two fragments of *Sweeney Agonistes*, an "Aristophanic melodrama." These later somewhat overly arch efforts to resurrect the "twentieth century man" of his earlier poetry are of interest today principally as the first evidences of what was soon to become Eliot's preoccupation with poetry for the theatre. The writer apparently turned to lyric or epic forms after *The Waste Land* only when he sought to dramatize some major change in his thinking.

"The Hollow Men" might seem to belie this theory, for it may strike one as simply a compressed version of *The Waste Land*, another exploration of the "dead land" and its empty people. The poem moves, however, through similar scenes toward a drastically different conclusion from *The Waste Land*'s and manifests repudiation of faith in any possible promise evoked at the end of the earlier poem. The events in Europe in 1922 and 1923 must have shaken Eliot's perilous hold on any promising fragments to which he clung. "The Hollow Men" emanates not the tough-minded cynicism of earlier poems, but the anguish of a weary oracle who has seen his worst prophecies coming true.

"Gerontion" had offered us a picture of a world exploding. *The Waste Land* presented a picture of a world collapsing (though the poem held out a hope that the collapse might be averted). Both foresaw violent Armageddons. "The Hollow Men" ends, however, with the chant, *"This is the way the world ends/ Not with a bang but a whimper."* The poem portrays the world not fracturing violently (as an exasperated young man would tend to see it), but drying up (as an aging man might suppose). Eliot now sees the world not—as he had earlier seen it—as willful, unruly, violently greedy and meriting castigation, but as pathetic and needing compassion—a vision that leads him to seek a spiritual solution that he cannot yet find, although "The Hollow Men" ends with a broken prayer that is resumed in *Ash Wednesday*.

Conspicuously missing from "The Hollow Men" are any references to the sacred Hindu writings that had colored with hope the final lines of *The Waste Land*. Immediately after World War I, Eliot had joined the many Western artists who went questing "after strange gods" for solutions to humanity's problems apparently not available in our Western tradition. While others continued this quest that still goes on with renewed vigor today, Eliot drew back. "The Hollow Men" suggests why.

Not only the epigraph for the poem, "Mistah Kurtz—he dead," comes from Joseph Conrad's *Heart of Darkness;* so also do the title and the controlling image. Conrad's Marlow twice applies the term "hollow" to Kurtz— ". . . he was hollow at the core," "The shade of the original Kurtz frequented the bedside of the hollow sham." Marlow also twice uses images of hollowness to characterize other employees of the company attempting to exploit the dark lands—"perhaps there was nothing within him," he says of the manager and he calls a brick-maker "this papier-mâché Mephistopheles."

Kurtz had gone to Africa with the idea that he could civilize it by suppressing savage customs. "Each station should be like a beacon on the road towards better things," he had annoyed the other employees by preaching, "a center for trade of course, but also for humanizing, improving, instructing." But things had not worked out as he had envisioned. Marlow finds Kurtz wanting in "restraint"—"the wilderness had found him out early, and had taken on him a terrible vengeance for the fantastic invasion."

What this portrayal of Kurtz could have suggested to Eliot

is that there is a profound danger in becoming involved with alien cultures, even from the loftiest motives. The danger in attempting to apply oriental philosophies to occidental problems—Eliot might have supposed—is that their principles would have been wrenched out of the cultural contexts in which they could only be fully understood (a fear certainly justified by the many faddish uses to which Eastern religious thinking has been put at times in the Western world). However sound these speculations, Eliot did come to believe that the only available hope for Western man lie in his rediscovery of his own tradition. In "The Hollow Men," the poet expresses little hope that this rediscovery will occur; but he is clearly moving toward taking his next great step in "Ash-Wednesday."

The meaning that Eliot attached to the term "hollow" is a metaphysical, spiritual one. For an explanation, we turn again to Conrad. Marlow says of his resistance to the appeal of the savage rituals to which Kurtz has succumbed, "Principles won't do. Acquisitions, clothes, pretty rags—rags that would fly off at the first good shake. No; you want a deliberate belief." The statement is puzzling, since we tend to equate "principles" with "beliefs" as though people actually act upon the premises they articulate. "Principles," Conrad suggests and Eliot apparently agrees, are only superficial things like clothes. Unless a man is filled with a consciously understood and accepted belief, he is hollow. The difference, however, between a man's principles and his beliefs—if indeed he has any—cannot be determined by listening to what he says—however eloquently—but only by observing what he does.

In an effort to bridge this gap between "saying" and "doing," Eliot presents *Ash-Wednesday* not as an exhortation, but as the evocation of an individual's trying agonizingly to recapture "a deliberate belief"—to move from the defeatist despair of "Because I do not hope to turn again" to the timorously flickering optimism of "Although I do not hope to turn again."

Analyzing the elaborate structure of *Ash-Wednesday* is beyond my purpose here, because the poem—especially the

third section that describes the ascent away from the
temptations of the sensuous world—is not an impersonal
record of dissociation from temporality and an attempted
dissolution of the tormentingly contending individual self into
a timeless, formless whole, but an account of the speaker's
own turning from the rewards of the material world ("Desiring
this man's gift and that man's scope"—an initial echo of
Shakespeare's Renaissance world which Eliot had much
admired) to the pursuit of spiritual satisfaction. The key to
understanding the movement of the poem is one of the final
lines—"Teach us to care and not to care." The statement is not
so paradoxical as it first sounds, for it describes the ambigu-
ousness of a genuine passion. We must want to have things
happen—the kind of things, for example, that Conrad's Kurtz
thought he wanted to have happen when he went to
Africa—things that might better the external world; but we
must not want to have them happen for our own personal
gratification. We must care that they happen for others; but
we must not be selfishly concerned that we profit materially
from them. The change that accomplishment brings about for
us must be internal. Perhaps this rare state of mind finds its
most explicit literary embodiment in Lambert Strether's
statement to Maria Gostrey as Henry James's *The Ambassadors* ends, "That, you see, is my only logic. Not, out of the
whole affair, to have got anything for myself."

While *Ash-Wednesday* has never enjoyed the response
of *The Waste Land* (it has been neither so much discussed nor
imitated), it remains a much admired and extremely influential
poem. Though Eliot spoke in it for fewer of his contemporaries than in his earlier long poem, he did in *Ash Wednesday*
present the most moving and memorable embodiment in
modern literature of the travail of a soul aspiring to escape the
trammels of a materialistic world and achieve spiritual tran-
quility, just as he had earlier provided "The Age of the Waste
Land" with the most articulate outpouring of its despair.

What happened thereafter (except in *Four Quartets*, a
meditative work that lies beyond the scope of an essay that

concentrates on the poet's involvement in the contemporary, material world) is that Eliot, understandably humanly, failed to achieve the serene state of caring yet not caring and became oftentimes a polemicist.

No account of the shift in Eliot's positions during the 1920s as reflected in his poetry can be completed without considering one later group of poems, the choruses from *The Rock*, "a pageant play," to quote the title-page of the first edition, "written for performance at Sadler's Wells Theatre, 28 May-9 June, 1934, on behalf of the forty-five churches fund of the diocese of London." The proceeds of this fund were to be used to build the first new Anglican churches in London in the twentieth century, an action that Eliot and others saw as a hopeful sign of a religious renaissance.

The choruses which Eliot provided for the performance contain the most explicit poetic statement that he made of his religious statements, yet despite their admirable technical proficiency and felicitous wording, they are less frequently discussed than most of Eliot's poems. One reason for their neglect may be their very explicitness—their return to the "prosiness" of "Gerontion" in an age that had learned—ironically—from Eliot and his disciples to admire principally cryptic, imagist verse. The choruses from *The Rock* provide little occasion for dazzling displays of critics' interpretive skill. Another reason is probably the distaste of many even of Eliot's admirers for the vehemence with which he states uncustomarily provincial religious positions. It is difficult to universalize statements like "I journeyed to London, to the timekept city,/ Where the River flows, with foreign flotations,/ There I was told: we have too many churches,/ And too few chop-houses."

Embedded in a matrix of local references, however, are a series of statements that demonstrate that even following his "conversion," Eliot had no anticipation that a rigidly fixed order of things could be established—that Utopia is possible. Rather he sees that the experience of worldly man—"fallen man"—must be a series of recurrent cycles of birth, decay, and rebirth. "And the Church must be forever building, and always decaying, and always being restored," the chorus recites. Later it continues in Chorus VI—the philosophical heart of the pageant:

> It is hard for those who have never known persecution,
> And who have never known a Christian,
> To believe these tales of Christian persecution.
> It is hard for those who live near a Bank
> To doubt the security of their money.
> It is hard for those who live near a Police Station
> To believe in the triumph of violence.
> Do you think that the Faith has conquered the World
> And that lions no longer need keepers? . . .
> . . . the Son of Man was not crucified once for all,
> The blood of the martyrs was not shed once for all,
> The lives of the Saints not given once for all:
> But the Son of Man is crucified always
> And there shall be Martyrs and Saints.
> And if the blood of Martyrs is to flow on the steps
> We must first build the steps;
> And if the Temple is to be cast down
> We must first build the Temple.

There are two conspicuous differences between the views expressed here and those dramatized in *The Waste Land* and related poems. First, although there is talk of violence and destruction, there is no mention of an ending. The world of *The Rock* moves toward neither violent nor whimpering end; it is not a world without pain and violence, but it is a continuing world. Eliot still feels as in "Gerontion" that "what is kept must be adulterated," but he is no longer made despondent by this contemplation, for he has learned that man cannot expect to keep, but must learn constantly to remake. Expressing this view, he remains a universal spokesman for those who can enough disentangle themselves from immediate sensations to perceive recurrent patterns.

The other, more parochial difference, however, lies in his

new faith that there may be a way out of the waste land, but that it must be a specific way. "Men have left GOD not for other gods, they say, but for no god; and this has never happened before," rises the plaint in Chorus VII:

> That men both deny gods and worship gods, professing first Reason,
> And then Money, and Power, and what they call Life, or Race,
>   or Dialectic.
> The Church disowned, the tower overthrown, the bells upturned,
>   what have we to do
> But stand with empty hands and palms turned upwards
> In an age which advances progressively backwards?

Eliot has never before in his poetry so specifically condemned recognizable social and political forces. It is hard to acknowledge this querulous posturing as the work of a man who only a few years later could write in "East Coker"—"But perhaps neither gain nor loss./ For us, there is only the trying. The rest is not our business." Perhaps I can suggest the difference between Eliot's impatience with "Life, or Race, or Dialectic" as commitments by quoting in comparison the concluding meditation in Thornton Wilder's *The Eighth Day* on these concerns:

> There is much talk of a design in the arras. Some are certain they see it. Some see what they have been told to see. Some remember that they saw it once but have lost it. Some are strengthened by seeing a pattern wherein the oppressed and exploited of the earth are gradually emerging from their bondage. Some find strength in the conviction that there is nothing to see. Some

And the book ends with an uncompleted sentence—"only the trying," not an outburst against "an age which advances progressively backwards."

By the 1930s Eliot had become specifically a Christian poet. He was quite a catch for the Christians, for he had few equals; but he was no longer the central spokesman for the age that he had been in the 1920s when—deliberately or not—*The Waste Land* epitomized the shocked vision and tentative hopes that animated nearly all thoughtful persons in our culture. We

must also finally observe that it is to the Christian tradition
(Jerusalem and Vienna) that Eliot returns, not the classical
tradition (Athens and Alexandria) espoused by Ezra Pound
and mourned by Reginald Pound in *The Lost Generation of
1914*. Eliot descended into the waste land from the University,
but he ascended back into the church. "When we have built an
altar to the Invisible Light, we may set thereon the little lights
for which our bodily vision is made," the choruses from *The
Rock* end. Generally, he remained there. Although through
Four Quartets he transcends temporal concerns—". . . history
is a pattern/ Of timeless moments," he is back to earth once
more in *The Cocktail Party*

> . . . that world does not take the place of this one.
> Do you imagine that the Saint in the desert
> With spiritual evil always at his shoulder
> Suffered any less from hunger, damp, exposure,
> Bowel trouble, and the fear of lions,
> Cold of the night and heat of the day, then we should?

Even Eliot's shift late in life to writing poetry principally for
the theatre is difficult to interpret as not evincing an increasing
concern for moving an audience. Except fitfully, Eliot does
not later transcend the stance of concerned Christian that he
articulates in the choruses from *The Rock*. I remark this
stability of Eliot's position after 1930 here only to indicate
that he himself never does relapse back into "the waste land
despair" that he gave poetic voice for a single decade though it
continues to dominate half a century later the vision of other
writers and critics.

POSTSCRIPT

The original version of the preceding essay was delivered as
a lecture several years before the publication in 1971 of
Valerie Eliot's "Facsimile and Transcript of the Original
Drafts" of *The Waste Land*. In subsequently revamping my
speculations I have not taken this recently available material
into account, because my interest was in the "public poem" as

it was known to readers during the 1920s and 1930s. Although rumors had circulated for years that Ezra Pound had assisted Eliot in substantially condensing the poem, the original version was unavailable; and the reputation of *The Waste Land* rested upon the form in which it appeared when published in 1922.

Now that the original typescript is available, however, questions are bound to arise about the perspective into which it may thrust my interpretation or any other. The cuts are extensive (though less so than long rumored): the 692 lines of the final typescript have been cut by over one-third to 433. The excisions, however, are principally from the opening sections of the first, third, and fourth parts of the poem. Except in the third section, few internal cuts are made; and the fifth section—which Eliot valued most highly—was scarcely touched. The reduction of the 92 lines of the original fourth section to the last ten was the most drastic.

None of these excisions, however, seem to me to have changed the world-view that the poem reflects; and a contemplation of them after completing my essay has not led me to wish to make any changes in my interpretation of the point of view the poem dramatizes.

After readings of an earlier version of this essay, I have most often been questioned—understandably—about Eliot's statement quoted in the edition of the original manuscript, "Various critics have done me the honour to interpret the poem in terms of criticism of the contemporary world, have considered it, indeed, as an important bit of social criticism. To me it was only the relief of a personal and wholly insignificant grouse against life. . . ."

First one must observe that the statement was recorded by the poet's brother from a lecture delivered by Theodore Spencer, presumably quoting Eliot. We thus receive it at third hand. Such evidence would be thrown out of any court of law, especially when the testimony comes from a world-renowned man's inconspicuous relative passing on some gossip.

Nevertheless, I am perfectly willing—for argument's sake—to accept the assertion as Eliot's and to maintain that it does not in any way invalidate the statements that I have made about *The Waste Land* as the embodiment of a world-view widely characteristic of thoughtful and sensitive individuals during the 1920s.

"Great poetry is the boiling over of great discontent," I wrote years ago. We need recall only that in 1922—as in any other year of this century—thousands of persons have recorded in verse and prose similar "rhythmical grumbling," as Eliot calls his work. Most of these remain unpublished or unread; a few are admired by cultists; only a handful win the world's attention, and only a few of these are favorably remarked upon. As the essays that follow in this book argue, almost all of the other significant writers of the decade—except William Carlos Williams (harbinger of an age yet to be born)—different as their works may superficially have been from Eliot's, reflected at heart his sentiments about the twentieth-century world as waste land. Carol Harter and Maurice Duke demonstrate especially in their essays on Dreiser and Cabell how very much beneath the surface the former's Naturalistic works and the latter's fantasies resemble Eliot's impressionistic masterpiece. The difference between Eliot's "personal grouse" and others is that he gave us in his poem what—in Alexander Pope's words—"oft was thought but ne'er so well expressed."

I have no doubt that the sentiments that prompted the poem were strongly personal; if they had not been, in fact, they would surely lack the passionate conviction that engulfs the reader in the poem (as the choruses from *The Rock* lack this passion when the poet deliberately strives for it). The poet must first come to terms with his own feelings; it can only be determined after the fact whether his feelings correspond closely enough to those of the artistically receptive members of his contemporary or some subsequent society to establish his reputation as a spokesman rather than an isolated grumbler. I would reject only Eliot's diffident dismissal of his own "grouse against life" as "insignificant," though we must honor his attitude even here; for had he viewed himself as writing "significantly," he would probably have written in the

ponderous, forgettable manner of many self-proclaimed geniuses whose self-evaluations have not been shared by the
world. On the one hand, paradoxically, every man's "grouse"
is significant as part of the human experience; on the other,
the measure of its significance can be determined only by the
audience. The artist must be humble in the face of his
passionate concerns. "Teach us to care and not to care," as
Eliot sings in "Ash-Wednesday." One achieves greatness only
unintentionally; those who like Richard Nixon set out to be
great create not *The Waste Land* but the waste-lands—perhaps
herein lies the difference between politician and poet.

The cuts in *The Waste Land* seem to me, furthermore,
efforts toward impersonalizing and objectifying the discontents. The removal of the gossipy introductions to the first and
third sections minimizes the personal grousing without substantially altering the animus of the poem. Certainly its impact
is strengthened by the excision of such anti-feminist bitching
about Fresca and Lady Katzegg as "Women grown intellectual
grow dull,/ And lose the mother wit of natural trull" and such
local reference as those to "the swarming life" that London
kills and breeds.

The most substantial cut of nearly eighty-per-cent of the
fourth section seems to me to reinforce my earlier argument
about the contemporary implications of the remaining ten
lines—Elliot's switching from a long account of a contemporary shipwreck to the final meditation on the dead sailor
clearly applies the term "Phoenician" to sea-farers of any era.

The principal effect of Pound's suggestions is to universalize the poem. He influenced the substitution of an epigraph
from the *Satyricon* for one from Conrad's *Heart of Darkness.*
It is not clear who decided that the original title, "He Do the
Police in Different Voices," drawn from Dickens' *Our Mutual
Friend* should be replaced; but the cumulative effect of the
two revisions is to lift the poem out of the mainstream of the
denunciation of the waste and insensitivity of arrogant
Victorian society and to focus attention through a classical
epigraph and timeless title upon the universality of the poem.

Even though Eliot at times reacted petulantly—as to Pound's excision of nearly all of the fourth section of the poem (" 'Perhaps better omit Phlebas also???' ")—he did accept the recommendations that were responsible for the elimination of most of the cryptically personal, ephemeral material from the poem. It is hard to believe anyway that an established master like Pound would have wasted his time on an "insignificant" grouse; the importance of the Valerie Eliot edition of the original version of *The Waste Land* is that it provides the evidence that the excisions and alterations from manuscript to published text were all directed toward turning a personal grouse into a universal statement of civilized man's discontents.

2

Edith Wharton:
The Nostalgia for Innocence

Eleanor Widmer

The ironic truth about the mistress of irony, Edith Wharton, was her inability to take sufficient risks. Born in 1862, into the old New York that prided itself on good breeding, good manners, and good language, Edith Jones was properly descended from those families who cultivated in her the sense of impeccable style that was to both determine and bifurcate her life. Raised to fear "people who wrote" and "fatiguing the brain," where authorship "was still regarded as something between a black art and a form of labor," Edith could not overcome her longing "to make up." One of her first writing efforts mentioned an untidy drawing room. This elicited from her mother an icy comment, "Drawing rooms are always tidy." The lesson did not go unheeded.

Constricted by a social milieu whose taboo was "the blind dread of innovation," Edith struggled to affect the compromise that would permit her to enjoy the advantages of class while avoiding the stigma of "people who wrote." When, at the age of seventeen, she sent her handwritten verses to Scribner's, she scrupulously enclosed her calling card. And, as a young bride, married to the proper Bostonian, Edward Wharton, thirteen years her senior, what could be more appropriate than her first book, co-authored with Ogden

Codman and called *The Decoration of Houses* (1897)? This
topic not only gained the approbation of her class, but at one
level served as a statement of her outward life. Edith's
existence, became, in fact, a series of houses: Pencraig in
Newport (her ancestral home), The Mount, at Lenox, Massachusetts (her bridal establishment), her Paris apartment on the
Rue de Varenne, and finally, the French summer house,
Pavillion Colombe. In these quarters, whose perfection some
visitors described as "chilling," Edith went to enormous pains
to elaborate her role as a lady, for she passionately believed in
her own comment, "In every society there is room, and the
need, for a cultivated leisure class; but from the first the spirit
of our institutions has caused us to waste this class instead of
using it." Surrounded by never less than a cook, a secretary,
and a chauffer (she was a zealous and compulsive early
motorist), Edith felt compelled to dress at the height of
fashion and to cease writing each day at noon in order to carry
out her function as a hostess. And she chronicled the social
and psychological topography of her class with equally
unremitting fastidiousness.

At the same time, one of her most charitable admirers and
a member of her immediate circle, Percy Lubbock, records
that she barely tolerated the company of women, that she
referred to herself as a "self made man," and that she came
alive only with her intimates: Walter Berry, Henry James,
Howard Sturgis, Charles du Bos. While she divorced her
mentally ill husband in 1913, no breath of her struggle taints
her strangely unmodern autobiography, *A Backward Glance*,
written as late as 1934, when the age of guarded propriety had
long since vanished. The dilemma of Edith Wharton was that
as much as she seemed to deride the society of the past that
equated conformity to its rules with personal fulfillment, she
could not break with it.

In like manner, save for the ubiquitous Undine Spragg of
The Custom of the Country, created the same year as her
divorce, none of her heroines, like herself, are free to place
love before duty. Despite Edith Wharton's vast intelligence,

despite the marvel and fluidity of her observations of her own society and her mockery of it, she was trapped by the antinomies of her "backward glance" and by her longing for the very era she satirized. Try as she might, she was unable to leap beyond the Georgian world. Once past her prime, after the writing of *The Age of Innocence,* Edith Wharton could do no more than recount, as a sleepwalker, the vision and dream of this lost and uncapturable past.

In that sense, and although she won the Pultizer Prize for *The Age of Innocence* in 1920, and produced a volume of fiction, essays, and poetry with monotonous regularity every eighteen months until her death at seventy five in 1937, it would be capricious to argue that hers was a voice of the 20s. In sensibility, perception, moral stance, she belongs to the period as yet untouched by the Great War. To her—perhaps more than to anyone else discussed in this book — the 1920s were indeed a waste land, a "wasted" land.

Like T. S. Eliot, Edith Wharton had an abhorrence of the megapolitan twentieth century; like him she became an expatriate—she returned briefly to America in 1923, but only to accept an honorary Doctor of Letters from Yale—and like Eliot she was driven by the exigencies of the war to reject the contemporary age which she physically inhabited. With undisguised nostalgia she wrote, " . . . as I look back at it across the chasm of the war and all the ruin since heaped up, every convention of that compact and amiable little world seems still to be standing." She comes achingly close to Eliot's "These fragments I have shored against my ruins." As with Eliot's Philomel, Edith Wharton mourned because "the world pursues,/'Jug Jug' to dirty ears," and her nightingale song trilled of that structured, rigid, reliable time whose uses "lay in preserving a few drops of old vintage too rare to be savored by a youthful palate."

Unlike the writers of the 20s whose banner spelled waywardness to all that was bourgeois and dutiful, the more Edith Wharton recognized the modern wasteland with its ash-heap of ossified bones, the more she fastened her eyes on the past. In her three most successful novels, *The House of Mirth* (1905), *The Custom of the Country* (1913), and *The Age of Innocence* (1920), her heroines are more multi-dimensioned than, say, Hemingway's simpering Catherine Barkley or the brittle Lady Brett Ashley. But whereas the latter are thrust into a fragmented and disintegrating society in which the old rules are wantonly disregarded, it is their element of risk-taking, rather than the explicitness of their sex life, that characterizes their modernity. From this contemporary land where custom is violated, where love comes before duty, where demands of the self take precedence over respect for convention, Edith Wharton retreated—more accurately, she never arrived. Problems of pregnancy, illicit love affairs, and the anguished turmoils of the heart permeated the Victorian novels—who can forget Dickens's Lady Dedlock of *Bleak House* whose studied ennui and emphasis on social correctness proved the mask behind which lay the frustrated illegitimate mother? But in Edith Wharton these crises had to be papered over with the stamp of legitimacy; indeed it was the theme of her best works—the cost of individual choices made within the confines of a fixed society.

In her earliest popular successes, *The House of Mirth*, the heroine, Lily Bart, is the victim of a moneyed society that not merely stifles freedom of choice in women, but in which one false move inevitably leads to another until the heroine cannot extricate herself from a crushing doom. When Lily Bart appears on the scene, literally in a tableau depicting the great masterpieces of art, she is under the aegis of one of the most respected hostesses in town, her promises all before her. In glowing beauty and health, she appears incapable of any but a glorious, if traditional, destiny. Yet the book could rightly bear the subtitle, *Opportunities,* for as each opportunity presents itself to Lily, she makes a decision which is esthetically and morally superior to the society around her, but which causes her to be rejected for it. Lily has the chance to marry the millionaire, Percy Gryce, and chooses to spend the crucial day with the attractive Lawrence Selden; though

Selden falls in love with her, Lily chooses to evade him; when the *arriviste* Simon Rosedale proposes, she is repelled, in an Eliotesque way, by his vulgarity, and rather than marry a *nouveau riche* and a Jew, she opts for the role of eternal houseguest, adrift in a tide of all that is mean and sordid in her hosts.

Though her tendencies and taste should place her at the apex of society, Lily moves slowly downward, losing the patronage of the best families, such as the Trenors, losing with the less accepted Dorsets, until ostracized on the Riviera for an alleged misalliance, she returns to New York and to Mrs. Norma Hatch, a divorcée from the West, "rich, helpless, unplaced," who resides, not in a fashionable house, but in a hotel. When the hapless Lily finally allows herself to consider marriage with Rosedale, her promises are squandered; her luster is gone; she is no longer socially desirable.

Why did Mrs. Wharton insist on grinding her heroine so finely under the heel of an irreversible fate? For one thing she wished to lay waste to the false values of a society that punished a sensibility as unique as Lily's. For another, she had an instinctive feeling for melodrama which in her novels of the 20s, *A Son at the Front* (1923), *The Mother's Recompense* (1925), *Twilight Sleep* (1927), *The Children* (1928), caused her writing to deteriorate to the level of popular womens' magazines. More important, she seemed incapable of projecting any but a weak, inadequate hero who would be of small help to the heroine in her struggle.

At the heart of *The House of Mirth* lies a muddled, if not soft center that even the grandeur of Mrs. Wharton's caustic style cannot disguise and that is directly related to Lawrence Selden, the lawyer whom Lily loves. Selden lacks decisiveness. When his love is freshest, he permits Lily to go her own way, and when her circumstances are most reduced, he does not possess the bravery of the traditional hero to right wrongs, to behave as protector and savior, and above all to declare the love that will prevent Lily's death. And Selden is cut from the identical cloth as Ralph Marvell (*The Custom of the Country*), and Newland Archer (*The Age of Innocence*). All are lawyers—the proper profession for men of the leisure class who dabble at some sort of work without straining the energies that belong to the primary obligation of the social round—and all are basically good. But these men are easily put off, hoodwinked, incapable of mustering their resources at the appropriate moment. These heroes acknowledge their deepest needs only when it is too late for impudent choices, when society has exacted from them the obedience to custom that robs them of initiative.

In her personal life, Mrs. Wharton had her pantheon of gods, her male writer friends including Henry James, whom, like Pound and Eliot, she revered. Ordinary mortals, like her husband, she viewed from a position of her own intellectual, moral, and esthetic superiority, and it is precisely such ineffectual men, who cannot measure up to the standards of the heroines, that she created in her books. This accounts for the basic pessimism in her novels. In a traditional society, where men must play strong roles, Mrs. Wharton insists on their playing the reverse, thus setting up the frustration and denial of happiness that eventuate when the heroine combats society alone.

Mrs. Wharton undercuts her pattern in *The Custom of the Country* where the absence of nicety and scruple are identical in Undine Spragg and Elmer Moffatt. In this totally unified novel that deals with the dissolution of the gentry at the hands of the grasping newly rich, we cannot help but admire Undine—named for her father's hair dressing product—for her energy, her aggression, and her willingness to stop at nothing to obtain social position and grandeur. A female embodiment of the American Dream—materialism and idealism, unscrupulousness and fastidiousness, in equal measure, Undine is the *parvenu* incarnate, born in the West and determined to acquire the heritage of the East and Europe, even if she has to conquer all the area in between. Married four times, though twice to the same man — to Elmer Moffatt first for girlish infatuation, to him again, and the rest for social position and power —

neither her morosely devoted *nouveau riche* parents, nor the genteel Roger Marvell, stand a chance once Undine has learned the value of social ascendency. Though the Spraggs reside in a hotel (a sign as with Norma Hatch, of not being established in New York), Undine manages to marry Roger Marvell and to move into the society of the prestigious Dagonets, only to find them painfully lackluster. Roger's poetry, the remote Italian towns of their honeymoon, and Roger's explications of the nuances of society bore Undine because she knows how life should be lived—not enchained in motherhood, not living in an unfashionable district, but at the hub of large parties where she can be admired and adored. Her love affairs and her marriages serve as her social education. Roger's suicide phases her not a jot, and she plots her marriage to the Marquis de Chelles with the naive purposefulness that brings positive results. Once disheartened with French provincial life—she longs for the Parisienne family seat, *hôtel* de Chelles, which she envisions as a literal hotel—Undine sees no reason for commitment to it. Divorced from the marquis and remarried to the now robber-baron Moffatt, ensconced as a powerful hostess in a Paris mansion replete with art treasures whose value she counts in dollars, Undine's final cry addresses itself to her denial of being an Ambassador's wife because of divorce: "It was the one part she was really made for."

The bouyancy in *The Custom of the Country* stems from Edith Wharton's unabashed delight in dealing with *parvenu* families whose foibles she can delineate without restraint and with a perfection toward detail that would make a social historian proud. The names alone tell much of the clash of values—the Abner Spraggs, Mrs. Heeny, Mabel Lipscomb, Elmer Moffatt, all without proper connections, versus the established Van Degens, Marvells, Raymond de Chelles. Equally at home in New York and on the Continent, Mrs. Wharton rarely fails to provide us with the subtlest distinctions of caste and class, in terms of dress, speech, taste; and she uses her brash though often naive heroine as the spokeswoman for the new American barbarians whose conquest of money, position, and even the treasures of art could not be impeded. With perfect symmetry, Undine Spragg is wedded to the wizard of Wall Street, Elmer Moffatt, the very man from her home town whose want of graces caused her parents to sever the earlier connection. Possibly the most satisfying of the Wharton novels because of the fulfillment of the heroine conjoined to a perfectly appropriate man, it lacks the cloying sentimentality of *The House of Mirth* or the regretful sense of loss engendered by her last fine novel, *The Age of Innocence.*

In this prize winner, written after the war, Mrs. Wharton attempted to justify and examine the old New York of her childhood, a regression necessitated by the upheaval in modern life that she sensed, rather than experienced. Faced with a choice of plunging into the chaos of the social revolution brought about by the war, she settled, not for what she knew of the period of the moneyed class just prior to 1914, but for the comfort of that "amiable little world," of the 1870s. With characteristic irony, she created her strongest heroine for what was to be her swan song as an innovative writer—several novels written after *The Age of Innocence* were serialized in "ladies' magazines" and several more, such as the novella *The Old Maid,* part of a quartet issued as *Old New York* (1924), bear the niggardly recollections of a writer already impatient with her themes, simultaneously facile and repetitive. But in *The Age of Innocence* Edith Wharton is at the height of her craft.

The heroine, Countess Ellen Olenska, is the composite of the most accomplished traits of Mrs. Wharton herself, the fusion of autobiography and romantic imagination. Like Mrs. Wharton, Ellen bursts with intelligence and keen perception, and while descended from one of the first families (ranked according to ancestry and finances) she chafes at the sterility of existence in which invitations to proper parties, one's box at the opera, the situation of one's house, bear frightening social implications. Ellen, the girl "who was allowed to wear black satin at her coming out ball," and who not only marries a Polish count but flaunts her independence by leaving him, represents all that is unconventional, high spirited, and authentic.

On her return from Europe, Ellen shocks society by appearing at an opera in a dark velvet empire gown, amidst the white clad assembly, and though tinged with scandal she brazenly sits beside her cousin, the virginal May Welland. Ellen lives in a bohemian quarter, befriends "people who write," welcomes married men in her salon, employs an Italian servant to whom she speaks affectionately in that tongue, and by her elegant taste savages the prudence of the restricted code of her class. She is the woman who places "two Jacqueminot roses (of which nobody ever bought less than a dozen)" in her living room, and who spontaneously sends her maid on an errand of mercy without the preliminary step of sending her calling card. Scandalous! But Ellen's insight into her society provides her with poignancy. "The real loneliness," she complains, "is living among all these kind people who only ask one to pretend."

Ellen shares neither the bathos of Lily Bart nor the brazeness of Undine Spragg. In a confining society that prides narrowness and stultification, her purity of spirit is misunderstood because the routinization of responses and feeling aims at "an artificial product."

Surely May Welland, with her aura of "whiteness, radiance, goodness," appears as the perfect symbol of the young girl whose blind obedience to convention prevents her encounter with "a new idea, a weakness, a cruelty or an emotion." And the hero, Newland Archer, applauds his engagement to May because of "her resolute determination to carry to its utmost limits the ritual of ignoring the 'unpleasant.'" As the archetypal Wharton hero, Archer practises law, equates the "pleasant" with the traditional, and cannot anticipate that his undoing will stem from May's false, and therefore annihilating, innocence. Pledged to marry Miss Welland, Archer is forced by society into the company of Ellen—the family prevails upon him to dissuade her from a scandalous divorce. In reluctantly undertaking this office, Archer falls in love with Ellen.

As in a fairy tale where the hero is put to the test with

feats that must be repeated three times, Archer is thrice presented with the opportunity to cast off false innocence, and each time he proves incapable of the task. Caught in a moral and psychological duality instilled by lessons from his childhood, he views with alarm the passionate life of the spirit and mind that Ellen holds out to him. Though on the verge of breaking his engagement, Archer settles for May's claustrophobic innocence simply because she has advanced the date of the wedding to please him, and he does not have the stamina to disappoint her. He makes the conventional choice, the while declaring, "Ah, no, he did not want May . . . to have that innocence that seals the mind against imagination and the heart against experience." Yet by casting Ellen aside, Archer commits himself to the dangerous form that innocence will play with his wife.

The victim of a prescribed destiny, Archer cannot rise above his ambiguities. Once married and at Newport, where May, an unchanging vision in a white costume, distinguishes herself in an archery contest—the perfect sport for the perfect married woman and the perfect, cold Diana—Archer has a nagging longing for Ellen. When he learns of her presence in Newport, and in fact is asked by his hostess to fetch her from the pier, he refuses to call out to her unless she turns and greets him. The swashbuckling hero who would leap across the pier in unbridled passion finds no place in the Wharton canon. Archer consigns himself to a trick of fate. *If* Ellen moves in his direction, he will greet her. Since she does not, he flees, incapable of risking the predictable for the unchartered ravages of passion.

But Archer's doom becomes sealed when for a third and last time he is prevented from giving in to his love for Ellen by running off with her. May announces her pregnancy to Ellen two weeks before its certainty, thus employing her lofty innocence for entrapment. "No; I wasn't sure then — but I told her I was. And you see I was right," she exclaimed, her blue eyes wet with victory." Though New York society believes that Archer and Ellen are lovers when they are not, its proponents close ranks behind May and show up for Ellen's farewell party before her embarkation for Europe. In the "hieroglyphic world where the real thing was never said or done or even thought," the desertion of the heart is a lesser sin than the desertion of a meaningless and destructive innocence of a mother-to-be.

It has been argued that Newland Archer, like John Marcher in Henry James' *The Beast in the Jungle,* was a man "to whom nothing was ever to happen." The comparison is unfair. What has *happened* to Archer is the knowledge of the cost of duty and his acceptance of it. After the death of his wife, when his son and daughter have been raised and Archer remains a respected, if unfulfilled, citizen, he admits that "it did not matter if marriage was a dull duty, as long as it kept the dignity of duty." His inability to confront Ellen after a lapse of twenty-six years is foreshadowed in his acceptance of having missed "the flower of life. . .a thing so unattainable and improbable that to have repined would have been like despairing that one had not drawn first prize in a lottery." In the heartbreaking last scene, where he gazes up at the windows of Ellen's apartment, and then walks away from it, we see the price paid for stale duty masking as commitment to conventional innocence.

The Age of Innocence was, in both an artistic and autobiographical sense, *un crie du coeur.* The "elaborate system of mystification" of the past was dead; morals and manners had taken a radical and disastrous course in the postwar era, and in her personal life, Mrs. Wharton, like Ellen Olenska, had been frustrated in her happiness. To her good friend Charles du Bos, Edith Wharton had confessed in anguish, "Ah, the poverty, the miserable poverty of any love that lies outside of marriage . . ."

A strong-minded intelligence about the conservative power of society and a brilliantly epigrammatic writer, Mrs. Wharton consigned herself to that not insignificant but nevertheless limited role of the writer who thrives only by looking back. With a disdain for the startling innovations of the 20s, and the rational awareness that even nostalgia could not justify the throttling innocence of the past, Edith Wharton, like her own heroines, was trapped by her edict, "The worst of doing one's duty was that it apparently unfitted one for anything else." And this duty toward her craft Edith Wharton continued long after her vision had cogency in a mirthless, uncustomary, anti-innocent world.

3

An Appointment with the Future:
Willa Cather

Bernice Slote

In 1919 and 1920 both T. S. Eliot and Willa Cather were in the process of becoming Knopf authors. That company published *Poems by T. S. Eliot* in February 1920 and Cather's collection of short stories, *Youth and the Bright Medusa*, in the fall of the year. Eliot had further correspondence with Knopf about another book, *The Waste Land*, but it was eventually issued in America by Liveright late in 1922, having first appeared in the *Dial* (October 1922). Although I have not yet found any mention of Eliot by Cather,[1] it is not unlikely that she would have seen at least his one Knopf volume (*Poems*); according to what I know of a portion of her library, she had in her possession many of her publisher's books. She did read the *Dial* occasionally, sometimes with amusement, but whether or not she ever read *The Waste Land* I cannot say. Still, from her college days on there is abundant evidence in her published journalistic writings that she had a habit of reading everything in sight.

It is safe to say, however, that Eliot's poem did not influence Willa Cather's writing of *One of Ours*, her 1922 novel, in which she developed something of the same kind of waste land Eliot created. She had finished writing the novel and had sent it to Knopf for a first reading by August 1921.

At that time Eliot was finishing *The Waste Land,* though he
did not work with Pound on it until early 1922 (when Cather
was already reading proof on her novel), and it was not
published until late in the year, long after *One of Ours* had
been published, had received very mixed reviews, and was on
its way to receiving the 1923 Pulitzer Prize. Nevertheless, *One
of Ours* is, like *The Waste Land,* in part the vision of sterility,
discordance, lost hopes, and human failure. That Cather's
novel allows for moments of splendor and a momentary
realization of ideals does not change the pattern of its
landscape, strewn with war and machines and silenced by
human inarticulateness.

One of Ours is the story of Claude Wheeler, bound on a
Nebraska farm and frustrated in his education by a sadistic
father and his own passivity, disappointed in a cold marriage,
yearning for something more than he has (something "splendid" in life), and delivered in the end to both a heroic triumph
and his death. The catapult is World War I. Claude's early life
is a rubble of money, machines (most of them useless), and
heavy-handed power. Symptomatic of this wasteland is what
Claude sees in the cellar of the Wheeler home: "Mysterious
objects stood about him in the grey twilight; electric batteries,
old bicycles and typewriters, a machine for making cement
fence-posts, a vulcanizer, a stereopticon with a broken lens." [2]
His younger brother, Ralph, collects these objects obsessively;
his older brother, Bayliss, is an implement dealer, successful
and unimaginative. That Claude is able to escape his dull
environment and go to France to be killed is, at last, an
accident of history. Yet *One of Ours* is not a "war novel," and
there is in it more of the horror than the glory of the war. It is
the story of the emergence of a human spirit from the prison
of self. [3]

The Waste Land and *One of Ours* meet at numerous
points. One of the most striking is that of the imprisoned self.
In Section V of *The Waste Land* ("What the Thunder Said")
we have a counterpoint of desert and rock with no water; of

thunder without rain. In this landscape of graves and bones it is said,

> I have heard the key
> Turn in the door once and turn once only
> We think of the key, each in his prison
> Thinking of the key, each confirms a prison
> Only at nightfall. . . . (11. 412-16)

One night Claude Wheeler bathes in the tin horse tank on his farm, the sky above like "warm, deep, blue water" with the moon floating like a water-lily in the sky's invisible current. The moon recalls the historic past of Egypt and Babylon, where slaves and captives languished in prisons. The passage continues: "Inside of living people, too, captives languished. Yes, inside of people who walked and worked in the broad sun, there were captives dwelling in darkness,—never seen from birth to death. Into those prisons the moon shone, and the prisoners crept to the windows and looked out with mournful eyes at the white globe which betrayed no secrets and comprehended all" (pp. 206-207).

There is another significant parallel. Eliot used the theme of the Fisher King, the dying old king of a wasted country redeemed by a young man—innocent, naive, but invested with the key to the symbolic Grail. This is, of course, the story of Parsifal, as well as a portion of Jessie L. Weston's *From Ritual to Romance,* which, according to Eliot, gave him his major theme. Willa Cather, by her own admission in a letter of November 17, 1922, created Claude Wheeler as a Parsifal figure (see James Woodress, *Willa Cather: Her Life and Art,* pp. 196, 279). Whether or not she ever read Weston, Cather was steeped in Wagnerian opera, knew *Parsifal* well and affectionately. (In later years she took the Menuhin children to *Parsifal,* I learned from them in interviews in December 1973.) She also knew Gertrude Hall's *The Wagnerian Romances,* for which she wrote an introduction in 1925. One time in the Southwest, she says in her essay on Hall's book, "I first read the chapter on *Parsifal,* with increasing delight. I was astonished to find how vividly it recalled to me all the best

renderings of that opera I had ever heard. Just the right word
was said to start the music going in one's memory" (*Willa
Cather on Writing*, pp. 61-62).

Claude is indeed that young man of *Parsifal*—strong,
inarticulate, naive—but he is the means by which the old land
is saved. No Fisher King is personified in the book; he is
developed three years later as Godfrey St. Peter in *The
Professor's House*. And Claude Wheeler is transmuted into
Tom Outland.

The Professor's House (1925) is in no sense confined to
the theme of the Fisher King; that is only one of perhaps five
or six strands of reference that operate through the book. And
the pattern is not definite, clearly defined and related; Cather's
habit of allusion is more indirect and momentary, more
suggestive than allegorical (I have previously called it "broken
allegory"). But the body of *The Professor's House* does
incorporate not only the desolation and sickness of St. Peter,
who has increasingly become remote from the creativity and
love which had once been the centers of his life, but also the
failures of others about him who live by the materialistic
values he cannot accept. Richard Giannone has commented in
Music in Willa Cather's Fiction that the "money motif" of
acquisition and envy (opposed to the motif of the ideal) is one
theme in the "sonata form" of *The Professor's House*. But it is
the young wanderer Tom Outland, discoverer of the cliff-
dweller ruins on the Blue Mesa, who becomes the Professor's
alter ego and restores him for a time: "Just when the morning
brightness of the world was wearing off for him, along came
Outland and brought him a kind of second youth" (p. 258).
Like Claude Wheeler, Tom Outland is swept away by the War,
and for the Professor the days after him have less delight.

In *Parsifal* the King is taken regularly to bathe in waters in
order to cure his sickness. So in *The Professor's House* the
motif of water is used to balance deserts, to evoke clarity in
place of confusion. Tom Outland finds the Mesa in snow and
stays with it through sun and bright air. A hidden spring is in
the depths of the rock. ("The shadow of a great rock in a

weary land," Isaiah 32.2.) St. Peter finds it necessary to live near Lake Michigan, and he goes there almost ritualistically to swim, to lie near its blueness, to be restored. "I sat upon the shore / Fishing, with the arid plain behind me / Shall I at least set my lands in order?" (*The Waste Land*, V, 424-26). In a sense, the Professor does set his lands in order. He eventually passes close to death, the ultimate wasteland, but goes on to a life that may be "without delight" but does have balance and realistic acceptance. Both Tom Outland and Godfrey St. Peter have come near the Grail — Tom perhaps best in his time on the Mesa and his vision there of completeness, the Professor in both the life created in his books and in his response to Tom's experience. And there is still help in the Professor's journey through the barren land from the wise, plain, and modest confidence of religious Augusta, the sewing woman, who saved his life. Augusta, like his primitive, essential self, which he recalls more and more, is tuned to the coming and going of seasons, to birth and death, to life.

One judgment by Willa Cather on the 1920s hardly needs to be repeated. She said in the prefatory note to *Not Under Forty* that "the world broke in two in 1922 or thereabouts, and the persons and prejudices recalled in these sketches slid back into yesterday's seven thousand years" (p. v). Virginia Faulkner has pointed out to me the close connection between this statement in *Not Under Forty*, published in November 1936, and Cather's "The Old Beauty," written (according to Edith Lewis) later that winter. "The Old Beauty" does take place in 1922. The story, with its encounter between Gabrielle Longstreet, a great beauty at the turn of the century, or before, and two knickered girls of the twenties, seems to be a fictional comment on the idea stated in *Not Under Forty.* The date of 1922 seems significant. I doubt that the reference has much to do with the publication of *The Waste Land*, but it might well relate to that of *One of Ours,* a book into which Willa Cather had invested several years of intense involvement and whose reception had greatly disappointed her. Most likely "1922 or thereabouts" should be taken to mean the beginning of the twenties, a time when the post-war disillusionment and changes in the temper of the people became inescapable. In the early twenties Willa Cather had also affirmed publicly many of the values she held and many of the shortcomings of American society as she viewed it then. In 1923 the *Nation* published her article "Nebraska: The End of the First Cycle," an essay which brilliantly summarizes the history of the West she knew and notes the change in the present generation from that of the more heroic pioneers. In 1921 she had lectured on art and American life in Nebraska.

When in October 1921 Willa Cather talked to the Omaha Society of Fine Arts, newspaper accounts of the lecture and interviews during the weeks she was in Nebraska gave some of her feeling about contemporary American life. Her chief criticism was exactly that which led the expatriates to Paris — that what retarded art in American life was standardization (why should everyone dress alike? all the cities look alike?), indiscriminate Americanism, false conventions of thought and expression, machine-made art, superficial culture (art out of encyclopedias rather than experience)[4] "Everyone is afraid of not being standard," she said. "There is no snobbishness so cowardly as that which thinks the only way to be correct is to be like everyone else." . . ."Any American housewife who teaches her good Bohemian or other foreign neighbor that it is as well for her to feed her family off a can of salmon as a roast goose is committing a crime against Americanism and art." She attacked restrictive laws in Nebraska — "Laws that put the state on a plane between despotism and personal liberty. Why, it costs two farm boys $5 and the filling out of a questionnaire as long as your arm if they want to go out in the barn loft and hold a wrestling match for the neighbors after the day's work is done." And by law the teaching of foreign languages under the eighth grade was barred in schools: "Will it make a boy or a girl any less an American to know one or two other languages? According to that sort of argument your 100 per cent American would be a deaf mute." She was exasperated about Prohibition. Though she lived in those years at 5 Bank

Street in the Village, she denied to a reporter that there was such a thing as Greenwich Village. "The Village doesn't exist," she said. "How could it in these times when the last cellar is empty?"

But whatever was wrong with American life in the 1920s, Willa Cather did not become an expatriate. "I cannot do my work abroad," she told Walter Tittle in 1925. "I hate to leave France or England when I am there, but I cannot produce my kind of work away from the American idiom. . . .I cannot create my kind of thing without American speech around me and incidents that cause memories to arise from the subconscious" (*Century*, July 1925, p. 312). And for the rest of the decade (after 1922, when the world broke in two), she continued to write of American life as she saw it — *A Lost Lady* (1923), *The Professor's House* (1925), *My Mortal Enemy* (1926), *Death Comes for the Archbishop* (1927), and several important short stories, including "Uncle Valentine" (1925) and "Double Birthday" (1929). They were all different in form, but all were concerned with the deepest problems of human life, individual and social. Unquestionably she saw a kind of watershed, a change in the post-war American life, even as many of us might say now that the world broke in two in 1960, or thereabouts. But I will stand with what Ellen Moers has written recently in "The Survivors: Into the Twentieth Century": "Willa Cather should instead have said, on behalf of herself and others of the survivors, that 'the world broke in two, but I did not' " (*Twentieth Century Literature,* January 1974, p. 9). In one way Willa Cather went strongly into the future. Her novels of the 1920s *were* all different. She was prepared for experiment, though she herself saw it less as experiment than submission to the novel's form. She might have preferred horses to automobiles (as she once said), but in her art she was ready for a new road. "The new American novel," she explained, "is better than the old-fashioned conventional one, with its plot always the same, its accent always on the same incidents. With its unvarying, carefully dosed ingredients, the old-fashioned American novel was like a chemist's prescription." That was on May 20, 1923, in a cabled interview from the Paris correspondent of the New York *World* at the time Willa Cather's Pulitzer Prize was announced. Two years later in April 1925, she was still saying, "You must work out your own fashion. . .work it out from under the old patterns." (*Nebraska State Journal* reprinted from the New York *World*).

Whatever there was of the wasteland — in both the human soul and the social values of the 1920s — Willa Cather countered that sterility with affirmations of life. These notes are not blatant, and so they are often overlooked. In the April 1925 interview, she called *One of Ours* a story of "youth, struggle, and defeat," and so, in a way, was Tom Outland's story in *The Professor's House.* Yet in both *One of Ours* and *The Professor's House* there is a movement toward life. Claude Wheeler is given a moment of splendor in his death, and Godfrey St. Peter is shown to have determined on life rather than death. As he lies on his couch in a room accidentally filling with gas, he considers whether he is obliged to struggle. Unconsciously he does make that effort toward life, for when he is rescued he has apparently risen from the couch in an effort to escape. Life, though on different terms from what he had hoped, is in the end the Professor's choice. "At least, he felt the ground under his feet" (p. 283), and he could face the future.

Marian Forrester in *A Lost Lady,* for all her disillusioning faults, had one great impulse: She was not willing to die with the pioneer period, but "she preferred life on any terms" (p. 169). She had always, recalls young Niel Herbert, "the power of suggesting things much lovelier than herself" (p. 172). The life force is also dramatized in "Double Birthday," which ends with old Uncle Albert's delight in young Marjorie Parmenter's admiration. For him the fires are not out, even at eighty, and " '*Even in our ashes,*' he muttered haughtily." In *Death Comes for the Archbishop* and the next novel, *Shadows on the Rock* (1931), written at the end of the decade, there are choices for the future. The Archbishop once thought of returning to retire in his native France, but when the time came he chose to spend his last years in the New World of the American Southwest — "that brilliant blue world of stinging air and moving cloud" (p. 234). There he was himself still a part of history moving onward. And Cècile Auclair in *Shadows on the Rock* also rejects the past, preferring Quebec to Old France, identifying with the Canada of the future.

Although Willa Cather was sometimes thought to be looking to the past rather than to the present, I suggest that in the 1920s she was actually writing for, and of, the future. Just as her short stories before 1905 and her journalistic comment in her early years anticipated much of the social criticism later developed by Sinclair Lewis and others, so many of her themes in the 1920s emerge as statements for the 1970s. Perhaps we can understand her concerns better now than we could fifty years ago. We understand, for example, the force of her urging for ethnic individuality and the recognition of the values in all cultures. Even before the 1920s two of her most important books, *O Pioneers!* (1913) and *My Antonia* (1918), developed fully for the first time in American literature the themes of immigrant participation in the settlement of the West. Her Swedes, Norwegians, and Bohemians with their old-world culture and language barriers are not figures of stage fun but are held as triumphant or tragic figures in the American scene. This view is closely related to her personal pleas for human individuality, for less imitation (plant native trees — cotton-woods and poplars and osage orange — rather than the Eastern maple, she told Nebraskans in 1921). And we also understand better now her perceptions of the differences between the Indian and the white man, and the necessary respect that must be given to the heritage of each. *Death Comes for the Archbishop* is deeply and sympathetically revealing of the Indian landscape, the Indian religion, the Indian people: "It was the Indian manner to vanish into the landscape, not to stand out against it" (p. 236). The Archbishop eventually learns to blend cultures: he sits looking at Santa Fe and his new cathedral for the last time — wrapped in Indian blankets.

Those who are now concerned with the environment may note Willa Cather's description in 1927 of the Navajo: "The land and all that it bore they treated with consideration; not attempting to improve it, they never desecrated it" (p. 237). In "Uncle Valentine," as well as in earlier stories, she commented on the destruction of the countryside. For example: "The wave of industrial expansion swept down that valley, and roaring mills belch their black smoke up to the heights where those lovely houses used to stand." She defended the right to something of America's natural wilderness. Captain Forrester in *A Lost Lady* kept a few acres of marshland; Ivy Peters, of the new breed of materialists, drained the marsh and put it into wheat. So he had "asserted his power over the people who had loved those unproductive meadows for their idleness and silvery beauty" (p. 106).

We can recognize the confusing and unfocused blundering of Washington bureaucracy and sometimes its disregard for real American values — as it is depicted in *The Professor's House* when Tom Outland tells of his abortive efforts to gain support for the preservation of historical artifacts on the Blue Mesa. And now we can recognize in *One of Ours* the battlefields that have circled the world since 1922 — the beaches of Normandy, of Korea, of Vietnam, and the soldiers who have returned. Some of those who died in Claude Wheeler's war "were merely waste in a great enterprise, thrown overboard like rotten ropes" (p. 319). The last pages of *One of Ours* show the wasteland of war to be the most futile of all. Afterwards, thinks Claude's mother, meanness and greed had engulfed everything at home again; nothing could come of it but evil. The worst was personal disillusionment: And "one by one the heroes of that war, the men of dazzling soldiership, leave prematurely the world they have come back to. . . .one by one they quietly die by their own hand. Some do it in obscure lodging houses, some in their office. . . .Some slip over a vessel's side and disappear into the sea" (p. 458). Willa Cather saw it all clearly, more than fifty years ago.

Willa Cather found both death and life in landscapes of the

spirit. If she wrote in the 1920s of something very like Eliot's "waste land," she also wrote of the shadow of the rock and of springs in the desert. And these themes were not confined to a date, or to a local habitation and a name.

Notes

1. Although I do not use them in this essay, there have been two good articles on some relationships between T. S. Eliot and Willa Cather: Bernard Baum, "Willa Cather's Waste Land," *South Atlantic Quarterly* (October 1949); and Philip L. Gerber, "Willa Cather and the Big Red Rock," *College English* (January 1958).

2. Willa Cather, *One of Ours* (New York: Alfred A. Knopf, 1965), p. 20. Hereafter pagination for quotations from this and other books by Willa Cather will be given in parentheses in the text, referring to the following editions, all published by Knopf: *A Lost Lady* (1923), *The Professor's House* (1925), *Death Comes for the Archbishop* (1927), *Not Under Forty* (1936).

3. See also the discussion of *One of Ours* in James E. Miller, Jr., "Willa Cather and the Art of Fiction," in *The Art of Willa Cather,* edited by Bernice Slote and Virginia Faulkner (Lincoln: University of Nebraska Press, 1974), pp. 135-37.

4. Quotations in this paragraph are from the Omaha *Bee,* October 31, 1921; Omaha *World-Herald,* October 31, 1921: Omaha *Daily News,* October 29, 1921.

4

Strange Bedfellows: *The Waste Land* and *An American Tragedy*

Carol Clancy Harter

It is difficult to imagine any two contemporary men of letters more dissimilar than Theodore Dreiser and T. S. Eliot. They are not merely unlike by virtue of ethnic, religious and economic background, professional interests, education, philosophy, and temperament; as artists they represent antagonistic — even irreconcilable polarities: Dreiser epitomizes the naturalist, journalist-fictionalizer, while Eliot remains the quintessentially allusive metaphysician, aesthetician-poet. Indeed, despite the fact that *The Waste Land* was published only three years prior to the publication of *An American Tragedy,* the dissimilarities between the two works are so profound they are rarely discussed in relation to one another. But that would not surprise either writer, for neither Dreiser nor Eliot seems to have been particularly aware of the other's artistic existence or impact on the literary scene, and there is no evidence whatever (in either his biography or letters) that Dreiser was in any way either impressed with or directly influenced by the publication of *The Waste Land.* Nevertheless, it seems remarkable that two monumental literary works such as *The Waste Land* and *An American Tragedy* were given the world within three years, and as yet have not been seriously discussed in the same critical context. Antithetical as they are, both works emanated from the rich artistic, socio-economic and cultural milieu of the twenties; and along with *Ulysses, The Sound and the Fury,* and *The Great Gatsby,* belong to an era of English and American letters as abundant and opulent as that of the Elizabethan theatre or the American Renaissance. Perhaps because of the distinctive quality of the milieu from which they evolved, both embody—however much they are diametrically opposite as literary forms—many of the same themes, symbolic motifs, and views of the human condition as it is manifested in the modern world. Each creates a metaphoric fabric whose design ultimately reveals the barren landscape of man's spiritual and moral wasteland. Frederick J. Hoffman notes some of the differences between Eliot and Dreiser's use of the wasteland landscape, but the similarities are equally apparent: "Since naturalism is, in literary terms at any rate, an extension of realism, the naturalist landscape incorporates not only the sordid detail used for a very much more complex purpose by Baudelaire, Eliot, and their contemporaries, but the scene itself in which social disparities can easily be imaged. Dreiser's concern with cities, hotels, clothes, and interiors helps to identify this landscape as a *social record of moral deficiencies.* But the landscape does not record merely despair over the disabilities of the modern world; it is asked as well to express externally the inner dispositions of its heroes" (my italics, "The Scene of Violence: Dostevsky and Dreiser," *Modern Fiction Studies,* Summer 1960).

It would not, I think, be unfair to him to suggest that the particular American tragedy Dreiser so memorably delineates through Clyde Griffiths is a projection of human loss and hopelessness conceived by (and in turn re-nourishing) the same wasteland that Eliot symbolically creates in his poem. For every landscape Dreiser paints—the natural, the "civilized," the urban, the psychological and moral—presents the bankruptcy of values and debasement of spirit which Eliot so forcibly perceived and made immanent in *The Waste Land.* However, while Eliot's panoramic view of human experience encapsulates all time, history, and culture, and filters it through the virtually omniscient consciousness of an androgynous Tiresias who despairingly contemplates the entire cosmos, Dreiser refracts the cosmic view and counterpoints it against the puny, never fully conscious sensibility of the lost Clyde Griffiths. The state of man and his universe is, nevertheless, strikingly similar in both works even though our vision of that universe is controlled by antipodal points-of-view. In *The Waste Land* we are behind the camera scanning the desolate ruins of the ash heaps, merely invited to identify with our brothers: " 'You! hypocrite lecteur—mon semblable—mon frère!' " In *An American Tragedy,* however, we are drawn inside immediately vis a vis the internalized controlling consciousness of Clyde Griffiths. (Perhaps this is Dreiser's most masterful technical accomplishment in *An American Tragedy,* one which he failed to perfect in *Sister Carrie.* In the later novel we are rarely exposed to the heavyhanded intrusions of the all-wise narrator who shapes the world from the outside as he did in *Sister Carrie.* As a result, Dreiser achieves in *An American Tragedy* a dramatic narrative which embodies his view of the wasteland of modern life. In its own way, *An American Tragedy* is as dramatic in form as *The Waste Land.*) If Eliot had chosen to present a fuller characterization of his "young man carbuncular," we would perhaps also experience *The Waste Land* from the inside, from the pathetic half-consciousness of a Griffiths-like sensibility. In both poem and novel, however, we the *hypocrites lecteurs,* are left with an overwhelming sense of futility and horror: institutions are hopelessly corrupt, Christianity is atrophied, nature is debased by industrialization, and the spirit of man is imprisoned: the secularization of the world and its values has resulted in an overriding materialism which leads, in both works, to death by drowning, death which offers little or no possibility for resurrection. Paradoxically, the "death by water" which Madame Sosostris warns against becomes the ultimate embodiment of human experience in both *The Waste Land* and *An American Tragedy.*

Ellen Moers is one of the few critics of Dreiser's work who articulates a symbolic link between *The Waste Land* and *An*

American Tragedy. Referring to the novel in *The Two Dreisers*, Moers remarks: "From its opening paragraph—an opening pared down to schematic starkness through the many stages of Dreiser's revisions—the novel unfolds as a fable of the 'Unreal City.' " She further suggests that the fable-like quality of Dreiser's city is emphasized by a "purposeful vagueness about time and place," a vagueness, I might add, resembling Eliot's own. While Moers does not pursue the comparison she introduces, one can trace the metaphors of urban life and landscape throughout each work and discover how analogous Eliot and Dreiser's views of the modern city were: each used the city as a metaphor for man's abuse of his resources, for his materialistic and destructive compartmentalization, and for his spiritual prison. While the image of the city as prison is symbolically suggested in *The Waste Land*, it is a literal reality for the convicted Clyde Griffiths, and is eventually transformed into an actual deathhouse. The city-as-prison-as-deathhouse in *The Waste Land*, while never literal, is invoked through Eliot's allusions to *The Inferno.*

Unreal City,
Under the brown fog of a winter dawn,
A crowd flowed over London Bridge, so many,
I had not thought death had undone so many.

Likewise, in *An American Tragedy* the Dantesque texture of the city is rendered imagistically in the opening paragraphs: "Dusk—of a summer night. . . .And the tall walls of the commercial heart of an American city of perhaps 400,000 inhabitants—such walls *as in time may linger as a mere fable.* . . . Having reached an intersection this side of the second principal thoroughfare—really just an alley between two tall structures—*not quite bare of life of any kind,* the man put down the organ . . ." (my italics, Modern Library, 1953, p. 15). This imagistic suggestion of an earthly Inferno, however, becomes explicit as Clyde awaits execution on murderer's row: "And in the meantime Clyde was left to cogitate on and make the best of a world that at its best was a kind of inferno of mental ills—above which—as above Dante's might have been written—'abandon hope—ye who enter here'" (p. 824). What Clyde's limited awareness cannot grasp is that the literal deathhouse he inhabits is simply an extension of the "unreal cities" to which he was continuously drawn. The difference is merely of degree: "The 'death house' in this particular prison was one of those crass erections and maintenances of human insensitiveness and stupidity principally for which no one primarily was really responsible. Indeed, its total plan and procedure were the results of a series of primary legislative enactments, followed by decisions and compulsions as devised by the temperaments and seeming necessities of various wardens, until at last—by degrees and without anything worthy of the name of thinking on any one's part—there had been gathered and was now being enforced all that could possibly be imagined in the way of unnecessary and really unauthorized cruelty or stupid and destructive torture. And to the end that a man, once condemned by a jury, would be compelled to suffer not alone the death for which his sentence called, but a thousand others before that. For the very room by its arrangement, as well as the rules governing the lives and actions of the inmates, was sufficient to bring about this torture, willynilly" (pp. 815-816).

Eliot's narrator, blessed with acute consciousness, sees and records the Styx-like quality of the "glorious" Thames; he recognizes his Inferno:

> The river sweats
> Oil and tar
> The barges drift
> With the turning tide
> Red sails
> Wide
> To leeward, swing on the heavy spar.
> The barges wash
> Drifting logs
> Down Greenwich reach
> Past the Isle of Dogs.

But Clyde, given the same opportunity to perceive the abuse of the Mohawk River and the town of Lycurgas, seems to be oblivious to the ramifications of what he sees: "The depot, from which only a half hour before he had stepped down, was so small and dull, untroubled, as he could plainly see, by much traffic. And the factory section which lay opposite the small city—across the Mohawk—was little more than a red and gray assemblage of buildings with here and there a smokestack projecting upward, and connected with the city by two bridges—a half dozen blocks apart—one of them directly at this depot, a wide traffic bridge across which traveled a car-line following the curves of Central Avenue, dotted here and there with stores and small homes" (pp. 197-198). These very bridges, evocative of the entrances and exits to various circles in the Inferno, become the dreary paths to and from the monotonous and uncreative work at the factory which lulls both Clyde and Roberta Alden into a lethargy only tempo- rarily alleviated by sensuality.

Like "those hooded hordes swarming / Over endless plains, stumbling in cracked earth / Ringed by the flat horizon only," Roberta and other factory workers partake of endless and meaningless journeys to and from the factories: "And im- mediately after breakfast joining a long procession that day after day at this hour made for the mills across the river. For just outside her own door she invariably met with a company of factory girls and women, boys and men, of the same relative ages, to say nothing of many old and weary-looking women who looked more like wraiths than human beings, who had issued from the various streets and houses of this vicinity. . . . And at night the same throng, re-forming at the mills, crossing the bridge at the depot and returning as it had come" (p. 273). Eliot's "hooded hordes swarming" are not unlike Dreiser's equally abstract and symbolic women "more like wraiths than human beings," mindlessly and hopelessly participating in (and hence in part creating and sustaining) the nightmare landscape of a world dominated by materialism.

Often in Dreiser's work, that world committed to materialistic values crystallizes in the urban hotel, essence of vulgarity, pretentious display, and garish pseudo-art to which Dreiser's romantic seekers are magnetically drawn. For Clyde Griffiths, the colorless poverty of his family's life and religion is easily superceded by the ersatz splendor of an American hotel. Kansas City's Green-Davidson, for example, represents to Clyde a palpable manifestation of the privileged life; it is a bower of bliss, a garden of earthly delights and a gauche monument to worldly success: "Under his feet was a checkered black-and-white marble floor. Above him a coppered and stained and gilded ceiling. And supporting this, a veritable forest of black marble columns as highly polished as the floor—glassy smooth. And between the columns which ranged away toward three separate entrances, one right, one left and one directly forward toward Dalrymple Avenue—were lamps, statuary, rugs, palms, chairs, divans, tête-à-têtes—a prodigal display" (pp. 41-42).

But like the sensuously stifling display of jewels, perfumes, colored glass, and "coffered ceiling" in Eliot's "A Game of Chess," Clyde's world of luxury masks a realm of boredom, frustration and meaningless activity. " 'What shall I do now? What shall I do?' " is echoed in *An American Tragedy* by Sondra Finchley and her circle as they continuously seek satiation in superficial pleasures to vitiate their idleness. Here, for the first time, in his voyeuristic initiation to the world of the Sondra Finchleys, Clyde becomes converted to the religion of materialism: the hotel and its occupants play heaven to Clyde Griffith's novitiate. Spying a young woman engaged in frivolous party conversation, Clyde imagines that "this sight was like looking through the gates of Paradise." At this early point in his development, Clyde makes the facile transition from the non-remunerative faith of his family to the cult of the rich and idle, and in so doing, naively imagines that freedom can thus be achieved: "Such grandeur. This, then, most certainly was what it meant to be rich, to be a person of consequence in he world—to have money. It meant that you did what you pleased. That other people, like himself, waited upon you. That you possessed all of these luxuries. That you went how, where and when you pleased" (p. 58).

Dreiser's Green-Davidson has its symbolic analogues in Eliot's Cannon Street Hotel and Metropole. For Eliot, the corrupting forces of materialism inevitably lead to the perversion of human relationships, and Mr. Eumenides's invitation to the reluctant narrator to join him for a weekend at the Metropole is suggestive of the debasement of sexual experience.

It appears, therefore, that in both works the hotel serves as a microcosm for the alienation, randomness, rootlessness, and lusts of 20th century man. H. L. Mencken perceived the importance of the hotel as symbol in Dreiser's work and suggested its relation to secularization and materialism, a relation Dreiser clearly shares with Eliot: "[Dreiser] is still engaged in delivering Young America from the imbecilities of a frozen Christianity. And the economic struggle, in his eye, has a bizarre symbol: the modern American hotel" ("Dreiser in 840 Pages," in *The Merrill Studies in AN AMERICAN TRAGEDY,* Columbus, Ohio, 1971).

The perversion of sexual relationships resulting from and contributing to spiritual and moral bankruptcy is at the center of both *The Waste Land* and *An American Tragedy.* For Eliot, the sources of fertility and creativity are dormant: "here is no water but only rock," "sweat is dry," and the sky reverberates with "dry sterile thunder without rain." The landscape of sterility forcefully mirrors the perversion of love that dominates the world in the shapes of lust. "The change of Philomel, by the barbarous king / So rudely forced," becomes an emblem in the poem for sexual uncreativity and the absence of love. The couple at the game of chess, the secretary, the young man carbuncular, and Lil, pathetically seeking abortion, are all variations on the theme of human sterility—for Eliot, the physiological and emotional consequences of the debilitation of spirit.

While Dreiser's brand of naturalism tends to ascribe overwhelming drives and instincts to man over which he has little control, and Clyde seems to be cursed with a preternaturally powerful sexual "chemism" (similar to that which Dreiser attributed to himself), Griffiths is nevertheless responsible for the debasement and abuse of other human beings through misguided sexuality. Roberta Alden becomes a Philomel-like creature "rudely forced" by Clyde's emotional blackmail and eventually she fills the desert of Clyde's world with an "inviolable voice" of pain, isolation and love that simply sounds "jug, jug" to Clyde's dirty ears. But Clyde is not wholly without conscience; indeed, while he refuses to respond to the pathetic voice of Roberta's suffering, he does respond to the "weird, haunting cry" of an "unearthly bird" at Big Bittern. "What was it sounding — a warning — a protest — condemnation? The same bird that had marked the very birth of this miserable plan. For there it was now upon that dead tree — that wretched bird. And now it was flying to another one — as dead — a little farther inland and crying as it did so. God!" (p. 529). But because he is unable to translate that cry (a warning — a protest — a condemnation?), it remains an ominous and mysterious "jug, jug," merely filling the unresponsive desert places of Clyde's soul.

Roberta Alden's weakness, on the other hand, while similarly originating in the rejection of her family's poverty and despair, is not due to tyrannical sexual impulses or to a destructive romanticism. Her need is for affection and approval, qualities which Clyde at first willingly provides in exchange for sexual intimacies. But Roberta's genuine potential for a creative relationship is immediately thwarted by Clyde's rejection of love and creative sexualtiy. Like the young man carbuncular, "his vanity requires no response," and when it receives one in the form of an unborn child, Clyde's immediate reaction is to conceive a means to induce abortion. And he naively proceeds to seek that abortion with utterly no consideration for the moral or human questions involved in the act. The thunder in Clyde's world is dry indeed, and like Lil in Eliot's poem, he views the potential birth of his child as a burden and an obstruction to life rather than as an

indispensable projection of it: "And so disturbed was he by
the panorama of the bright world of which Sondra was the
center and which was now at stake, that he could scarcely
think clearly. Should he lose all this for such a world as he and
Roberta could provide for themselves—a small home—a baby,
such a routine work-a-day life as taking care of her and a baby
on such a salary as he could earn, and from which most likely
he would never again be freed! God! A sense of nausea seized
him" (p. 449).

This acute sense of nausea which seizes him whenever he
imagines a mundane family life with Roberta and their child is
symptomatic of Clyde's conversion to the religion of materialism—a cult over which Sondra Finchley rules as a pagan
priestess. For Clyde never relates to Sondra as a man to a
woman: he worships her as a goddess, much as he did Hortense
Briggs, the first Sondra in his life. "For apart from her local
position and means and taste in dress and manners, Sondra was
of the exact order and spirit that most intrigued him—a
somewhat refined (and because of means and position showered upon her) less savage, although scarcely less self-centered,
Hortense Briggs. She was, in her small, intense way, a seeking
Aphrodite, eager to prove to any who were sufficiently
attractive the destroying power of her charm, while at the
same time retaining her own personality and individuality free
of any entangling alliance or compromise" (p. 350).

His Aphrodite is not so much an object of lust as an *object
d'art* and Clyde's desire is "to constrain and fondle a perfect
object" (397). In Clyde's consciousness, in fact, Sondra comes
to represent a degree of perfection that utterly removes her
from the world of mundane human experience of which
Roberta is so much a part: "He lifted his hands as though to
caress her gently, yet holding them back, and at the same
dreamed into her eyes as might a devotee into those of a saint
. . ." (p. 398).

This destructive idol worship is not unfamiliar to Eliot,
and in "A Game of Chess," he presents us with a woman who,
like Sondra Finchley, occupies the throne of a traditional love

STRANGE BEDFELLOWS: ELIOT AND DREISER 61

goddess and appears to embody the passions which have the
potential to re-vitalize the arid landscapes of the wasteland.

> The Chair she sat in, like a burnished throne,
> Glowed on the marble, where the glass
> Held up by standards wrought with fruited vines
> From which a golden Cupidon peeped out
> (Another hid his eyes behind his wing)
> Doubled the flames of sevenbranched candelabra
> Reflecting light upon the table as
> The glitter of her jewels rose to meet it,
> From satin cases poured in rich profusion; . . .

But also like Sondra's, this imitation Cleopatra's allure is based
on the illusions of her "strange synthetic perfumes" which
"troubled, confused / And drowned the sense in odors." And,
of course, Clyde, prisoner of his senses and his fantasies,
associates the "synthetic perfumes" of Sondra's world with
genuine passion: "Sondra, Twelfth Lake, society, wealth, her
love and beauty" (460). For Clyde, this ingenuous linking of
society, wealth, and love ultimately focuses on life at Twelfth
Lake, for it is there that Clyde experiences his most splendid
moments with Sondra amidst the frivolous activity of the
resort population: "And then this scene, where a bright sun
poured a flood of crystal light upon a greensward that
stretched from tall pines to the silver rippling waters of a lake.
And off shore in a half dozen different directions the bright
white sails of small boats—the white and green and yellow
splashes of color, where canoes paddled by idling lovers were
passing in the sun! Summertime—leisure—warmth—
color—ease—beauty—love—all that he had dreamed of the
summer before, when he was so very much alone" (p. 482).

This lake country becomes symbolic of the possibilities of
a new life for Clyde; he imagines a veritable rebirth occurring
there. In Clyde's obsessive pursuit of that new life, however, it
becomes clear to him that in order to achieve it, he must
dispose of all remnants of his past. Having already deceived
Sondra and her peers concerning his family and their life in the
West, Clyde gradually concludes that Roberta and his unborn
child are the only remaining links with what he considers his

sordid past. They too must be destroyed. It is not surprising then that the very lake country which seems to symbolize the new life becomes the means to the destruction of the old. The lake, previously evocative of love, is transformed into a symbol of death: "And as they glided into this, this still dark water seemed to grip Clyde as nothing here or anywhere before this ever had—to change his mood. . . . And yet, what did it all suggest so strongly? Death! Death! More definitely than anything he had ever seen before. Death! But also a still, quiet, unprotesting type of death into which one, by reason of choice or hypnosis or unutterable weariness, might joyfully and gratefully sink. So quiet—so shaded—so serene" (p. 527).

The same strange sense of peace in death which mesmerizes Clyde as he gazes on the waters in which Roberta will momentarily sink in horror and incomprehension, accompanies the death by drowning of Phlebas the Phoenician in the "Death by Water" section of *The Waste Land.*

> A current under sea
> Picked his bones in whispers. As he rose and fell
> He passed the stages of his age and youth
> Entering the whirlpool.

But the ostensible peace in the death by drowning is a superficial and transitory peace; it precedes the final descent into the churning whirlpool and gives no hint of resurrection. If Phlebas is a corrupt version of the fertility god, and if his death signals finality with little or no hope of regeneration, then it is clear that Dreiser uses the death of Roberta Alden analogously in *An American Tragedy.* For Clyde Griffiths, Roberta and her child should represent fertility and its fruits. But he destroys them in order to procure his own "resurrection" into the new life which Sondra Finchley—as idol—represents. However, that destruction by drowning results merely in death for Clyde Griffiths—Roberta's, his child's, his own. Water, potential symbol for love and creativity in both poem and novel, becomes the emblem of sterility and death. For both Eliot and Dreiser "there is no water" imminent to quicken the "dried tubers" of the modern landscape.

While the cleansing and rejuvenating waters of spiritual rebirth are not immediately forthcoming for Eliot, there are nevertheless signs that the forces of creativity are not altogether lost: the thunder brings hope that self-control, giving, and compassion can re-awaken the deadened spirit of humanity; and, the narrator sits upon the shore, fishing, with the arid plain behind him, seeking the means to regeneration. There is guarded optimism in *The Waste Land* and hope that "these fragments I have shored against my ruins" (perhaps the poem itself) will prevail against the ubiquitous forces of destruction.

But for Clyde Griffiths there is no such promise. He has shored up no fragments against his ruin. He has changed little, understood less. Indeed, his last-minute conversion from a worship of the material to the religion of his mother and the Reverend McMillan is ironically undercut by the tone and texture of the imagery Dreiser uses to describe Clyde's last moments. "And his feet were walking, but automatically, it seemed. And he was conscious of that familiar shuffle—shuffle—as they pushed him on and on toward that door. Not it was here; now it was being opened. There it was—at last—the chair he had so often seen in his dreams—that he so dreaded—to which he was now compelled to go. He was being pushed toward that—into that—on—on—through the door which was now open—to receive him—but which was as quickly closed again on all the earthly life he had ever known" (p. 870).

Even the potentially purgative "fires" of the electric chair seem destined to work utter confusion on Clyde Griffiths. Reverend McMillan himself appears to recognize the desperation of Clyde's situation and remembers his final forlornness with horror: "He walked along the silent street—only to be compelled to pause and lean against a tree—leafless in the winter—so bare and bleak. Clyde's eyes! That look as he sank limply into that terrible chair, his eyes fixed nervously and, as he thought, appealingly and dazedly upon him and the group surrounding him" (p. 871).

Indeed, the minister's profound fear that Clyde died with no genuine understanding and no faith to transcend his earthly experience is reinforced by the barren images which Dreiser creates to describe Clyde's death. While his mother and the minister offered Clyde the opportunity to embrace religious acceptance (". . . how easy it was—if Clyde would but repeat and pray as he had asked him to—for him to know and delight in the 'peace that passeth all understanding' " [p, 784]), his response to their zeal was mechanical, half-hearted acceptance.

But as Eliot suggests, the state of "shantih"—"the Peace which passeth understanding"—is far more difficult to achieve than Reverend McMillan would like to believe. And for Dreiser, traditional modes of Christianity simply cannot lead man to that achievement; he makes his rejection of Christian salvation eminently clear with the masterful last chapter of *An American Tragedy* in which the cycle of Clyde's life is about to be repeated by another restless and lost boy.

Where there is hope in *The Waste Land*, there is despair in *An American Tragedy*. All Dreiser seems to leave us is "the vast skepticism and apathy of life."

5

Sherwood Anderson
and the Lyric Story

Eileen Baldeshwiler

At this date, not much remains to be done by way of
appointing Sherwood Anderson a place among American
writers; in fact he himself succinctly indicated his own
position when he remarked in the *Memoirs* that "For all my
egotism, I know I am but a minor figure." There is little
disagreement, either, about the work on which Anderson's
reputation rests — *Winesburg*, "Death in the Woods," a few
stories from *The Triumph of the Egg*. When we come to
estimate the accomplishment represented by *Winesburg*, however, things are not quite so clear. There are those who wish,
still, to view the collection as a frame-story, but they then
must reckon with the difficulty of seeming to reduce all the
stories to the dead level of equivalent exhibits. Those on the
other hand who want to read *Winesburg* as an initiation novel
about George Willard have to face the problem of resting their
case upon a character who in the end remains the thinnest
figment. To choose to relegate Anderson and *Winesburg* to the
limbo of regionalism is no longer acceptable.

Perhaps the sanest way is to view *Winesburg*, an uneven
collection, as a special kind of amalgam of naturalism and
lyricism. Every reader, whether approvingly or not, acknowledges the lyric intensity of the best Anderson stories. To

Herbert Gold, Anderson is "one of the purest, most intense poets of loneliness," while Irving Howe (who has also called Anderson a "pre-poet") holds that no other American writer "has yet been able to realize that strain of lyrical and nostalgic feeling which in Anderson's best work reminds one of another and greater poet of tenderness, Turgenev." Robert Gorham Davis ascribes the "great impression" made by *Winesburg* to its "freshness and lyric intensity." It is Paul Rosenfeld, however, who has seen most clearly that Anderson's lyricism is a method as much as an effect, for to this reader, Anderson's narratives "really are lyrics with epic characteristics, lyrics narrative of event."

In analyzing the elements that go into Anderson's lyricism, Rosenfeld notes the "legendary tone, the repetitions of slow rhythms and the loose joints" of the American tale, as well as the personal feeling that rises from the region between Anderson's "conscious and unconscious minds." But Rosenfeld places greatest stress on the purely verbal aspects of Anderson's poetic quality, for

> Anderson's inclusion among the authors of the lyric story . . . flows first of all from the fact that, using the language of actuality, he nonetheless invariably wrings sonority and cadence from it; unobtrusively indeed, without transcending the easy pitch of familiar prose . . . He sustains tones broadly with assonances and with repeated or echoing words and phrases. He creates accent-patterns and even stanza-like paragraphs with the periodic repetition or alternation of features such as syllables, sounds, words, phrases, entire periods . . .
> (Introduction to *The Sherwood Anderson Reader*, pp. xiv-xv.)

Many readers of Anderson will see these assertions as a part of Rosenfeld's special pleading and will doubtless be more inclined to share Irving Howe's belief that amidst the "chaos of his creative life Anderson had to cast around for a device with which to establish some minimum of order in his work" and found it "in the undulations of his verbal rhythms . . ." Indeed, it is precisely in those pieces where he was "most at sea imaginatively" that "the rhythm is most insistently established."

Rosenfeld, I think it can be shown, is on much stronger ground when contending that Anderson's stories are — in other ways — "lyrics with epic characteristics," and in holding that

> As for his own specimens of the lyric story-kind, they have 'inner form' like Gertrude Stein's, but their rhythms are livelier, longer, more self-completive than those of the somnolent lady-Buddha of the *rue de Fleurus*. While wanting the suavity of expression in Turgenev's lyric tales, Anderson's share the warmly singing tone of the Russian's, surpass them of course in point of tension, and have the Andersonian qualities of subtlety of attack and humorous and acute feeling, perceptions of the essential in the singular, glamour over the commonplace, boldness of image . . . Wonderfully they 'stay by us.' *(Sherwood Anderson Reader, p. xix.)*

What, precisely, is the "inner form" of Anderson's stories and how can they be said to be "lyrics with epic characteristics"?

In the first place it must be noted that the best Anderson stories always contain and lead up to a *revelation,* epiphany, or state of realized experience. Robert Morse Lovett has said that Anderson's stories "reach outward into the unknown," while Granville Hicks asserts that "Surfaces, deeds, even words scarcely concern him; everything is bent to the task of revelation." To Herbert Gold, "The experience of epiphany is characteristic of great literature, and the lyric tales of Anderson give this wonderful rapt coming-forth, time and time again." Irving Howe — uncomplimentarily — notes that Anderson "wrote best when he had no need to develop situations or show change and interaction —," but Anderson's own ideal of art is expressed precisely in his idealization of "the tale of perfect balance," with all its "elements . . . understood, an infinite number of minute adjustments perfectly made . . ."

Summaries of Anderson stories reveal even less than is usually the case about the significance of the narratives; obviously in Anderson what is at stake is not histories, biographies, gossip, or even tales. From Anderson's best work one does derive an unmistakable sense of authentic experience being worked out from within, in the manner of the great

Russians — Turgenev and Chekhov — with their unparalleled suggestiveness and extreme economy of means. Like the Russians, Anderson does not "import his poetry into the work — he allows only the poetry that is *there*" (Herbert Gold). The significance of an Anderson story has very little to do with the "facts" that are related but it has something to do with the arrangement of those facts and with the relationship of these "epic" elements to other, more properly poetic strains.

Anderson's abandonment of pure naturalism involved him in a movement away from structures dependent upon sequential action or gradually increased intensity and toward an arrangement of events which would better dramatize the centrifugal, diffused, resonant effect his materials called for. The halting, tentative, digressive style, and the circular, hovering or "Chinese box" approach to "what happened" thus do not so much demonstrate Anderson's affectation of the manner of oral tale-telling as they illustrate his understanding that the "epic" base of the story must be manipulated in such a way that weight is thrown upon the significance of the happenings as it reveals itself to the central consciousness and to the reader, rather than upon the events themselves. This is, of course, essentially a "poetic" strategy.

Moreover, as Jon Lawry has demonstrated in his reading of "Death in the Woods," the narrative strategy, by which the story is not really "told" to any assumed audience, makes it possible that "its process of growth and contact is discovered by the audience, through the act itself rather than through the narrator's relation of the act," for "The audience is invited to enter as individuals into a process almost identical with that of the narrator and to reach with him for contact with another life." This narrative method makes it possible for the "unacknowledged audience" to "share directly not only the narrator's responses but his act of discovering and creating those responses" — and this is precisely the "method" of the post-symbolist lyric. It is also the technique by which in Anderson fantasy is most controlled, or, "if not exactly controlled, simplified, given a single lyrical line," and ambivalent — if not contradictory — emotions enfolded within one action.

Before turning to an analysis of stories by Anderson which illustrate the lyrical effects we have been describing, we may mention briefly other marks of the poetic character of his narration: non-realistic, ritualistic dialogue, the use of symbols to embody and dramatize themes, and the exploitation of suggestiveness, "the art of leaving out." In thinking of the whole of Anderson's achievement it is well to bear in mind that he began his writing career "under the influence and patronage of the realists at the time when realism was being modified by symbolism" (Robert Morss Lovett).

The first story of *Winesburg*, "Hands," affords a vivid illustration of one of the ways in which Anderson manipulates his story-line in such a way as to evoke a maximum resonance from the events narrated. Normal time sequence is almost obliterated as Anderson penetrates with the reader further and further into the mysterious recesses of Wing Biddlebaum's mind. The tragedy of Wing Biddlebaum is of course presented by means of the things that happened to him — not even the lyric story can totally dispense with the "epic" elements essential for the narrative genres — but the events of Biddlebaum's life are presented neither straightforwardly nor in a conventional flashback sequence. Rather, Anderson uses a kind of box-within-box structure as he takes us into the interior mystery of his character by means of a series of vignettes in which Biddlebaum is revealed first through the eyes of George Willard (whom Anderson cunningly utilizes as both the confidant the plot requires and as an objective correlative for all that Biddlebaum seeks), and finally through the protagonist's own sense of himself. But these sections flow so smoothly through the story-teller's hands, and are so completely suffused with Wing Biddlebaum's consciousness, that we are not aware of any awkward juncture between sections. In this structure, the first event in Biddlebaum's "chronological" life becomes the last in the record of his emotional life, because the beating of the schoolmaster was the one event which both precipitated and contained the entire mystery of the man. With the presentation of this event, also, Anderson has brought his story to its maximum level of universalization, for without resorting to allegory but by remaining wholly within the confines of realism Anderson has made us feel that we are all Wing Biddlebaum and that we are also the men who cast him out of the village half dead, and that Biddlebaum's situation enfolds within it the entire condition of man. The last section of the story is a beautifully falling cadence; coming after the event of the beating, it simply shows us Wing Biddlebaum as he now is, as we have made him, as we are:

> When the rumble of the evening train that took away the express cars loaded with the day's harvest of berries had passed and restored the silence of the summer night, he went again to walk upon the veranda. In the darkness he could not see the hands . . . Although he still hungered for the presence of the boy, who was the medium through which he expressed his love of man, the hunger became again a part of his loneliness and his waiting. Lighting a lamp, Wing Biddlebaum . . . prepared to undress for the night. A few stray white bread crumbs lay on the cleanly washed floor by the table; putting the lamp upon a low stool he began to pick up the crumbs, carrying them to his mouth one by one with unbelievable rapidity.

Anderson's exploitation of the symbolic aspect of the eating of bread, and of the hands themselves, requires no commentary.

Other kinds of dislocation of the narrative line appear in "Adventure," in "The Thinker," and in "Sophistication." In the first story, a report of the exterior events of Alice Hindman's life is counterpointed by an account of the development of her inward, emotional life. The patterns move in opposite directions, for while Alice's outward existence appears to run steadily downhill into dull meaninglessness, her inward life climbs with increasing intensity toward a climax of desperation and hysteria. A review of only the story's outward events would seem to confirm the frequent accusation that Anderson is given to assembling large, undifferentiated narrative masses out of which he is unable to bring order or illumination, yet when he is at his best, Anderson's unfolding of inner life — even when it is not so strongly cross-grained as in "Adventure" — does provide a sufficient make-weight for outward event, and in fact the outcome toward which the narrative strives is precisely an evocation of the *quality* of the relationship between inner and outward event. In Anderson, this evocation is essentially poetic or musical. And while restraint is not a trait usually ascribed to Anderson, it is this virtue of tact which rules such sections of his narrative as the conclusion of "Adventure," in which Alice Hindman, recalling herself from the wild scene in the street, goes weeping to bed with the words,

> "What is the matter with me? I will do something dreadful if I am not careful," she thought, and turning her face to the wall, began trying to force herself to face bravely the fact that many people must live and die alone, even in Winesburg.

In "Sophistication," the "epic" elements are arranged in such a way that George Willard's restlessness and puzzlement are dramatized — rather than merely reported — through the structure itself with its jerky, spasmodic focusing and re-focusing. Anderson, moreover, demonstrates a high degree of cunning in not attempting any sort of philosophic resolution of George's dilemmas but by providing instead a rather quiet culminating scene in which all the contradictory aspects of George's and Helen's consciousness are caught up in a symbolic action (is it ludicrous to see a resemblance to Yeat's use of the great-rooted blossomer?):

> It was so they went down the hill . . . Once, running swiftly forward, Helen tripped George and he fell. He squirmed and shouted. Shaking with laughter, he rolled down the hill. Helen ran after him. For just a moment she stopped in the darkness . . . when the bottom of the hill was reached and she came up to the boy, she took his arm and walked beside him in dignified silence.

Other symbol-like devices appearing in the story are the cornfields, the dry leaves and trees, the stallion, and the grandstand. Anderson's conducting of the narrative is too loose and diffuse for these objects to form a genuine symbolic pattern, but their presence does add power to the lyric suggestiveness of the narrative.

Structure in "The Thinker" is much more complex. As in "Hands," the problem here is to develop for the reader the sense of a particular personality, in this case one not nearly so unusual as Wing Biddlebaum, and that of a much younger man. Anderson begins the story by describing in his rambling, tentative manner Seth Richmond's house, the circumstances of his mother's widowhood, and her present feeling for the boy. A quarter of the story elapses, before we hear any words from Seth himself, but with his return from the runaway trip we are moved directly into his consciousness and from then on the story is told from Seth's point of view. At the same time, the eerie disjointedness of experience is conveyed directly with (for Anderson) surprisingly little editorializing as we follow the young man through his brief visit with George Willard, his eavesdropping on the quarreling hotel men, his meeting with old Turk in the street, and his unsatisfactory encounter with Helen. At almost exactly midpoint in the story comes the devastating self-revelatory comment that Seth "was not what the men of the town, and even his mother, thought him to be," for "No great underlying purpose lay back of his habitual silence, and he had no definite plan for his life." Observing from afar the sullen, furious baker with the empty milk bottle in his hand, Seth "wished that he himself might become thoroughly stirred by something . . ."

For the elucidation of Seth's identity, Anderson has ranged around the central silence and dumbness of the young man various "talkers," including Turk Smollett with his "absurdly boyish mind," the half dangerous old wood chopper "who hurries along the middle of the road with his wheelbarrow and its nicely balanced dozen long boards." Seth knew that

> when Turk got into Main Street he would become the center
> of a whirlwind of cries and comments, that in truth the old

man was going far out of his way in order to pass through Main
Street and exhibit his skill in wheeling the boards. "If George
Willard were here, he'd have something to say," thought Seth.

Along with the windy political quarrelers briefly overheard in
the hotel lobby is grouped the emptily ebullient George
Willard who announces, "I know what I'm going to do. I'm
going to fall in love. I've been sitting here and thinking it over
and I'm going to do it." The climax comes as Seth, equally
disgusted and bored with George's prattle and his own silence,
seeks out Helen White, who utters almost no words during
their walk together.

The central meaning of the boy's encounter with all these
persons is conveyed in two interpolations. In the first, during
the silent walk with Helen, Seth remembers the moment the
day before in a field where he had heard "A soft humming
noise" and looking down "had seen the bees everywhere all
about him in the long grass":

> He stood in a mass of weeds that grew waist-high in the field
> that ran away from the hillside. The weeds were abloom with
> tiny purple blossoms and gave forth an overpowering fra-
> grance.

Now imagining himself with Helen in that field, Seth thought
he would lie "perfectly still, looking at her and listening to the
army of bees that sang . . . above his head." But a little later,
as the distant thunder moves closer and the spot where they
are sitting is momentarily illuminated by lightning, "The
garden that had been so mysterious and vast, a place that . . .
might have become the background for strange and wonderful
adventures, now seemed no more than an ordinary Winesburg
back yard, quite definite and limited in its outlines." Unable
either to go forward into a meaningful existence or to preserve
his integrity by a return to innocence, Seth Richmond can
only stand, after Helen's departure, "staring, perplexed and
puzzled . . . as he had been perplexed and puzzled by all the
life of the town out of which she had come." Again, it is
through the arrangement of actions and by a quiet exploitation of the symbolic aspects of objects and events that

Anderson succeeds in bringing before us a full-dimensioned protagonist fraught with the burdens and fleeting joys resembling our own.

It is in the *Winesburg* stories such as "The Thinker," "Adventure," "Hands," "Sophistication," and "The Untold Lie" that Anderson manages to reinforce a certain surface fidelity with what Ernest Boyd has called the "deeper realism which sees beyond and beneath the exterior world to the hidden reality which is the essence of things." By combining in a special manner the story's "epic" elements with characteristic lyric devices, Anderson is able, at least on occasion, to reach the "something totally private, untouchable, beyond appearance and action, in all of us" and thus exemplifies his own belief that "To live is to create new forms: with the body in living children; in new and more beautiful forms carved out of materials; in the creation of a world of the fancy; in scholarship; in clear and lucid thought . . ."

6

The Baroque Waste Land of
James Branch Cabell

Maurice Duke

James Branch Cabell, the author of fifty-two books and
the creator of an elaborate system of mythology which forms
the basis of his fiction, seemed to be different from most of
the major American writers of the 1920s. While other novelists
were realistically dissecting the society in which they had been
raised, often fleeing from that society in order to do so,
Cabell, living comfortably in Richmond, Virginia, was headed,
in matters of art, in quite another direction. Seemingly
uninterested in the Carol Kennicotts, the Jay Gatsbys, the
Jake Barneses, and people such as Eliot's narrators, in whose
fictional lives we find a major part of the era's ethos, he
interpreted the twentieth century, particularly the years
between World War I and the stock market crash, with the use
of both real and imaginary historical characters, most of whom
he placed in a mythological land which he named Poictesme. It
was a realm in which time and space dissolved, leaving only the
imagination to grapple with the vast fictional illusion he had
created.

Considering Cabell's background, education, and temperament, perhaps one would conclude that it was inevitable that
he should come to interpret the world in which he lived
through the medium of myth, which allowed him considerable

esthetic distance between himself and his subjects. Born into a
family, and a region, that was quite conscious of its past, he
was educated and lived almost all of his life in that region.
Paris and New York of the 1920s, so much in vogue with the
major writers of the day, held little to excite him. Rather, he
preferred the solitude of his family, first at Dumbarton
Grange, located a few miles north of Richmond, and later on
Richmond's prestigious Monument Avenue, where he lived
from 1925 until his death in 1958. By all odds, Cabell seemed
to be a man out of step with his times, truly the "scarlet
dragonfly embedded in opaque amber," as H. L. Mencken
called him in "The Sahara of the Bozart."

Cabell, however, is not as he appears at first sight.
Although in subject matter he remained apart from the literary
mainstream of the 1920s, his world view belies, as do the
world views of many of the decade's major writers, his concept
that life is an emotional, cultural, and intellectual vacuum. For
Cabell the dream may be the ultimate reality, but it offers no
more than a diversion from those parts of existence which
man, because of various self-constructed codes by which he
lives, will not allow himself to face. Thus, from the point of
view which forms the philosophical basis of the Cabellian
world, existence offers only appearances, never realities. And,
if the appearance is the reality, then there is no still point, no
central solid core in human life.

One can best understand Cabell's world view from his
ambitious eighteen-volume Storisende Edition, published by
Robert M. McBride and Company, between 1927 and 1930.
Although this multi-volume edition is sometimes said to
contain both the best and the worst of Cabell side by side, it is
the place in which one finds the majority of his works as he
chose to leave them for posterity. He wished all future reissues
of his books to be based on the Storisende Edition. And so
concerned was he about the integrity of the edition that after
it was completed, he began to publish under the name Branch
Cabell, because, as he wrote in the Introduction to *These
Restless Heads* (1932), he wished to allot to the Storisende

Edition, which he also called the Biography of the Life of Dom Manuel,

> its own exclusive author; and [thus to limit] the output of this now delimiting writer to the Biography alone.
>
> For yet another affair [Cabell continues] I am minded to render. . .the literary career of my predecessor unique, in that his Collected Works must now stand, and so perish by-and-by, in the exact form he designed and completed,—no blunders save his own, with no inclusions untivitated by him, with no loose ends anywhere, with no incongruous editing by other hands, and (above all) with no lackwit replevinings from his wastepaper basket conducted by his heirs and creditors. . . .

In the Preface to the second edition of *Beyond Life,* published first in 1919 and again in 1927 as the first volume in the Storisende Edition, Cabell presents the schema which, as he says, governs the whole Biography:

> Above all does this book attempt to outline the three possible attitudes toward human existence which have been adopted or illustrated, and at times blended by the many descendents of Manuel. I mean, the Chivalric attitude, the Gallant attitude, and what I can only describe as the poetic attitude. The descendants of Manuel have at various times variously viewed life as a testing; as a toy; and as raw material. They have variously sought during their existence upon earth to become—even by the one true test, of their private thoughts while lying awake at night—admirable; or to enjoy life; or to create something more durable than life.

Maintaining steadfastly that the Biography of the Life of Dom Manuel should be read as one gigantic book, with each individual novel forming one of its chapters, Cabell explored his three themes of chivalry, gallantry, and poetry in minute detail in the Storisende Edition.

The first of the themes, chivalry, is introduced in *Figures of Earth,* actually the second volume in the Storisende Edition. First published in 1921, when Cabell was at the height of his powers, this book introduces Dom Manuel, who is an important figure in the Biography. A young pigtender upon whom lies his mother's *geas*, as Cabell writes, "to make

myself a splendid and admirable young man in every respect,"
Manuel, in his ignorance, attempts to follow his mother's
wishes by forming a model of a man out of clay. Later, as he
leaves his pigs and comes to operate as an allegorical figure in
the realm of Poictesme, we learn that Manuel is a person
whose every action has been prefigured by his failure to
understand the true nature of the geas which his mother had
laid upon him. He cannot understand, of course, because, as
the subtitle of the book, "A Comedy of Appearances,"
indicates, one cannot firmly grasp reality. For Manuel—and, as
we subsequently learn, for all Cabellian characters—life is only
appearance, reality being that which we create in our search,
doomed to failure, for order.

This abortive search for order, and the way in which,
craving perfect order and failing to find it we attempt to create
our own, are the subjects of *The Silver Stallion*, the next book
in the series. In this volume, first published in 1926 and one of
the best of the Cabellian romances, we find that a myth has
sprung up about Manuel. Now dead, he has become deified,
and in the process the myth has become far greater and more
satisfying than the actual accomplishments of the man could
ever have been. Closely paralleling Christ, the mythic Manuel
of *The Silver Stallion* lives in the memories of people as being
the saviour—"redeemer," as Cabell calls him—who someday
will return to Poictesme, thereby blending the myth and the
reality and causing perfect understanding among the inhabitants, his followers. Ironically, the source for his statement
that he will return is the young Jurgen, the central character in
another novel, who fabricates a story about having personally
witnessed the deification of Manuel. Jurgen does so in order
that his father, one of Manuel's followers, will not whip him
for having stayed too long away from home. From Jurgen's
story springs the myth, neatly paralleling the subtitle of the
novel, "A Comedy of Redemption." Chivalry, then, as well as
all its attending virtues, is born of misunderstanding and of
fabrication, and the world in which it lives, Poictesme, is, of
course, a touchstone for the real world.

Moving to *Domnei,* the third book to treat the theme of chivalry, we find the central idea slightly altered. Cabell defined the concept of Domnei as woman worship, considering it an offshoot of the central chivalric ideal. Couched in the style of late nineteenth century romance, *Domnei* chronicles the love, estrangement, and final reconciliation of two people named Perion and Milicent. Overly stylized and highly lyrical, the book's artistic beauty is no parallel for its negative philosophical statement, however. A good part of the story is given over to Perion's search for his abducted love. But when he finds her he realizes that he and she are not the same two people who loved formerly. "He found a woman," the narrator says, who was

> still a compelling beauty. Oh, yes, past doubt: but this woman was a stranger to him, as he now knew with an odd sense of sickness. Thus, then, had ended the quest of Melicent. Their love had flouted Time and Fate. . . . For this was not the girl whom Perion had loved in far-away Poictesme.

Further, the narrator says, "I cannot even tell you just what mystery it was of which Perion became aware." Once again, as Cabell dramatizes it, we find a severe disparity between what one would wish and what actually is. And, once again, because ideals and reality have conflicted with each other, the human heart goes wanting.

In *Chivalry* and *The Rivet in Grandfather's Neck,* the last two volumes treating the theme of chivalry as it descended from Manuel, and in *The Line of Love,* which treats all three themes, we find the chivalric attitude as it passed through the English renaissance and finally into Virginia in the late nineteenth century. *Chivalry* and *The Line of Love* are comprised of short stories which Cabell published early in the twentieth century. *The Rivet in Grandfather's Neck,* first published in 1915, is a full-length novel which best carries forth the ideas of chivalry, as Cabell sees it, in modern times.

In the 1927-30 Author's Note to *The Rivet in Grandfather's Neck,* Cabell notes that Colonel Rudolph Musgrave, like his ancestor Manuel, had a charge placed upon him. "He served his geas," Cabell writes, "in so far that he frankly accepted, in theory at least, every obligation which life laid upon him. But he, almost as frankly, preferred to the performance of a mere drab obligation the executing of a fine gesture which he himself could cordially admire. He was, in short, a gentleman. . . ." Here, of course, is the central problem. But in order to understand Musgrave's dilemma, we need to be mindful of the way he is reacting to his recent past. As the novel unfolds, we find that his greatest flaw is his Southern chauvinism. A genealogist engaged by the local historical society, he, like the stereotyped white Southerner, has a nostalgic sense of longing for the ante-bellum past. This is his geas, the rivet in his neck. Because he is a gentleman, he must live within the confines of the code which he has inherited; but because of a change in Southern society—the Civil War, Reconstruction, the redistribution of wealth, and the change in the culture—the code is no longer viable. Living in the modern world, and longing for the past one which is irretrievable, his life is, as the subtitle of the novel makes clear, "A Comedy of Limitations."

But if chivalry is indeed a myth, a fabrication made by man in his feeble attempt to elevate himself, what of gallantry, the second of Cabell's main themes in the Biography of the Life of Dom Manuel? Chivalry, we recall, had to do with a self-imposed testing, and we clearly see from the novels which treat this theme, that the test was not really worth having taken, as the rewards for having passed it are indeed meager. Gallantry, however, one might expect to be different. After all, if, in the Cabellian world, the test yields unsatisfactory results, perhaps the answer lies in viewing life as a toy, from which one can detach oneself. Thus one becomes an existentialist, seizing the moment for what it has to offer, and ignoring any attempt at personal elevation.

In the Author's Note to *Gallantry*, first published in 1907 and incorporated into the Storisende Edition in 1928, Cabell makes a statement which sums up the gallant mode of living quite succinctly. Although supposedly written to introduce that single volume, the preface can be taken as encompassing all the volumes of the Biography which deal with the gallant mode:

> Each one of these persons [those who follow the way of gallantry] dealt with hereinafter, I repeat, accepted his terrestial surroundings without really bothering about the inner being of himself or of his companions, or about any other matters either above or below his chance-assigned orbit in life. These people, in fine, were worldings, although not necessarily in an ignoble sense of the word.

Thus it is that the main character in *Jurgen,* by far Cabell's best known novel, owing to its famous seizure and trial in New York City in 1920, takes a year-long odyssey, during which time he has exotic, often sexual, adventures with people from both myth and imagination. At the end of the time, however, he shrugs—the way in which Cabell's gallant persons accept the adversities of life—and goes back home with his wife, Dame Lisa. Thus it is also that Florian, the protagonist in *The High Place,* has an extended dream in which he is clearly bisexual at one point, seduces numerous women at others, and finally murders four wives. Ironically, when he awakens from the dream and goes about the business of living his life, we see, from Cabell's epilogue, that he is doomed to live in real life the actions about which he dreamed. Subtitled "A Comedy of Disenchantment," this book gives us a view of the dream and the reality when they blend together, making gallantry not a toy, but actually a code which degrades self and destroys others. Again, in *The Cords of Vanity,* which is to the theme of gallantry what *The Rivet in Grandfather's Neck* is to the theme of chivalry, in that both novels treat their respective themes as they are found in the Virginia which Cabell was raised, we find the same kind of thing. Subtitled "A Comedy of Shirking," this novel is a first-person narrative spoken by Robert Townsend. A latter-day Florian, Townsend repeats his ancestor's actions, but in a kind of mauve decade Virginia setting. His libertinism, coupled with his confession-like statements to the reader, both indicate a person, who although

he may be trying to espouse the ideals of gallantry, actually
belies his inability to cope with the world in which he lives.

About the way of gallantry, then, one might generalize as
follows: Although, under the dictates of this code one should
view life as a toy, as a pleasant diversion, not aspiring to life's
highest ideals, nor disdaining its more mundane aspects, such a
view is really impossible. Why, we cannot really say, because
Cabell does not clearly tell us. The implication seems to be,
however, that chivalry is of a higher order than gallantry. But
chivalry, as we have already seen, is a myth, man's longshot,
but failing, attempt to lend meaning and thus permanence to
his life. So, too, is gallantry a failure, in that man, because of
his idealizing faculty, wants more than gallantry; he wants
chivalry, although ironically he may not know that he does.
Thus far, the Biography of the Life of Dom Manuel has
implied that neither of them is attainable.

Finally, however, there is the way of poetry. If man,
seeking chivalry, reaches out from the center of his existence
and fails, and if, seeking gallantry he looks around him and
fails, he still may be able to look within himself, finding there
the ability to shape life through art, thus giving to the flux the
permanence that he so ardently desires.

In the extended Auctorial Induction to *The Certain Hour,*
a collection of ten tales centered on the way of poetry, the
earliest of which was written in 1907, Cabell addresses his
reader directly. Noting that man has always had an innate
desire "to write perfectly of beautiful happenings"—to create
perfection through art—he goes on to make a statement that
comments significantly on the creator, in this case the poet:

> People whose tastes happen to be literary are entirely too
> prone to too much long-faced prattle about literature, which,
> when all is said, is never a controlling factor in anybody's life.
> The automobile and the telephone, the accomplishments of
> Mr. Thomas Edison and Mr. Luther Burbank, and it would be
> permissible to add, of Mr. Henry Ford, influence nowadays, in
> one fashion or another, every moment of every living
> American's existence; whereas had America produced, instead,

a second Milton or a Dante, it would at most have caused a few
of us to spend a few spare evenings rather differently.

Although Cabell did not mean this statement to introduce the
theme of poetry as it is treated in the Biography of the Life of
Dom Manuel, it is tempting to so use it, as it focuses so neatly
on the problem of the artist as his lot is dramatized in several
of the books in the series. Clearly, this extended statement,
when contrasted with the latter one about man's desire "to
write perfectly of beautiful happenings," gives us a strong
indication that, in the long run, the way of poetry will offer
no more than the ways of gallantry and of chivalry. And,
indeed, when one looks at the major novels which deal with
the poetic approach, that being the idea that life is raw
material which has the potential of being made permanent
through art, he finds that such is the case.

Published first in 1927, *Something About Eve* is one of the
major source studies for the way of poetry. In that book,
incorporated into the Storisende Edition in 1929, Cabell
dramatizes the ways in which his protagonist, the poet Gerald
Musgrave, fails to achieve, as Cabell calls it, *Antan,* the perfect
point, at which the poet, after conceptualizing the ideal, is
able to record it for all time, thus satisfying both himself and
his audience.

In many ways a typical Cabell hero, Gerald Musgrave,
living in Virginia in the first decade of the nineteenth century,
has a prolonged love affair with Evelyn Townsend, a sexually
insatible, but genteel, married woman, the wife of one of his
friends. A writer who has pretensions of producing immortal
works of literature, Musgrave has a dream in which he
exchanges places with someone who agrees to assume his
duties as both writer and lover. After the two have changed
lives, however, Musgrave the poet does little with his newly
found freedom. Following his consorting with figures from
myth, imagination, and history—reminiscent of Jurgen—he
succumbs to the allurements of a domestically oriented
temptress, wasting away his precious time sitting peacefully on
her porch, eating her cooking, and wearing clothes she has

provided for him. Here Cabell is pointing out the inability of
the way of poetry to move outside the confines of purely
human limitations. Perhaps the poet, symbolized by Musgrave,
may aspire to seek permanence through art, but he fails. In the
end Musgrave returns from his dream and must take up his life
where he left it. His surrogate neither satisfied Evelyn's
nymphomania nor completed any work on Gerald's most
important manuscript, which, because he now knows it will
never be finished, Gerald destroys.

Yet, as Cabell further noted in the Author's Note to
Something About Eve, "to fail as a poet may very well be to
succeed as a human being." In order to explore this idea we
need to turn to the ten tales in *The Certain Hour.* In the
author's Note for this volume, the eleventh in the Storisende
Edition, Cabell comments that Gerald Musgrave of *Something
About Eve* gained success as a human being, although he failed
as a poet. "Now the ten with whom we deal hereinafter," he
continues, "all more or less brilliantly succeeded" as poets.
"Yet as human beings no one of them might be ranked as
successful." Although Shakespeare, Sheridan, Pope, and
Herrick, along with others, are seen as being successful
practitioners of their art and thus giving permanence to a part
of the flux of existence, their lives, Cabell intimates, belie their
contribution because in the Cabellian world practical action,
and the theoretical contemplation which results in perfect art
must harmonize. "In brief," Cabell writes of the ten people in
The Certain Hour, "they lived as poets; and all poets, until
Time and Conformity have subdued them into rational beings,
must live as exiles." If, in *Something About Eve,* Cabell is
pointing out, as I have suggested, the inability of the way of
poetry to lead one outside the confines of purely human
limitation, then in *The Certain Hour* he is most likely further
pointing out that the way of poetry, which creates a law unto
itself, may also very well rob its followers of their basic
humanity. The final statement thus indicates that the way of
poetry is no more attainable, or satisfying for that matter,
than the ways of chivalry and of gallantry. All indications are

that man cannot shape life through art because in the process of the quest to do so he either succumbs to worldly pleasures or loses so much of his humanity that he really does not know what life is.

Where, then, do we stand? What is the statement made by Cabell's ambitious Biography of the Life of Dom Manuel, a work which occupied him for the latter part of the 1920s?

If we use Eliot's *The Waste Land,* probably the central poem of the first half of the twentieth century, as a touchstone or organizing metaphor, we see that in subject matter and social comment, the two writers are poles apart. *The Waste Land* paints for us a world in which we hear the pub keeper calling time, in which the sex act is as mechanical as putting a record on the gramophome, in which the meaning of our myths and the richness of our culture have somehow been inverted, a world in which "in this decayed hole among the mountains" we stand waiting for cleansing and renewing rain but hearing only thunder. On the surface, Cabell's world is obviously not like this. Cabell chides us with his urbanity, dazzles us with his ironical wit and captivates us with the beauties of Poictesme, a realm which is more perfect than any which we will ever be privileged to see. Beneath the surface, however, lies a kind of spiritual wasteland, not unlike Eliot's, in that in Poictesme nothing is really worth the effort because nothing can really ever be accomplished. Cabell's chivalric heroes, those who view life as a testing, find that there is really nothing to test oneself against because the myths which form the core of existence have been fabricated both by chance and by opportunism. The gallant figures, those to whom life is a toy, a diversion, find a similar world facing and opposing them. These characters—Jurgen, for example—are the defeatists who live their lives by compromise. Knowing full well that their codes of behavior and the operation of the real world are alien to each other, they nevertheless, like J. Alfred Prufrock, "prepare a face to meet the faces" that they meet, perennially venturing forth to attend their ritualistic, and metaphorically insignificant, tea parties. The way of poetry offers little more, because in the Cabellian world it is impossible to be both poet and person. One must choose, and in the choosing one will invariably feel unfulfilled because he can have only half of what he feels the life of art should afford him.

Eliot's waste land and Cabell's Poictesme are not too far apart then. In the former, man is out of touch with his mythology; in the latter his mythology is seen as being his hostage against mediocrity, but it is false. Again, in the former the mainstream of western culture—its art in the largest sense—is seen as being degraded while in the latter we see a world in which art counts less than the inventions of a Thomas Edison and a Henry Ford. Finally, in the former there is a cancerous malady at the core of society. In the latter the same malady is obviously there, but Cabell attempts to conceal it in artifice. These two writers never met. The one was a central figure in both the European and American literary scene while the other worked quietly in his private study in Richmond, Virginia. There can be little doubt, however, that both saw the world from a quite similar point of view.

7

Baedekers, Babbittry, and Baudelaire

David G. Pugh

If T. S. Eliot published a Baedeker's Guide to the landmarks of a spiritual wasteland in 1922, then in the same year Sinclair Lewis constructed a sociologist's Ideal-Type to analyze a cultural wasteland, both on Main Street in smalltown Gopher Prairie and in Zip City, George F. Babbitt's Zenith, Winnemac, U.S.A. The first one-fourth of the novel closely follows Babbitt's daily routines and rituals, as the individual's symbolic behavior surfaces in his use of artifacts and in his social contacts, revealing the spirit and unspoken assumptions of an era. Often, one vivid image will encapsulate an entire spectrum of attitudes, as does the billboard of Dr. Eckleburg's eyeglasses over the valley of ash heaps at the dump outside New York City. Once visualized in the pages of F. Scott Fitzgerald's, *The Great Gatsby,* the eyes become a quick shorthand reference, a symbol of the wasteland for the reader to absorb, to recall, and along with Eliot, to have "shored against my ruins."

Is the image of George F. Babbitt, Realtor, still this encapsulated shorthand? Even though Lewis predicted accurately in a letter to his publisher (Dec. 17, 1920) that in two years the country would be talking of 'Babbitry', is it still a *potent imagent,* (as is Don Quixote, tilting at windmills, impossible dream or not) or has it joined many others, once trippingly on the tongue,—a Pecksniff? a Malaprop?—now smelling of the academic lamp or attic dust? Lewis, in his 1930 Nobel Prize address, himself accused the American Literary Establishment of preferring its literature "clear and cold and pure and very dead," and offered Henry Wadsworth Longfellow as a horrible example, from fifty years before, of such embalmed, boring, genteel artistry. Should we now, another half-century later, insert Lewis' name in Longfellow's place? Is Babbittry dead? Geoffrey Moore, an Englishman, writing a few years after Lewis' death, asked if we had outgrown *Babbitt*— had it gone the way of the flivvers, Kitty Hawks, and the unfenced prairies; . . . yet hypocrisy, provincialism, prejudice, all forms of materialism, have only changed their clothes, (and not just in America). Babbitt: alive, readable? . . . or cold, boring, and very dead?

Recently, attempts to interest new readers in Lewis have emphasized his "sociological imagination," his documentation, his early use of concepts and reportorial devices since popularized by David Riesman, C. Wright Mills, and Erving Goffman, among others, such descriptions of behavior as Inner-and Outer-directed, as alienated, or as gamesmanship. Ever since the Lynds, analyzing Muncie, Indiana as *Middletown* (1927, 1936), social scientists have fashioned their prose techniques after ones Lewis had already used, so that now he reads (more so than in 1922) "just like a sociology book." Sophistication about peer-group pressures is much more likely these days, when sociograms of who prefers whom for "best friend" can be charted and interpreted for fifth graders. There are still signs around us today revealing a wasteland of boredom and conformity, and we may be even more willing than readers in 1922 to look for symbolic significance in ordinary behavior, to "read meaning into" surface details of a small incident in daily life.

Do the surface incidents in *Babbitt* (or *Main Street*, 1920) provide enough cues and contexts to relate them to our habitual daily behavior? Are the images in Eliot's *Waste Land* also discernible in Lewis' prose reporting life in the 'Unreal City', *Zenith*? Will observing George F. Babbitt serve as an objective correlative, a tangible image for a feeling, a state of emotion, as Eliot theorized? As readers, are we able to recognize part of ourselves in Babbitt's behavior? Can we simultaneously discern the "state of feeling" Lewis furnished us? A reader can obtain an image of daily life from a Sears Roebuck or Monkey Ward catalog, although the esthetic goal of also deriving a state of feeling from any image may require noticing rhetorical forms of presentation which are somewhat different from those found in most sociology books.

One way of getting at the "state of feeling" evoked by Babbitt is to compare the original impact with the retrospective interpretations after his death. *Babbitt* was read in 1922 partly by young rebels fleeing the bourgeois middle class backgrounds in which they had grown up, venerating H. L. Mencken, who having coined a label, the *Booboisie,* quite understandably felt in his review of the novel that *Babbitt* was a "social document of a high order." May Sinclair, acknowledging the realistic effects, predicted, however, that "though nobody will recognize himself. . . everybody will recognize somebody else." One small phrase in her review is suggestive of our reactions to the book so many years later. "You can smell the ash heaps behind every house." This minor image can evoke a not so minor feeling in anyone who has removed large clinkers and either powdery or wet ash from a coal-fired grate furnace; it evokes a multi-sensual kinesthetic effect—but most of us now have experience only with oil or gas heat.

Lewis may be ". . . cold, and very dead" for readers today, unless they can enter the social world the novelist very clearly created at the time he wrote. This holds true for any non-contemporary work. If Thackeray mentions a young woman wearing lavender gloves and a yellow scarf with a purple and wine-red shot silk dress or notes that there were fires (fireplaces) in the bedrooms of a house, some awareness of the significance, of the *variation from the norm,* is helpful. Heated bedrooms are not likely to seem luxurious to a reader today. Babbitt's clear-glass bathroom towel-racks set in nickel wall brackets have to be compared to porcelain or wood-dowel racks, (the 1922 norm) to feel their 'uptodateness'.

Literature is not so much a mirror which *reflects* life realistically as it is a prism or lens which *refracts* selected, condensed aspects of thought and feeling. This refraction exaggerates, as does a convex mirror such as a shiny chrome hubcap, and one frequent justification for scholarly labor is the need to give a reader in a later time some sense of the actual knowledge of the world possessed by the readers at the time of original composition or publication—knowing that it is, indeed, an impossible dream to evoke 100% of it. Any work which has staying power transcends these limitations and offers enough internal clues of tone and context to remain intelligible without recourse to guide books or prefatory essays or 'bogus' footnotes like Eliot's to *The Waste Land*. But isn't a Baedeker for a foreign city similar to footnotes and explanations? Should one read it before a trip, or carry it along and stop at every street corner, or read it afterwards?

Mark Schorer, summing up his massive 867 page biography of Lewis, emphasizes Lewis' *documentation*, his creation of Babbitt, showing the "standardization of business culture and the stultification of morals under middle class convention," concluding that as Americans, even today, we can hardly imagine ourselves without drawing upon Lewis' writings as a background. As recently as April 1968, in a CBS TV documentary filmed in Duluth, Minnesota, a Lions Club heard Pat Hingle deliver a speech spoken by Babbitt to a Booster Club in the 1922 novel and reacted favorably to its sentiments. His values live on. D. J. Dooley, on the other hand, feels that it is not documentation, but satiric exaggeration, the shaping by genre and formal technique, by literary convention, which enables the book to affect us, by *intensifying* and *ordering* our experiences, pointing out to us, Baedeker-fashion, what we then perceive. If art historian Ernst Gombrich is right that in viewing a painting "the innocent eye sees nothing," because it is both naive and untutored in what to look for, the same conclusion seems doubly applicable to the reader of such a genre as satire. How do you tell photographic realism from the satirical warping of the shiny hubcap?

Lewis, especially in later life, when he went camping with some Duluth real estate men, gave evidence of liking much of George F. Babbitt as an individual. Some of his readers, in 1922 and later, selected only the details they wished to dislike; and many times over the past several decades, particularly during the booming enrollments of the 1960's, academics in English departments have snorted at poor Babbitt playing with his new toy, an automobile dashboard cigar lighter, while themselves fingering the latest cassette or photocopy gadget and measuring the zip in their department in quantified terms. (They are more likely to recognize Babbittry and Boosterism in an administrator's request for the total number of student credit hours produced in their classes, however.)

Any cluster of literary or cultural conventions can trip up "the innocent eye"; conventions, by their nature, are often common, unobtrusive, accepted as a matter of course, as unspoken agreements by writer and reader, speaker and hearer, agreements 'to act as if X were really so', even though both know that it is not true.

When Lewis mentions the German immigrant farm women in Gopher Prairie waiting patiently for their men while sitting in the wagons hitched outside the saloon on Main Street, we can, fifty years later, recognize some shift in the cultural "convention." (Don't kid yourself, though, that all the wives would now be in the bar, too.) Lewis was capable, even as late as 1949, failing in health, two years before his death, of recording significant small changes in the details of daily life, changes in fashion and cultural conventions. On returning from a year in Italy, he noticed that men's clothing was more colorful, that moccasins were worn in public *even* by elderly men, and that TV was becoming common in bars. In an introduction to David L. Cohn's *The Good Old Days* (1939), a collection of materials from old Sears, Roebuck catalogs, Lewis himself judges the value of reporting "things", the social and material surface of life. He put it this way: "Mankind is always more interested in living than in Lives . . . . By your eyebrow pencils, your encyclopedias, and your alarm clocks shall ye be known."

There are, in addition to cultural conventions, cues for the reader in the conventions and techniques of humor: dialect, exaggeration, juxtaposition, all embodied in this sample by Finley Peter Dunne, creating the comments of Mr. Dooley, an Irishman in a tavern on Archey Road back of the stockyards in Chicago at the turn of the century—the cultural tradition for Mayor Daley, if you please. Discoursing to the bartender and all the others, Mr. Dooley packs into one sentence many of the shifts of tone which let us know that satire, even with a straight face, is not the same as a tape recorder set next to the draft beer spigot. The subject is the benefits of progress and inventions during the reign of Queen Victoria: "An' th' invintions — th' steam-injine an' th' printin'-press an' th' cotton-gin an' th' gin sour, an' th' bicycle an' th' flyin' machine an' th' nickel-in-th'-slot machine an' th' Croker machine an' th' sody-fountain an'—crownin' wur-ruk iv our civilization—th' cash raygisther." Readers can leap the seventy year barrier here by noting the contrasts and the build-ups: locomotives to one-person wheels, the pun on gin, the latest (airplane experiments) to the less lofty items, including the New York City political machine of Boss Croker, from the productive to the consumptive — sody fountains — and finally to the basis of it all, money. This is not too far a cry from the satirical accumulations of detail in both *Main Street* and *Babbitt.*

Some critics, even in the twenties, perceived Lewis as sharing one traditional frame with Eliot, feeling that both men evoked comparison with Dante's *Inferno.* Such a suggestion for reading a work "places" it, offering a perspective for the innocent eye. Alfred Kazin has suggested that the "sheer terror immanent in the commonplace" makes Lewis' picture of Babbitt's unsuccessful rebellion and return to the values of conformity and boredom more terrifying than some of

Faulkner. Lewis was reacting against a romanticizing taste which was either interested only in the distant (long ago or far away) or could treat the commonplace only by glamourizing, falsifying, sentimentalizing or prettifying it. This "literary" tone contrasts with the clichés Babbitt and his cronies use, or with Eliot's colloquial description of Lil in the pub or of Madame Sosostris with her *wicked* pack of cards, drawing ironically on both the older use by non-card playing Methodists and the more contemporary use as a term of approval. Today, furnishing a Baedeker for Babbitt's desert (placing it in the tradition of the dark night of the soul would be a bit much) and sharpening the reader's reactions to the details in texture and surface, the effects of language, may be the most effective helpful guides.

'Jug, Jug' to Dirty Ears

One major problem in reading a Lewis novel after fifty years have passed concerns its accessibility. Eliot, for instance, footnoted *The Waste Land* in 1922 to make it a thicker book, and in doing so mentions much which he assumed was out-of-the-way reference: Jessie Weston's *From Ritual to Romance,* Tarot, Fisher-Kings, and allusions to Elizabethan drama. He did *not* footnote (although college undergraduate texts now wisely do so) references to the City of London banking district, paintings, St. Augustine, Hamlet-Ophelia, *the Tempest,* the Bible, or the meaning of the nightingale's cry, "Jug, Jug." Lewis, also, does not explain allusions, mimicry or traditional references that he assumed would be clear. For the reader today, these sounds may well fall on dirty ears, which miss the tone, just as the innocent eye fails to perceive the structure and symbolic shorthand behind the surface "things" in a painting. (Editor's note: Reading *Main Street* recently, some of my students expressed a desire for notes about the topical allusions.) Isn't a stock response to "Jug, Jug" likely to link it to moonshine whiskey, hillbillies, or maybe a crock? Or, for those more genteel, not in associations to L'il Abner or

Daisy Mae in the comics, but possibly to a link with a loaf of
bread and a Thou under a tree somewhere?

In *The Waste Land,* a brief sample of the multi-leveled
problem is the reference, which Eliot notes only to an
Australian Ballad, for "O the moon shone bright/ on Mrs.
Porter/ and on her daughter/ They wash their *feet* in soda
water." A Romantic American Indian Maiden often sung
about in Eliot's youth in St. Louis, Mo. was Pretty Red Wing,
and the lyrics of the refrain indicated that the moon shines
bright on pretty Red Wing, with a lot of sighing and crying and
some dying thrown in. The opening lines, however, use a
fairy-tale convention which was soon turned obscenely into an
infantry marching song. There once was an Indian maid, who
said she wasn't afraid . . . the military version (known to
American Legionnaires and high school students between the
wars) continued "to lie on the grass . . ." etc., etc. Old Wives'
Tales and such Southern folklorists as William Faulkner have
also sensitized readers nowadays to the effects of lying out
under the naked moon, like Eula Varner and others in
Yoknapatawph County. Such echoes of old popular songs
may fall on deaf or innocent ears now, just as the title of
Faulkner's short story "That Evening Sun Go Down" (which
includes a reference to St. Louis in the text) may escape any
linkage with "St. Louis Blues." Lurking even further under the
surface of Eliot's supposed Australian ballad is the question of
tone which shows up in the reference to "feet" as a
euphemism and to soda water as a possible douche or VD
prophylaxis. Mrs. Porter can be a conventional reference for
brothel-keeper. A reader who picks up the ballad associations
only, classifying it as a song of former love, may have enough
to move through Eliot's mind-set here, but some of the "Jug,
Jug," is falling on dirty ears.

When George F. Babbitt, dressing for work in the first few
pages of the novel, puts in his pocket a loose leaf address
notebook containing many items, including a curious
inscription: DSSDMYPDF (an item Lewis uses the whole
paragraph to build up to and leaves unexplained), the function

of the detail, like the function of the ballad for Eliot, is clear enough from the context without a footnote — it is a motto or a reminder to himself. Does it gain from a gloss? Lewis wrote to his publisher (Dec. 28, 1920) that Babbitt would be a GAN about a TBM, and we have not lost the facility for using abbreviations over the intervening decades. It is psychologically fitting that Babbitt himself do such things and that in this Great American Novel the Tired Business Man may be telling himself 'Don't Say Something Dumb-Mouthed You Poor Damn Fool'.

Lewis indicated in an interview later published in the *University of Kansas City Review* (1958) by Allen Austin that he had deliberately had Carol Kennicott in *Main Street,* decorate a room in bad taste to show that while she was bright, she was not *that* bright. The old golden oak table, brocaded chairs, and family photographs were replaced with a japanese obi hung on the maize wall, sapphire velvet pillows with gold bands, and in keeping with the yellow and blue color scheme, a squat blue jar was placed on a square cabinet, between yellow candles. Since Lewis arranged the list in this order, ending climactically with the jar, a reader today might have some contextual cues for the "bad taste" in her decorating.

When Chum Frink (the "poet") tells his fellow Booster Club members that they ought to Capitalize Culture (supporting the symphony orchestra for instance), is the pun for capital as $ and capital as emphasis — big letter C — sufficiently clear? Babbitt's son, Ted, was named for the President in office at his birth, Teddy Roosevelt, a good liberal reform Republican. Even this small detail gives some insight into George F's penchant for conforming to current fashions, for admiring the powerful, and for respecting the Great Institutions of American Life.

Lewis could be blatant in his choice of names or his characteronyms. The evangelist, Billy Sunday, turned ever so slightly into Mike Monday preaching at a revival meeting. Babbitt was first tentatively named George Pumphrey, then

Fitch, but whether Lewis intended to evoke all the associations since discovered in the sound of his final name, Babbitt,
is unanswerable. Does the name currently suggest any of the
following—B.T.Babbitt Household Cleaner (and who remembers Bab-O and Sapolio?); a frictionless metal used in machine
tool work (the Realtor in the gears of Commerce); *babble*, as
the talk in the novel goes on and on; or *babyish*, as his details
of dreaming at the beginning are added to later in the novel?
As with reading a Baedeker *afterward,* these can be fitted into
the experience of reading the novel on recalling it, but do they
jump out crying "Jug, Jug" on first reading?

When Genevieve Taggard, commenting upon a machine age
exhibition of artists in New York, quoted one artist, Louis
Lozowick, approvingly from the viewpoint of the *New Masses,*
the Marxist magazine she was writing for (July 1927), she used
the word 'plastic' in a different sense than it is likely to have
for many readers now: "The artist must objectify the
dominant experience of our epoch in plastic terms that possess
value for more than this epoch alone." (Printed in F. J.
Hoffman, *The Twenties,* p. 291.) Here 'plastic' seems to have
favorable connotations of shapable and adaptable, without the
negative, imitative, unnatural, unfeeling associations more
likely today. Does Lewis, conveying the tedium of the porch
swing and the mosquitoes on a hot summer night in Gopher
Prairie, or the boredom and ennui of George Babbitt as he
moves daily through his 'plastic' life—in the recent sense—
objectify the emotional experience for the reader so that it
now possesses value for us? Just such shifts in the tonal
resonance for common words can impede our access to an
earlier work, Eliot's, Lewis' or that of any other author.

Lewis' most widely recognized technique, however, is the
catalog, probably epitomized in the two views of Dyer's drug
store in *Main Street,* when both Carol and Bea Sorenson (a
Swedish farm girl just coming into town who becomes the
Kennicott hired girl or maid) see greatly different details for
the soda fountain. Carol's "electric lamp with the red and
green and curdled yellow shade over the greasy marble

fountain," becomes Bea's "huge fountain of lovely marble with the biggest shade you ever saw — all different kinds of colored glass stuck together; and the soda spouts they were silver, and they came right out of the bottom of the lamp shade!" In *Babbitt*, this device was augmented by the description of daily rituals, dressing, starting the car, filling the gas tank on the drive downtown, each with their own style of ceremonial behavior and speech. These devices offered readers in the 1920's a fresh way of looking at the routines of life around them, but they were not likely to accept that view as factually accurate, since they could discount exaggeration on the basis of their own experiences. While they might find Veblen's notions of conspicuous consumption should lead them to the conclusions, as Anthony Hilfer puts it, that Babbitt, like his dashboard cigar lighter, was decorative but non-productive, and that many of the real estate subdivisions really were the way Lewis described them, they knew life around them and how people actually spoke. They could recognize the half-truths and mimicry on a different plane of experiential evidence than we do fifty years later, when we must pay more attention to stylistic devices and stock responses in order to recognize Babbitt as a real toad, maybe, but in an imaginary garden. Some readers and critics in the past have reversed this order; Lewis reported parts of a real garden, but created a cardboard toad. In contrast to this, there are still some students, after finishing their reading, who will sigh, "but he sounds just like my father."

The ultimate question, then, for investing time and energy in reading *Babbitt* or about a woman's life in a small town before the automobile changed things, as in *Main Street,* is whether or not the plastic terms, the technique and surface texture of the novels, clear in their own epoch, can transmit to a later time a feeling about values, ennui, a wasteland or a wasted life. Do the details we notice in reading *order* and *intensify* our own experience(s)? Do we experience, and not just cognitively recognize, the stultification, the boredom, the desire for escape, and gain insight into what Lewis (at age 46) writing to his publisher (Dec. 28, 1920) called Babbitt's life of compromises: "He is all of us Americans at 46, prosperous but worried . . . wanting — passionately — to seize something more than motorcars and a house *before it's too late*".

The opening paragraphs of the novel show Babbitt dreaming of a faery child before the alarm goes off in the morning. In the last sentences of the novel, Babbitt, dreaming now while wide awake, tells his son to live life however he wishes, "Go ahead . . . The world is yours". The myth that youth will be better off dies hard in this country. But his own motto, in the small loose-leaf notebook in his pocket is not the Rabelaisian motto over the abbey of Theleme (masterfully ironic satiric statement about Calvinistic predestination in itself) — *fais ce que vouldras* (Do what you will). The notebook page, impermanently recorded, loose-leaf, as Babbitt's magic motto, his talisman to ward off evil, his rabbit's foot, is DSSDMYPDF. And this is the way the world ends, not with a bang, but a whimper. (Which quotes another tag line that, like Dr. Eckleburg's view of the ashheaps, we often use as a fragment to shore against our ruins.)

It is a whimper of and for the main character and the society in the novel, not necessarily for a great part of the psyche of the reader. What *Babbitt,* as a good read, can become for us now is a fragment shored against the ruins, against our own psychological memories, our own potential half-forgotten dreams, our own responses to the Sears' and Ward's ads in the Sunday paper. To make this possible requires revivifying, recreating some of the era of 1910-1922 and of attitudes toward spiritual wastelands and backyard ashheaps then, and also requires paralleling those ash heaps from our own experiences.

As Eliot's old man epitomizes it in "Gerontion," "Whatever is kept must be adulterated." We cannot help but adulterate what a reader of 1922 might have responded to, and we cannot help but add, with an uninnocent eye, not only our own experiences (plastic and otherwise), but also those conventions, literary frames, traditional references, ("Jug,

Jug!"), which enable us to sense the boredom, as well as the pleasures of George F. Babbitt's day in the life.

Some travelers may require a Baedeker before the trip, rather than afterward. Even knowing what to look for may not completely suppress the potential for inattentive boredom. The motiviation of nostalgia, particularly for an era prior to one's birth, is a very tricky bit of magic. How does Lewis show us How We Live Today? The best advice before picking up the book is that which Eliot uses to close the first section of *The Waste Land:* Baudelaire's Preface (about ennui) to *Fleurs du Mal:*

> You know him, [boredom], hypocrite lecteur, mon sembable, mon frere. [My hypocritical reader, my double (or shadow), my brother.]

8

Ring Lardner:
Not an Escape, but a Reflection

Jonas Spatz

The twenties were an age of humor. The list of names—
Mencken, Benchley, Thurber, Parker, Lewis, and Lardner, to
mention a few—is impressive. And there was plenty to laugh
about. The war to end all wars had ended. Prosperity was in
the air, and with it arrived what we have come to recognize as
a particularly modern brand of hedonism, compounded of
potent drugs, constant movement, and uninhibited sexual
expression. What gave the twenties their special character
(achieved again in the sixties) was this feeling of having been
freed from traditional moral and social restraints. Comedy
was, in this sense, an overflow of animal spirits, a celebration
of the pleasures of this world and of the present moment. The
Puritan, defined by Mencken as one who is tortured by the
thought that somewhere, somehow, somebody is enjoying
himself, was in retreat on all fronts. Much of the urban humor
of this period depended on the consciousness of having
escaped from those barren small towns which still stubbornly
adhered to the old values. Its targets were personal quirks and
eccentricities, lapses from fashionable or enlightened behavior
which exposed the clumsy provincial to gentle ridicule. *The
New Yorker,* founded in 1925, dispensed a brand of wit which
was definitely "not for the little old lady from Dubuque." The

adventures of the rube in the big town were, of course, the foundation of Lardner's early work, and the homespun wisdom of Will Rogers exploited the same relationship from the other side. The Scopes Trial of 1924 was from this point of view the zenith of the genre. It was high vaudeville, with William Jennings Bryan as the Top Banana. In any case, this comedy was essentially tolerant and indulgent because it was condescending, subordinating the old to the new and the ingenuous to the sophisticated.

On the other hand, the most important contemporary comic form was social satire. Here the past was the normative voice, and its antagonist was more powerful and impersonal. The civilization built by industrial capitalism was denounced for its physical ugliness, its vacant and banal culture, its greed and hypocrisy, and above all its replacement of individual creativity with the mechanized conformity of the bureaucrat and the corporation employee. The satirical tone is cynical and resigned, perhaps because outrage no longer seemed an appropriate reaction to the triumph of bourgeois values. Shock and anger imply the possibility of significant political and social action. The tone of *Babbitt* or "The Love Nest," however, is beyond hope and, in Lardner's case, beyond frustration itself. The statement is simply, "Here is modern man; look on his works and despair."

The development in satirical style from the genial to the bitter and from the personal to the societal accompanied the disillusionments of World War I. The belief in human progress and rationality no longer appeared tenable in the face of this conclusive demonstration of man's capacity for self-destruction. Similarly, the "waste land" image arose as a spontaneous expression (although it had long been a popular literary and religious symbol) of ultimate cynicism about man's nature and spiritual condition. As Warren French points out, Eliot himself began with rather trivial portraits of the decadent aristocracy. "The Love Song of J. Alfred Prufrock" suggested that the failures and eccentricities of his early characters were somehow related to the general alienation in

modern society. By 1920, Eliot had progressed to a comprehensive vision of universal desolation, later realized in
"Gerontion," *The Waste Land,* and "The Hollow Men."
Certainly the first three parts of *The Waste Land* are great
satire, peopled with unforgettable representatives of a faithless
and materialistic age: Madame Sosostris, Mrs. Porter and
Sweeney, Albert and Lil, "the young man carbuncular" and
his typist, and the Cleopatra figure whose eternal question,
"What shall we do tomorrow? /What shall we ever do?",
haunted a generation of booze-soaked romantics from West
Egg to Pamplona.

The direction of this development, from detached amusement to anger, and finally to despair, links Ring Lardner, one
of the greatest satirists of his time, with the central tendencies
of the serious literature of the twenties. "The horror and the
boredom" of ordinary middle-class life became his main theme
and turned him from gentle humor to Swiftian satire. He saw,
as Eliot did, that man was becoming increasingly isolated from
his environment, from other men, and from himself. Although
terms like fragmentation, isolation, and alienation are now
little more than cultural clichés, their emotional equivalents
captured the spirit of the period. They account both for the
appearance of *The Waste Land* and for the growing pessimism
of Lardner's writing. Throughout his career, Lardner remained
ambivalent toward his characters, alternately poking fun at
their ignorance and savagely condemning their greed, egotism,
and hypocrisy. But as in most of the comic writing of his time,
the balance in Lardner's fiction shifted until laughter itself
symbolized the cruel joke that life had become. As his vision
expanded, he could see connections between his ballplayers,
movie producers, song writers, suburban housewives, and golf
caddies. They were no longer simply individuals; they were all
part of the banality and dishonesty of contemporary society.
He continued to write funny stories and fracture the American
language, but eventually the vice itself came to matter more
than its comic expression.

What happened to Lardner's idealism and tolerance of

human failings was metaphorically described, perhaps inadvert-
ently, in "There Are Smiles," one of the few sentimental love
stories he ever wrote. The hero is a traffic policeman,
"distinguished from the rest by his habitual good humor,"
who charms guilty motorists with comic descriptions of their
driving feats. One day he falls in love with a young girl he has
stopped for speeding. Nothing much happens. He is married;
she is engaged. She drives him home twice, but he can't say
what he feels. Then he reads in the paper that she has been
killed in a car crash. He goes back to work, but everything has
changed:

> Well, on an afternoon two or three weeks later, a man
> named Hughes from White Plains, driving a Studebaker, started
> across Forty-sixth Street out of turn and obeyed a stern order
> to pull over to the curb.
> "What's your hurry?" demanded the grim-faced traffic
> policeman. "Where the hell do you think you're going? What's
> the matter with you, you so-and-so!"
> "I forgot myself for a minute. I'm sorry," said Mr. Hughes.
> "If you'll overlook it, I'll pick you up on my way home and
> take you to the Bronx. Remember, I give you a ride home last
> month? Remember? That is, it was a fella that looked like you.
> That is, he looked something like you. I can see now it wasn't
> you. It was a different fella."

Finally, even his fury subsided. Guilt or innocence didn't seem
to matter so much anymore because almost everyone was a
victim.

During the first stage of this process, Lardner was writing
primarily about sports. His earliest stories about Jack Keefe,
the Busher with the major-league ego, became the most
popular with the general public. Like most male Americans,
Lardner spent his youth idolizing sports heroes. The influence
of fictional characters like Frank Merriwell—who despite his
exploits on the field remained modest and generally decent—
had placed athletes beyond criticism. But Lardner's ten-year
apprenticeship on various newspapers had shown him what
they were really like: stingy, ignorant, selfish, egotistical—

children playing a children's game for the adulation of other children. Yet *You Know Me Al* was an immediate sensation in spite of the fact that it subverted the most sacred of popular American myths because it allowed the reader to feel superior to the small-town hick. The Busher constantly pits his narrow provincialism against the demands of the big town and is defeated by one or another of his vices or stupidities. In letter after letter, Keefe presents his side of the story at the expense of his tormentors—stone-fingered and weak-hitting teammates, ignorant managers, disloyal sweethearts, and various predatory waiters, bellboys, cabdrivers, and landlords—only to betray unwittingly the true situation. Although Keefe never shares the credit for his ephemeral victories or admits his inevitable failures, we can hear the offstage laughter of those around him, to whom he will always be bush-league.

In many ways the portrait is devastating. Yet the Busher remains sympathetic. He yearns to return to his home town where he can drink beer and trade stories with his social and intellectual equals, but the city's glitter is irresistible, and he is destined to be unhappy there whatever his success. The Busher's worst qualities are elicited by his removal from his natural environment where his vices could have masqueraded as Puritan virtues. He is no noble savage, but civilization has made him worse than he might have been.

Lardner's relatively benevolent treatment of the baseball hero continued into the twenties. The Busher's rather inocuous traits were, however, only one side of the picture. In "Alibi Ike," Keefe's tendency to excuse or deny his mistakes becomes an obsession. Ike never drops his guard, hiding not only his motives but his real self. The Busher's taste for women becomes in Hurry Kane an all-devouring desire that almost ruins his career. And Keefe's mild screwiness, characteristic of all of Lardner's ballplayers, is in Buster Elliott of "My Roomy" a violent psychosis. Each of Lardner's athletes possesses an epic talent marred by one comic flaw, which, as he recognized, could also lead to tragedy. Each withdraws deeper into himself until he loses touch with reality. Ike constructs a fantasy life for himself that changes in detail whenever anyone else tries to make logical sense out of it. Buster Elliott won't read letters from his girl because she can't tell him anything he doesn't already know. When he discovers that she has jilted him, he tries to brain her with a baseball bat and ends up in a lunatic asylum.

Yet humor still outweighs any serious criticism or psychological analysis in these stories because baseball is, after all, a game and ballplayers remain innocent rubes whose exploits strike us as ludicrous and touchingly heroic. By the mid-twenties, Lardner stopped writing about them altogether. Perhaps by then athletes, except for Midge Kelly of "Champion," weren't appropriate symbols of that single-minded devotion to self which is a major concern of Lardner's best work and also at the heart of Eliot's diagnosis of the modern disease.

In the books that immediately followed *You Know Me Al,* which were also about the rube in the big city, Lardner's point of view and attitude toward his material began to change. The Busher had been so naive and self-centered that he never fully understood or consciously conveyed what was happening to him. The narrators of *Gullible's Travels* (1917) and *The Big Town* (1921), although still from the sticks and relatively easy marks, have a degree of self-knowledge and moral awareness which makes them reluctant to join their wives in the mad pursuit of respectability and social position. They are virtually anonymous commentators whose sardonic asides approximate Lardner's own growing skepticism. Lardner continued to be amused by his characters, but he also began to judge them, sometimes harshly.

Lardner's city, like Eliot's, is alien and forbidding. Its inhabitants are either idle and bored or predatory and ambitious. The characters in stories like "Quick Returns," "Lady Perkins," and "Three Without, Doubled" are always looking for "the real people" of the wealthy aristocracy whose friendship will provide the key to an exciting and meaningful life. But they never seem to find them. They meet only con-men and adventurers who deceive them or snobs who reject them because of their déclassé speech and manners.

The social failures of the "Gullibles" and the Finches, however, are not permanently damaging, partly because they intuitively reject the pretensions of the "high polloi." *Gullible's Travels* ends with a hilarious and nightmarish bridge party at which the narrator destroys his wife's last chance to break into society. "Gullible" acts only half-consciously, but once he has been banished he feels somehow relieved, as if he has avoided an impending disaster. The situation is a bit more ambiguous in *The Big Town,* where it is the cynical materialism of the narrator's wife and sister-in-law that preserves them. Mrs. Finch, newly enriched by her dead father's war profits, decides to go to New York to "get ahead" in society and to marry off her sister Katie. Katie falls in love with a young inventor who later plunges to his death during a test flight of his airplane. Here is her reaction:

> While I and Ella was getting ready for supper I made the remark that I s'posed we'd live in a vale of tears for the next few days.
> "No," said Ella. "Sis is taking it pretty calm. She's sensible. She says if that could of happened, why the invention couldn't of been no good after all. And the Williamses probably wouldn't of give him a plugged dime for it."

After a series of disappointments, the Finches eagerly return to the Midwest and a more modest existence. These reversions to simpler life-styles imply, as Lardner did in *You Know Me Al,* that these are basically harmless people who, for the moment, have been morally disoriented by money. They have been bitten by "society bacillus," but the sickness is not fatal.

Throughout his career, Lardner also reacted angrily to the greed and ambition that infected his contemporaries. In these stories, everyone is on the make with no regrets, as the cruelties of "Champion" and "A Day with Conrad Green" and the air of corruption permeating "A Caddy's Diary" and "Rhythm" certainly illustrate. "Champion" is patterned after the typical rags-to riches tale, but with interesting variations. The irony in the powerful first paragraph, for example, depends on its "Official Biography" tone:

> Midge Kelly scored his first knockout when he was seventeen. The knockee was his brother Connie, three years his junior and a cripple. The purse was a half dollar given to the younger Kelly by a lady whose electric had just missed bumping his soul from his frail little body.

In a series of brutal scenes parodying the storybook version of the rise of the boxing hero, Kelly throws fights, seduces his friend's sister, abandons her on their shotgun wedding night, betrays his manager, and in a final reversal winds up on top, praised for public consumption as "a regular boy," because, as Lardner knew, "The people don't want to see him knocked. He's champion." Only those willing to violate every rule of decency and live completely without feeling can become champions in the ring and, by extension, in the American marketplace. Sports were no longer an escape from reality but a reflection of it. Similarly, in "A Day with Conrad Green" Lardner's rage is overwhelming. Green is a monster of avarice, self-pity, deceit, and ingratitude, and the story consists of little more than a succession of despicable acts, each of which boomerangs and leaves him more miserable, but no less powerful, than before.

Anger, however, is not dominant in the later stories. Except for "Haircut," it is difficult to find anything comparable in tone to "Champion" and "A Day with Conrad Green." Lardner began to write not in terms of ruthless competition or the obsessive drive for success but of the boredom, frustration, and loneliness that Eliot had portrayed in *The Waste Land.* His characters are unable to communicate with or care about one another or to find meaning in their useless and unhappy lives.

Lardner's treatment of marriage is an example of his mood during this period. In his early work, marriage is a fight promoter's mismatch, punctuated by wisecracks, if not real blows. These encounters, however, like those in Hollywood movies or in comic strips, never lead to meaningful emotional confrontations because neither partner takes the other, or the marriage, very seriously. They are simply empty rituals exploited by the author for their stock-comic possibilities. Tom Finch and his wife are always disagreeing about something, but he can still muster up enough feeling to slug a Wall-Street broker who makes a pass at her. But in *The Love Nest* (1926) and *Round Up* (1929), the bantering, almost cheerful tone of combat is replaced by long desperate silences, born of weariness and repression. The wife in "Anniversary" plays countless games of Solitaire while her stolid husband monotonously reads fillers from the newspaper. Finally, on the evening of a wedding anniversary he has forgotten, she is driven to request a punch in the eye as a gift—a sign that he still knows that she is alive. In "The Love Nest," husband and wife trade elaborate endearments, although she secretly drinks so that she can tolerate her frustration and resentment. The once jealous and passionate husband in "Now and Then," recognizing that his wife now bores him, at first looks for excuses to avoid spending time with her, but finally simply abandons her to her loneliness. Even when the marriage survives into old age, as in "The Golden Honeymoon," it is only a feat of endurance, a conquest of everything but mutual indifference: "Mother set facing the front of the train, as it makes her giddy to ride backwards. I set facing her, which does not affect me." Lardner doesn't ordinarily take sides in these battles, even if his reader does. His point is only that this is the way people live: selfish, unsympathetic, sometimes cruel, but punished, perhaps disproportionately, by their inability to give or receive love.

In a real sense, this isolation was always Lardner's subject. Although many of his best stories were written in the third person, Lardner, from the beginning, specialized in one-sided forms—letters, diaries, monologues, first-person narratives—all emphasizing how difficult it is to transcend the self and reach out to another person. Lardner exhibits an impressive number of variations on the same theme. Some stories, like "Travel-

ogue," "Zone of Quiet," and "Sun Cured," begin as conversations but become monologues immediately, as one ego quickly
overwhelms the other. Others, like "Now and Then" and, of
course, *You Know Me Al,* consist of one side of a correspondence. Each letter seems to take up where the last ended; no
answer is necessary, since the writer isn't paying attention.
Still others are exchanges of letters which people write at, not
to, each other. In "Some Like Them Cold," for example,
Mabelle Gillespie is so wrapped up in herself and in her desire
to trap Charles Lewis that she can't see what his letters make
obvious: he doesn't care about her at all. "Ex Parte" could
easily have served as the title of Lardner's collected works,
instead of just one story.

There was one final stage beyond despair. It is no surprise
to discover that Lardner turned to writing nonsense plays and
fairy tales in which the main source of humor is the
unintentional pun and the *non sequitur.* From one viewpoint
they were simply extensions of what he had been describing all
along. Here, however, the isolation is so absolute and abstract
that it sheds its human dimension and becomes an exercise in
the absurdity and impotence of language itself. But in another
way, these diversions recapture some of the childlike joy that
must have made life seem so fresh to Lardner in those years
when he was deciding to make his living by making people
laugh—before he, like his characters and his age, had wised up.

9

Fun at the Incinerating Plant: Lardner's Wry Waste Land

Forrest L. Ingram

The first thing I generally always do is try and get hold of a catchy title, like for instance ... "Fun at the Incinerating Plant."

Preface, *How to Write Short Stories*

The road leading from New York to the towns on Long Island's north shore is, for the most part, as scenically attractive as an incinerating plant. Nevertheless, Jennie kept saying "How beautiful!"

"Reunion" in *The Love Nest*

To pass an evening sipping Lardner's wry wit often means waking with ashes on the tongue. His landscape of characters during the 20s is often "as scenically attractive as an incinerating plant." But Lardner rarely fails to evoke from his readers a grimacing smile of self-recognition. His braggarts and bullies lead the reader on with their fascinating self-justifying patter. And too often for comfort, the reader finds that he is laughing at himself.

Lardner developed his satiric style during the years (1914-1919) when he was writing the Jack Keefe stories. Throughout those stories, he maintains an ironic contrast between the narrator's inadequate self-perception and the (hopefully) more critical awareness of the reader. Jack Keefe's

image of himself diverges widely from the image which he
unwittingly presents to Al and to the reader. The same may be
said of many of Lardner's later stories such as "Haircut," "I
Can't Breathe," "The Golden Honeymoon," "A Caddy's
Diary," and "Who Dealt?".

Critical opinion of Lardner has ranged from those who
describe him as a popular light humorist to those who praise
him for his bitterly pessimistic criticism of American society.
Indeed, before the 20s, Lardner was best known as a sports
writer, columnist, and popular verbal comedian. Apparently,
few people noticed the serious criticism which lurked just
beneath the surface of the Keefe stories.

The sheen of humor with which Lardner polished his
stories allowed him covertly to criticize athletes and other
middle-Americans without incurring general public rancor. In
"Champion," however, Lardner clearly condemns the manly
art of boxing, and there is no smile in his prose. Only
extremely dense sports fans could have missed the harsh
ridicule which Lardner hurls at an insensitive public in the
final paragraph of that story. "The people don't want to see
him knocked," a sports editor says of Midge Kelly—one of the
most despicable characters in American fiction. "He's
champion."

Although Lardner's early stories concentrated mainly on
figures from the world of sports, on a deeper level his satires
were aimed principally at the foibles of human beings—their
pettiness, foolishness, hypocrisy, greed, insensitivity, and even
cruelty. More and more during the 20s, Lardner's theme
became: *homo homini lupus.* He expanded his vision during
this period to include the wider world of corrupt business
executives, middle-class social climbers, husband-hungry girls,
plagiarizing song writers, old folks abandoned by insensitive
children, and married couples undermining each other's lives.
Before the decade was over, literary critics such as Mencken,
Canby, Seldes, and Wilson hailed Lardner as one of America's
harshest and most talented satirists—and this in a decade
loaded with satirists of American society.

Lardner's fiction-writing career peaked during the 20s. He entered the decade with the stories of *The Big Town* (1921) and exited with *Round Up* (1929). *The Big Town* closed the door on Lardner's apprenticeship years; *Round Up* collected in a single volume all the stories of *How To Write Short Stories [With Samples]* (1924) and *The Love Nest and Other Stories* (1926) as well as sixteen previously uncollected stories. It represents, therefore, a compendium of all the mature fiction Lardner wrote during the 20s. The rest of this essay will deal primarily with *The Big Town* and *Round Up*.

The Big Town is a cycle of five stories which were published serially at wide intervals between March 1920 and May 1921. Although each story presents a single complete action, the cycle as a whole develops a single major theme which builds up from story to story. Further, it presents, as a whole, an overall pattern of actions in which the major characters reveal themselves through their reactions to thematically developing sets of circumstances. Therefore, although each story is relatively independent, its full significance can be appreciated only after all the stories have been read.

The static structure of *The Big Town* closely resembles that of an earlier Lardner cycle, *Gullible's Travels, Etc.* (1917), which is also composed of five stories and which also deals with a "wise boob," his wife, and his wife's unmarried sister. In both cycles, the first and fifth stories pair off, as do the second and fourth; and the third story stands as a pivotal center.

The dynamic structure of *The Big Town* may best be described in terms of physical and thematic movement, development of characters, and the repetition in varied contexts of situations and motifs.

As far as physical and thematic movement is concerned, the narrator (Bob Finch) and his wife (Ella) travel from South Bend, Indiana, to New York "to see life and get Katie [Ella's sister] a husband." The movement from midwest to east and back west again parallels, in thematic intent as well as in geographical symbolism, Nick Carraway's odyssey in *The*

Great Gatsby, which Lardner's friend and neighbor on Long Island, F. Scott Fitzgerald, wrote in 1925. The Finches do indeed "see Life" in New York; and what they see makes them eager to return to South Bend.

As far as character development is concerned, there are only three characters who occur in all the stories of the cycle: Finch, Ella, and Katie. Ella initiates the action of the entire book with her insistence that the Finches go to New York to find Katie a husband from among "the right kind of people" and "to see Life." Further, she is always the most eager to embark on new adventures and is the least likely to become disillusioned. When, therefore, she agrees to go back to South Bend, and even encourages Finch ("Get uppers if it's quicker") to speed up the process, the reader knows a change has occurred in her which is directly traceable to the series of experiences through which she has had to pass. She goes back to the midwest, as Nick Carraway did, a wiser person.

Kate's case is more interesting. The title page of *The Big Town* carries a two-inch drawing of a young gay twenties girl, kicking up her heels and throwing money by the handfuls into the air. Like Fitzgerald, Lardner was both fascinated and repelled by a generation of *nouveau riche* middle-class people with reckless habits of spending. Kate is clearly a member of that generation and that class. Her stepfather died just after the war and left Kate and Ella $75,000 apiece from his war-profiteering leather factory. Kate and Ella want to put the whole amount into a checking account, but Finch persuades them "to keep five thousand apiece for pin money and stick the rest into bonds."

But then the spending spree begins. Kate and Ella go to Chicago to "buy all the party dresses that was vacant." And once in New York, Kate spots a "brand new model Bam Eight" which costs $4000 and she wants one immediately. But the car salesman puts her off and tells Finch:

> "Listen . . . I'll be frank with you. We got the New York agency for this car and was glad to get it because it sells for

four thousand and anything that sells that high, why the
people will eat up, even if it's a pearl-handle ketchup bottle . . .

Finch asks him what makes it worth $4000. "Well," he replies,
"what made this lady want one?" Neither Kate nor any
member of the quick-spending set could have answered him.

Kate's mercenary mind is further revealed in the third
story. She displays a romantic interest in an aviator/inventor
Bill Codd when she thinks he is going to make a million on his
new model plane. But when Codd crashes and dies, Kate
wastes no tears on him: "why the invention couldn't of been
no good after all. And the Williamses probably wouldn't of
give him a plugged dime for it."

In the final story, Kate withdraws $50,000 from her
capital in order to buy herself a husband. Kate wants to be a
star, so she finances the short-lived career of a two-bit
comedian from the Follies who promises her a part in his new
drama. The play flops, and Kate wants to withdraw her money
from the venture. But then Ralston, the comedian, asks her to
marry him. And Kate, aware of the role her money plays in
the relationship, accepts.

Cynicism reeks in the final lines of the cycle:

> So here we are, really enjoying ourselves for the first time
> in pretty near two years. And Katie's in New York, enjoying
> herself, too, I suppose. She ought to be, married to a
> comedian. It must be such fun to just set and listen to him
> talk.

Yes, such "fun." Fun at the incinerating plant.

Finch's own development throughout the cycle traces a
different arc. He is narrating the entire cycle after the two-year
odyssey is over. He could, therefore, color scenes to his own
advantage, inserting witicisms which at the time he may have
been unable to conjure up. But for the most part, this does not
seem to be the case. Rather, he maintains an ironic distance
which helps him to laugh at his own folly and to reflect upon
the more serious implications of his actions.

Finch wins the reader's respect in the first story. He
dislikes Griffin on first meeting, and notices early the

attentions Griffin pays to his (Finch's) wife. When Ella tells
him of Griffin's improper advances to her, Finch "floored"
Griffin nine times, "kicked him for eight goals from the field"
and "hit him over the fence for ten home runs."

Finch never shows any enthusiasm for the life of the rich.
An ex-cigar salesman, Finch did not receive any of the money
left to Ella or Kate, and even while the "old codger" was alive,
Finch refused the position of foreman at the leather factory
"at only about a fifty per cent cut." [sic] He constantly
argues with Ella and Kate to be more conservative in their
spending, but they remind him that the money is theirs, not
his.

Finch wins the reader's respect in other stories by his
critical observations of the habits of the rich and the upper
crust. In describing the crowd at the racetrack in "Only One,"
Finch says:

> Lots of them was gals that you'd have to have a pick to break
> through to their regular face. Since they had their last divorce,
> about the only excitement they could enjoy was playing a long
> shot.

And in "Lady Perkins," Finch describes the Long Island hotel.

> Well, I s'pose it's what you might call a family hotel, and a
> good many of the guests belongs to the cay-nine family. A few
> of the couples that can't afford dogs has got children, and
> you're always tripping over one or the other . . .

And when he is dressing to go out for dinner, he remarks:
"They was one advantage in dolling up every time you went
anywheres. It meant an hour when they was no chance to do
something even sillier."

For the most part, then, Finch himself is not taken in by
the glitter which surrounds him on his trip east. And he is
not taken in by Ralston's overstatements about his salary or
braggadocio about his "suite." Generally, he is an upright man,
even though he never hesitates to break the prohibition law.

But on several occasions, Finch bends his morality for the
sake of advancement in social status or increase of finances. In
"Lady Perkins," for instance, he lies about having "yap-

hounds" who are in the hospital with an otherwise unknown dog disease called "blanny." He lies in order to make contact with Lady Perkins and introduce Ella and Kate to her. More seriously, in "Only One" he bets all his money on a horse named Sap when he finds out that the jockey of the favored horse is going to throw the race. "I don't know if you'll think I done right or not," he tells his fictional South Bend friend.

> Or I don't care. But what was the sense of me tipping off a guy [Daley] that had said them sweet [read: nasty] things about I and Ella? And even if I don't want a sister-in-law of mine running round with a guy that's got a jail record [Mercer], still Daley squealing on him was rotten dope. And besides, I don't never like to break a promise . . .

These rationalizations do not completely calm Finch's conscience. And later, he is forced to lie about his bets to Kate and Ella: "I must of went crazy and played him for a thousand men."

Finch, then, undergoes a minor moral decay during his trip to the east. But the harm done is not irreparable. As soon as Katie finds a husband, he and the Mrs. head home.

The final page of the cycle returns the reader to its beginning. Finch tells his wife:

> "Do you remember what we moved to the Big Town for? We done it to see Life and get Katie a husband. Well, we got her a kind of a husband and I'll tell the world we seen Life. How about moseying back to South Bend?"

Finch is not deceived into believing that he has really seen "Life." Nor is he convinced that they have been successful in finding Katie a husband. But partial success is sufficient for any realist. Finch has had his "fun" at the incinerating plant. And he's ready for home.

As the 20s progressed, Lardner's disillusionment with America took a bolder and harsher fictional shape. The mild satire Lardner displayed in *The Big Town* grew blacker and grimmer and his humor more self-deprecating in *How To Write Short Stories* and *The Love Nest*.

The preface to *How To Write Short Stories* burlesques

both the writing handbooks which had become popular around the turn of the century and Lardner's own reputation as a literary artist. You can't find "no school in operation to date," he asserts, "which can make a great author out of a born druggist." He jokingly describes his own methods of writing a story:

> The first thing I generally always do is try and get hold of a catchy title, like for instance "Basil Hargrave's Vermifuge," or "Fun at the Incinerating Plant."

Speaking about the development of a story, Lardner first introduces three characters in a banal situation and then adds:

> From this beginning, a skilled writer could go most anywheres, but it would be my tendency to drop these three characters and take up the life of a mule in the Grand Canyon. The mule watches the trains come in from the east, he watches the trains come in from the west, and keeps wondering who is going to ride him.

America is Lardner's mule, dumbly staring at the traffic east and west.

Even more non-sensical are the self-debunking introductions Lardner places before some of the stories. For instance, his brilliant story "Champion" bears the inscription: "An example of the mystery story. The mystery is how it came to get printed." Some of these introductions, however, are genuinely humorous; others, in the spirit of the preface, ridicule the reader for his gullibility. For instance, Lardner entices the reader to plunge enthusiastically into "The Golden Honeymoon" (the story of a golden wedding anniversary) by giving it the heading "A story with 'sex appeal.'" "My Roomy," a cruel story about a mad baseball player who almost murders his fiancee and her new boyfriend with a bat, is introduced with the sentence:

> A house party in a fashionable Third Avenue laundry and the predicament of a hero who has posed as a famous elevator starter form the background of this delightful tale of life in the Kiwanis Club.

Lardner knew that some of his readers would take his

playfulness, his black humor, and even his self-debunking non-humor seriously. In 1926, he wrote a spoofing introduction to *The Love Nest* under the pseudonym Sarah E. Spooldripper. A footnote informs the reader that Miss Spooldripper used to take care of the Lardners' wolf. "She knew all there was to know about Lardner," the note continues, "and her mind was virtually blank. It was part of her charm."

Miss Spooldripper lets the reader in on some of the "secrets" of Lardner's private life: "Lardner always bolted his food. He was afraid the rats would get it. It was part of his charm." At the end of the introduction, Miss Spooldripper laments that "The Master is gone," and asks "who will succeed him? Perhaps some writer still unborn. Perhaps one who will never be born. That is what I hope."

The final absurdity occurs in the final footnote, which informs the reader that Miss Spooldripper is gone too. "Two months ago she was found dead in the garage, her body covered with wolf bites left there by her former ward, who has probably forgotten where he left them." Despite the obvious absurdity of this introduction, there were critics who took every word seriously and bemoaned the passing of Ring [gold Wilmer] Lardner. Lardner did not misjudge the gullibility of the American public.

The stories of *How To Write Short Stories* and *The Love Nest* reappear, in indiscriminate order and mingled with sixteen previously uncollected stories, in *Round Up.* (The preface and introductions were left behind.) The thirty-five stories of *Round Up* unquestionably contain Lardner's best stories of the decade, indeed, the best stories of his entire career. Some few of the stories are mildly humorous, others mildly critical. But many are definitely "wasteland stories."

One of the most cynically satirical is "Haircut." The barber/narrator tells a newcomer in town about the short happy life of Jim Kendall, a salesman whose main occupation was hurting other people. A thoroughgoing sadist, Jim enjoyed destroying human beings and would have lived long and

happily at his task had it not been for a "cuckoo" kid named
Paul Dickson who was sane enough to shoot Jim and
"cuckoo" enough to get away with it.

Lardner levels his grimmest satire at the barber and people
like him who interpret evil as "fun." The barber still
remembers Jim with kindly affection: "He certainly was a
caution!" "He was really a card!" punctuate his narrative.
Lardner and his readers not only condemn Jim, but also stand
horrified at the density of the garrulous barber, at his
insensitivity and crass complicity with Jim's destructiveness.
The barber would notice no incongruity in such a title as "Fun
at the Incinerating Plant."

"Who Dealt?" is another first person monologue which
operates on several levels of recognition. Two couples are
playing bridge: Tom and his wife (whose monologue Lardner
records), and Arthur and his wife Helen. Tom's wife drinks,
but Tom doesn't—until the end of his wife's persistent talking.
Little by little, the evening wilts and then collapses. For the
wife unwittingly reveals to Arthur the story of Tom's love for
Helen. At one point, she tells Tom's "friends" about a story he
had written:

> It's a story about two men and a girl and they were all
> brought up together and one of the men was awfully popular
> and well off and good-looking and a great athlete—a man like
> Arthur. . . . the well-off man kept after the girl to marry him.
> He didn't know she had promised the other one. Anyway she
> got tired waiting for the man she was engaged to and eloped
> with the other one. And the story ends up by the man she
> threw down welcoming the couple when they came home and
> pretending everything was all right, though his heart was
> broken.

And after she recites a poem Tom had written about Helen's
broken promise, Tom, who had been off liquor for some time,
begins guzzling Scotch.

Throughout the story, Tom's wife is enjoying herself
immensely with her new friends. She constantly misinterprets
Tom's bids, just as she misinterprets his blushes. There are

some laughs for the reader, but again, Tom's wife's fun dooms her to a wasteland marriage.

Lardner's most universally admired story contains his blackest satire. Among the effects of the late Miss Sarah E. Spooldripper, I have discovered a first-hand account of a dramatic rendition, directed by Lardner himself, of the story "Champion." One of Lardner's close associates in his Vanity Fair puppet show wrote the account in a letter to a dear friend and garbage collector on Long Island. I include it here solely in the interests of scholarship—and also because it mentions the word "wasteland" at least once.

Dear Joe,

You should be here Joe. They'd be lots of work for you here. We's always cracking jokes and telling funning stories, like we used to do down at the incinerating plant.

I'm still doing vaudeville Joe with this guy Lardner. I've took a job as one of his puppets. I walks in one day and he looks me over and says You'll do, just like that. What for? I says. I need some body to play wasteland, he says. I nearly fell over laughing. Can you imagine anyone saying that kind of thing Joe?

He makes up these skits you see Joe and then reaches down in his bag and pulls me up. Oh, he's got some mean skits Joe. And when the skit's over, who's laying on the side of the stage in a heap? Me, that's who.

You ever seed any of Lardner's shows? We been doing one called "Champion." I have to keep running backstage changing clothes, cuz there ain't no really good puppets around anymore. Another guy helped the story along too. He played Midge Kelly, the boxer. What a jerk! The whole show was a kind of boxing match, although there weren't no other boxers in it. Cept me and Kelly.

Well, the first scene, I plays Connie, Midge's cripple kid brother. In comes Midge and whammo! I'm down on the floor and Midge is snatching up my four-bits. Then he hauls off and kicks me in my lame leg. That's when the audience gets an idea about what a wasteland character is.

Next thing, I runs off and slips on a dress—don't laugh Joe. I couldn't stand it. Midge comes in and says Hi Ma and I says something about Connie and Midge smashes me. So I lay there like dirt again.

Then off with the skirt and on with the pants. Midge borrows some dough off me which I lets him have cuz I don't want him to hit me for real. Midge skips town. A real honey.

So I slips on another skirt and I'm Emma. Midge borrows some money from me and tries to skip town again. But my brother catches him and I marries Midge. On wedding night, Midge comes in and knocks me for a loop. When I comes to, he's gone. Good riddance. Cept I still got Midge's kid in me.

Sometimes I looks out in the audience about this point. They're setting there like mules. It takes a lot of punching to open an audience's eyes.

Anyways, I switches dresses and sends Midge some letters. Emma dear needs some dough for the kid—he's dying from nothing to eat by this time. Midge throws the letter away. Then I writes saying Mama needs some dough and Connie would sure like a little letter. He throws that one in the wastebasket too. See what he thinks of me Joe?

Well, to make a short story of it Joe, I gets knocked down a couple more times, jilted, betrayed, and abused by Midge Kelly. And all the while he's getting closer and closer to being top dog on the boxing ladder.

But the crowd ain't seed the last punch yet. A guy named Wallie Adams comes in to tell some sports reporter what a great guy Midge is—an ideal father, how he loves his little wifey and just adores his bouncing babies. Midge just can't stand nothing but good clean living it seems.

Wallie don't say nothing about the wasteland Midge left behind him—wife, brother, mother, managers, friends, all wasteland and ashes. That's me Joe.

The crowd should be steaming mad by this time. But Lardner hasn't landed the last punch yet. A sports editor rares back and says: "The people don't want to see him knocked. He's champion."

Some of 'em got it, but most of 'em just set there wide-eyed like a cow.

Well Joe that's the kind of wasteland I been playing. You can have your broken pillars and rats running across glass in empty cellars and desert rock with no water. That's pretty and all. But the human wasteland is the worst kind of all. Take it from me Joe. I been there.

Well Joe why don't you come up and see me in "The Love Nest." You'll die laughing.

Your old pal,

Puppet Pete

10

Dos Passos in the Twenties

A.S. Knowles, Jr.

It is true of John Dos Passos, as it is of any other writer, that he was a product of certain influences. Yet he stands in retrospect as an artist who was, more than anything else, himself. It is not simply that his response to outside influences was unslavish and selective; it is that far more than some of his great contemporaries, he was able in his best work to subdue the debilitating influence of an ego that requires one's art to reflect a certain image of one's self. The illegitimate child of a corporation lawyer and his mistress, Dos Passos experienced the kind of dispossessed childhood that could have produced yet another example of that hero-figure of all Romantic ages, the wounded, self-conscious artist; and, in fact, his auto-biography is never absent from his work. Nevertheless, there is a simple and fundamental difference between Dos Passos and, say, Hemingway. In Hemingway, the sense of self shaped the writer. In Dos Passos, the writer shaped the sense of self.

Or so Dos Passos appears in retrospect. At his death in 1970, his reputation was just beginning to recover from three decades of decline brought about partly by a falling off of his art, partly by the disenchantment of left-liberal critics with a writer who had not only deserted the cause, but had seemed to go over to the other side. Yet by the later 1960's even those who shook their heads over his politics had to admit that there was something indomitably independent about the man, some refusal to accept anyone else's conception of what he ought to be—as a man or as a writer—that demanded admiration. He was very nearly the sole survivor of a generation of troubled geniuses in whom the worm of self-destruction had somehow done its work. That he should still be alive and productive in the late 1960's seemed to affirm that there was yet another way in which he was different. Of the whole lot, "Dos" seemed to have found, in going his own way, some extra portion of not merely physical, but moral health.

If we consider the beginning of his career, however, his independence will have to be understood as a latent quality that will emerge only as the young Dos Passos moves through and beyond an apprenticeship in which there is every kind of shaping influence. There is the matter of his birth and childhood. There is Harvard. There are the first World War and socialism. And beyond events, there are literary movements— determinism and expressionism especially. Beyond literary movements there are impressionist music and cubist painting. In the beginning, these are the shapers of his art. When he reaches the height of his powers, in U.S.A. (1930-36), the roles have reversed; Dos Passos' art has taken command, and what were once "influences" have become elements of a complex masterpiece utterly dominated by its creator.

"WHERE THE WOMEN COME AND GO . . . "

While there is some justice in thinking of Dos Passos as one of those young writers who were shot out of the cannon's mouth, he had begun to write before he entered the first World War. His first published novels come after the war and are about the war, but Streets of Night (1923), his third novel, was begun at Harvard before Dos Passos joined the Norton-Harjes ambulance corps in 1917, put aside, then finished some

five or six years later. It is not the sort of novel with which
Dos Passos would later be associated, yet there are elements of
Dos Passos' mature sensibility that are better understood after
one has glanced at this early work. Principally, *Streets of Night*
reminds us that the young Dos Passos was an inhabitant of the
same milieu that produced T. S. Eliot and the poems of
Prufrock and Other Observations (1917). Pre-1918 Cambridge
was the center of an American post-Decadence, nourished by
the young Harvard aesthetes who were in varying degrees
shaped by fashionable attitudes of despair, boredom, self-
doubt, anti-Philistinism, anti-respectability, and a tremulous
commitment to Art. It was a sometimes languid, sometimes
highly charged sub-culture that could not abide the "Cambridge ladies who live in furnished souls . . . and have comfortable minds," as Dos Passos' friend E. E. Cummings was to put
it in his famous condemnation of local mores. *Streets of Night*
is Dos Passos' slightly callow expression of the torments of
youth, bearing much the same relationship to his career as
Fitzgerald's *This Side of Paradise* did to his. Its three principal
characters find their hopes for a fulfilling existence stifled by a
society that, long after the demise of the Puritans, continues
to be fundamentally puritanical and inimical to that still
fashionable remnant of nineteenth century philosophy, the
life-force. Wenny, the embodiment of joy, freedom, and
physical life, kills himself when he finds he cannot escape the
web of the past. Fanshawe, the intellectual (an echo of
Hawthorne?), resigns himself to the world of Prufrock: "And
I'll go back and go to and fro to lectures with a notebook
under my arm, and now and then in the evening, when I
haven't any engagement, walk into Boston through terrible
throbbing streets. . . ." And Nan, the girl who could neither
give herself to Wenny nor resign herself to Fanshawe, retreats
behind the blind doors of Boston to attempt to summon up
Wenny's spirit with a ouija board.

Eliot's "The Love Song of J. Alfred Prufrock" appeared
first in 1915, probably before Dos Passos' novel was begun.
The year before the novel was completed and published *The*

Waste Land was in print. While Dos Passos was in many respects to become one of the later chroniclers of the waste land, it is Eliot's earlier poetry that echoes through *Streets of Night*. Dos Passos' Cambridge is a city of yellow fogs, sputtering arclights, sombre evenings, chattering teacups. The "lonely men in shirtsleeves" are there as well. Dos Passos' sense of the evocative power of physical detail is as acute as Eliot's, although his expression of it is less terse:

> There were puddles in the road. It was dark between arclights, a few glows from windows loomed distant among weighty shadows. Shadows seemed to move slouchingly just out of sight. Fanshawe felt he was walking unawares through all manner of lives, complications of events. Thoughts of holdups brought a vague fear into his mind. There ought to be more lights.
>
> * * *
>
> They had reached the long brightly lighted oblong of Central Square where the fog was thinned by the shine of the plateglass windows of cheap furniture stores and the twisted glint of tinware in the window of Woolworth's.

Passages such as these not only echo Eliot, but give some indication of the way in which Dos Passos' interest in painting acted upon his imagination. It would be going much too far, however, to say that *Streets of Night* ought still to be read by anyone but a devotee. It would be more reasonable to say that it ought to be read about, in order to understand that the writer who was later to become famous for a massively realistic chronicle of American experience served his apprenticeship as Eliot served his, detailing the essentially trivial failures of Boston.

"ALL THE CIRCLES OF HELL"

Yet the novels that follow (published though they were before *Streets of Night* was finished) have not entirely freed themselves from the concerns of their predecessor. *One Man's Initiation: 1917* (first published abroad in 1920, in America in 1922, but given its first unbowdlerized printing in 1969) and *Three Soldiers* (1921) both confront the great trauma of their age, the war of 1914-18. The war is unquestionably more "important" as a subject than the frustrations of Cambridge, but both works, in large measure, see the war in terms of its impact upon a sensitive young man from Harvard. This is natural enough. Dos Passos was such a young man, and both novels draw upon his own experiences on the Western Front. Bringing Harvard to the war, however, meant bringing certain stock attitudes or postures; these tend to produce a triteness of ideas and, more seriously, of style. Hemingway is remembered for a passage on abstract words in *A Farewell to Arms* which reads in part:

> I was always embarrassed by the words sacred, glorious, and sacrifice and the expression in vain. We had heard them, sometimes standing in the rain almost out of earshot, so that only the shouted words came through, and had read them, on proclamations that were slapped up by billposters over other proclamations, now for a long time, and I had seen nothing sacred, and the things that were glorious had no glory and the sacrifices were like the stockyards at Chicago if nothing was done with the meat except to bury it.

In *Three Soldiers,* there is a meditation on the same subject:

> Were they all shams, too, these gigantic phrases that floated like gaudy kites high above mankind? Kites, that was it, contraptions of tissue paper held at the end of a string, ornaments not to be taken seriously. He thought of all the long procession of men who had been touched by the unutterable futility of the lives of men, who had tried by phrases to make things otherwise. . . . And he felt a crazy desire to join the forlorn ones, to throw himself into inevitable defeat, to live his life as he saw it in spite of everything, to proclaim once more the falseness of the gospels under the cover of which greed and fear filled with more and yet more pain the already unbearable agony of human life.

The comparison is a little unjust. The first passage is by a writer who was consciously crafting an original style and working seven or eight years later in a career that ran roughly parallel with Dos Passos'. But the point remains: finding a true and unaffected style was a longer process for the well-schooled Dos Passos than for the less educated Hemingway.

Three Soldiers, nevertheless, brought Dos Passos fame. The earlier *One Man's Initiation* had not; published in England, its sales for the first six months amounted to sixty-three copies. This first of the two war novels had been conceived in Dos Passos' mind as a large work incorporating *Streets of Night*. It turned out to be a novel of less than two hundred pages that may now be read as a modest prelude to *Three Soldiers*. Its hero, Martin Howe, is autobiographical, his adventures presented through a series of impressionistic sketches of soldiering on the Western Front. Martin is a sensitive young intellectual of his time and place. Revolted by the war, he nevertheless is gripped by the Romantic desire for experience: " 'I am going to do something some day,' " he says, " 'but first I must see. I want to be initiated in all the circles of hell.' " The novel ends with Martin joining in a debate among a Catholic, a Communist, and an Anarchist that concludes with the hope of coming revolution. Dos Passos later wrote that despite its failures as art, the debate "still expresses, in the language of the time, some of the enthusiasms and some of the hopes of young men. . . ." The same could be said for the novel as a whole. Whatever grandiose plans Dos Passos had for *One Man's Initiation* at its inception, it turned out to be a fundamentally modest and convincing work.

Three Soldiers, on the other hand, was conceived and carried out on a large scale. Over four hundred pages in length, the novel is an attack upon war as the lethal agency of a civilization intent upon crushing the freedom of the individual. To give breadth to his attack, Dos Passos selected a trio of national types: Fuselli is an Italian-American from the streets of San Francisco, Chrisfield a farm boy from middle America, and John Andrews a well-bred Virginian who has been studying music at Harvard. In one way or another all three are overcome, not by the enemy on the field of battle, but by the military machine they are made to serve and that, in turn, serves a repressive society. It is a powerful idea and one that remains decidedly modern; yet the novel finally seems forced, as polemical novels often do. That Fuselli, who wants nothing so much as to become a corporal, should end up in a labor battalion; that Chrisfield should kill not a German but one of his own sergeants and become a fugitive; and that John Andrews should be arrested for desertion as he sits composing his first major work, are ironies too perfect to seem uncontrived. The anger of *Three Soldiers* is real, but its expression is labored.

For a number of reasons, however, *Three Soldiers* stands as one of Dos Passos' major works. First, it brought him recognition. H. L. Mencken called it "unquestionably the best war novel yet produced in America, and other reviewers praised its frankness, power, and "extraordinary beauty." The novel received an initial printing of three or four thousand copies and went on to become widely read; from the appearance of *Three Soldiers* on, Dos Passos would not be an obscure writer. Second, the novel required Dos Passos to enlarge the scope of his fiction so that it could traverse contrasting scenes and moods, in this instance the suffocating grimness of the Western Front and the liberal pleasures of student life in Paris. To give some sense of the universality of his theme, he was compelled to create a varied group of characters. Choosing Fuselli, Chrisfield, and Andrews, Dos Passos had his first opportunity to cut down through a society and show how the malevolent machinery of authoritarian capitalism could destroy those who did not understand or would not embrace the system, whatever their background. Finally, as one reads *Three Soldiers* he can feel Dos Passos testing and stretching what are to become formidable powers of observation. The sharpness of eye and ear for which he would become famous is honed repeatedly here, urged on by the vision of a painter-novelist working in the mind of a musician:

He hurried along the road, splashing now and then in a shining puddle, until he came to a landing place. The road was very wide, silvery, streaked with pale green and violet, and straw-color from the evening sky. Opposite were bare poplars and behind them clusters of buff-colored houses climbing up a green hill to a church, all repeated upside down in the color-streaked river. The river was very full, and welled up above its banks, the way the water stands up above the rim of a glass filled too full. From the water came an indefinable rustling, flowing sound that rose and fell with quiet rhythm in Andrews's ears.

Andrews forgot everything in the great wave of music that rose impetuously through him, poured with the hot blood through his veins, with the streaked colors of the river and the sky through his eyes, with the rhythm of the flowing river through his ears.

The writing remains romantic and, here and there, trite, but passages such as this remind us of something the more controlled writing of U.S.A. may conceal. In Dos Passos' fiction, more than in that of other American writers of his generation, we are exposed to a broad spectrum of twentieth century art. Dos Passos has a comprehensive sensibility, absorbing the imagery of Cezanne and Monet into the texture of *Three Soldiers* as he was to draw Cubism and Expressionism into the fabric of later works. In the Paris scenes, the sound of Debussy can be sensed as clearly as the tauter rhythms of ragtime and Tin Pan Alley in the fiction to come.

If *Streets of Night* had echoed Eliot, *Three Soldiers* seemed not to. It would be a year before *The Waste Land* was published, and there was little in Eliot's earlier poetry that could apply to Armageddon. Eliot had virtually ignored the first World War, confining himself (as E. M. Forster put it) to the "slighter gestures of dissent." For Dos Passos, the war was ˑd would remain the great betrayal, the long moment when ˑern industrial capitalism could clearly be seen holding ˑn by the throat. It required major gestures of dissent, ˑJohn Andrews' changing his projected tone poem ˑˑ based on a vision of the Queen of Sheba to one ˑBody and Soul of John Brown." Yet Andrews does not assume that his waste land will be greatly revivified by revolution:

> "It seems to me," he said very softly, "that human society has always been like that, and perhaps will be always that: organizations growing and stifling individuals, and individuals revolting hopelessly against them, and at last forming new societies to crush the old societies and becoming slaves again in their turn. . . ."

It is a melancholy statement that could well stand as a motto over all of Dos Passos' work, and might long ago have been noted by those who could not understand why the writer who spoke so eloquently against Capitalism was to turn just as vehemently upon Socialism, Communism, Fascism, and Unionism.

"O CITY CITY . . . "

We speak of Dos Passos' "novels," and the term suffices for the longer fiction from *Streets of Night* to the first volume of *U.S.A.* (*The 42nd Parallel*, 1930). The author came to prefer the term "chronicles," implying that he no longer wished his fiction to be regarded as primarily an art form, and that he had come to regard himself as an historian more than an artist. Whatever the merits of Dos Passos' terminology, it can be argued that *Streets of Night, One Man's Initiation,* and *Three Soldiers* are all to some degree unrealized works and that Dos Passos was not comfortable with the "pure" novel. In the late years of his long career, Dos Passos was to produce several historical studies; in the twenties he published two books of travel, two dramas, and a volume of poetry, suggesting that even in the early years he was by no means satisfied that fiction was his most secure form.

Although Dos Passos' first appearance between hard covers had been in the collection *Eight Harvard Poets* (1917), *A Pushcart at the Curb* (1922) was to be his only further attempt

to achieve recognition as a poet. Most of the poems in
Pushcart are terse impressions of places at home and abroad,
reflecting Dos Passos' travels in the post-Harvard years; there is
no evidence of greatness in his verses, but neither are they
incompetent:

> Buildings shoot rigid perpendiculars
> latticed with window-gaps
> into the slate sky.
>
> Garment-workers loaf in their overcoats
> (stare at the gay breasts of pigeons
> that strut and peck in the gutters).
> Their fingers are bruised tugging needles
> Through fuzzy hot layers of cloth,
> thumbs roughened twirling waxed thread;
> they smell of lunchrooms and burnt cloth.
> The wind goes among them
> detaching sweat-smells from underclothes
> making muscles itch under overcoats
> tweaking legs with inklings of dancetime.
>
> Bums on park-benches
> spit and look up at the sky.
> Garment-workers in their overcoats
> pile back into black gaps of doors.
>
> > Where the wind comes from
> > scarlet windflowers sway
> > on rippling verges of pools,
> > sound of girls dancing
> > thud of vermillion feet.

The poems are a further storing up of images, many of which
will be absorbed into the poetic prose of the chapter
introductions of *Manhattan Transfer* and the Camera Eyes of
U.S.A. The same gathering of experience and insight occurs in
the travel essays of *Rosinante to the Road Again* (1922) and
Orient Express (1927, with illustrations by the author), in
which Dos Passos is always voyaging on two levels, into the
world and into the self, and observing both with disarming
objectivity:

> Telemachus had wandered so far in search of his father

that he had quite forgotten what he was looking for. He sat on
a yellow plush bench in the cafe El Oro del Rhin, Plaza Santa
Ana, Madrid, swabbing up with a bit of bread the last smudges
of brown sauce off a plate of which the edges were piled with
the dismembered skeleton of a pigeon. Opposite his plate was a
similar plate his companion had already polished. Telemachus
put the last piece of bread into his mouth, drank down a glass
of beer at one spasmodic gulp, sighed, leaned across the table
and said:
    "I wonder why I am here."

(Rosinante)

We look upon the poetry, the books of travel, and the
dramas (*The Garbage Man*, 1926; *Airways, Inc.*, 1928) as minor
works, but *Rosinante* and *Orient Express*, especially, are still
fresh and often charming; when we see these "other" writings
of the Twenties standing in their diversity before *U.S.A.*, we
understand how important they were in providing Dos Passos
with some portion of the great bulk of experience—both real
and literary—his masterpiece would require. In that respect,
the most important single work published by Dos Passos in the
Twenties was *Manhattan Transfer* (1925). There, for the first
time, Dos Passos saw what his apprenticeship was leading to, a
densely populated and many-layered novel of the American
character.

Considering the nature of Dos Passos' fiction to this point,
readers of the newly published *Manhattan Transfer* might have
expected it to have been an attack upon the big city as an
expression of the power of industrial capitalism—New York as
another kind of battlefield, Manhattan as a symbol of
civilization's compulsion to crush the individual in a machinery of streets and buildings. In fact, some such meaning is
present in the work. Yet the novel is far more a moral work
than a political one, with Dos Passos using New York much as
Eliot uses London, to provide a hectic but fundamentally
sterile setting for a study of man's failure to conquer his own
depravity. Thus, *Manhattan Transfer* looks directly forward to
U.S.A. which, in its three volumes, examines not so much the
failure of a system as the moral decay of those individuals—

both the powerful and the powerless—who are the system.
Like *U.S.A.*, *Manhattan Transfer* has no heroes, for Dos Passos
had now put behind Romantic conceptions of young heroes
ranged against the world. The partially autobiographical
Jimmy Herf is only an observer-protagonist, last seen quietly
leaving the waste land after the collapse of his marriage to
Ellen Thatcher:

> Sunrise finds him walking along a cement road between
> dumping grounds full of smoking rubbishpiles. The sun shines
> redly through the mist on rusty donkey-engines, skelton
> trucks, wishbones of Fords, shapeless masses of corroding
> metal. Jimmy walks fast to get out of the smell. He is hungry;
> his shoes are beginning to raise blisters on his big toes. At a
> cross-road where the warning light still winks and winks, is a
> gasoline station, opposite it the Lightning Bug lunchwagon.
> Carefully he spends his last quarter on breakfast. That leaves
> him three cents for good luck, or bad luck for that matter. A
> huge furniture truck, shiny and yellow, has drawn up outside.
> "Say will you give me a lift?" he asks the redhaired man at
> the wheel.
> "How fur ye goin?"
> "I dunno. . . . Pretty far."

Behind Herf's tentative farewell lies not a single story but a
network of stories of people moved largely by their appetites:
simple greed, the lust for power, sexuality. Running through
the network is a central strand, the career of Ellen Thatcher.
She is brought into the world in the first paragraph of the
novel, squirming "feebly like a knot of earthworms." With
that image Dos Passos establishes his theme: whatever our
pretensions to moral superiority, we are dominated mainly by
our reflexes. Ellen grows up, becomes an actress, marries and
divorces a homosexual, marries Jimmy Herf, becomes a
successful editor, enters the world of the powerful, divorces
Jimmy. She is a great beauty, a magnet to men, but like
Dreiser's sister Carrie, Ellen finds that her conquests leave her
unfulfilled. Lacking the moral energy to inject meaning into a
shallow life, she can only go on responding to her instincts.
Near the end of the novel, she is buying a dress at "Madame

Soubrine's" when a seamstress is accidentally burned. Ellen is momentarily shaken by this brief exposure to tragedy, but the instincts regain control; we catch our last glimpse of her entering the Algonquin, "advancing smiling towards two gray men in black with white shirtfronts getting to their feet, smiling, holding out their hands."

Around Jimmy Herf and Ellen Thatcher, others dance to the hectic rhythms of the city: Stan Emory, an ebullient but drunken architect who commits suicide; Joe Harland, a failed financier turned alcoholic; George Baldwin, an ambulance chaser who pursues, and catches, the brass ring; Bud Korpenning, a country boy who is driven to his death by fear of the city. The novel has an enormous cast of characters, but only one who seems to possess a significant measure of simple moral health. Armand Duval (called "Congo"), a former seaman, an anarchist, has a hard-headed knowledge of himself and his goals that makes it possible for him to maintain his equilibrium. What Congo wants above all is to be his own man, and he succeeds. His frequent appearances in the novel, moreover, assure us that Dos Passos was not asserting a flatly deterministic view of man; although the majority of his characters are letting themselves be pushed about by their appetites, Congo demonstrates that it is possible to be sane, resourceful, self-reliant, and yet cheerfully human.

With *Manhattan Transfer* Dos Passos took a full stride into the territory of *The Waste Land.* The first words of the novel, poised above the opening sentences of narration, recall Eliot's description of the Thames in "The Fire Sermon:"

> *Three gulls wheel above the broken boxes, orangerinds, spoiled cabbage heads that heave between the splintered plank walls, the green waves spume under the round bow as the ferry, skidding on the tide, crashes, gulps the broken water, slides, settles slowly into the ship. . . .*

Indeed the whole novel is a fire sermon, full of references to fire engines, sirens, buildings in flames; Stan Emory and the seamstress, Anna Cohen, suffer death or injury by fire. When George and Cecily Baldwin quarrel over his unfaithfulness and

her fear of sex, it is as if we were reading the tense dialogue of
"A Game of Chess": " 'All right ... leave me alone. ... I
don't care about anything.' " After George has left, she echoes
the desperate yearnings of "What the Thunder Said," musing,
"Oh if it would only rain. As the thought came to her there
was a low growl of thunder above the din of building and of
traffic. Oh if it would only rain." In the pages that
immediately follow, Ellen Thatcher advises a friend to have an
abortion. In both *Manhattan Transfer* and the later *U.S.A.*,
Dos Passos shared Eliot's sense of how banal and degrading our
casual eroticism is likely to be (" 'Well now that's done: and
I'm glad it's over.' "). He wrote brilliantly of the sexual itch:

> "Get up on your toes and walk in time to the music. ...
> Move in straight lines that's the whole trick." Her voice cut the
> quick coldly like a tiny flexible sharp metalsaw. Elbows
> joggling, faces set, gollywog eyes, fat men and thin women,
> thin women and fat men rotated densely about them. He was
> crumbling plaster with something that rattled achingly in his
> chest, she was an intricate machine of sawtooth steel white-
> bright bluebright copperbright in his arms. When they stopped
> her breast and the side of her body and her thigh came against
> him. He was suddenly full of blood steaming with sweat like a
> runaway horse.

In *Manhattan Transfer*, Dos Passos all but completely
broke away from the perspective of the Harvard aesthete.
Impressionism gave way to pungent illustration: George Grosz
instead of Monet. The wounded sensibilities of Martin Howe
and John Andrews flickered in the personality of Jimmy Herf,
but the more important legacy from the early fiction was the
further development of characters from the grittier world of
Fuselli and Chrisfield. Above all, Dos Passos had begun to
discover how to live within not just his own personality (as
with Howe and Andrews), but within the personalities of a
broad range of American types. Living within them, he was
able to portray them with an uncanny faithfulness to reality
that moved Jean-Paul Sartre to call him, in 1938, "the greatest
writer of our time."

By the end of the Twenties, Dos Passos was preparing *The*

42nd Parallel. With its appearance in February, 1930, he had begun an epic chronicle of America from the turn of the century to the early years of the Depression, called, when its three volumes were gathered together in 1938, *U.S.A.* The Romantic egotism of the early fiction had been largely subordinated in *Manhattan Transfer;* in *U.S.A.* Dos Passos would move still closer to the objectivity of the Classical Humanist. Insofar as it is influenced by any other works in what might be called its moral perspective, *U.S.A.* is touched by the spirit of Plutarch's *Lives* and Gibbon's *Decline and Fall of the Roman Empire,* sharing their conviction that the story of a society is the story of its individuals. Ironically, both works had been urged upon the young Dos Passos by the father who had contributed so much to Dos Passos' Romantic sense of alienation.

To reach this point Dos Passos had had to live and write expansively, redefining his talent as it matured. The works of the Twenties were essential to his greatest achievement and became part of it: lyrical autobiography controlled and molded into the Camera Eyes; real men and events into the Biographies and Newsreels; the vision of a culture in terms of a vast network of interrelated lives, into the fictional narratives. It would, however, be an achievement that Dos Passos could not repeat. As the pace of events quickened through the later Thirties, he would find himself compelled to respond more quickly to the crises around him. There would be no time for experimentation, no time for the slow ripening of art.

11

The Death Ship: B. Traven's Cradle

Philip Melling

> Lyke as a myrrour doth represent agayne
> The fourme and fygure of mannes countenance
> So in our ship shall he see wrytyn playne
> The fourme and fygure of hys mysgovernance.
>
> Sebastian Brant's *Narrenschiff*

B. Traven's *The Death Ship,* a product of the author's experiences in the International Merchant Marine in 1922, was first published in Germany as *Das Tottenschiff* in 1926. Traven, a Wisconsin immigrant of Scandinavian extraction, abhorred the commercial ballyhoo of the East Coast literati and refused to allow the novel's publication in the United States until 1934, preferring to risk the distortions of retranslation into English. This implied no racial or regional preference, but rather a distrust in proportion to the degree of exposure involved in contemporary publicity. The advertising industry symbolized to Traven a world in which "Human beings must be kept under control. They cannot fly like insects about the world into which they were born without being asked." This situation existed for no other reason than "to show the omnipotence of the state, of the holy servant to the state, the bureaucrat" (177).* To compensate for the

---

*All page references are to B. Traven, *The Death Ship* (London, 1967).

removal of freedom, Traven rejected the American dream and ridiculed his national identity with a gallery of masks and deceptions.

Traven's anti-capitalist leanings, however, allowed cultural Stalinists on the *New Masses* to evaluate *The Death Ship* as a contribution to the collectivist school of art. Herbert Klein, writing under the name of "Arthur Heller," asked whether there was "anywhere an intenser apotheosis of wage-slavery carried to the ultimate of exploitation" (June 12, 1934, p. 24). In support of this viewpoint it should be acknowledged that Traven is often prolix in the worst collectivist manner. His excessively lurid descriptions of life aboard the *Yorikke* and naturalistic accumulation of details of horror is frequently reminiscent of Dalton Trumbo's technique in *Johnny Got His Gun*. The effect is self-neutralizing; it tends to leave the reader immune to the subject matter. Yet *The Death Ship* is not important as a muckraking diatribe on labor conditions at sea or an attempt to inspire maritime reform; with its footloose American sailor disloyally abandoned by his ship without any source of identification, *The Death Ship* provides an early perspective on the disengagement, dispossession, violence, and social overturning that dominated American literature beginning in the 1930s.

Gerald Gales is a rootless, migrant outsider, looking up at society from the lowest social rung. From his low-milieu, episodic confrontations there emerges not merely an authentic strain of vernacular expression, but also a bitter and sardonic analysis of society, not to be confused with such a tired and fragile collection of anti-bureaucratic cliches as Dalton Trumbo's *Washington Jitters*. Gerald Gales sings the song of the self-educated worker, in the bitter, sardonic language of suffering. At his most effective he deserts the obligatory eloquence of literature for a language that is simple, a style that suits his natural simplicity, and what W. M. Frohock describes as "a wry tendency to see himself as something much closer to a comic than a tragic figure." The polyglot ship *Yorikke*, on which he willingly sails toward an unknown end, is an absurdity; but Gales faces death with puns and jests upon his lips, for if life cannot be outwitted at least it can be laughed at.

Picaresque irony is an individualistic exercise locating a condition of rootlessness which is at the heart of Gales' situation. As a victim of "superstition" and the open-road, Gales is consumed by what F. W. Chandler in *The Literature of Roguery* calls "Gypsydom." But the nature of Gales' nomadism—grave-digger's assistant in Ecuador, seller of "splinters from the very cross of Our Saviour at country fairs in Ireland for a half-crown" (95) — precipitates a detachment from community and an existential dilemma. (Individuation is achieved through the apprehension of space and the constraints which are placed upon Gales by the *Yorikke.*). The commencing irony of *The Death Ship's* narrative, therefore, exposes a disillusioned romantic entrapped by the meaningless respectability of the *S. S. Tuscaloosa,* a distinctly non-romantic cargo freighter, "a fine ship, an excellent ship, true and honest down to the bilge. First-rate freighter. Not a tramp" (7). Gales' sarcasm and fondness for irony implies a defensiveness and insecurity, a need to assert his self-importance by creating an invulnerable pose. He becomes the sly-gushing sermonizer whose tongue-in-cheek pride and hortatory admiration for the commercial philosophy which the *Tuscaloosa* represents gives way to a mood of disaffection and cynicism:

> What a ship the *Tuscaloosa* was! The swellest quarters for the crew you could think of. There was a great ship-builder indeed. A man, an engineer, an architect who for the first time in the history of shipbuilding had the communistic idea that the crew of a freighter might consist of human beings, not merely of hands (7).

But "full-fledged sailors aren't needed" aboard such a modern ship, which is merely "a floating machine" designed to make money for the company. The "real sailor" is deprived of identity, function and purpose and is actually reduced to a "deck hand" or "handy man" (8). The modern ship demotes the "real sailor" from Emerson's "Man Thinking" to man "metamorphosed into a thing," a creature engaged in the purposeless service of industry. The sea ceases to be a location of human adventure, initiation and heroism and becomes either an instrument of profiteering technology or the victim of a synthetic "romance" manufactured by the Hollywood dream factory and pulp magazines. "The song of the real and genuine hero of the sea has never yet been sung," announces Gales, because it is "too cruel" for a people committed to narcotic "ballads" and bland mythologies (8). This statement is prophetic but intentionally ironic since Gales is himself a victim of myth and romance like those "many fine youngsters who fell for those stories (sea romances) and believed them true, and off they went to a life that destroyed their bodies and their souls" (8).

On docking at Antwerp Gales retrieves his nomadic zest and renounces his vow to "Honey," his New Orleans sweetheart, to stay clear of other dames. The sight of empty buildings and offices on the pier to which the ship is moored—"bleached human bones found in a desolate place in the open sun. . .so utterly hopeless like a world going to pieces without knowing it" (10)—convey a sense of disintegration and sterility about commercial life that Gales can never tolerate. In a more characteristic act of curiosity and adventure, he disembarks from his "smart American freighter" in search of ". . .people hustling about. . .doing business, making money, getting drunk, laughing, cursing, stealing, killing, dancing, falling in love, and falling out again" (10). After spending a night in a brothel, he returns to the docks the following morning to find that the Tuscaloosa has departed for New Orleans. The casual, parental betrayal underscores his suspicion of bureaucratic methods. Without money, legal identification and social recognition—a touchstone of the insane nationalism fanned by World War I—Gales discovers that he has "no established home anywhere in the world" and no "legal existence" (20). His position in the world is adequately summarized by the Belgian interpreter: " 'In any

civilized country he who has no passport is nobody. He does
not exist for us or for anybody else" (23).

William Doerflinger in *The Saturday Review Of Literature*
(May 5, 1934, p. 677) called *The Death Ship* "a blasting satire
against bureaucracy" and "the arbitrary irrationality of petty
legal regulations as they obstruct the free life of the
individual." The novel traces the narrator's betrayal and
disenchantment by a world which contradicts its own dream
of liberty, through the slow erosion of his personality to his
gradual awakening as a creative consciousness.

Gerald Gales initially responds to his new environment by
challenging, through caricature, the established codes of
behavior. (Although not until he is interred in the *Yorikke* and
the initiating world of pain does Gales fully evade occasional
self-pity and petulance and a romantic indulgence in the role
of an outcast.) In the Low Countries he begins to caricature
respectable institutions and officialdom in order to expose
their absurdity, but caricature has a paradoxical effect. On the
one hand, the artist, through the exaggeration of his strokes
can create the impression of an unusual intensity of life in his
creatures. The element of expressionistic distortion in caricature, however, leaves the reader with the feeling that such life
is virtually surreal. This sense of the not-quite-real filters
through from Gales' world as humanity is monstrously
transfigured.

Gales becomes the slightly jocular and ribald commentator
who maims and mocks the declamations of others in a
reportage as ruthless, impolite and elaborately bitter as the
world it describes. Like the fictional persona of E. E.
Cummings' *The Enormous Room*, Gales slyly ridicules his
interrogators who, by adopting the lofty and uncommuni-
cative language of the power-dream, have divorced themselves
from the world of the vernacular. The American consul in
Holland, stultified and incapable of discretionary judgment, is
recorded as saying: " 'Cawn you prove thawt you hauve been
on the *Tuscaloosa*?. . . Pshaw! Tsey, tsey, tsey, Nonsense.
Where did you pick up that story? Out of a magazine? Come

clean, come, come' " (28). The Dutch police, for example, are exposed as witless and inept. Their commissioner—"What a man! He was a thinker. . . .Back home he would have had the capacity of solving problems of national economy or be dean of Princeton" (40) — confined to a traditional language. He poses questions in the tired cadences of bureaucratic cliches, but equipped only with inherited language responses, he stands feeble and confused before Gales' verbal evasions. Gales assumes the multiple task of demonstrating the correspondence between language and experience and its corrosive effect on the psyche. English sailors speak in a language which reflects their national chauvinism. "They shout as they owned the world" in a boorish limey slang, "Hey, submarine admiral, Nancy of the gobs. Tell us real sailors who won the war. . . .Hello, Yankey, what're you doing here?. . .Now it is too hot for you, isn't it? Polishing anchor chain, hey' " (44). The language and accent of the French prison chaplain demonstrates the false solemnity, decadence and aloofness of the man as an official, "He spoke good English. It must have been the English William the Conqueror spoke before he landed on the coast of old England. I did not understand a word of his English" (47). Gales can "not understand" because the official religion which the priest represents is impervious to Gales' needs — a fact which he interprets through caricature, "Whenever he mentioned God, I thought he was talking about a goat" (47).

Like Thoreau, Traven saw the state with its creatures—big business, bureaucracy, institutionalized morality, messianic war—as Behemoth crippling and deforming mankind out of all human semblance and conditioning him to a sterile acceptance of its values. The American Consulate in Paris is rife with time-servers and poltroons, whose function it is to persecute "the plain people like me" with defunct clichés concerning freedom, liberty and material wealth. Moreover, ...

> "the whole thing was no longer an affair of human beings; it had become an affair of papers, blanks, affidavits, certificates, photographs, stamps, seals, files, height-measuring, and quarrel-

ling about the colour of the eyes and the hair. The human
being himself was out and forgotten. A piece of merchandise
would not have been treated so" (51).

Over this cattle market absurdly hangs the American flag—
traditional symbol of refuge, sanctuary and dream—and two
other pictures. One is of a man

"who said something about the country being created by the
Lord to be the land of the free and for the hunted. Another
picture of another man who has said great things about the
right of human beings, even Negroes, to unrestricted freedom"
(51).

The only people who can acquire such "freedom" in the
twentieth century however are the grossly rich and privileged
classes who have appropriated the dream for themselves. The
short, fat banker's wife, Mrs. Sally Marcus, can acquire her
"pacepot" by bribing the officials with money, but "the
hungry men and women waiting in the room" who had never
been in God's country before "can only look on with envy and
defeat" (53).

The perpetrator of this charade is the American Consul
himself, an insidiously hollow individual who possesses the
grotesque and unpronounceable name of "Grgrgrgrs." He can
only reiterate the familiar absurdity that Gales does not exist,
because officialdom has no record of his identity — " 'Think it
silly or not. I doubt your birth as long as you have no
certificate of your birth. The fact that you are sitting in front
of me is no proof of your birth. Officially it is no proof' "
(57). And though the pictures on his wall portray "lovers and
supporters of freedom " (59) Gales' particular case is not
relevant to their conception of "freedom." But "Grgrgrgrs"
pleads that this is not of his doing since " 'It is the system of
which I am a slave' " (60).

Freeing himself of a child-like dependence on official
non-definitions of his existence Gales moves away from the
Low Countries and into Spain where he travels unimpeded
between Seville, Cadiz, Barcelona and Marseilles, searching for

"risks" and "the true satisfaction of having done at last
something while you were alive on this crazy earth" (217).
Spain is a contradiction in terms, politically oppressed yet
spiritually relaxed, the precise inverse of those countries which
have been supposedly liberated by a war fought for democracy:

> The people who sang and made music and made love were
> mostly in rags, but they were smiling and friendly, and lovely.
> Above all there was so much freedom. . . .Why should I
> condemn Spain because of what I had heard? . . .No cop comes
> up and wants to search my pockets to see if he can find a lost
> formula for the manufacture of unbreakable wine-glasses. . . . .
> Such a country I should leave? Such people I should spoil by
> chasing jobs and looking busy and hustling? Not for the world
> (81-84).

When Gales does leave Barcelona it is to board the mysterious
unworldly death ship *Yorikke* for perverse and irrational
reasons:

> I could not remember ever having seen anything in the world,
> ship or no ship, that looked so dreadful and hopeless, and so
> utterly lost, as did the *Yorikke*. I shivered. It was better to be a
> stranded sailor and hungry man than to be a deckhand on this
> ship (93).

But the very fact of the *Yorikke*'s grotesqueness appeals to
Gales' "superstitious character." As he confesses, "Suppose I
should say no—all my luck, for the rest of my life, would be
lost. I might never again get a ship to sail on back home to
New Orleans" (95). Wish-fulfillment and the need to move on
determine his actions: "It seemed utterly ridiculous. No one in
the whole world could force me to sign on with that ship, and
yet—Guess it is always like that. If you are happy and
contented, you want to be still happier. You want a change"
(96).

The *Yorikke* is an antique hulk which operates by
gun-running, trafficking in dope and illicit migrants, but is
subject to no laws of the sea. It is crewed by passportless
sailors from many nations, polyglot outcasts who have lost

their papers, nationality and right to consular protection. Officially non-existent their culture is one of common degradation and illiteracy and their destiny—commonly—death. The description of the ship if one of Traven's most evocative set-pieces. Livid and lurid the *Yorikke* is a cell-like sliver torn from life and its character is sheer monstrousness. It is so atrocious as to be absurd, for it mingles comedy with the bizarre exaltation of horror. Gales reacts to the *Yorikke* as "a huge joke," yet instinctively with some affinity, since the ship—like its detractor—is without birth certificate or registration papers:

> There was something wrong with the *Yorikke*. . . .I felt real sympathy for the frightened *Yorikke,* who had to leave the calm, smooth water of the sheltered port and be driven out into the merciless world to fight against gales and typhoons and all the grim elements under heaven. . . .None of her men had mercy on her (89).

The kinship he intuits with this "old hussy trying to dance the rumba" (93) is based on an almost mystical appreciation of her "personality" and "intelligence" (92), qualities which, later in the novel, Gales defines in terms of trustworthiness. The *Yorikke,* like Melville's *Pequod,* is a mythological symbol. W. H. Auden suggests in *The Enchafed Flood* that "if thought of as isolated in the midst of the ocean, the *Pequod* can stand for mankind and human society moving through time and struggling with its destiny." Gales embarks to escape a spiritual condition of spleen and powerlessness; the sea has become to him what Auden calls, "a place of purgatorial suffering." The horror of the ship and Gales' introduction to pain is forecast by a sign that reads:

He
Who enters here
Will no longer have existence (99).

The ability of an accomplished picaro to look at himself from a distance as though he were someone else, to step outside himself and defuse a potentially nightmare situation is an important, redeeming trait; it prevents him from taking his situation too seriously and enables him to see objectively what is ridiculous about his station. On boarding the *Yorikke* Gales attempts to assuage his initial loneliness with a sardonic and whimsical celebration of his experiences:

> One should never cease to learn. If you cannot go to college because you have no money and you have to sell papers to make your own living, you should nevertheless not miss any means by which you can get educated. Travelling, and having lots of experiences in life, are the best education for any man (66).

Gales indulges in maudlin rhetorical outbursts which detract from his growth:

> We, the gladiators of today, we must perish in dirt and filth. . . .We die without the smiles of the beautiful ladies, without holding their perfumed handkerchiefs in our hands. We die without the cheering of the excited crowd. We die in deep silence, in utter darkness, and in rags. We die in rags for you, O Caesar Augustus! (125)

As coal-drag, mess boy and Rat Watch on the *Yorikke*, Gales' life is a form of cheerless and unremitting suffering. His tasks multiply, his pay is reduced, food and sleep are denied him. At the lowest point in his depression he contemplates suicide as an escape from the burns and scalds which he acquires when scouring out the *Yorikke*'s boilers:

> Make a clean short cut, old boy from Sconsin, chuck the coal drag, and hop over; have done with that filth and dung. Make the hop and enter the good old sea while you're still a clean Yank sailor; and before you get soiled all over and make the sea ashamed of you when you come to kiss her good-bye (136).

But there is yet another catch. Gales realizes that were he to commit suicide, his tasks and burdens would merely be placed on the shoulders of some other "poor, overtired, ragged, starved, and tortured coal-drag who would have to go in double watch" (136). Gales, therefore, rejects the mesmerism

of the sea and re-accepts the challenge of the stokehold. This
may involve a pioneer acceptance of "filth and dung," but it
may also lead him toward a new awareness of life through a
triumphant assertion of the will, "Damn it, damn it all, the
devil and hell. Now, listen here, boy from Sconsin, that pest
Yorikke cannot get you. Not you. And all the Consuls neither.
Chin up and get at it. Swallow the filth and digest it. Quickest
way to get rid of it" (136). In his newly found rage to live
Gales spits defiance at the insidious comforts of tradition and
society and accepts the challenge of work.

> "Save your soap and crash it down your wind-pipe. I do not
> need it any longer. But you shall not hear me whine again. I
> spit into your face. I spit at you and your whole damn breed.
> Swallow that. I am ready now for battle" (137).

He thus resolves his situation by learning the process of
unlearning and demanding his release from an official non-
existence so that he may create an elemental identity.

To help him realize this desire is the other coal-drag
Stanislav Koslovski of Poznan, an experienced sailor whose
homeland was wiped off the map by the Treaty of Versailles.
Stanislav is one of E. E. Cummings' "Delectable Mountains,"
an inarticulate "soothing savage" like Melville's Queequeg. In
the face of mounting oppression and suffering Stanislav
propounds an illiterate's philosophy of endurance and hope. In
other words. . . .

> "even if we are all dead ones; all of us, it is not worth the
> trouble to lose heart. Don't get down on your knees. Blare
> them all in their stinking faces even when sighting your last.
> You cannot live beyond for a thousand years or a hundred
> thousand with the feeling eating at you that you gave in during
> your last hour. Don't lose heart. Stick it, and stick it hard. It
> can't come worse. I ought to know" (147).

Through Stanislav, Gales experiences a more selfless understanding of the other boiler men in the stoke-hold, men who
confront even greater physical suffering than himself. He
appreciates slowly their anger, patience, bitter humour, loyalty

and hopelessness: "They were dead. Without a country. Without nationality. Without birth-certificates with which to prove that they were citizens of the earth" (150). Gales can no longer despise those men who, like him, have "forgotten their own selves" (150), and he rejects his pretense of superiority by identifying their suffering with his own. Gales' attempts to overcome torture and return into life are carried out both on his own behalf and on the behalf of these living dead so that they might share with him in the conquest of death. "...why do I permit myself to be tortured? Because I have hope, which is the blessing, the sin, and the curse of mankind. I hope to have a chance to come back to life again" (151).

Through monotonous rituals of abnormal physical and mental pain Gales acquires a resiliency, toughness and an enduring immunity from depression. He overcomes insanity, and, by expanding his capacity for understanding and love, accomodates the world without disarming himself of knowledge of its grim realities. His triumph is one of the human spirit unaided by external forces and one which leads to a supreme exaltation.

> "I am free. Unbound. I may do now whatever I wish. I may curse the gods. They cannot punish me any more. No human law, no divine commandments, can any longer influence my doings, because no longer can I be damned. Hell is now paradise. However horrible hell may be, it cannot frighten me any more" (166).

Like the narrator of Cummings' *The Enormous Room* Gales has freed himself from a world of traditional emotion, morality, and institutionalized religion by simply inverting familiar values. But if E. E. Cummings achieved his release through the world of the imagination Gales has achieved it through a medium of pain. Purgation of the senses allows him to interpret life outside the self with a heightened consciousness. Consequently he experiences a transcendental relationship with inanimate existence, a more profound sense of unity with the by-passed hardware of life.

"Before I shipped on the *Yorikke* I never thought that a thing like a burned match, or a scrap of paper in the mind, or a fallen leaf, or a rusty worthless nail might have a soul. The *Yorikke* taught me otherwise. Since then life for me has become a thousand times richer, even without a motor-car or a radio. No more can I ever feel alone. I feel I am a tiny part of the universe, always surrounded by other tiny parts of the universe, and if one is missing, the universe is not complete—in fact does not exist" (170).

This new found simplicity and freshness is mirrored in his brand new name, Pip, which provides another link with *Moby Dick*. This name, being the same forward as it is backward, becomes a convenient linguistic symbol of recognition, rather than some enigmatic imposed adornment of self. "Rebirth had taken place" (174) and this rebirth, though primarily a stripping away of the inner consciousness, is also demonstrated by the metamorphosis in Gales' attitude toward Yorikkian English. Initially Gales was contemptuous of the language spoken by the *Yorikke*'s crew; but after experiencing the frustrations of stoking the furnaces in the womb of a death ship, he refuses to apologize for any impoliteness, especially of the firemen whose discourteous expletives would be offensive to conventional society. "One must not expect clean speech from a mass compelled to live in filth and always overtired and usually hungry" (163). For Pip the bleak, crude, primitive mutterings of the stokehold Yorikkians possesses a beauty all its own. Only "three hundred words common to all the crew" are "understood by all" (193-4) but that is sufficient in an enslaved society, for "the gallimaufry language, the "Yorikkish" spoken, is a link between those in desperate exile" (B. Lynn, "The Works of B. Traven," *Arena*, I 1950, p. 92). Thus the apparent linguistic confusion aboard the Death Ship contains a primordial meaningfulness since the communal personality is founded on a common illiteracy. By proposing illiteracy as the major virtue of the collective hero of the novel, Traven discredits the traditional language system. Toward this end he creates a hierarchy of articulateness in which the most verbal are the most villainous, such as the

life-denying verbosely professional bureaucrat to whom Stanislav applies for citizenship in Hamburg, whose negative,
uncreative, inherited expressions derive from nothing but
" 'hypocrisy, egoism, and an insane nationalism' " (211).

It was an "insane nationalism" which condemned Pip to
the life of a disinherited disillusioned outcast. But in the
stokehold of *Yorikke* he has, ironically, been forced to
confront a starker reality, that of the self; a reality which
contemporary man has timorously evaded. Thus *Yorikke*
becomes an "Honest" ship for Gales because she "did not
pretend to anything she was not" (203). Pip celebrates her
reliability and consistency, albeit one of horror, for allowing
him to discover an awareness of truth and joy. "So I found
one day that the *Yorikke* had actually become a ship on which
I could live and even laugh" (248).

During most of his sojourn in the bowels of the ship Pip
resides in a limbo between loss of an official external self and
the discovery of an essential inner being. Deprived of the
necessity for motivated action he functions as an intensely
aware but frozen intelligence. His search for an authentic self
is a search from within for a nucleus of original goodness;
before rebirth he needs self-knowledge. His forty days in the
wilderness are similar to the journeyman's movement through
the dark night of the soul in T. S. Eliot's *Four Quartets* and in
a similar manner discovery of the self is characterized by a
suspension of time, the dissolution of external bases of
identity, and a change in physical appearance—the most
superficial basis for a definition of self in the objective world.
Gales wallows deliberately in dirt. "The filth in the quarters
had become thicker, but I was now used to it. In this way the
Yorikke once more proved an excellent teacher, making it
quite clear that the saying: " 'All civilization is only a thick
layer of varnish on the human animal' has a lot of truth in it"
(248). Consequently Gales has the ability to transcend
squeamishness by creating a new life based on hardship and
filth from which he derives humility and sympathy:

"Looking at my fellow sailors now and then, I could not

imagine how it had ever been possible that, seeing them for the
first time, I had thought them the dirtiest and filthiest bunch
of guys I had ever seen. They looked quite decent" (249).

In Pip's inverted scale of things cleanliness is next to
ungodliness and the most despicable characters are those
immaculate bureaucrats who "sit at their desk, scratching and
filing and polishing their finger-nails" (230). These creatures
live meaninglessly; they have no talent for developing what is
peculiarly human, tenderness and sadness. They are truly living
dead, hollow men, unthinking, unfeeling, ungod.

In contrast the common hero of the *Yorikke* is the
illiterate saint; the coal shoveller who lives perpetually in
"filth, in soot, in dirt, in ashes" (231). Thus "Nobody could
blindfold" Stanislav Koslovski "with slogans and success
yarns" for he is a benevolent giant who deduces "a wisdom
and philosophy" from every experience he encounters. Pip
also fosters a new relationship with the firemen, A.B.'s, and
other hands whom, Pip surprisingly discovers, are not like the
"ordinary kind of human bugs" (249). They are not mindless
or conventional because they still retain that spirit of priceless
curiosity which first they displayed by signing on the *Yorikke.*
They become the true pioneers of the twentieth century,
orphaned by a society which has rejected that energizing spirit.
They are truly living—simple, brave and generous—and they are
capable of growth, as is Pip. In his last act on board the
Yorikke he rescues one of them from certain death when
scaling out a red hot boiler. In this newly discovered
humanistic spirit Pip holds a debt of gratitude to the *Yorikke.*
"All right, I cannot pass by you, *Yorikke;* I have to tell you I
love you. Honest, baby, I love you" (263). He has suffered
honestly because his torment has been neither synthetic nor
futile and in that achievement he feels an infinite superiority
to the deluded creature he once was on the *Tuscaloosa.* In a
world full of double standards, meretriciousness and deception
the *Yorikke* has constituted, through its gallery of unswerving
horrors, a unique symbol of stability, direction and ethical
morality. "You are no hypocrite. Your heart does not bleed

tears when you do not feel heartaches deeply and truly"
(263-4). The *Yorikke* has become a symbol of protection and
paternalism allowing Pip to discover an absolute source of
happiness, trust and reassurance. He confesses, "I never want
to leave you again, honey. I mean it."

But contentment is still not that easily maintained against
the machinations of fate. Whilst on shore in Dakar he and
Stanislav are shanghaied onto another death ship, the *Empress
of Madagascar,* and forced to work in the stokehold. However
the ship founders awkwardly and unexpectedly on a reef when
being scuttled off the West coast of Africa. Although Pip is
able to rescue the negro coal drag, Daniel, from the exploding
boiler room, only he and Stanislav are left alive when a rowing
boat with the crew in it is swamped and capsizes. They return
to the *Empress,* which by now has settled down between a
group of rocks and, finding themselves the only remaining
survivors, live sumptuously from a well-stocked galley. For a
time they gluttonously indulge their appetites and their wit in
the midst of desperation and hopelessness as an absurd defence
against the reality of imminent destruction.

Divorced from his familiar world of honest labour and the
dignity of toil, however, Stanislav becomes increasingly de-
pressed. His humourless despair—' "Everything we have here is
too good to last. It can't last, I tell you; I am suspicious of the
whole safari here" ' (287)—is in blatant contrast with Pip's
jocular optimism: " 'You are ungrateful, that's what you
are. . . .You are rich, Stanislav, did you ever realize that? You
are a ship owner' " (289).

When the ship disintegrates in a violent storm their raft is
narrowed down to a single wall of the ship's wooden cabin.
Pip's immersion in the sea and his acceptance of the stars'
message ("Do not long for us if you are in want of peace and
rest; we cannot give you anything which you do not find
within yourself!' " (292)) is the final consummation of his
spiritual metamorphosis. It constitutes the climax of his
baptismal rebirth, his final acceptance of man and his world,
their glorious possibilities and glorious disabilities. In this

vision he refuses to make ritual observances to Nature but celebrates an enjoyment of life that he has created for himself. "All we have is our breath. I shall fight for it with teeth and nails. I won't give up and I won't give in. Not yet" (295). But if Pip emerges into a new life and survives (partly also by chance for he, too, perceives the *Yorikke* and yet recognizes it as a mirage after being unable to untangle the knots that bind him to the raft), Stanislav capitulates to the past. His once noble illiteracy degenerates into incomprehensible gibberish and finally, amid hallucinatory visions, he jumps into the sea in chase of his only salvation, an imaginary Marie Celeste Yorikke.

In its emotional and frantic intensity the conclusion of *The Death Ship* is both powerful and moving.

> "I yelled at the hole: "Stanislav. Laski. Brother. Comrade. Sailor. Dear, dear comrade. Come here. Ahoy! Man, ahoy! Sailor, ahoy! Come here. I am standing by. Come on!" (303)

Pip survives; Stanislav does not. Here is the perpetual and dramatic contradiction in most of what B. Traven writes, the constant inward struggle between optimism and despair; a symbol of that struggle between the decency of humanity against its impulse toward viciousness and greed; the triumph of the individual will against its secession and obliteration. B. Traven, through the fate of Stanislav, displays his contempt for the monster of civilization which has the power to destroy all that is simple, primitive and good. This monster may be fed on anything from celluloid to gold but the result is the same: the debasement of all human values and the human spirit.

Traven's novel, in spite of its extremely troubling message of man's inhumanity to man, is ultimately positive in tone and affirms the value of living by reaching beyond desperation into hope. Civilization may yet be saved through the courageous endurance of Pip, who refuses to succumb to the corruptions of society and achieves a silent and personal victory.

Through Traven's savage humor, the caricature of suffering, his mystic sense of man's relation to his work, the interplay of coarseness and a continual shifting of the plane of meaning whereby anger slides into satire, satire into despair and despair into hope, *The Death Ship* achieves a remarkable power. As an anonymous reviewer said in the *Saturday Review of Literature* (April 28, 1934, p. 671), "Beginning as a kind of humorous satire on government bureaucracy and the absurdity of passports, it rises into powerful fantasia and ends as a *Moby Dick* of the stokehold."

12

The Becoming of Gertrude Stein's
The Making of Americans

Kenneth Frieling

Although the early series of portraits and the first of her landscape dramas constituted the bulk of Gertrude Stein's productions during the twenties, I consider a work of earlier composition, *The Making of Americans,** to best represent this decade since many of her later techniques and aesthetic postures first appear in this novel—a work which she pronounced as equal to the works of Proust and Joyce. The publishing history of *The Making of Americans* clearly indicates that few shared Stein's opinion of its worth.

---

* I will not refer to the original 925 page version of *The Making of Americans* even though it is again available from Peter Owens (England) and the Something Else Press (USA). Instead all page references are to the abridged 1934 Harcourt, Brace and World edition which (as reprinted in 1966) represents the most approachable, available, and economical text for the non-scholar. This abridged version retains virtually all the passages essential for an essay of this brief scope as well as the complete last section of the novel. Incidentally, this version also provided the essentials for Stein herself, as she referred exclusively to it during her lecture tour of the United States. For references to her lectures I have used the readily available paperback, *Gertrude Stein: Writings and Lectures 1909-1945*, edited in 1971 by Patricia Meyerowitz for Penguin (page references preceded by *Lectures*).

Although intermittently written and extensively revised
between 1903 and 1911, this novel was not published until
1925 at Robert McAlmon's Contact Press—and then, only
because some interest in the work had resulted from Hemingway's prevailing upon Ford Madox Ford to print several
installments of it in his *Transatlantic Review.*

Appropriately, the intent—but perhaps not the result—of
the novel seems entirely relevant to the decade of its
publication. In this work, subtitled "History of a Family's
Progress," Stein faced the impending wasteland of her chosen
subject material and the void of any audience, then attempted
aesthetically to transcend the dreary, banal history of immigrant families in America by developing a processual style
increasingly concerned with the form of the writer's consciousness and with the medium's gradual rarefication into a
non-representational, rhythmic "becoming."

The seven sections comprising *The Making of Americans*
clearly show this change of direction. In the first, "The
Dehnings and the Herslands," Stein suggests that the novel will
deal with the first sixty years—three generations—of American
living of four immigrant couples: "And these four women and
the husbands they had with them and the children born and
unborn in them will make up the history for us of a family and
its progress" (4). However, the developing focus centers on the
third generation of Julia Dehning and her impending marriage
to Alfred Hersland—with lengthy digression on the American
fixation upon washing.

While the next two sections announce the Herslands as
their subject, the bulk of the family material centers on the
Hissings and their daughter Fanny, whose husband is the
second David Hersland and whose friends, the three Shilling
women, provide the occasion for increasingly lengthy passages
of repeated phrases such as "trickling weeping" and "important feeling." The modulating phrases first emblemize, then
subsume the characters. Similarly, Fanny Hersland's three
seamstresses and their three children's three successive govern-
esses provide material for growing patterns of phrases and

thematic motifs; most importantly, they constitute pallid
illustrations of Stein's tentative theory of human personality
as either "independent-dependent" or "dependent-
independent." But realizing that she has left the specific
members of the families as well as the families, Stein declares
she will now deal with individual characters and ends section
three with "To begin then" (208). This promise is immediately
forgotten.

The names of Fanny and David Hersland's three children
head the next three sections. Increasingly insistent waves of
repeated motifs and word patterns nearly submerge the vague
depictions of the two eldest childrens' disastrous marriages:
Martha Hersland's loss of Phillip Redfern in section four, and
Alfred Hersland's evasion to Julia Dehning in five. The sixth
section presents the abstracted David Hersland who dies
young, forestalling any plot of failing fortune in marriage. In
this section Stein increasingly eliminates not only characters,
but even the direct naming of people and objects (except,
significantly, knives and scissors). David's feeling that immortality has no meaning for him prefigures the non-
representational seventh and last section.

This final section's title repeats the novel's subtitle:
"History of a Family's Progress." But it includes no dates, no
genealogy, no allusion to the successively more tawdry lives of
the novel's original families; it is a brief section of rolling
modulations of progressive verbs; a seventh-planed coda
beyond colloquial, polemic, or literary speech—no names, no
places, no objects appear. At this point Stein has achieved an
essentially alogical language which has distilled or dissolved the
particular family members, their history, and her own games
of systems of categories and types into a final rhythmic
motion of "Everyone is being living" (402).

The novel opens with an anecdote from Aristotle illustrat-
ing a son's limit of rebellion and an accompanying didactic
commentary: "It is hard living down the tempers we are born
with." (3 *MA*). Both this technique of using an exemplum as
well as any naturalistic dictum have totally disappeared by the

novel's close. Stein eventually discards plot, illustration of
anecdote and description, statements of theme—all basic to the
traditional novelist's craft—and allows the characters to gradually become tangential and finally disappear as well. Admittedly, at best her characters are lifeless. Stein does not present or
show her characters; she makes pronouncements upon them.
Indeed, not one line of conversation exists in the novel. We are
given Stein's attitudes to them, not their feelings; thus, a
central recorded character, Martha Hersland "was really not
very interesting to anyone" (214). Stein's typical attitude
manifests itself in her pronouncement on Mr. Hersland's
"failing in succeeding" and "succeeding in failing" (318); her
disinterest in her recording that the Hersland's child "got sick
and died of something" (334). Her interest lasts as long as her
rhythmic encapsulation of the character persists.

Probably these characters demand salvaging in the novel's
patterns of style because their sixty years of American culture
fail to give them a distinct sense of self or of tradition. Stein
early declares that in the United States "Custom, passion, and
a feel for mother earth are needed to breed vital singularity in
any man, and alas, how poor we are in all these three" (20).
High school education acts as a leveller for the Herslands;
college painfully throws the lack of Martha and Phillip
Redfern's sense of heritage and birth into bland relief.
Evidently, Stein did not start *The Making of Americans* with
the intent of denigrating American middle class life. Yet, while
variously professing to applaud the solid middle class values of
Americans, Stein belies her protestations in her depiction of
the bourgeois' love of respectability and suspicion of any
diversity (19), the monotony and "ethically aesthetic aspiration of the spare American emotion" (31), or of the "crude
virginity" of the "western woman" (13, 262). America
emerges as a nation of dislocated, rootless people; a bland
wasteland where families decline and marriages fail—indeed the
few surviving plot lines in the novel trace the failure of
marriage for the Dehnings, the Redferns, and two generations
of Herslands.

As the potential in the subject of America's generations fails Stein, she becomes increasingly intrigued with what she described later in "The Gradual Making of *The Making of Americans*" as the characteristically American

> sense for combination within a conception of a given space of time that makes the American thing the American thing and the sense of this space of time must be within the whole thing as well as in the completed whole thing... it is strictly American to conceive a space that is filled with moving, a space of time that is filled with moving and my first real effort to express this thing which is an American thing began in writing *The Making of Americans* (Lectures, 98).

This concern with the form—to the eventual exclusion of the subject content—of this peculiarly American vision increasingly asserts itself in the novel. The patterns of the characters' "histories" soon obfuscate any individual traits.

Thus, Stein announces the eventual appearance of a history of "stupid being" in everyone, of how feelings "came out" in everyone; "there will be such a history of every one who ever was or is or will be living . . . it makes it so of them real being" (150, 130, 123). The recording will not elucidate them in terms of some outside verisimilitude, but give them real existence within their space of time, "an orderly history of every one who ever was or is or will be living" (206). But such a history including every individual and type must predict, ultimately, a literature of exhaustion. Perhaps recognizing this, Stein alters her intent by section five: "Sometime then I will give a history of all of them and that will be a long book and when I am finished with this one then I will begin that one" (279). However, after she finds her essential voice at the close of *The Making of Americans* such a project becomes unnecessary.

She can abandon the original scope of her histories because the constant movement of varied repetitions emerge unequivocably as the central technique capable of merging time and space in the novel. The modulating repetitions of various word, phrase, and sound motifs gradually merge the various generations and categories from the initial thinly sketched individuals and settings to the rolling coda of the entirely non-representational plastic form of the final seventh section.

Stein reiterates in the first sections of the novel that a character's "bottom nature" emerges from his repeatings; in his history "slowly everything comes out from each one in the kind of repeating each does in the different parts and kinds of living they have in them . . . Every one then has in their living repeating" (128). This is extended to become the vehicle of compositional activity:

> always I am looking and comparing and classifying them, always I am seeing their repeating. Always more and more I love repeating, it may be irritating to hear from them but always more and more I love it of them . . . the being in them, the mixing in them, the repeating in them, the deciding the kind of them every one is who has human being (211).

Gradually Stein, like her characters, achieves her permanence through the modulating repetitions of her immediate consciousness which initially engulfs the specific data shards of her characters' lives, discerns their various rhythms, then incorporates these rhythms into the evolving novel's ineluctable progress toward the final abstract rhythms of the coda. As the discontinuous realities of individual Americans and of the wasteland of American culture find in the core of Stein's consciousness or being a fusing rhythm, I am reminded of Whitehead's concept of "prehension" as a possible paradigm of Stein's processual "entity" forming itself as it absorbs, then modifies the actual and imaginative realms into itself. Through such a rhythmic entity the objective past becomes a part of the form of the present work. If *The Making of Americans* is autobiographical, it is so only in the sense of recorded present consciousness—the novel is not about Stein's past except as it exists in the shifting rhythmic patterns of present and progressive tense memory.

She is not unaware, however, of the void outside the

energy fields of her rhythmic prose. Just as her original subject in the novel fails her, so does any audience of readers or even friends:

> I am writing for myself and strangers. This is the only way that I can do it. Everybody is a real one to me, everybody is like someone else too to me. No one of them that I know can want to know it and so I write for myself and strangers (211).

This feeling is amplified in the next (fifth) section:

> Disillusionment in living is the finding out that nobody agrees with you not those that are and were fighting with you . . . Then you say you will write for yourself and strangers and this then makes an old man or an old woman of you (282).

As she feels the novel's movement away from connections with her American subject and potential audience, she at first fears its movement to a self-sufficient world where the medium would express no outside nature to any outside viewer but would manifest the artist's nature rarefied—a concept expressed by the contemporary 1919 *De Stijl* epigraph,

> The object of nature is man
> The object of man is style.

Stein's lingering fear that her novel will never communicate, as expressed in the opening of section two, seems to prefigure the minimal position of Samuel Beckett's protagonists several decades later:

> Bear it in your mind my reader, but truly I never feel it that there ever can be for me any such creature, no it is this scribbled and dirty and lined paper that is really to be to me always my receiver (37).

This minimal world continues to distress her as she admits being "all unhappy in this writing, disillusioned since "no one can believe as you do about anything," or simply being "altogether a discouraged one" (229, 281, 308).

Nonetheless, as she transcends the banal wasteland of her subject, she also overcomes her sense of creating merely an isolate monologue by discovering and entering the rhythms of her characters: "This is a comforting thing in being a great author inside one that always even with much lonely feeling and much sighing in one;" and this new mode of existence takes form as a "very somber burden then that one is beginning having coming saying that pleasant living is a pleasant thing and to be explaining how some are liking pleasant living" (314). Characters such as Alfred Hersland increasingly function as tools for her evolving patterns of rhythmic motifs:

> Repeating and repeating and repeating and beginning and ending and being a young one and then an older one and then a old one and then not any longer one one; I am sometimes inside and sometimes including this realizing. The relation of content and reflection, the relation of being and living, the relation of learning and stupid being, this is in me in my feeling, certainly in me now and I will now be doing expecting (319).

Thus, Stein loses interest in both the problems of narrative and exegesis of characters. The "making of Americans" modulates into the "thinking of Stein" as even characters are distilled from the pure, clear rhythms. The novel form becomes her experiential "space of time" world which disperses her feelings of discouragement, futility, and solitude. Its evolving repetitions of progressive verbs removes her from her characters' fatally static condition of "living copying their own repeating . . . with an automatic copying of their own repeating rather than really live inside them their repeating" (132).

But before she discovered that by not "copying" but evolving and rarifying her attitude toward her thematic motifs (such as the cycle of birth, aging and death in the passage above) as she evolves her verbal motifs into a purer, abstract form, she had wished to "know" the exterior world. Earlier she wondered at her resistance to the religion which buffers

Old Hissen and others from their deaths, to the "believing" which leads a Plymouth Bretheren woman to consider her periods atypical, or the self-esteem which destroys the sense of immortality or others; she is "such a one" as those "who want to know about anything about everything" (309). But as earlier her urge for the concrete America disappears so does her desire for any polemically expressed theory of reality. The epistemological act increasingly consists of not knowing outside phenomenon or theories, but recognizing the rhythmic core of her won "existing being;" by the fifth section she recognizes that "I know very well I am not knowing all the ways any one can have living have meaning. . . .I know I am quite a happy one knowing something of being" (324). Later, "I am almost not hoping that I will sometime know everything about everyone" (335).

However, many commentators (possibly baffled by the endless pages of undulating repetition, bloodless characters, and ambiguously explained categorical terms) present definite identities to the characters and carefully regimented explanations to the categories. Biographical criticism and exegesis by lists of tables must, however, always fall. The urge of many to see blends of Leo Stein, Leon Solomons, and even Picasso in her characters and Los Angeles or Baltimore in the settings suggests the continuance of the old problem of Gertrude Stein's personality preceding her literary achievement. Intrinsically, the characters exist as means to other ends: for example, Julia Dehning's determination to marry Alfred Hersland tells nothing of her, but does repeat the theme of failed marriage, repeat the key sectional motif of washing, and illustrate a discussion of types of women.

Similar traps exist for those attempting to establish rigid explanations of the lists and various systems in the novel. While various rambling lists of ways women like men, need others, or want to know (184, 116, 309) occur throughout, the central categories concern independent-dependent and the antithetical dependent-independent type of personality. This distinction seems analogous to the "bottom Nature" theory of women who "have attacking as their way of fighting, some such of them have resisting as their way of winning" (179). But soon the parallel is broken by various extraneous "subduing" and "resisting-loving"—Stein's love of modulating repetitions breaks the two categories analogy and finally with the discussion of seamstress Mable Linker reptures each from within. Stein seldom makes any reference to them in the last half of the novel where "bottom nature" is replaced by such categories as "instincts" and "ideals." Also, throughout Stein uses other systems to explain personality, such as inherited traits in the Wyman children (196) or the behavioristic theories for the Hersland children's being raised in a poor section of town. Critics' charts cannot make consistencies here.

And yet, this constant variation is totally consistent with Stein's central mode in *The Making of Americans.* The novel, as her consciousness records successive and thus variant versions of her shifting relational, patterns to her actual and fictional materials. The categories' mutability accurately reflects the pervasive rhythms of the modifying consciousness of Stein.

Her consciousness in the novel becomes inseparable from the novel. She and it embody the processes of doing, thinking, knowing, being the immediate recorded thought. As Stein told John Hyde Preston, when one evolves a new form, "it is not the form but the fact that *you are the form* that is important." The overwhelming presence of progressive verb forms express this fusion of the space of time. In section five whole paragraphs are comprised of extended variations on such phrases as "there ever can be of thinking feeling believing knowing doing is common" (287); by this section's end, waves of verbals and strings of dangling clauses distend over pages. Characters' names become personal pronouns and then the indefinite "such a one"; humans become "being" or "someone" and "man's life" becomes "man's living." Thus past and present become the amorphously fluid present where characters are rarefied out of existence and systems of categories are relinquished. Stein indeed shows the uniquely American space of time to be "filled always filled with moving."

Using her professor William James's term in her lecture "Composition as Explanation," Stein observed that in *The Making of Americans* after creating a prolonged present, it was natural to create "more and more complicatedly a continuous present" (lectures, 25). After being disjointed by the lack of any distinct chronology of generations and by constant digressions, sequential time disappears into the floods of verbals. Similarly, the antithetical distinctions of "bottom nature," names and concrete noun hierarchies dissolve as an anabasis of incantatory, hypnotic prose expresses the immediate movements of Stein's consciousness. Since early she discovers with external objects the difficulty "to describe what I mean by the names I give to them" (133), and recognizes that everyone conceives things differently: "no one can believe as you do in anything" (281), Stein increasingly employs words of greater arbitrary value and relative meaning. As she had "gotten rid of nouns and adjectives as much as possible by the method of living in adverbs in verbs in pronouns, in adverbial clauses written or implied and in conjunctions" (Lectures, 136), eventually the words simply disengage themselves from identifiable exterior actualities and become self-sufficient tautologies—"dead is dead" (288)—of the thing in itself: "every word I am ever using in writing has for me very existing being" (306).

Thus, by the final section, a coda entitled "History of a Family's Progress," no names, places or objects appear. In the undulating, always slightly varying repetitions a series of earlier verbal motifs—doing, standing, needing, remembering, being, existing—occur along with occasional references to "family," "dead one," and "any one." Style eloquently contains all. The landscape of language fuses the fragments of Stein's meandering consciousness into a processual artifact, a plastic form without definite center or containing frame. The varying rhythms are comprised of the totally existing word. Stein pronounces that in talking one can "be saying mostly anything" thus employing many words unsuitable for writing, since "in writing a word must be for me really an existing thing, it has a place for me as living, this is the way I feel about me writing" (306). These elements echo the phenomenology of the act of art current among several painters contemporary to the novel's composition.

In Mondrian's theory of "Plasticism" the figurations of representational art were to be avoided as obstacles to clarity. Mondrian asserted that "nonfigurative art demands . . . the destruction of the particular form and the construction of a rhythm of mutual relations, of mutual forms of free lines." Stein's feelings seem even more completely congruent with the observations of Robert Delaunay: "Art in nature is rhythmic and has a horror of constraint. If art relates itself to an object, it becomes descriptive, divisionist, literary" and thus loses its "clarity."

This quest for the clarity of a non-descriptive, non-literary mode seems the best metaphor for the structure of the novel. As I indicated earlier in briefly outlining the seven sections' gradual swell to achieve the final coda, the determined anabasis toward this end constitutes the overall progress of the overall form of *The Making of Americans.* Having established Stein's employment of characters as illustrative objects rather than individual entities, I can most concisely indicate the overall progress of the novel in technique and theme by presenting its three David Herslands.

The first David Hersland is a colorful butcher whose poignant reluctance to leave his village in "the old country" results in an extended anecdote about his wife's repeated returns to fetch him for the journey to America. No such characterization delineates his son who emerges from variously repeated references as a large progressively minded, yet anxiety-ridden man raising his family in Gossols, where he expects vaguely to "find his fortune" but fails. His son, the third David Hersland, is even less immediately a human personality—as he "becomes a dead one" before his "middle living," very little comment is made on his life. Instead, we know him essentially through his sharing of some of the thoughts and concerns with essentially formal problems which fascinate Stein herself. Like her, he considers that "each one has their own way of having connection between what that one is meaning and what that one is thinking . . . is saying" (364); also, like the Neoplasticists Mondrian and Delaunay's concern with achieving clarity, a central characteristic of David was his being "of a kind in men and women having it in them to have feeling clearly in them, to be telling clearly the feeling they have in them" (365).

The third David Hersland does not exist outside the rhythms of Stein's repetitions. His undeveloped personality in his (sixth) section reflects the incremental dissociation of character with anecdote, setting, or human relationships. His section resembles increasingly a Mondrian painting as the undulating prose abandons all representational items in its final abstract dirge's conclusion, "Any one could remember this thing, his having been a dead one, his having been a living one" (391). In Stein's rhythmic consciousness of being, death and life form interpenetrating continuities. In this transcendent fusion of the immanent past upon the present, "He was not being living beyond the ending of the beginning of being in the middle of being living" (378). The processual "being and becoming" achieve an equilibrum beyond the literature of represented reality as well as the literature of polemical ideas.

Then, in the final section Stein's plastic consciousness evolves a non-representational mode of vision from the rhythmic energy fields of the mutating repetitions of constant "becoming"; a "being" in which memory and death exist only as a part of the actual flux of the present. She has conquered the problems of depicting the banal American cultural wasteland, of her anxieties about a non-existent audience, and of the frustrations in mapping unstable psychological and sociological theories of human personality. By filling that peculiarly American "space of time" with the varying rhythms of plastic consciousness, Gertrude Stein achieves a transcendent mode for the process of her subject, the making of Americans: "Any family living can be one being existing and some can remember something of some such thing" (416).

13

Glenway Wescott's Variations on The Waste Land Image

Sy Kahn

When T. S. Eliot published "The Waste Land" in 1922 he gave to the decade a vital and compelling image. Whether poets or not, young American writers who were to establish their reputations in the 1920s found in the poem a symbol answerable to their own sense of pervasive moral and cultural failure. The prosperity, the new social freedoms, the increased mobility, the magnetic urban centers, the accelerated technological discoveries that characterize the decade did not succeed in dulling our writers' perception and sense of moral decay and the loss of values and dreams. The images and scenes of emotional and spiritual aridity in "The Waste Land" made of the title of the poem not only an encapsulating image of its content but also an explanation and reference point for young novelists such as F. Scott Fitzgerald, Ernest Hemingway and Glenway Wescott.

Less concerned with theology and the loss of specific classical and Christian tradition than Eliot, each of these novelists reinterpreted the image to suit his own sense of failed values. Eliot had struck a telling and tolling note; development and variations would follow in a number of virtuoso performances. There were many kinds of "wastelands" to be revealed, many chronicles of broken illusions and failed or abandoned ideals.

Consider Fitzgerald's *The Great Gatsby* (1925), a novel as emblematic of the decade as is Eliot's poem. Jay Gatsby's quest for shining truths and golden moments, his romantic idealization and pursuit of Daisy, fixed now in our literature as firmly as the lovers on the famous Grecian urn, ultimately suggests an analogue for the failure of questing America to attain its dream. Surely the dream takes many forms: the search for a new Eden or new Jerusalem, for religious and political freedom, for social equality and justice, for material wealth, for the "pursuit of happiness," or for the perfection of self. Whatever green light was seen winking in the distant dark at the end of the dock near Daisy's house, the 1920s discovered that the light too often was a will o' the wisp in an insidious bog. Bullet-riddled at the end of the novel, Gatsby attains stature because, against all odds and evidence, he pursues an ideal, a "Platonic" image of himself and of love, once imagined as possible and still recaptureable. However, scene after scene reveals human corruption, frivolous and frantic hedonism, and reckless and careless action. By contrast, Gatsby's idealism makes him "great."

That Gatsby is doomed is prefigured early in the novel when Fitzgerald depicts an area of land between "West Egg" Long Island and New York City through which Gatsby drives as a literal wasteland — the "valley of ashes." Amidst the smoke and dust move men who seem fashioned from the gray material itself. It is a landscape that will become, reflexively, emblematic of Gatsby's world. For despite the wealth and glitter of Daisy and her set, the golden girl proves a corrupted creature of dust after all, even though of gold dust. The landscape simply makes apparent what the novel increasingly reveals: the human wasteland of cynicism, betrayal and moral aridity.

Equally expresive of the mood of general despair are Hemingway's two novels *The Sun Also Rises* (1926) and *A Farewell to Arms* (1929). Both works are chronicles of disillusionment during which Jake Barnes, the sexually disabled war veteran of the earlier novel, and Frederick Henry, a wounded American deserter from the Italian army and the war, attain a Gatsby-like stature by contrast to the fools and failures among whom they live. Though neither of these protagonists are killed, as is Gatsby, both physically wounded men suffer repetitive psychological wounding and stoically endure. Jake cannot, because of his wound, consummate his desire and love for Lady Brett. Lt. Henry must suffer the loss of Catherine, his lover, and their child in childbirth. These situations and events intensify the sense of loss and failure that pervade the worlds of both novels.

In each of these three novels it is the narrator who is instructed through a series of disillusioning events, Nick Carraway, Gatsby's friend, in Fitzgerald's novel, and Jake and Henry in Hemingway's. Loss sharpens their sensibilities, their talent for moral distinctions, and accounts for the ironic tone by which they condemn the fatuous and frivolous. Whether the setting is West Egg, Montparnasse or the battlefields of Italy, the moral wasteland is there.

We look to the work of Eliot, Fitzgerald and Hemingway as among the major literary achievements of the decade — for compelling image in Eliot and for rich variations in the novelists. I wish now to turn to a writer who, like Fitzgerald and Hemingway, was an expatriate Midwesterner writing in France, and who provided an additional and special amplification of the wasteland image. Glenway Wescott during the 1920s enjoyed a reputation that rivalled Fitzgerald's and Hemingway's, and he seemed then a writer of equal promise. Born in Wisconsin in 1901, now living in New Jersey, Wescott mainly lived and wrote in France during the 1920s, not returning to live again in the United States until 1933. During the 1920s he produced two novels, *The Apple of the Eye* (1924) and *The Grandmothers* (Harper's Prize novel for 1927), an essay and ten short stories under the title *Goodbye Wisconsin* (1928) and a privately printed small edition of a short work *The Babe's Bed* (1930). All of these works, though not to the same degree, explore the past in an attempt to understand, define and exorcise it. Among Wescott's complex motives was his desire to account for the cultural wasteland he felt Wisconsin, and by implication the Midwest and the United States in general, to be. Troubled, even haunted by the past, Wescott sought self-definition through an imaginative rendering of family history in his major work of the 1920s, *The Grandmothers.* He also wanted to understand the sadness and sullenness of failed pioneers, their narrow Protestantism, their repressed lives, their suspicion of, even hostility toward a child of esthetic and creative impulse. To Alwyn Tower, his protagonist of the novel, as well as of *The Babe's Bed,* the return to the past is necessary to gain knowledge and to go forward. In the last chapter of *The Grandmothers,* Wescott wrote:

> So some of these feverish, reactionary ones (he himself, for example) went back, in imagination, to what had produced them; their hope, anxiety, and interest went back. Against the law. The weak stayed; the strong returned once more to the place from which they had gone back, from which they would have to go forward. Backward and forward, two continual motions of the imagination making up that of their lives. Forward finally . . .

In Wescott's work of the 1920s fictive narrator and author are never far removed from each other — persona is almost person, fiction almost biography, or discovered biography. One has the impression that the past is not simply recalled for its record of things past but imaginatively evoked for the purpose of exploration and definition, that the work itself is the definition. The setting for all of Wescott's work of this period is Wisconsin, but that is simply the stage, not the substance, of these works. Indeed, the region is richly evoked in a highly distinctive lyrical and imagistic prose, and through the strategies of this style, Wisconsin becomes the microcosm by which the American experience and *mythos,* as Wescott understood them, is rendered.

In the essay "Goodbye Wisconsin," which gives the book its title, Wescott speaks to us, as it were, in his own voice and makes explicit those loves, concerns and rejections fictionalized and symbolized in the stories and novels he wrote in the 1920s. For Wescott, Wisconsin is the place you cannot go back to after such knowledge and experience Europe offers. The Wisconsin towns, bleak in winter, but with a new material prosperity that might have dazzled the pioneers of a previous century, suggest to Wescott that materialism has displaced imagination, that dowry has replaced dream. The rural landscapes still invite the imagination, stimulate it to speculate upon the older ideas of exploration, virgin territory, human restlessness and courage that propelled people toward the west, toward the beckoning rather than the rising sun. But now, in the 1920s, Wisconsin seems to him an enervated cultural wasteland, a barren ground for artists, and its human native crop "seedless." Surely many of Wisconsin's character-istics that urge Wescott's departures during the 1920s are the same ones that prompted other artists to abandon the Middle West: its melancholy atmosphere, its materialism, its moral taboos and drab religion, and its depressing towns. Now even more alienated from home because of his expatriate life, Wescott concludes that life in 1927 has outdistanced to a greater degree than in his youth the "poetry" of pioneer times.

The essay opens with Wescott on a train going home, north from Milwaukee, with a blizzard coming south. In contrast to the bleak landscape he recalls that "stiff carnations of the Mediterranean are in bloom." He is his own symbol of exotic change and the estranged with his Basque beret, his gloves, cigarette lighter and foreign cigarettes, and with Thomas Mann's *Hochstapler Krull* in his hands. If he has changed, so has Wisconsin. The house in town where his family lives is not like the old "fruitful and severe" farmhouse of his youth that "seemed to have an immortal soul . . ." Now there are a bathroom and waxed floors; carpets like everyone else's have replaced the rag rugs of his grandmothers. "Progress," he thinks. "Deprivation is dead . . . I rejoice, but regret some of his poetry." The town too is without "poetry." There can be no idylls, no pastorals in the "lamentably impressive" town. The essay strikes the notes here of dirge and lament for a way

of life regrettably and permanently lost. The old "rustics" had
become "provincials." Urbanization has unsettled the youth,
keeping them uneasy and discontent, but at the same time
they are not strong enough to break away. Movies, "imagination's chapel in the town," keep them stimulated and nervous
— but the final effect is narcotic. Impulse and imagination are
indulged in vicariously.

Since the morality of the town recognizes no sexual
liberty, there is either early marriage or bad reputation. The
former means "Wisconsin forever, with never any wholesome
dissipation of a thousand chimeras — travels, ambitions,
curiosities." For some there is fever. Erotic songs, "syncopated
bewilderment on the dance floor" and "the disastrous and
vacillating ease in Miss Garbo's face" create vibrant, anxious
nights. Nevertheless, the young people are disturbingly herd-
like. Group-consciousness rather than self-awareness motivates
their actions; there is a lack of courage and candor. He
concludes that the chief work of the fraternity he visits is "to
beat out of each other all conceit and incivility."

In 1927 Wescott found Wisconsin more comfortable but
less comforting than was the former rustic life. What was
ardent feeling and compelling dream is now nervous indeci-
sion; what was a kind of pagan pleasure, because of, or in spite
of, hardship is now sterile luxury. With a book of Gide's in his
hand this time, he takes his leave and returns to Europe. For
him the road back, as for Alwyn Tower, is the road ahead.

However, the land outside the towns, outside the train
windows, has not changed. Its natural beauty endures, yet
unspoiled by the towns, and the old enchantment of the land,
evoked in the lyrical manner of the earlier novels, takes hold
of him again as he rides away through the cold, Wisconsin
night. The land still enchants, and glimpses of people working
their farms, or remembered glimpses in other seasons, stimulate Wescott to render them in classic, statuesque images of
dignity and endurance. It is the land, stretching out and
gigantic, that makes for the seemingly heroic stance and
gesture of its workers, in contrast to the urbanized lives that

seem to him cramped, dessicated, and repressed, and whose horizons, physical as well as emotional, are short and limited.

Both Wescott and Hemingway have used the land as a purgative against the glutted human scene, as a corrective for urbanized Wisconsin, or, as in *The Sun Also Rises,* for the dissipations of the Left Bank in Paris. Certainly the differences between the work of the two men, not to mention the men themselves, are profound and numerous, but there is parallel purpose here. In the fishing interlude that takes Jake Barnes and his friend Bill Gorton to the Burguete, the honest simplicity of action and pleasure gives their activities a ritual purity, much as the actions and emotions of Wescott's remembered "rustics." The unsullied land in both works inspires purified action. Indeed, Hemingway has remarked that the true hero of his novel is the land, as the title of his novel taken from Ecclesiastes suggests. It is interesting to note that Hemingway ridiculed Wescott in *The Sun Also Rises,* a *roman à clef,* by casting Wescott as Robert Prentiss, an unlikeable rising young novelist Jake meets in Paris. (In an early draft of the novel Wescott was less masked as Robert Prescott.) Nevertheless, in works of great dissimilarity in style and technique, both Wescott and Hemingway make the land prevail as counterbalance to scenes of human emotional wastelands. At this point, one may recall Hemingway's earlier stories of his boyhood in Michigan which celebrate the land. Michigan and Wisconsin, parallel states with similar landscapes, are recalled by both writers for a similar purpose—and in Hemingway's novel, Michigan is translated to Burguete as well. Not so in Fitzgerald's *The Great Gatsby.* As we have noted, the land itself is wasteland, as if feverish human corruption had incinerated it.

The ten stories in *Goodbye, Wisconsin* that follow the essay were written during 1921 to 1927 and in one sense are a record of various disillusionments. Wescott has remarkable capacity for variations on this theme. He expresses the disappointments of expatriation, maturity, labor, faith, art and love. In consequence, there are sorrow, tears, drunkenness, terror and murder, in a crescendo of reactions. In commenting on his work, Mary Butts, a writer and critic of the 1920s, said of *Goodbye Wisconsin* that it was "The book of a man fallen out of love, and in his embarrassment likely to overscore his subject than show the least ingratitude or brutality." She concludes, "So much for the adieus of a young man supremely sensitive to 'sacra' and 'rite,' whose childhood was passed without them, among a people with taboo for ritual, prosperity for imagination."

Wescott's disillusionment with the Middle West reflected his feeling of a general cultural failure in America. To him there were so few memorable Americans—Lincoln, Lindbergh, the "gloriously bizarre" Isadora Duncan—so few genuinely artistic accomplishments. He missed the "whole-heartedness" and the "desire for immortality" that he felt marked and animated ancient Greek culture. In the essay he compares the "dead-leaf complexion" of American youths to the "marble-headed Greeks." Americans seemed intense only about wealth. Its youth are corrupted; their potential comes to nothing. Sex replaces or defeats intellectual activity and creativity, and a nation only physically creative Wescott thought was beneath contempt.

Catching the sense of malaise, the failed tradition, the empty social rituals, the creative and spiritual aridity above all, of Eliot's poem, Wescott, as Fitzgerald and Hemingway, responded in ways suitable to his experience and talent. In the 1920s it was the Midwest that Wescott best understood, and making the region a metaphor for America in general, he, along with many other American writers of the period, found it culturally wanting. The pervasive and persuasive image of the wasteland that Eliot objectified in his adroit poem, that caught so well the mood of an age, was amplified by Wescott, a writer who, as Marjorie Brace has noted ("Thematic Problems of the American Novelist," *Accent*, Autumn, 1945), marks in his entire work a "progressive exploration of every American theme in a kind of aesthetic pilgrimage. . . ."

As Eliot's poems and Hemingway's novels of the period

make clear, the sense of cultural and moral wasteland was not peculiar to America and Americans; Europe and Europeans are equally indicted. Eliot was writing of a condition and an age, not a location or a particular people. Like Shelley's "traveller" in the poem "Ozmandias," the speaker in "The Waste Land" has a tale of deserts to tell. Shelley's traveller "from an antique land" tells us of his seeing "two vast and trunkless legs of stone," and nearby a half sunk, shattered visage. From these remnants, and an inscription on the pedestal, the traveller can surmise that these are the relics of a once powerful and prideful dynasty and culture. Nothing remains except "colossal wreck," and "boundless and bare/ The lone and level sands stretch far away." Shelley's poem mocked pride and power, and the stretching sands make the ironic comment that a civilization may be reduced to a wasteland. Eliot turns the image. In his poem we are located in the wasteland, figurative rather than literal, and travellers stumbling upon relics would only know them as "withered stumps of time," since those travellers would have no historical, cultural or religious contexts by which to understand either the artifact or its symbolic meaning. Those stretching sands, whether they mock or magnify a cultural condition, touched many shores. Certainly there is nothing new in depicting spiritual "dryness," in making images of failed hope and the loss of tradition and its vital roots. That story is old and repetitive; but Eliot gave it a fresh imprint in the 1920s, and under his seal each writer unrolled his own scroll.

Wescott's testimony during the decade, unique by virtue of his special style and sensibility, made an important, sometimes brilliant, contribution to the literature of disillusionment. That disillusionment was redeemed, if by nothing else, by the variations that gave it complex shape and meaning.

14

Fitzgerald's *Gatsby:*
The World as Ash Heap

James E. Miller, Jr.

It was about twenty-five years ago that I spent my days and nights writing a doctoral dissertation at the University of Chicago on F. Scott Fitzgerald. It is hard to remember that in those distant days, in the late 1940's, there wasn't much of a bibliography on Fitzgerald to read. I was working on his fictional craft, and there wasn't very much on fictional technique to digest either (the "new criticism" stuck pretty much to poetry). I spent a lot of time going through magazine files in Chicago and newspaper files in Minnesota. There were no paperback reprints, and even some of the hardcover editions were missing from the library. I picked up original editions in small second-hand bookstores in Chicago for around a dollar each, including (as it turned out) a first edition of *The Great Gatsby*.

I published my dissertation some years later (1957), and then revised and added to it slightly to make *F. Scott Fitzgerald: His Art and His Technique* (1964). In the meantime, articles and books on Fitzgerald poured forth in rich abundance, his work became widely read even in high school, and Fitzgerald was firmly lodged with Hemingway and Faulkner as one of the three "great" writers of the 1920's— and some bold critics today see even more in Fitzgerald than in Hemingway.

Fitzgerald now appears to be central, somehow, however vaguely, to American self-conception (he has, perhaps, replaced Hemingway in this role), and *The Great Gatsby* appears to be central to Fitzgerald's meaning and significance. My work on Fitzgerald's *Gatsby* a quarter of a century ago was on craft, on technique, on art. It is time that I had my say on the book's meaning, its themes, its moral implications.

I
"the deeper psychology"

In a famous letter to Fitzgerald, T. S. Eliot wrote of *The Great Gatsby:* "In fact it seems to me to be the first step that American fiction has taken since Henry James. . . ." This statement might have seemed, at one time, a forgivable exaggeration, but by now serious critics begin to wonder whether it is indeed true. And if true, what it means. Unfortunately, Eliot never got around to explaining his meaning.

The more we stare at Eliot's letter, the more it seems to sound like another famous letter in American literature, Emerson to the unknown Whitman in 1855, saying: "I greet you at the beginning of a great career." Eliot said that he had read *The Great Gatsby* three times, and he added: ". . .it has interested and excited me more than any new novel I have seen, either English or American, for a number of years." It is possible that it has taken us as long (in the case of Fitzgerald) as it did Whitman's readers to catch up with that writer's first distinguished critic.

When Eliot wrote, his masterpiece, *The Waste Land,* lay three years behind him, and it is possible that he saw in *The Great Gatsby* a reflection of some of the kinds of images of the horror of modern life that he himself had given currency in his poem. And a review of the "waste land" images of *Gatsby* is in order. But it is worth dwelling briefly first on Eliot's invocation of the name of Henry James. F. Scott Fitzgerald and James? Who besides Eliot could link them so casually?

Eliot might have had in mind Fitzgerald's craft, but it is

more likely that he was thinking of something in addition and beyond. And Eliot's 1918 essay on James, written for the special memorial issue of *The Little Review,* might provide some clues. It is in that famous essay that Eliot paid his notorious compliment to James: "He had a mind so fine that no idea could violate it." Eliot did, of course, make his meaning about "idea" clear by noting the universal tendency that destroyed art: "...instead of thinking with our feelings... we corrupt our feelings with ideas; we produce the political, the emotional idea, evading sensation and thought." James, Eliot contended, maintained a "viewpoint untouched by the parasite idea. He is the most intelligent man of his generation."

In a later part of his essay, Eliot linked James with Hawthorne, quoting James's compliment paid his compatriot in his book on the New Englander: "...the fine thing in Hawthorne is that he cared for the deeper psychology." This "deeper psychology" (missing, says Eliot, in English contemporaries of the American writer such as Dickens and Thackeray) was central to the achievement of both James and Hawthorne: "The point is that Hawthorne... did grasp character through the relation of two or more persons to each other; and this is what no one else, except James, has done. Furthermore, he does establish, as James establishes, a solid atmosphere, and he does, in his quaint way, get New England, as James gets a larger part of America, and as none of their respective contemporaries get anything above a village or two, or a jungle." (It should be parenthetically noted that among the James titles that Eliot lists for his examples, perhaps the most relevant in a discussion of F. Scott Fitzgerald are *Daisy Miller* and *The American,* the one work a classic portrait of the uninhibited American girl, the other a portrait of a rich American entrepeneur.)

Clearly Eliot's hostility to "idea" in fiction (or art) does not hinder his appreciation for Hawthorne's "getting" New England and for James's "getting" America. It might be difficult to say just what the "solid atmosphere" is that enables these novelists to "get" the places they "get," but obviously such "getting" makes, in Eliot's view, for major achievement in fiction. And it is tempting to see Eliot's analysis thus: that, as James represented a step (or perhaps several steps) beyond Hawthorne, so Fitzgerald represents a step beyond James (or through him) in his avoidance of contamination of "idea," and his ability to "get" not only America but the modern age: that same modern age that Eliot "got" so brilliantly in *The Waste Land.*

It takes only a casual acquaintance with Eliot's work to know that his conception of James's term, "the deeper psychology," could not have implied protracted and direct psychological analysis by a novelist, nor could it have had reference to Freud and his followers. James used the term in a discussion, mostly unfavorable, of Hawthorne's tendency toward allegory (in his 1879 book on Hawthorne): in spite of this tendency, the "fine thing" about Hawthorne was that he cared for the "deeper psychology." Both James and Eliot, then, must hold in common the view that the "deeper psychology" is that which is revealed by the novelist through dramatized relationships among people and through the use of powerfully charged concrete images. In short, Eliot must have seen (as in the passage above) in the achieved "deeper psychology" of Hawthorne and particularly James something in the nature of a successfully realized "objective correlative"—a concept which he was shortly to elaborate in his essay on "Hamlet and His Problems" (1919).

We might translate Eliot's praise of *Gatsby* into a paraphrase of Eliot on James: *The Great Gatsby* is a book that has not been "violated" by an idea, but is one of the most "intelligent" books of Fitzgerald's generation. It "gets" America and the modern age, not through direct proclamation of a set of ideas (as in Sinclair Lewis, for example), but through dramatization of Gatsby's pursuit of Daisy, through dramatic presentation of a number of other intricately related characters (Tom, Nick, Jordan, Wolfsheim, Owl Eyes, Gatsby's father), and through a sequence of powerful, pervasive, and devastating images that force the reader to "think with his feelings" (as does the reader of *The Waste Land)*. Thus without writing allegory, Fitzgerald has provided a commentary on his country, his time, and the contemporary era through his intuitive understanding of the "deeper psychology." And Fitzgerald's achievement is both a triumph of technique and a triumph of meaning or theme.

With the recent publication of the original version of *The Waste Land,* we are beginning to understand how stubbornly personal in its origins was that most impersonal poem of the twentieth century. We have long known that *Gatsby* also grew out of personal agonies of the spirit. Both poem and novel clearly transcended the personal not by ignoring it but by drawing on the instinctive wisdom it bestowed, and, through the "deeper psychology," discovering the universal malaise in the particular "sickness," the common darkness in the individual gloom (it was, of course, Ezra Pound who helped Eliot pare his poem to its hard core of enduring matter; Ernest Hemingway through example may have indirectly helped Scott Fitzgerald discover the durable in his material).

Let us turn briefly to this "deeper psychology" (as defined above) in both Eliot and Fitzgerald. In Part II of *The Waste Land,* "A Game of Chess," we find what is in effect the juxtaposition of two dramatic scenes of sexual intrigue or malaise or conflict. The first scene is one of meaningless elegance and profound boredom, shot through with the echoing question—"What shall I do now? What shall I do?" and concluding,

> The hot water at ten.
> And if it rains, a closed car at four.
> And we shall play a game of chess,
> Pressing lidless eyes and waiting for a knock upon the door.

The next scene shifts to a lower class pub and tunes in on a conversation about Lil and her husband Albert—he recently "demobbed" and set on "a good time," she spending his money not on her teeth but on abortion pills (she has five children already, "and nearly died of young George"):

> The chemist said it would be all right, but I've never been the same.
> You *are* a proper fool, I said.
> Well, if Albert won't leave you alone, there it is, I said,
> What you get married for if you don't want children?

Several generations of Eliot interpreters have pointed out that these ingeniously juxtaposed scenes not only ring true in detail, idiom, rhythm, but they also suggest much about the sterility, aridity, vacuity of modern life: sexual relationships have been diminished, devitalized, debased, and thus life at its vital center has dwindled into meaninglessness and banality.

The first two chapters of *The Great Gatsby* similarly juxtapose two separate but intricately interrelated worlds, the rich and baroque world of the East Egg mansion of the Buchanans and the mean and grotesque world of the Myrtle Wilson—Tom Buchanan trysting apartment in New York. When Nick visits the Buchanans shortly after the novel opens, he walks in on a scene as filled with boredom and meaninglessness as that portrayed by Eliot described above:

> The only completely stationary object in the room was an enormous couch on which two young women [Daisy and Jordan] were buoyed up as though upon an anchored balloon. They were both in white, and their dresses were rippling and fluttering as if they had just been blown back in after a short flight around the house. I must have stood for a few moments listening to the whip and snap of the curtains and the groan of a picture on the wall. Then there was a boom as Tom Buchanan shut the rear windows and the caught wind died out about the room, and the curtains and the rugs and the two young women ballooned slowly to the floor.

The slow motion of the scene, together with super-sophisticated conversation about nothing at all and the suggestion of sexual intrigue in Tom's mysterious telephone conversations, reveal a life lived on meaningless and purposeless levels and surfaces in which sex is no more than a "game of chess."

In the chapter that immediately follows, we find ourselves in the apartment rendezvous of Tom and Myrtle:

> The apartment was on the top floor—a small living-room, a
> small dining-room, a small bedroom, and a bath. The living-
> room was crowded to the doors with a set of tapestried
> furniture entirely too large for it, so that to move about was to
> stumble continually over scenes of ladies swinging in the
> gardens of Versailles. The only picture was an over-enlarged
> photograph, apparently a hen sitting on a blurred rock.
> Looked at from a distance, however, the hen resolved itself
> into a bonnet, and the countenance of a stout old lady beamed
> down into the room.

In the drunken brawl that ensues, the conversation is as
meaningless, and as revealing, as that in Eliot's pub scene: "I
almost married a little kike who'd been after me for years. I
knew he was below me. Everybody kept saying to me:
'Lucille, that man's 'way below you!' But if I hadn't met
Chester, he'd of got me sure." (This from Mrs. McKee,
Myrtle's sister.) The scene concludes with Tom breaking
Myrtle's nose for daring to mention his wife's name. Meaningless sex and meaningless conversation resolve into meaningless
violence, in a life as empty and shallow and sterile as any
described in *The Waste Land.*

II
"night scene by El Greco"

If my conjectures are right about Eliot's conception of
"the deeper psychology," it involves not only characters but
images, particularly as they might be assembled to "get" a
place and time. In his own poem, *The Waste Land,* we
encounter a great collage or assemblage of images only
subterraneously connected but which are so powerful and so
intricately orchestrated as to haunt the imagination for long
after the encounter. Eliot's mind, too, is so fine that it cannot
be violated by an idea, but he thinks powerfully with his
feelings and that means, surely, that he "thinks" in images,
and compels his readers to do likewise. And in *The Waste
Land,* those images are most frequently of death—

> Unreal City,
> Under the brown fog of a winter dawn,

> A crowd flowed over London Bridge, so many,
> I had not thought death had undone so many.

The most horrible death in *The Waste Land* is, like that in these lines, a living death.

In a similar way, but without the concentration of poetry (though often with its ingenuity of language), *The Great Gatsby* progresses by images. At the opening of Chapter II, Fitzgerald reveals what might be called the controlling image of the book, the first of a series of subtly interrelated images of death in life, life in death:

> About half way between West Egg and New York the motor road hastily joins the railroad and runs beside it for a quarter of a mile, so as to shrink away from a certain desolate area of land. This is a valley of ashes—a fantastic farm where ashes grow like wheat into ridges and hills and grotesque gardens; where ashes take the forms of houses and chimneys and rising smoke and, finally, with a transcendent effort, of men who move dimly and already crumbling through the powdery air. Occasionally a line of gray cars crawls along an invisible track, gives out a ghastly creak, and comes to rest, and immediately the ash-gray men swarm up with leaden spades and stir up an impenetrable cloud, which screens their obscure operations from your sight.

The reader may hear himself murmur, as he reads, "I had not thought death had undone so many." Fitzgerald's waste land scene is clearly a scene of a living hell, an assemblage of "grotesque gardens" that parody in ashes the vital world of growing things; and it is peopled by living dead men who crumble away even as they rehearse their pointless activities, swallowed finally from view by the clouds of ash-dust raised by their meaningless movement. Over this bizarre scene stare the gigantic eyes of Dr. T. J. Eckleburg, the fading sign of a long-forgotten oculist. Those weather-dimmed eyes, as they "brood on over the solemn dumping ground," will reappear in the novel, coming to haunt it and the reader: the world as ash heap, presided over by the vacant stare of a billboard deity.

Though confined geographically to the area near the Wilson garage, the valley of ashes spreads like a contagious fungus psychically through all the novel, leaving in its wake a trail of images of death. They appear sometimes only on the periphery of vision, as on the drive to New York (Nick with Gatsby): "A dead man passed us in a hearse heaped with blooms, followed by two carriages with drawn blinds, and by more cheerful carriages for friends. The friends looked out at us with the tragic eyes and short upper lips of southeastern Europe, and I was glad that the sight of Gatsby's splendid car was included in their somber holiday." The hearse and its contents may serve as an omen for Gatsby's car, which in spite of its ministering so spectacularly to all the comforts of life (". . .bright with nickel, swollen here and there in its monstrous length with triumphant hat-boxes and supper-boxes and tool-boxes. . .terraced with a labyrinth of wind-shields that mirrored a dozen suns") becomes the novel's chief vehicle of death, leading directly to Myrtle's. Her death, within easy view of the valley of ashes, is as grotesque and meaningless as her life, ripping asunder the body that was the repository of her cheap successes and minor ambitions: ". . .when they had torn open her shirtwaist, still damp with perspiration, they saw her left breast was swinging loose like a flap, and there was no need to listen for the heart beneath. The mouth was wide open and ripped at the corners, as though she had choked a little in giving up the tremendous vitality she had stored so long."

Gatsby's gorgeous cream-colored car is also the indirect cause of his own death, as it is the deep imprint of the fantastic car on his excited brain that enables Wilson (through Tom Buchanan) to track Gatsby down and to shoot him (erroneously, of course) for killing Myrtle. At this critical moment, Gatsby has gone to his pool for a swim, and Nick speculates that for Gatsby it might well have been a moment of awareness—awareness that he had lost Daisy to Tom, and that he had lived "too long with a single dream." As Nick imaginatively recreates the scene, Gatsby is touched with terror at the discovery that the world is not a garden of delights but something of an ash-heap: "He must have looked up at an unfamiliar sky through frightening leaves and shivered as he found what a grotesque thing a rose is and how raw the sunlight was upon the scarcely created grass. A new world, material without being real, where poor ghosts, breathing dreams like air, drifted fortuitously about. . .like that ashen fantastic figure gliding toward him through the amorphous trees." *Ashen*. By now the signal is unmistakable. Though driven by a dream of splendid life, Gatsby plays out his role (like the others) on the dumping ground of ashes. But in contrast with the violence of Myrtle's death, Gatsby's seems hardly noticeable as his body floats silently on the swimming pool surface:

> There was a faint, barely perceptible movement of the water as the fresh flow from one end urged its way toward the drain at the other. With little ripples that were hardly the shadows of waves, the laden mattress moved irregularly down the pool. A small gust of wind that scarcely corrugated the surface was enough to disturb its accidental course with its accidental burden. The touch of a cluster of leaves revolved it slowly, tracing, like the leg of transit, a thin circle in the water.

It is surely the vacuous eyes of Dr. T. J. Eckleburg with their uncomprehending and meaningless stare that preside over this scene of the pneumatic mattress floating aimlessly on "its *accidental* course with its *accidental* burden." In a world become ash-heap, one's fate has no relevance to one's life: *accident* rules supreme.

As the valley of ashes is introduced early in the novel to become a kind of pervasive presence, gradually becoming the psychic setting for all the novel's action, so "the night scene by El Greco" in the last chapter tends to take over the reader's memory of the novel and to distort the action into a kind of surrealist dream. In trying to sum up, finally, his inexplicable feelings about the East, Nick reports the way it appears in his "more fantastic dreams": "I see it as a night scene by El Greco: a hundred houses, at once conventional and grotesque, crouching under a sullen, overhanging sky and a lustreless moon. In the foreground four solemn men in dress suits are walking along the sidewalk with a stretcher on which lies a drunken woman in a white evening dress. Her hand, which dangles over the side, sparkles cold with jewels. Gravely the men turn in at a house—the wrong house. But no one knows the woman's name, and no one cares." The "day scene" of *The Great Gatsby* is surely the valley of ashes, and its night scene is this El Greco dreamscape, with its meticulously dressed characters performing meaningless actions in a meaningless world. But there is, perhaps, more connection between these two powerful images than is explicitly stated. The night scene by El Greco seems to be the dark underside of the valley of ashes, the night of its day, the nightmare of its reality. The one posits the other. And there seems to be a continuity in the gigantic, vacant oculist's eyes of the valley of ashes and the "sullen, overhanging sky and . . . lustreless moon" of the El Greco night scene. The worlds merge and meld into each other. And in that world, if one looks over his shoulder, he might well notice a scene out of *The Waste Land,* Part V:

> A woman drew her long black hair out tight
> And fiddled whisper music on those strings
> And bats and baby faces in the violet light
> Whistled, and beat their wings
> And crawled head downward down a blackened wall. . . .

III
"looking for a business gonnegtion"

Although *The Great Gatsby* conveys much of its meaning obliquely through its imagery, it still is filled with what Henry James called "solidity of specification" and what T. S. Eliot named "a solid atmosphere." Although *The Great Gatsby* is much more than a book about the 1920's, it remains solidly based in the era and place that gave it birth. But it is not only based there: it also provides, in some sense, a commentary on the times.

The 1920's saw the enshrinement of business as the religion of America, and at the same time saw some of the most pervasive business and governmental corruption the country had ever experienced. One president gave the country the Teapot Dome scandal, a rip-off of oil resources to stagger the imagination; another president proclaimed that "the business of America is business." The decade opened with a scandal of the "fixing" and "wheeling-dealing" that will never be wholly unravelled. It was the era of Al Capone in bootlegged booze and Harry Sinclair in Teapot Dome oil lands. For the first time in history, members of the presidential cabinet were jailed for bribery. With such national heroes for models, what more can a country ask for?

Fitzgerald's novel is a more powerful embodiment of the spirit of the times than the collected works of Sinclair Lewis, perhaps because Fitzgerald *dramatised* while Lewis *stated*. The corruption of the 1920's saturates *The Great Gatsby*. Gatsby's "greatness" is constructed in part on illegal activities that are never fully and clearly defined — bootlegging in a string of drug stores? the handling of bonds from governmental bribes? big-time gambling and gangster war-fare? No matter. Our imagination improves on the withheld reality (as in James's *Turn of the Screw* and *The Ambassadors*). Even the narrator Nick Carraway is infected with the "business ethic" of the time as he pursues his career as a bond salesman and confesses: "I bought a dozen volumes on banking and credit and investment securities, and they stood on my shelf in red and gold like new money from the mint, promising to unfold the shining secrets that only Midas and Morgan and Maecenas knew."

Tom Buchanan comes from the world of established wealth, which, though contemptuous of the blatant kinds of corruption represented by Gatsby and his associates, itself indulges quietly and discreetly in bribery, blackmail, and manipulation (preferably legal) to maintain and consolidate its power. It is a world that has lines into the more obviously corrupt world, as witness Tom's friend Walter Chase, a one-time associate of Gatsby, who is willing to spy on Gatsby for Tom (and no doubt for a price). In many ways Tom Buchanan is the most sinister character in *The Great Gatsby*, as he seems to typify the American business man (man of power) who remains the perpetual adolescent intellectually: "Tom would drift on forever seeking, a little wistfully, for the dramatic turbulence of some irrecoverable football game." "Something was making him nibble at the edge of stale ideas as if his sturdy physical egotism no longer nourished his peremptory heart." Tom is presented as circling around an idea that might provide the means for the application of his brute strength and financial power—racial suppression: "Civilization's going to pieces . . . I've gotten to be a terrible pessimist about things. Have you read 'The Rise of the Colored Empires' by this man Goddard? . . . The idea is if we don't look out the white race will be—will be utterly submerged. It's all scientific stuff; it's been proved."

If Tom Buchanan appears sinister in all his respectability, Jordan Baker appears pathetic in her petty cheating at golf. But her corruption cannot be dismissed as minor, as it suggests the contagiousness of the 1920's disease (the disease is not, of course, confined to the 1920's, but it reached epidemic levels in that age). In a few swift strokes, Fitzgerald through Nick reveals her character and her world: "When we were on a house-party together up in Warwick, she left a borrowed car out in the rain with the top down, and then lied about it—and suddenly I remembered the story about her that had eluded me that night at Daisy's. At her first big golf tournament there was a row that nearly reached the newspapers—a suggestion that she had moved her ball from a bad lie in the semifinal round. The thing approached the proportions of a scandal—then died away. A caddy retracted his statement, and the only other witness admitted that he might have been mistaken." It is not surprising that, given her allies in the world of the rich, the unpleasant incident would be "fixed." But the point revealed in the novel is that however easily a cheating episode can be hushed-up, a debased spirit cannot so quickly be mended or fixed. Jordan Baker remains what she is, a product of the pervasive corruption of the period: she will cheat her way through life.

Meyer Wolfsheim is the most clear-cut figure of 1920's

gangsterdom. He lurks in the shadows behind Gatsby throughout, and when he emerges briefly in the restaurant scene in
New York to have lunch with Gatsby and Nick, we glimpse
something of his career in his short and sweet tale of the
"night they shot Rosy Rosenthal." It was at "the old
Metropole": "It was six of us at the table, and Rosy had eat
and drunk a lot all evening. When it was almost morning the
waiter came up to him with a funny look and says somebody
wants to speak to him outside." Over the protest of his
friends, Rosy "went out on the sidewalk, and they shot him
three times in his full belly and drove away." It is at this point
that Wolfsheim turns to Nick and says, "I understand you're
looking for a business gonnegtion." Later, Gatsby tells Nick:
"Meyer Wolfsheim?. . .he's a gambler. . . . He's the man who
fixed the World's Series back in 1919."

Although the foreground of *The Great Gatsby* is largely
filled with the super-sophisticated life of the rich and
pleasure-bound figures of the jazz age, the "roaring twenties,"
not far in the background are the Rosy Rosenthals, the Meyer
Wolfsheims, the Walter Chases, in violent pursuit of money
and the good, easy life. The two worlds share in common the
universal desire for the right "business gonnegtion," and the
reader may be sure that at the edges, where the two worlds
meet in the shadows, such "gonnegtions" are negotiated and
consummated continually.

IV
"a vast, vulgar, and meretricious beauty"

Gatsby's own "corrupted innocence" lies at the heart of
the meaning of the novel. And although he is quite obviously a
figure of the 1920's, he is also something more. Although *The
Great Gatsby* is deeply rooted in its time, it is considerably
more than a revelation of life in the jazz age. It transcends its
time to reveal something about America, American character,
and the American dream. Tom Buchanan and the others

exploit the American "business ethic" (or "gangster ethic") for their own sordid advantage. But Gatsby is as much victim as exploiter. From the moment that we (with Nick) first set eyes on him, we sense that he is vulnerable in his innocence in some way that all the others are not. He is standing outside in the dark night, looking over the waters from West Egg to East Egg: ". . . he stretched out his arms toward the dark water in a curious way, and, far as I was from him, I could have sworn he was trembling. Involuntarily I glanced seaward—and distinguished nothing except a single green light, minute and far away, that might have been the end of a dock. When I looked once more for Gatsby he had vanished, and I was alone again in the unquiet darkness."

Trembling? Perhaps Gatsby is the only character (except Nick) capable of *trembling* in the "unquiet darkness" of the novel. Surely he is the only character in pursuit of something transcendent and worthy of his own submission. And it is his tragedy that his vision of transcendence comes to focus on an object that is enchanting on the surface, rotten at the core.

To trace the origins of Gatsby's dream means beginning near the end of the novel and zig-zagging back and forth in order to piece together the broken pieces of his life. For example, it is only in the last chapter that we encounter (through his father come East for the funeral) Gatsby as a boy. And in that mid-western boyhood we discover the roots of Gatsby's transcendent vision. Gatsby's father shows Nick a tattered copy of an old *Hopalong Cassidy* book, and there on the flyleaf are the resolutions that the boy James Gatz made for his self-improvement and "getting ahead." They include such touching items as, "Practice elocution, poise and how to attain it . . . 5.00-6.00 p.m." and "Read one improving book or magazine per week." This schedule and list of "General Resolves" look as though they have been copied from the pages of Benjamin Franklin's *Autobiography.* They constitute, of course, but one of the many suggestions throughout the novel that Gatsby's dream is rooted deeply in the American dream, here manifested in its materialistic bias as it conjures up visions of crafty and thrifty Benjamin Franklin and his solemn advice on the "Way to Wealth."

From Gatsby's boyhood we must jump to his young manhood (and Chapter VII) for our next glimpse of the development of the dream. We learn only the bare outline of his life on Dan Cody's yacht, encountered on Lake Superior. It was at this time that Gatsby began the remaking of himself, beginning with the change of name from James Gatz to Jay Gatsby: "The truth was that Jay Gatsby of West Egg, Long Island, sprang from his Platonic conception of himself. He was a son of God—a phrase which, if it means anything, means just that—and he must be about his Father's business, the service of a vast, vulgar, and meretricious beauty. So he invented just the sort of Jay Gatsby that a seventeen-year-old boy would be likely to invent, and to this conception he was faithful to the end." Thus, even before the encounter with Daisy, the dream appears unworthy of the dedication of the dreamer, and curiously at odds with his astonishing innocence. The adventure on the Cody yacht concludes with Gatsby as victim (cheated of the money left him by his rich patron).

The next transformation in Gatsby takes place on his initial encounter, as a young officer in the army, with Daisy Fay in Louisville, and for this event we have only fragmentary accounts in scattered chapters. But from these it is clear that the vague, inchoate dream alights on Daisy, and romantically transfigures her into a creature of Gatsby's imagination: "He knew that when he kissed this girl, and forever wed his unutterable visions to her perishable breath, his mind would never romp again like the mind of God. So he waited, listening for a moment longer to the tuning-fork that had been struck upon a star. Then he kissed her. At his lips' touch she blossomed for him like a flower and the incarnation was complete." Whatever the "incarnation" is, we can be sure that it is not the real but a transcendent Daisy commensurate with the energy and compatible with the innocence of the dream creating her. Something of the nature of this transfigured Daisy is suggested in another passage (in Chapter VIII): Gatsby "had intended, probably, to take what he could and go—but now he found that he had committed himself to the following of a grail."

Gatsby's re-encounter with Daisy is, of course, the action represented in the foreground of the novel as constructed, but the fate of Gatsby's dream is not so fully delineated. We must speculate with Nick as to Gatsby's feelings and insights: "There must have been moments even that afternoon [their first rendezvous after five years] when Daisy tumbled short of his [Gatsby's] dreams—not through her own fault, but because of the colossal vitality of his illusions. It had gone beyond her, beyond everything. He had thrown himself into it with a creative passion, adding to it all the time, decking it out with every bright feather that drifted his way. No amount of fire or freshness can challenge what a man will store up in his ghostly heart."

In the confrontation scene between Gatsby and Tom, in the New York hotel room, when Tom reveals to Daisy what his spies have learned about Gatsby's activities, Gatsby appears to lose control as he begins to talk excitedly and irrationally, "defending his name against accusations that had not been made." At this critical turning point, we are told that "only the dead dream fought on as the afternoon slipped away, trying to touch what was no longer tangible, struggling unhappily, undespairingly, toward that lost voice across the room." Was the dream dead or dying for Gatsby at this point? Although he plays out the role he has assigned himself in relation to Daisy, there are hints that he might have developed some self-awareness. But there is suggestion too that he preserved his illusion intact. When Nick leaves him standing outside the Buchanan house, after Daisy has killed Myrtle Wilson with Gatsby's car, and after we have just glimpsed (with Nick) the cosy, conspiratorial scene of Tom and Daisy at a kitchen table holding cold fried chicken and bottles of ale—Gatsby appears to be devoted to the "sacredness of the vigil." But does he sense, on some level of consciousness, what Nick tells us and we know to be true—that he is "watching over nothing"?

The complexity of Gatsby's illusion, and his own complicated feelings about it, are suggested in a number of
astounding remarks that he drops in off-hand manner in casual
conversation. For example, as Nick at one point (before the
New York confrontation scene) is trying to find the right
description for Daisy's voice, Gatsby says: "Her voice is full of
money," and Nick is overwhelmed with the aptness of the
metaphor. In another instance, after the confrontation scene,
as Nick and Gatsby are discussing the relation of Tom and
Daisy, Gatsby suddenly says: "In any case, . . . it was just
personal." And Nick asks the reader: "What could you make
of that, except to suspect some intensity in his conception of
the affair that couldn't be measured?"

It is no doubt this immeasurable and indefinable "intensity" of Gatsby's dream that induces Nick to call out to him,
on their last meeting (when Gatsby is still waiting for the call
from Daisy that will never come): "You're worth the whole
damn bunch put together." Nick adds: "I've always been glad
I said that. It was the only compliment I ever gave him,
because I disapproved of him from beginning to end. First he
nodded politely, and then his face broke into that radiant and
understanding smile . . ." And as Nick senses something of
Gatsby's embryonic awareness, he remembers his first encounters with Gatsby at his big parties: "The lawn and drive had
been crowded with the faces of those who guessed at his
corruption—and he had stood on those steps, concealing his
incorruptible dream as he waved them goodby." At Gatsby's
death, we must again speculate with Nick as to the extent of
Gatsby's self-knowledge: "I have an idea that Gatsby himself
didn't believe it [the call from Daisy] would come, and
perhaps he no longer cared. If that was true he must have felt
that he had lost the old warm world, paid a high price for
living too long with a single dream." But whatever the extent
of Gatsby's final insight, Nick's judgment remains clear from
the moment it is presented on the second page of the novel:
"No—Gatsby turned out all right at the end; it is what preyed
on Gatsby, what foul dust floated in the wake of his dreams

that temporarily closed out my interest in the abortive sorrows and short-winded elations of men."

How can it be that Gatsby, surrounded by so much corruption, can remain innocent? We know something of the sordidness of the sources of his fortune, and we witness the moral shallowness of Daisy, about whom he has spun the gossamer foundations of his fantastic and colossal dream. We cannot even be sure that he has, in the face of defeat, achieved that kind of self-knowledge that would render his fate genuinely tragic. We can only speculate, as Nick speculates, on what he has learned in his obsessive pursuit of so unworthy an object. But Nick's judgment is clear in Gatsby's defense, and after all is said—it is only Nick's Gatsby that we come to know in the novel. But even as Nick asserts Gatsby's worth above all the others, he is compelled to add that he "disapproved of him from beginning to end." It is the moral awareness that Nick achieves in the progress of the action of the novel that enables him, in spite of Gatsby's "corruption," to affirm that he came out all right in the end. His ambivalent moral judgment is not unlike that of Owl-Eyes, the party guest who earlier was startled to find the books in Gatsby's library real. He is the only one of the multitudinous party-goers to attend Gatsby's funeral, and he says the final word at the graveside: "The poor son-of-a-bitch." (It is to be precisely this moral judgment that, later, Ratliff was to pass on the Snopeses at the end of William Faulkner's *The Mansion* [1959].) It is moral sympathy for a victim whose innocence transcended his corruption.

Whatever the extent of Gatsby's moral awakening, it could not have embraced the totality of vision that Nick has at the close of the novel. As Nick sits on Gatsby's beach, his imagination reaches back into history: ". . . as the moon rose higher the inessential houses began to melt away until gradually I became aware of the old island here that flowered once for Dutch sailors' eyes—a fresh, green breast of the new world. Its vanished trees, the trees that had made way for Gatsby's house, had once pandered in whispers to the last and greatest of all human dreams; for a transitory enchanted moment man must have held his breath in the presence of this continent, compelled into an aesthetic contemplation he neither understood nor desired, face to face for the last time in history with something commensurate to his capacity for wonder." From Benjamin Franklin's plan for moral improvement, which incidentally showed the way to wealth, all the way to the "greatest of all human dreams," whose fulfillment seemed to require destruction of the very wilderness which inspired it (the "vanished trees") — Gatsby was as much the victim of his American heritage as he was of Tom, Daisy, and George Wilson. His innocence was his persistence in the belief in the American dream as he carried it with him deep in his psyche, unaware that it contained the seeds of its—and his—destruction. He could "tremble" in the unquiet darkness as he gazed at the beckoning green light, just as the settlers must have been caught up in overwhelming "wonder" at the sight of the new continent. He and they could submit themselves to a vision that was, however distorted with materialistic bias, touched with the ideal or transcendent. The others, the "foul dust that floated in the wake of his dreams," were incapable of comprehending dream or vision: "they smashed up things and creatures and then retreated back into their money or their vast carelessness. . . ."

V
"borne back ceaselessly into the past"

Although *The Great Gatsby* is deeply rooted in the 1920's, and at the same time appears to provide a commentary on American character and the American dream, it is still something more—something reaching out beyond its time and beyond its place. In short, the novel embodies and expresses the simple, basic human desire and yearning, universal in nature, to snatch something precious from the ceaseless flux and flow of days and years and preserve it outside the ravages of time. This is obviously a theme that is not confined to the 1920's or to America. Although it may not win the designation of "archetypal," it is hard to imagine a time when human beings did not feel it deeply.

The Great Gatsby is a novel relentlessly devoted to the present, set, as it is, in its total action in the summer of 1922. But it is a novel that is haunted by the past—Gatsby's and America's—and it is the past which reaches into and shapes the present. Gatsby himself embodies in a grotesque way the desire to transcend time. When Nick repeats to him a truism, "You can't repeat the past," he astonishingly replies: "Can't repeat the past? . . . Why of course you can!" To Gatsby time appears as submissive to his will as wealth or power: "He looked around him wildly, as if the past were lurking here in the shadow of his house, just out of reach of his hand." And he cries out: "I'm going to fix everything just the way it was before." Gatsby's desire is not peculiarly American, but his stupendous self-assurance that he can recreate the past may well derive from the dark underside of the American dream. But time will run out on Gatsby, as it has on the American dream—and as it does on all human dreams and desires and aspirations.

It is this theme, more feeling than statement, that is evoked by the lyric style of *The Great Gatsby.* Throughout the novel, Nick responds in a deeply personal way to the events he witnesses, translating them into feelings that lie so deep as to defy precision of language. For example, at the end of Chapter VI, after Gatsby has tried to explain Daisy's meaning for him and the absolute necessity of recovering that lost past, Nick muses:

> Through all he said, even through his appalling sentimentality, I was reminded of something—an elusive rhythm, a fragment of lost words, that I had heard somewhere a long time ago. For a moment a phrase tried to take shape in my mouth and my lips parted like a dumb man's, as though there was more struggling upon them than a wisp of startled air. But they made no·sound, and what I had almost remembered was uncommunicable forever.

"An elusive rhythm, a fragment of lost words" —we feel

with Nick a sense of loss of the past that cannot be articulated. This sense of loss becomes acute and central in the closing lines of the novel, as Nick meditates on Gatsby's abortive dream: "He had come a long way to this blue lawn, and his dream must have seemed so close that he could hardly fail to grasp it. He did not know that it was already behind him, somewhere back in that vast obscurity beyond the city, where the dark fields of the republic rolled on under the night." Nick has come to realize that Gatsby's dream was lost before it was even dreamed, as the American dream itself had been frittered away, squandered in the past. But Nick's last thoughts move away from Gatsby to himself—and to "us"—as he meditates on time, and present, past, and future: "Gatsby believed in the green light, the orgiastic future that year by year recedes before us. It eluded us then, but that's no matter—tomorrow we will run faster, stretch out our arms farther . . . And one fine morning—" Nick here breaks off, the vision intercepted before it is launched, and speaks his last words on Gatsby's, his, the American, the human predicament: "So we beat on, boats against the current, borne back ceaselessly into the past."

With these closing words we find that we ourselves have become participants in the novel's meaning, as the action has broadened out to include us all. It is impossible to respond to those final words without being thrown back into one's own past, in painful memory of those momentous events of purely personal meaning that have slipped away to be lost forever. We are all Gatsbys yearning to recreate the past; we are all Nick Carraways lyrically regretting the rush of time swiftly past our grasp. And as we close the book and look about us, touched by an "elusive rhythm, a fragment of lost words," we may feel something of the impulse of the protagonist at the end of *The Waste Land* —to gather fragments to shore up against our ruin.

15

Hemingway: The Recoil from History

C. W. E. Bigsby

Few writers captured that sense of disillusionment and despair, which Eliot had identified, as effectively as Ernest Hemingway. The 'lost generation,' which he described with all the clarity and simplicity called for by Ezra Pound, inhabited a wasteland every bit as ironical and dessicated as Eliot's. The echoing "nothing and again nothing," of the second section of "The Waste Land," becomes the "nada y pues nada y nada y pues nada" of "A Clean Well-Lighted Place." The gulf which Hemingway saw as having opened up between cause and effect, aspiration and realisation — a gulf which seemed to deny the very notion of historical process — is essentially that of "The Hollow Men."

> Between the conception
> And the creation
> Between the emotion and the response
> Falls the Shadow.
>
> > *Life is very long*
>
> Between the desire
> And the spasm
> Between the potency
> And the existence
> Between the essence
> And the descent
> Falls the Shadow

Of course the shadow was more than simply that cast by the war. But, for Hemingway, there was a clear division not only between two generations whose experience had been so radically dissimilar, but between those who recognised reality for what it was and devised the strategy necessary for bare survival, and those who continued to live with romantic notions of faith and conduct.

The America of Prohibition, the Hays Office and the Scopes trial obviously had a fairly low commitment to reality. Faced with a disturbing present many tried to sustain a threatened sense of moral order by invoking pre-Darwinian and even pre-industrial values. The Fugitives in the South resurrected an agrarian dream as though industrialism as such were the root of evil rather than the visible evidence of a more fundamental disjunction between man and his situation. Eliot and Pound looked even further back. At the same time the emergence of a self-consciously urban Negro literati was reflected not so much in the forging of new concepts of social and artistic possibilities as in a romantic nostalgia for the pagan simplicities of Africa. In fact Warren Harding's desire for normalcy was widely shared in a society disturbed by the implications of twentieth century reality. Even the expatriate flight to the Old World was more than a quest for artistic stimulation or simply a retreat from the anti-intellectualism of Babbitt and his fellow Boosters. It was in part at least a search among the debris of war for some structure which could be imposed on an experience which increasingly refused to conform to any of the patterns invoked with decreasing confidence by a Puritan nation suddenly alive to the in-adequacy of a world view forged in New England settlements and Mid-Western towns. The war, itself an elegy to 19th century notions of rationality and human progress, seemed to many to suggest a general principle of disorder which validated an intuitionist philosophy. If no external absolutes operated then who could the individual turn to but himself? He alone could create an order which no longer seemed to be implicit in existence itself. If Hemingway's heroes cling so stubbornly to the integrity of their own actions and see morality as "what you feel good after," this apparently romantic stance is a desperate device and not a confident assertion of romantic egotism. Indeed, the various roles which Hemingway played with such enthusiasm throughout his life arguably evidence a retreat from a full sense of individuality and identity which is perhaps reflected in the reified characters of his novels — a retreat from self-conscious individuality and complexity which betrays a lack of faith in anything but the bare bones of experience. Just as the New Critics were intent on expunging the personality of the author from literary study so Hemingway distrusted everything but the integrity of the concrete fact and action. He set out to capture the living event; not to record an emotional diary but to describe "the sequence of motion and fact which made the emotion" — a version, clearly enough, of Eliot's objective correlative. In his early work he trusts the validity of the object, of the simple action, and distrusts emotions and rationality alike. His characters avoid thought because rationality has been exposed by the logical commonplaces of war and because memory is simply an avenue to trauma. Like Krebs, the protagonist of "Soldiers Home," his characters want to live "without consequences" and if, in a sense, Hemingway's world was perpetually frozen in the youthful Mid-Western all-male society of his own past — a society of permanent adolescence in which experience is indeed without consequence — it is because complexity as such threatens a potentially disastrous loss of control. In "Big Two-Hearted River" the wounded protagonist has to take each event separately; every action has to be self-contained. Only such a strategy as this can evade the vulnerability which marks such a character as Frederic Henry when he abandons his emotional neutrality for the complicated biological determinism of his affair with Catherine. To this extent his characters are an extension of his spare style. The rich texture of the 19th century novel gives way to a simple unadulterated style. The circuitous ambiguities of Henry James had reflected so well his sense of a rich and complex world: the deracinated form of Hemingway's work accurately reflects his own sense of an existence which must be codified if the individual is to exist with any dignity.

The war destroyed every kind of framework and model. It dismembered the human body and annihilated the patterned grace of Europe's cities. It destroyed the dignity of death and undermined the confidence of those who pictured history as a steady and logical progress. In desperation they reasserted the old verities, or lived out the absurdity of their age in a chaotic materialism. To others there appeared to be form even in formlessness. Darwin, Marx, Freud and Spengler all seemed to suggest the existence of a kind of order, a governing principle, a key to the cipher of existence, even if the order was simply systematised disorder, the principle only a description of process and the key merely an interpretation of observed phenomena. Fitzgerald, who, like his protagonist Dick Diver, saw himself as a creator of consonance, was naturally enough drawn to the work of all four men — seeing not only an explanation and justification for the contrary forces which tore at his own personality but also a central impulse towards the elaboration of some kind of balance which was his own social and psychic need. Hemingway, who felt the same need, affected contempt for intellectual theorisers who constructed flawless models of experience in their heads without confronting the brute and inchoate realities of existence for themselves. For the individual confronting the senseless pain and pointless butchery of warfare, for the man learning to live with the bitter irony of his own emasculation, spiritual and physical, there was no meaning in historic process or social system and though he could recognise the truth of psychological trauma this could not be cauterised by the neat retracing of experience suggested by Freudian analysis. For Hemingway's heroes were all too aware that you could not go back again, and that relief could only come through the manufacture of a structure manifestly absent from life itself. His fascination with the bull-fight, his elaboration of a code depending on the authenticity of experience, the courageous confrontation of an ineluctable reality, and a refusal to acknowledge defeat, are the strategies adopted by a man who does not believe that science, history or political theory can invest the life and death of an individual with the dignity necessary for continued existence. Each man is alone without the consolation of shared experience. Manuel Garcia, in "The Undefeated," fights a personal battle in the bull-ring – a battle whose essential meaning cannot communicate itself to those who merely watch and consequently fail to understand his anguished fight for self respect. The true Hemingway hero is Jake Barnes, rendered incapable of sharing his most intimate experiences and cut off, in a fundamental way, from those around him; or it is Frederic Henry, walking back to his hotel in the rain; or, prototypically, Christ, cut off from God and man, but dying well on the cross, transforming defeat into a kind of victory because he imprints his own meaning through personal integrity, on an otherwise meaningless death. Fitzgerald's characters are destroyed because they are unable to mould the world to match their visions. They try to project their dreams of order onto a society which he saw as fundamentally entropic but, lacking a personal integrity which can sustain such a reckless challenge to reality, they are destroyed. They are corrupted because they collaborate in the general disorder which is the antithesis of their search for pattern. Hemingway's heroes avoid this error. They declare a separate peace; they insulate themselves as far as possible, and conform to a code which provides an alternative to the threatening disorder of society and historical reality. Hemingway places emphasis on performance not because of some misplaced sense of virility but because, deprived of ultimate purpose, the individual is forced either to create an objective of his own or to see virtue as residing in the ability to function from day to day. Thus, in the bull-ring, death has a meaning conferred on it which is absent in the haphazard killing of warfare. Speaking of the disembowelling of the horses Jake explains that "it became something that was going on with a definite end, and less of a spectacle with unexplained horrors."

To Barnes the only meaning in life was that derived from the experience of living. "I did not care what it was all about. All I wanted to know was how to live in it. Maybe if you found out how to live in it you learned from that what it was all about."

The bullfight is important because, though an artificial construct, it offers an ordered experience in which it is possible to distinguish the authentic from the sham, the true from the merely plausible. The bullfighter, true to the standards and traditions of his craft, like the writer anxious to strip his work of all pretence and dishonesty, is pitching himself against both a form of spiritual decadence and the constant threat of dissolution. He challenges death, the final anarchic impulse. He challenges the principle of disorder, creating a discrete universe, outside of time, in which control, personal courage and purity of style have a meaning denied the individual faced with the anti-tragic banalities of the modern wasteland.

In a recent book, *The American Novel and the Nineteen Twenties* (London, 1972), Malcolm Bradbury asserts that the purgatory in which Hemingway's characters live is "in history; it has a specific place in time, for Hemingway's elect is the elect of modernity" and the wound of war is "an initiation not only into the human condition but into the conditions of history; it is a place in time" which "creates the communal consciousness of a generation." While it is true that the cause of his disaffection and the root of his trauma is historical, there is another sense in which this is merely fortuitous. The catalyst might just as well have been the senseless violence of pain and fear pictured in "Indian Camp" or the casual inhumanity of "The Killers." Frederic Henry joins in the war in Europe not because of any sense of real commitment or any understanding of political realities but simply because he happened to be in Italy and to speak Italian. The war is a game, as is his sexual adventuring. When the seriousness of both becomes immediately apparent he is trapped in a world which can have no future. Where can he go after the retreat from Caporetto except to that long-established escape from historical reality—Switzerland; where can he go in his emotional life after the death of Catherine and her child—a son strangled by its own umbilical cord in a painfully precise image of a world with no discernible future? Similarly, in *The Sun Also Rises*, though Jake Barnes' injuries were sustained in the war and thus, to that extent at least, he is ineluctably tied into history, his response from that moment on is profoundly ahistorical. Life becomes an attempt to "play it along and just not make trouble for people" and the attraction of the fiesta, which gave the book its English title, is precisely its evasion of causality. "Everything became quite unreal finally and it seemed as though nothing could have any consequences. It seemed out of place to think of consequences during the fiesta." The Hemingway protagonist is caught outside of history. As Frederic Henry knows well enough, "You could not go back again." But equally well you could not go forward either when all normal standards are reversed. Unable to contemplate a past which seems to have lost all meaning or to be the source of unbearable pain, and yet unwilling to conceed a future in which he might be required to accept responsibility for the present, the hero's only solution lies in dissociation, an ironic detachment such as that which Jake Barnes affects in *The Sun Also Rises* when he finds himself trapped in a world in which desire seems permanently sundered from fulfillment. The abandonment of historical process becomes a necessary tactic for survival. Leaving aside the spurious social commitment of *To Have and Have Not*, it was not until Robert Jordan levelled his sights on Lieutenant Berendo, at the end of *For Whom the Bell Tolls*, having put aside his perhaps more important psychic battle, that Hemingway's heroes stride back into the historical arena again.

   The fact that his early heroes serve so effectively to create "the communal consciousness of a generation" does not so much prove that they are "in history" as indicate a flight from history which was shared by many others who discovered themselves to be cut off from the past while unable to discover any new values which could sustain a coherent vision of the

future. Hemingway did capture the mood of his time but that
mood was itself profoundly ahistorical. "The snow of 1929
was not real snow," Fitzgerald remarked in a story, "if you did
not want it to be real snow you paid some money." The gaudy
spree which he took part in and criticized was simply another
version of the frenetic cafe society, the trip to Pamplona and
the pointless and necessarily sterile sexual intrigues which
Hemingway pictured in *The Sun Also Rises*. It is no accident
that books written in the 1920s should be so full of perverted
love, for anything else would have implied a faith in the future
which was simply not held by writers who had witnessed for
themselves the apparent collapse of every structure which had
previously supported the individual.

Hemingway had no respect for history as such; only for
personal histories. Each generation had to re-learn the essential
truths of life which could never be simply passed on as part of
a developing body of knowledge. History was there, of course,
as First Cause, a sense of what Hemingway called "an ignored
tension." But salvation lay not in the public world of passing
time and social responsibilities, but in a private world in which
the real battle is for control of a psychic terrain. It is no
accident that his heroes should be expatriates, cut off from
their own American past and living life as detached outsiders
who feel no real commitment to the cause which they have
embraced. What they do choose to acknowledge is a personal
code which has meaning precisely because it is unrelated to a
historical process which seems to allow no place for the
courage and integrity essential to Hemingway's sense of a
meaningful existence. Like the returned soldier of "Soldiers
Home" the Hemingway hero discovers early that "the world
they were in is not the world he was in." Removed from those
around him by a physical wound, like Jake Barnes, or by a
necessary act of desertion followed by harrowing emotional
trauma, like Frederic Henry, they step out of history to
confront themselves, like so many American heroes from
Leatherstocking to Ahab and Huckleberry Finn, against a
timeless setting of the natural world.

The attraction which Hemingway felt for the simple facticity of the countryside, the trout stream, the African bush, had little to do with Jacksonian agrarianism. It was simply that this was a world removed from time and the society of man. The title of his first novel expressed precisely this sense that the only certainty lay in the biblical assurance that the earth endureth forever. Beside this assurance, social and political commitment, personal relationships and the urgencies of the moment are seen in a perspective which owes nothing to history; the physical and psychological detritus of life is subsumed in a natural cycle which simultaneously mocks and consoles. The separate peace declared by Frederic Henry was a tactic which carried the full force of Hemingway's own commitment. If neither author nor character could as easily evade the implications of the 'biological trap,' one could always detect the timeless outline of nature—not a romantic resource expressing beauty and truth but a constant comment on man's insignificance. As late as 1936 he could still assert that "if you serve time for society, democracy, and the other things quite young, and declining any further enlistment make yourself responsible only to yourself, you exchange the pleasant, comforting stench of comrades for something you can never feel in any other way than by yourself." Nature, eternal and inescapable, washes away not only the responsibilities of Frederic Henry, as he plunges into the River Tagliamento, but all signs of man's cruelty, pain and fear. It annihilates history as it absorbs all evidence of man's victories and defeats, neutralizing the power of time and the destructive spirit of an era born out of senseless slaughter and coming of age in a period of reckless materialism. The image now is no longer that of the therapeutic river found in "Big Two-Hearted River" and *The Sun Also Rises* nor even the cool high mountains of *A Farewell to Arms*. In *The Green Hills of Africa* it becomes the Gulf Stream, a current which "will flow, as it has flowed, after the Indians, after the Spaniards, after the British, after the Americans and after all the Cubans and all the systems of governments, the richness, the poverty, the martyrdom, the sacrifice and the venality and the cruelty are all gone as the high-piled scow of garbage, bright-coloured, white flecked, ill-smelling, now tilted on its side, spills off its load into the blue water . . . the palm fronds of our victories, the worn light bulbs of our discoveries and the empty condoms of our great loves float with no significance against one simple, lasting thing—the stream." This was Hemingway's response to the waste land. You responded to the savage irony of a "burned over land" with an equally deracinated selfhood in the knowledge that sceptical detachment was finally the only safe method of picking one's way through the ashes of a dying civilization. Meanwhile, in the background, offering a mute but ironic comment on human activity, is the stream flowing on to the sea as part of an endless cycle of ebb and flow, life and death which seems to offer the only kind of meaning which can be won outside of the arena of personal integrity. Yet in Hemingway's world no less than in Eliot's even the imagery of the natural cycle is subverted. Spring no longer represents an unqualified renewal of life. The prospect of birth and vitality merely precipitates a sharper consciousness of imminent death. Frederic and Catherine live through an idyllic winter, their child slowly maturing in the womb:

> Winter kept us warm, covering
> Earth in forgetful snow, feeding
> A little life with dried tubers.

But with the arrival of the rain they descend from the mountains for the April birth of their son and discover the true extent of an anarchy which they had thought restricted to the social world:

> April is the cruellest month, breeding
> Lilacs out of the dead land, mixing
> Memory and desire, stirring
> Dull roots with spring rain

Eliot's fisher king and Hemingway's Jake Barnes seem to suggest a radical disjunction in the natural order—a dislocation which runs deeper than fashionable despair or personal alienation. Both men turned naturally enough to apocalyptic imagery as they detected what seemed to be a loss of will and energy at the heart of the organism—a decline which led to the brink of dissolution. But where Eliot looked to the past for evidence of organic integrity, Hemingway set himself the task of reconstructing form and purpose in the blighted world of the present. And if his resistance to a reductive vision of human nature implied an exaggerated concern for physical courage and personal integrity and could only be achieved at the cost of abandoning social commitment and historical consciousness, this was a measure of the profound sense of spiritual malaise which characterized his generation and the desire for meaning which sent Hemingway from battlefield to battlefield, from the open challenge of the big game hunt to the structured drama of the bullfight.

16

Phlebas Sails the Caribbean: Steinbeck, Hemingway, and the American Waste Land

Richard Astro

Though John Steinbeck and Ernest Hemingway are, with William Faulkner, the foremost heirs of the American naturalistic tradition, their works have rarely been studied together for the purpose of yielding the kind of reciprocal insights which might broaden our knowledge about both Nobel prize-winning novelists. One reason for this lack of comparative critical interest is that Hemingway, whose works so often reflect his infamous ingratitude towards those from whom he learned, took little or no interest in Steinbeck's work. Nowhere in Hemingway's canon is there even a passing reference to Steinbeck. Steinbeck often told his wife Elaine that Hemingway was the greatest influence on western writing in the twentieth century. But the Californian was as typically reticent about comparing himself to Hemingway as to any of his contemporaries. And all we really know about Steinbeck's attitude toward Hemingway is that he genuinely admired his work.

But perhaps the central reason why Steinbeck and Hemingway are rarely scrutinized together is that their novels and short stories seem at least a continent and a generation apart, and their styles are almost the direct antithesis of one another. Steinbeck's best writing is marked by a genuinely simple and objectively clear prose idiom which presents, evaluates and gives meaning to uniquely beautiful descriptions of the American landscape and the simple people who live on the land by a code of guileless human virtues. Less concerned with presenting what "could be" or "should be," Steinbeck usually tells us only what "is," a way of seeing he learned from his closest friend, marine bioligist Edward F. Ricketts. In such memorable works as *Of Mice and Men, In Dubious Battle* and *Cannery Row*, Steinbeck employs what Ricketts called the philosophy of "non-teleological thinking" as fictional method and achieves what T. K. Whipple in *Study Out the Land* calls the "middle distance" in which characters are placed "not too close nor too far away" so that "we can see their performances with greatest clarity and fullness."

As an undergraduate at Stanford, Steinbeck learned from Edith Ronald Mirrielees, his creative writing teacher, that the story writer's "medium is the spot light, not the search light." Hemingway's medium, on the other hand, is the search light as well as the spot light, though his "iceberg" technique keeps hidden from view the intelligence behind it. Hemingway rarely comments on the action in his stories, but his strong autobiographical presence and his deliberate creation of a space made meaningful by the author's insistence on what is left out makes it necessary to approach his fiction differently than that of his California contemporary.

Moreover, we generally think of Hemingway as operating within the psychic community where the chief task of the writer is to "create living people; people not characters," since "a *character* is a caricature (*Death in the Afternoon*, p. 191)." But we regard Steinbeck as a novelist of the physical community, and we accept as thematically consistent characters whom Hemingway would surely call caricatures.

Those works by which Hemingway's achievement is usually judged are set primarily in post-World War I Europe, while Steinbeck's most important fiction is set in pre-World War II California. And while we view Hemingway as a two-fisted champion of the individual in a world in which, as the novelist concludes in *Death in the Afternoon,* "the individual is all you ever have and schools only serve to classify their members as failures" (p. 100), we think of Steinbeck as a celebrant of the "school or group consciousness." Following the sound advice of Philip Young, we define Hemingway's world as a constant state of war where morality is harshly pragmatic ("what's moral is what you feel good after") and in which the novelist insists "that we honor a stubborn and nearly hysterical pre-occupation with the profound significance of violence in our time." But we think of Steinbeck as a novelist of affirmation and, in later life, as a rigid moralist who urged man to seek the possible in a world of ever-shrinking possibilities. Hemingway's is the world of the shelled Italian hillside, the bull ring, and the Spanish front. It is, as Young notes in *Ernest Hemingway: A Reconsideration,* an American Guernica where "things do not grow and bear fruit, but explode, break, decompose, or are eaten away." But Steinbeck's is a world of coastal tidepools and long valleys which the novelist studied with enthusiasm and affection and in which he found evidence that "all things are one thing, and one thing is all things."

And yet, despite stark contrasts in style and subject matter, Steinbeck and Hemingway did not think along wholly dissimilar lines. Both were men of this world and they responded in their fiction to conditions commonly felt and interpreted. That Hemingway turned for meaning to the individual as he learns "how to live in it," whereas Steinbeck turned to a broadening group consciousness in the fruit orchards and cotton fields of the Salinas and San Joaquin Valleys, simply reflects two ways of reacting to a common vision, a common experience.

This, of course, was the vision of the 1920's; a vision of the world as a valley of ashes as it is embodied, dramatized and mourned in the most famous and influential poem written in English during the first half of the twentieth century, T. S. Eliot's *The Waste Land* (1922). For in two lesser regarded but nevertheless vitally important novels, Steinbeck's *Cup of Gold*

(1929) and Hemingway's *To Have and Have Not* (1937), the
authors employ the central premises of Eliot's outlook (as it
appears in his masterpiece as well as in such lesser works as
"Gerontion" and "The Hollow Men") to depict the American
wasteland, to portray a world of broken images, a chaos of life
destroyed and meaning shattered.

Cup of Gold is Steinbeck's first novel, written after the
novelist's retreat to California after an unsuccessful venture to
the teeming, frenzied city of New York. Hemingway, on the
other hand, had been concerned with the wasteland theme in
virtually all of his important fiction preceding *To Have and
Have Not.* There are traces of Eliot, whose poems Hemingway
borrowed from Ezra Pound in 1923, in some of the stories in
In Our Time. And in *The Sun Also Rises,* the novelist
transmutes Eliot's wasteland materials into a hard-headed
evaluation of man's stumbling and largely unsuccessful efforts
to achieve that peace "which passeth understanding." As too
many critics have already noted, Jake Barnes is Hemingway's
fisher-king, complete with problems of sexual inadequacy and
a love for angling. The wasteland motif is again present in *A
Farewell to Arms* in which there is not only death by water,
but a protagonist (Lieutenant Henry) who ignores the subjective vision (exemplified by the sensitive priest from Abruzzi)
and makes a spurious and destructive "separate peace."

But it is in *To Have and Have Not* that Hemingway
climaxes his consideration of the fate of the individual in the
wasteland. It is true, of course, that because Hemingway's tale
of Morgan deals with a uniquely American brand of individual
in an unusual wasteland setting, the novel seems less wasteland
fiction than does his treatment of Gertrude Stein's lost
generation in *The Sun Also Rises.* Similarly, the wasteland
motif in Steinbeck's first book is subtle and less distinct than
that in his last novel, *The Winter of Our Discontent.* But
Eliot's poem is chiefly valuable for its power as a universal
metaphor, not confined to specific localities. It is vital and
relevant wherever and whenever the spiritual condition it
depicts exists, and so it interprets not only F. Scott Fitz-

gerald's world of Jay Gatsby, but gives meaning to the quality of life in the small Texas town in Larry McMurtry's *The Last Picture Show*. The condition of *The Waste Land*, as Frederick Hoffman suggests in *The Twenties*, is supra-historical and archetypal. It exists wherever there are crowds of people walking in circles—seeing nothing, knowing nothing. Certainly, Eliot's poem depicts a local situation (post-War London) and contains — as Warren French points out in the opening essay in this book — precisely that topical image of accelerated grimace demanded by Pound in "E. P. Ode Pour L'election de son Sepulchre." But it simultaneously reveals a universal dilemma: Man's loss of meaning and his inability to believe, and his concomitant sentencing to the "rotting house" of a fragmented and rootless society. *The Waste Land* is a searing analysis of the modern condition, and it provided Steinbeck and Hemingway with the category and the imperative for their respective tales of Morgan. So while the violent dreams of primitive freedom embraced by Hemingway's Harry Morgan and Steinbeck's Henry Morgan are distinctly American and find closer parallels in Frank Norris' Moran and A. B. Guthrie's Boone Caudill than in Eliot's Smyrna merchant, what really defeats the Morgans is not their election of violence in and of itself. Rather Henry and Harry Morgan are American Pheonicians who reach the extremities of their conquests and are unable to respond to the demand to "give, control and sympathize."

Just as Eliot drew heavily from Jessie Weston's history of the Grail legend for the title, plan and incidental symbolism of *The Waste Land*, so Joseph Fontenrose finds that the cup symbol accompanied by "frequent round and concave images, and the climactic event, the taking of Panama, the 'Cup of Gold,' indicate that the Grail legend provided the central structure of this [Steinbeck's] novel" (*John Steinbeck: An Introduction and Interpretation*, p. 10). Henry Morgan is Steinbeck's Grail knight who dreams of going to sea and becoming a great adventurer. In a seaport, as he is trying to secure passage to the West Indies, he is betrayed and sold as an

indentured servant to a harsh but foolish and easily manipulated colonial planter. Using his period of indenture to gather
knowledge of the Indies, Morgan later organizes a pirate band
and becomes a daring and much feared buccaneer. Eventually,
he completes his Grail quest by capturing the city of Panama
and the beautiful woman known throughout the Caribbean as
La Santa Roja. But Morgan's golden cup proves counterfeit
when he finds that his successes give him little pleasure.
Finally, he deserts his companions, gains a pardon as well as
knighthood from the British king, marries a beautiful but
banal woman of high station, and retires to Jamaica where he
serves as Lieutenant-Governor of that island until his death.

The finest passages in *Cup of Gold* are those lyric sections
in which Steinbeck celebrates the natural world and depicts its
effects on man; passages which indicate that the novelist was
already beginning to recognize the intricate relationship
between man and the natural environment which serves as a
thematic substratum in so much of his best fiction. But *Cup of
Gold* is really Henry Morgan's story, a study of a human
wasteland in which, as Peter Lisca suggests, Morgan's "exclusive attention to a single purpose [the quest for wealth and
empire] separates him from humanity—the unforgivable sin"
(*The Wide World of John Steinbeck*, p. 27). Morgan captures
his Cup of Gold, but it does him little good. Isolated from his
fellow man, Morgan becomes "a lumpish man," a fool who
searched for meaning through power and "was idiot enough to
think he could get it" (New York: Bantam, 1953, p. 184 — all
subsequent page references are to this edition).

Henry Morgan was not always "a lumpish man." As a child
living in the lush glens of Wales, where "in the pastures great
work horses nervously stamped their feet" and small brown
birds "flew twittering from tree to tree and back again" (1),
Henry's eyes "looked out beyond the walls and saw unbodied
things" (4), and there was "a great quantity of decision" in his
face. Robert Morgan, Henry's father, perceives the "quick,
hard set of his chin," and he knows that " 'this son of ours will
be a great man' " (12). But he simultaneously recognizes that

Henry's greatness will prove meaningless because " 'he will murder every dream with the implacable arrows of his will. This boy will win to every goal of his aiming; for he can realize no thought, no reason, but his own' " (12). In *Cup of Gold,* Steinbeck defines temporal "greatness" as a concomitant of folly, distorted vision and the solipsistic pursuit of empire. Early in the novel, the young Henry learns from Merlin, the strange seer, that he who seeks a material Grail can succeed only if he remains a child:

> "You want the moon to drink from as a golden cup; and so, it is very likely that you will become a great man—if only you remain a little child. All the world's great have been little boys who wanted the moon; running and climbing, they sometimes caught a firefly. But if one grow to a man's mind, that mind must see that it cannot have the moon and would not want it if it could—and so, it catches no fireflies" (19).

Henry remains a child long enough to catch his firefly, but cut off from humanity, he grows lonely. " 'Old Merlin had spoken truth so long ago,' " concedes a grown-up Morgan. For as a man, he is "alone in his success, with no friend anywhere" (91).

Gradually, Henry learns "he had touched all things and watched them pale and shrivel at his touch. And he was lonely" (93). And "April is the cruellest month" when, in the spring of the year, Morgan captures the Cup of Gold only to find it and himself tarnished by the quest. Called by La Santa Roja " 'a babbler, a speaker of sweet considered words, and rather clumsy about it' " (144), Morgan sickens and loses his sense of purpose. Whereas he was once "terrifically constant," he suddenly finds himself " 'dragging a frayed rope, and my anchor gone' " (167). And it is only in the gold he has plundered that he hopes to find the materials "for the making of a new anchor."

> "This is hard and heavy. Its value may fluctuate somewhat in the economic currents, but at least it has a purpose, and only one purpose. It has an absolute assurance of security. Yes, perhaps this is the one true anchor; the one thing a man may

be utterly sure of. Its claws hook tightly to comfort and
security" (167).

Morgan "hooks his claws" to the comfort and security of
material wealth, but still he has " 'no lusts, and my desires are
dry and rattling' " (162). As Lieutenant-Governor of Jamaica,
his duties are, by his own admission, "the duties of appearances," so that he even orders the death of two former pirate
companions simply to maintain his respectability. And on his
deathbed, he is a hollow man who wants little more than to
depart the world "with a decent supply of clean linen."

Like Eliot's Gerontion, another wasteland resident, Morgan has dried out and become dull-headed. He sits in the
"decayed house" of his own rotting dreams, one of Eliot's
"tenants of the house," and "old man driven by the Trades/
To a sleepy corner." And the "deep, mellow pulsation of the
Tone" he hears at the moment of his death is only the last
thought "of a dry brain in a dry season."

Morgan experiences the truth of Gerontion's message that
"unnatural vices / Are fathered by our heroism" and that
virtues "Are forced upon us by our impudent crimes." He is a
western Phlebas, an American Phoenician who, like Fitzgerald's Dan Cody in *The Great Gatsby*, deals in metals. He
"passed the stages of his age and youth/ Entering the
whirlpool," clinging in the end to "the profit and loss." He is a
man who once lived, but who dies "with a little patience."

Clearly then, *Cup of Gold* is Steinbeck's critique of the
solipsistic pursuit of wealth and empire. But problems arise
when one inquires as to the nature of Steinbeck's stated
alternatives to Morgan's distorted Grail quest. For upon
reflection, it becomes apparent that if there is an alternative to
"greatness" in *Cup of Gold,* it is mediocrity. After Morgan
takes Panama, he is told by La Santa Roja that " 'all men who
break the bars of mediocrity commit frightful sins' " (162).
And when he asks Merlin if he ever wanted the moon, Merlin
responds that he did, but failing, found a new gift in failure.

"But there is this gift for the failure; folk know he has failed,
and they are sorry and kindly and gentle. He has the whole

world with him; a bridge of contact with his own people; the cloth of mediocrity" (19).

Merlin attempts to vindicate his philosophy of failure by noting that boys become men when, like great black ants grown to adulthood, they drop their wings and indulge in a "magnificent crawling." But nowhere in *Cup of Gold* does Steinbeck suggest that Merlin's crawling is magnificent at all. The seer recalls when " 'my bitter wings dropped, I was a man and did not want the moon' " (109). But while he tells Henry he is sorry for him, he simultaneously concedes, " 'Mother Heaven! how I envy you' " (20). Similarly, old Robert Morgan admits that " 'my youth went out of me sticking to coins,' " and he admires his son who " 'finds it in his power to vault the mountains and stride about the world' " (10-11). Robert complains bitterly that " 'the only possession I carry about me is a bag of losses' " (108), and he is jealous of young Henry who " 'tests his dreams,' " while " 'I — God help me! — am afraid to' " (109, 12). Little wonder then, that Henry, who drops his wings and ends up "a bound slave on a whole slab of marble" feels sick " 'with a disease called mediocrity' " (161).

It might be argued that *Cup of Gold* is a weak novel because in it Steinbeck is unable to provide his leading character with the kind of meaningful alternative to the pursuit of wealth and power that he later developed with the help of Ed Ricketts and which distinguishes the life styles of the protagonists of such novels as *Tortilla Flat* and *Cannery Row*. But a novel must be judged on the basis of what it contains, not what it leaves out. And *Cup of Gold* does contain a picture of the world as a waste land and in which a Grail quest is undertaken, not by a Faustian character of tragic stature as Peter Lisca suggests, but by an idle dreamer turned sullen bully whose fate seems less tragic than pathetic. And the real horror of *Cup of Gold* is that the novelist poses no satisfying options to Morgan's drive for power, nothing but Robert Morgan's "bag of losses."

Late in the novel, after he is securely established in Jamaica, Henry tells the two pirates whom he has just sentenced to die, that " 'civilization will split up a character, and he who refuses to split goes under' " (187). It is in the nature of things, Steinbeck seems to say, that in the wasteland of the world man has no choice but to "split" in order to survive. So Henry "splits" and follows the mechanical gestures of an existence which is no better than death in life. His is a failure in love, like that of Eliot's Elizabeth and Leicester in *The Waste Land*, and even his marriage (to another Elizabeth) and a life of luxury fails to conceal the emptiness of his passion. Steinbeck's wasteland novel closes without even the possibility of redemption. There is no thunder, no prayer for peace; just a broken Grail knight, a hollow man living in "a cactus land" for whom life ends, not with a bang, but with a whimper.

The central difference between Steinbeck and Hemingway's tales of Morgan is that Hemingway's Morgan does not "split" and so instead "goes under." Like Steinbeck's Henry, Harry Morgan is alone, isolated from humanity by a dream of freedom which is really no more than a dream of violence and unrestraint. But he does not become an old man "driven by the Trades / To a sleepy corner." Ferocious, gloomy, and unsociable, he has so given himself to savagery that for him no compromise with civilization is possible.

Hemingway's only American-based novel (if one excludes *The Old Man and the Sea*), *To Have and Have Not*, initially seems to be Harry Morgan's story, a study in what Hemingway called "the decline of the individual." But for a number of reasons, among them Hemingway's peevish desire to chastise his friends (in this case John Dos Passos and Jack Coles), the Morgan story gradually gives way to a chronicle of Richard Gordon's failing marriage and an account of a group of wasteland creatures aboard yachts in the harbor at Key West. And while Hemingway sacrifices the severe stylistic discipline which accounts for much of the excellence of the Nick Adams stories and *The Sun Also Rises*, in that the book's narrative strands do not cohere or counterpoint, Hemingway does succeed in creating a vivid wasteland panorama, as severe an indictment of the modern world as anything in his entire canon.

Ostensibly a contrast between society's "haves" and its "have-nots" in which the wealthy are really the "have-nots," Hemingway concludes that we are all really "have-nots." Sterility, violence and death are the realities which most comprehensively express Hemingway's sense of the world in the novel. There are no genuine heroes who, according to the precepts of the Hemingway code, acknowledge *nada* but abhor it and struggle courageously and heroically against the void. There are none of Philip Young's "tutors or tyros," who win Pyrrhic victories and impose meaning on chaos.

Carlos Baker sees Hemingway's Morgan, an ex-policeman turned charter-boat fisherman and rum-runner (significantly named Harry instead of Henry — perhaps the counterpoint of the dying writer on the slopes of Kilimanjaro), as a distinctly American type. He is, insists Baker, a nineteenth century frontiersman in a twentieth century situation, a civil disobedient unwilling to content himself with passive resistance. (*The Writer as Artist*, pp. 210-11).

At the beginning of the novel, Morgan tries to support his wife and daughters by chartering his boat to a vacationing sportsman in Havana. When the client loses Morgan's expensive fishing gear and absconds without paying his charter fee, Morgan enters into an agreement to transport some illegal Chinese. In the process, he doublecrosses and murders his associate. Later, he is wounded and loses an arm on a rum-running expedition. His money gone and his boat confiscated, Morgan makes with some ruthless Cuban revolutionaries a desperate bargain which kills him.

Baker is quite accurate in the sense that he defines Morgan as "a lineal descendant of the American frontiersman." He resembles Guthrie's Boone Caudill in *The Big Sky* as Delbert Wylder suggests in *Hemingway's Heroes*, and he possesses qualities which do merit admiration. But he clings to a life-style that is no longer profitable except by violating the law. So while he is a civil disobedient, he is no noble savage.

Hemingway, much like Guthrie, shows that the lapse from
civilization is fatal. Harry's flaw, like Boone's, is the flaw of
the great American myth — his savagery — he becomes a killing
machine, and that course leaves him nowhere to go. In a very
real sense then, Hemingway's westernmost novel is particularly
western in that it reveals the decline of the American west.
Hemingway's Harry is like Guthrie's Boone and unlike
Steinbeck's Henry in that he cannot change his ways. He is an
untamable, but despite Hemingway's life-long admiration for
men with "cojones," he does not apotheosize Morgan as a
"mythic Untamable." Instead, as Wylder suggests, Hemingway
presents Morgan as an Ahab, but a wasteland Ahab whose
monomania does not challenge the meaning of the universe.

"April is the cruellest month" in *To Have and Have Not* as
it is in *Cup of Gold*. For from the opening of Part I
(significantly subtitled "Spring") which details a particularly
violent shoot-out on the streets of Havana, Harry Morgan
learns that murder is the easiest way of doing business. As
Harry learns to live in the terror-ridden world of the novel, he
becomes a selfish man with the courage and integrity of a
bully. " 'You ain't human,' " he is told by Wesley, his Black
rum-running companion, " 'You ain't got human feelings.' "
(New York: Scribner's, 1937, p. 86 — all subsequent page
references are to this edition).

Not only is Harry Hemingway's nautical version of the
American frontiersman attempting to survive in a frontierless
land, he is also his wasteland fisher-king, a fisherman with
limited intelligence and without humility or compassion, who
fishes alone (" 'Anything is better alone,' " [105] Harry
insists), and only for himself (and for his family, he claims,
though he seems not to care for his children). Politically
uncommitted (" 'I ain't no radical,' " Harry tells Albert Tracy,
the pathetic WPA sewer digger who cannot find work "at
living wages anywhere"), Harry is a "bad-spoken bully," a
"bad dream man" who agrees to carry the Cuban revolutionaries solely from self-interest and not from any sense of
commitment to their political objectives. " 'F--- his revolu-

tion,'" Harry thinks to himself after one of the Cubans tells him about the political tyranny which extends over that island state. " 'The hell with their revolutions. All I got to do is make a living for my family and I can't do that'" (168). Described by his wife Marie as "snotty and strong and quick, and like some kind of expensive animal" (258), Morgan is a hostile, insolent man with only his "conjones to peddle," and they prove not to be enough. " 'I guess I bit off more than I could chew.'" Morgan concedes after he is fatally wounded. " 'I shouldn't have tried it.'" (174).

Perhaps the reason why Sheridan Baker sees Morgan as "the last individual," as a beaten but undefeated man of "single-handed and single-minded integrity," is that he does seem almost a tragic figure in comparison with the novel's other characters, some of whom have brief contact with Harry and are humiliated by him. Compared to Morgan who is, as Oscar Cargill puts it in *Intellectual America*, "good in a boat, good in a bed, [and] good in a fix," Richard Gordon is an empty soul who is not good at anything. Gordon is a writer who claims he is writing the great proletarian novel. Really though, he is one of Eliot's hollow men, synthetically stuffed with attitudes and faiths he cannot feel. He and his wife are true wasteland figures for whom love "smells like lysol." Theirs is a kind of "picknose love" which "hangs up behind the bathroom door" (186).

Hemingway peoples the Florida keys with a veritable rogues gallery of the wasteland rich, vacationers from Fitzgerald's "East Egg." Sterile and passionless, they are people with no standards who face no consequences. Some are in flight from reality and follow the tradition set by American literature's premier escapee, Rip Van Winkle, by drinking too much. Seeking freedom and solace, they drink their way through life, never realizing that "plus ca change, plus c'est la même chose." There is Herbert Spellman, an intellectual Mr. Eugenides who describes himself as "a lovely little stork" (198). And there are the miserable Mr. and Mrs. Laughton and the obscenely promiscuous Helenè Bradley. Even Professor

MacWalsey, whom Hemingway treats gingerly (he is based on a composite of two men the novelist admired) and who sobers up long enough to realize that " 'the operations of life must be performed without an anaesthetic' " (221), admits he will return, if only temporarily, to " 'the anaesthetic I have used for seventeen years' " and " 'which is probably a vice for which I only invent excuses' " (222).

Then there are the lost souls on the yachts at the Finger Piers: Henry Carpenter, who plays a machine that "doesn't pay jackpots any more" and who is simply postponing an inevitable suicide; a sixty-year old merchant who thinks "in deals, in sales, in transfers and in gifts" and quiets his worries with Scotch highballs. He is a character with a "bloated little belly" and "now useless equipment that had once been his pride" (234) and is the kind of man who led his business victims to use on themselves "those admirable American instruments so easily carried, so sure of effect, so well designed to end the American dream when it becomes a nightmare. . ." (238). On another yacht there is a "pleasant, dull and upright family" whose money has come "from selling something everybody uses by the millions of bottles, which costs three cents a quart to make, for a dollar a bottle. . ." (340). And on the *Irydia IV,* there is the wanton and solipsistic Dorothy Hollis who, like the women in Eliot's "A Game of Chess," has a severe case of bad nerves. She masturbates and takes luminol in search of the sleep which might ease the pain of a life in which, she concludes, "we all end up as bitches. . ." (245).

Hemingway's "have-nots" fare no better than his "haves." Almost without exception they are "rummies" who reel aimlessly through the pages of the novel. The drunken veterans in Freddy's bar are accurately described by one of their number as " 'the very top cream of the scum' " (205), completely brutalized men who " 'have been beaten so far that the only solace is booze and the only pride is in being able to take it' " (206). Hemingway's treatment of the veterans in *To Have and Have Not* is particularly interesting in view of the fact that in 1935 he championed their cause in *The New*

Masses after 200 of them were drowned in a hurricane through what seemed to Hemingway to be needless bureaucratic neglect. But the epitome of the futile lives of the "have-nots" occurs when the screaming Mrs. Tracy falls into the water after learning of her husband Albert's probable death at sea. Having lost her dental plates, her pathetic cries of " 'Basards! Bishes!' " make her seem more ludicrous than justifiably angry, more a fop than a tragic victim whose "grief is more than she can bear" (253). In this scene, Hemingway has imaged, as Maxwell Geismar notes in *Writers in Crisis*, "our national dental plate" wherein "the rare and few accents of humanity's divine articulation have been reduced to a sort of grotesque mumbling." Interestingly enough, in one of his close-up shots in "A Game of Chess," Eliot notes: "Albert's coming back, make yourself a bit smart. / He'll want to know what you done with that money he gave you / To get yourself some teeth." But in the wasteland of *To Have and Have Not*, Albert will never come back, and it is unlikely that his widow will ever have enough money to get another set of teeth.

Hemingway convincingly demonstrates, as does Eliot in *The Waste Land*, that there is no more vitality among members of the lower class than among those of higher station. Not the class-conscious depression novel that some readers have supposed, *To Have and Have Not* reveals Hemingway's distrust of the usual proletarian panaceas of the 1930's. His proletariat is no more liberated than Eliot's, and like Eliot's, his lower class wastelanders are "red sullen faces [who] sneer and snarl / From doors of mudcracked houses," characters unable to use their consciousness to direct the paths of history. With the exception of Harry, Hemingway's people are essentially one person—practicing the automatic gestures of a life lived in death. As Marie Morgan soliloquizes when she realizes that eventually "you find out everything in this goddamned life," "you just go dead inside and everything is easy. You just get dead like most people are most of the time" (261).

Faced with unsatisfactory options, Hemingway's fisher-frontiersman does merit admiration for his stubborn refusal to "go dead inside." And in a sense, he can hardly be blamed for deciding that "anything is better alone." But though, unlike Steinbeck's Morgan, he does not capitulate to the standards of aristocratic mediocrity (actually, he has no choice in the matter), he is, like Steinbeck's Henry, a Phlebas who dies by water. He too is an American Phoenician, "a dealer in metals," who takes dangerous changes in the pursuit of gain. His death is no heroic sacrifice and results from insufficient cause. Hopelessly trapped in the mire of the American wasteland, his life is a protracted series of negatives in which, as he realizes after he is fatally wounded, a man " 'ain't got no hasn't got any can't really isn't any way out' " (224).

Much has been made of Harry's last remark that " 'a man alone ain't got no bloody fucking chance' " (225)—words which Hemingway tells us had taken Harry all his life to learn. And there are those who would argue that Harry's statement is really Hemingway's call to arms, despite the fact that the novel is not political. But if we regard Harry as Hemingway's fisher-frontiersman as well as his dying Phoenician who fishes but catches nothing in dirty wasteland waters, it seems credible to conclude that Harry's dying statement, which comes as suddenly and as unexpectedly as Eliot's peals of thunder, is but a fictional correlate of Eliot's plea for those human qualities of giving, controlling and sympathizing which, if followed, might "redeem the time." And like Eliot's three verse fragments which offer at least a minimum of hope, Morgan's last words are fragments he has "shored against his ruins." Hemingway's fisher-king is left alone on the Queen Conch, "with the arid plain behind him." But though his London Bridge has fallen down, he attempts to set his own lands in order. Of course, like Hieronymo, he appears "mad againe" to those who hear him ("He had told them," notes Hemingway, "but they had not heard" [225].) But Hemingway, like Eliot, does seem to suggest that recovery is possible.

Steinbeck's Henry and Hemingway's Harry are by no means identical, but they are alike in many ways. Both are "buccaneers" who roam the waters where their namesake's treasure is perhaps still buried. Both are sullen bullies, not very intelligent men, whose schemes of morality are alien to any behavioral code of civilized society. Both are proud men whose pride is the foundation of their aloneness, their refusal to acknowledge their dependence upon others. Both are mythic figures (a Grail knight and a fisher-king) who try to flee the empty mediocrity they see about them, but whose hollow ships collide on the islands of their aloneness. But unlike Steinbeck's Henry, for whom the "deep, mellow pulsation of the Tone" obscures all understanding, Harry Morgan glimpses the promise which exists in what for him, as for Eliot, is an alien culture.

Cup of Gold and *To Have and Have Not* contain similar pictures of an American wasteland. But despite appearances, occasioned by the heavy amount of violence in Hemingway's novel, Steinbeck's vision is the grimmer of the two. For whereas *Cup of Gold* ends with "thoughts of a dry brain in a dry season," Harry Morgan's dying words suggest the tentative hope of a prayer for peace. At the end of *Cup of Gold*, "there was no light anywhere," but at the conclusion of *To Have and Have Not* there is still "the sea looking hard and new and blue in the winter light" (262)

The protagonists in Steinbeck and Hemingway's next novels seek and attain (in alien cultures) that promise of peace glimpsed by Harry Morgan. And while Steinbeck's *To a God Unknown* (1932) and Hemingway's *For Whom the Bell Tolls* (1940) are in many ways wholly dissimilar novels dealing with mutually exclusive settings, characters and situations, the mythic quests by Steinbeck's Joseph Wayne and Hemingway's Robert Jordan are curiously similar. It is impossible and would be inappropriate to examine at length Hemingway's longest and perhaps most important novel and Steinbeck's most cryptic work in the context of this study. But it should at least be pointed out that Wayne and Jordan become true mythic heroes (Wayne is almost a literal Frazerian fisher-king) who plunge through the life's apparent chaos to unite experience and restore meaning.

What Wayne and Jordan learn as they complete what Joseph Campbell calls in *Hero With A Thousand Faces* the "nuclear unit of the monomyth," as they transcend and transmute the infantile images of their personal pasts in a process of mythic self-purification, is that there is a far larger world than that represented by the self. In their journeys they undergo rites of initiation and installation which teach the lesson of the essential unity of the individual and the group. They become dislocated from time and space as they seek and find meaning, not in power or violence, but in being able to give, control and sympathize. And what they find as they soar above the insane, ruthless tragedies of life, what in *Ash Wednesday* Eliot calls the "twisting, turning below," is that for the man who can view life whole—who can become one with all men—and who can, in effect, "care enough not to care," the world is no longer the Morgans' vale of tears, but a bliss-yielding manifestation of presence. Wayne and Jordan come to know eternity and that makes them comprehensive. Both must die, of course, but not before they open the path to what Campbell calls "the light beyond the dark walls of our living death." Each in his own time and in his own tempo fulfills the modern hero-deed: he brings "to light again the lost Atlantis of the living soul."

In a very real sense, John Steinbeck and Ernest Hemingway are authors of and for our time. Despite the obvious differences in plot, character and style in their overall canons, both were similarly affected by and wrote out of the wasteland vision defined by Eliot in 1922, but applicable to the entire western world for a good portion of this century. And both men, after creating American wastelands in their respective tales of Morgan, directed their greatest mythical heroes to the almost unfathomable realization that there is no separateness; and this realization enabled them to achieve Eliot's peace which passeth understanding. Above all, what Steinbeck and Hemingway learned from their wasteland visions is that it is not society that is to guide the creative hero. Rather it is precisely the reverse. Born of two drowning

Phoenicians, Robert Jordan and Joseph Wayne become the archetypal heroes who break through the spheres of their own existence to accomplish that supreme ideal.

17

Faulkner: The Way Out
of the Waste Land

Gene W. Ruoff

Toward the end of the war a party of British infantry, stranded in the barrage zone, attempts to work its way back to the Allied lines. The men blunder into an unmapped depression, which broadens and deepens into a "miniature valley," which seems "a region, a world where the war had not reached, where nothing had reached, where no life is, and silence itself is dead."* As the soldiers follow the valley, they see that it is "a series of overlapping, vaguely circular basins formed by no apparent or deducible agency" (p. 468). Grass bayonets slash at their legs, and odd chalky knobs, which appear at first to be natural formations, are revealed to be the tops of half-buried skulls. As the men descend further, a landslide dumps them into a cavern filled with the reeking

---

*William Faulkner, "Crevasse," *Collected Stories of William Faulkner* (New York, 1950), p. 468. All references to Faulkner's short stories, hereafter cited parenthetically, are to this edition. Other editions cited in the text are *Soldier's Pay* (New York, 1926); *Sartoris* (New York, 1929); *The Sound and the Fury* (New York, 1929); *Sanctuary* (New York [1962]). I have omitted discussion of *Mosquitoes* (1927), which is in many respects very much a Twenties novel; however, it bears little relation to Faulkner's predominant concerns during the decade and has even less relation to his later thematic development.

skeletons of Senegalese troops, still sitting or reclining as they
were when they were killed by gas in the spring of 1915.
Throughout the party's efforts to escape from the tunnel, an
injured man protests, shrilly and deliriously but appropriately,
"A'm no dead! A'm no dead!" (p. 471). Reaching the end of
the cavern, the men break through, out of the putrescent
stench and into open sunlight; but their emergence leaves them
as lost as before.

Faulkner's "Crevasse," which borrows upon the traditional
landscape of Hell in order to portray a landscape of ultimate
waste, is a story in which the demonic elements are all the
more chilling because they are presented (and accepted by the
soldiers) as part of the "natural" produce of war. With such
abundant and efficient human workmanship available, this
valley of death has required few touches of the devil's hand.
"Crevasse" was initially published in *These 13* (1931),
Faulkner's first collection of short stories. It was the last of a
group of four stories—"Victory," "Ad Astra," and "All the
Dead Pilots" are the others—all devoted to the war and all
apparently written after his pilgrimage to Europe in 1925.
Faulkner made the collective subject of these works clear in
1950, when he brought together his *Collected Stories:*
organizing the volume into geographical units, such as *The
Country* and *The Village,* he placed these four stories (together
with "Turnabout," a slightly later work) in a category entitled
The Wasteland.

Although this late classification suggests the degree to
which Faulkner associated the concept of the wasteland with
the ravages of World War I, and "Crevasse" demonstrates the
rather modish skill with which he was able to elaborate this
dominant motif of the Twenties, it was not a central concern
of his writing during the decade. Not until *A Fable* (1954),
Faulkner's attempt at the definitive war novel, does he
organize the torn landscape of Europe into a symbolic
structure as comprehensive and intricate as those which
control such Yoknapatawpha novels as *Absalom, Absalom!*
(1936) and *Go Down, Moses* (1942). During the Twenties

Faulkner's attention is absorbed by the human waste of the war; his settings, both in Europe and in the American South, tend to serve as the grounds of human action and passion rather than their emblematic fulfillment.

The war stories of *These 13* provide an interesting perspective on the concept of waste which runs through the bulk of Faulkner's fiction during the Twenties. The sense of loss which afflicts his characters seems to begin in their deracination. The narrator of "Ad Astra" begins his tale in the following way: "I don't know what we were. . . . we had started out Americans, but after three years, in our British tunics and British wings and here and there a ribbon, I don't suppose we had even bothered in three years to wonder what we were, to think or to remember" (p. 407). All of the characters in the story respond in some way to a fundamental awareness of discontinuity. Even Gerald Bland, the womanizing, self-confident Southerner who appears as one of Quentin Compson's nemeses in *The Sound and the Fury* (1929), has invented the "sweetest little wife" (p. 408) back home, who is the subject of his drunken reveries. Monaghan, Bland's nouveau-riche antagonist, keeps insisting, "I'm shanty Irish. . . . That's what I am. My father was shanty Irish, by God" (p. 415). Comyn, the Irishman who is the only native Britisher of the group, denounces the English monarch and claims "no king since the Ur Neill, God bless the red-haired stern of him" (p. 420). A captured German pilot dragged along on the pilots' barhopping expedition has renounced his aristocratic heritage ("I still say baron I will not be, for it is not good" [p. 418]), and the sensitive and intelligent Indian subadar, considered good enough to attend Oxford but not good enough to become an officer, will endure the racial humiliations of exile rather than return home to power.

The most seriously alienated character of these stories, though, is Alec Gray of "Victory," whose career reveals the psychological perils of military success. Coming from a long line of Scottish shipwrights, Gray enlists in the army, only to be thrown immediately into a penal batallion for refusing to shave. He is returned to his original platoon on the eve of its entry into combat, and as a result of its first raid, during which he brutally murders his sergeant-major, he is cited for heroism and selected to attend a school for officers. Gray rises to the rank of captain and wins another medal before he is gassed and mustered out. He will not or cannot return to the shipyards on the Clyde, electing instead to accept a gentleman's position in London; its duties are ambiguous, but his primary credentials seem to be a proper address, proper clothing, and business cards which read "Captain A. Gray, M.C., D.S.M." (p. 455). After a nostalgic visit to the scene of his triumphs, he returns to England to find that his position has evaporated, and he sinks from guiding Midlands businessmen through "the flesh-pots of the West End" (p. 457) to selling encyclopedias door to door to selling matches on a streetcorner—still ramrod straight and properly attired, however ill and frayed. Gray's military career has unfitted him for civilian life. His potential for violence, which the war revealed and rewarded, has been used for the greater cause, and he has been discarded as so much embarrassing refuse.

For Faulkner the casualties of the war were not just its obvious victims, the physically maimed. Only in his first novel, *Soldier's Pay* (1926), where the flyer Donald Mahon returns to Georgia with his face horribly disfigured and quickly goes blind, do we find any great emphasis on the soldier's symbolic wound. More frequently Faulkner's victims have, like Bayard Sartoris of *Sartoris* (1929), apparently returned whole. Young Bayard's wound is psychic, ostensibly stemming from the loss in combat of his brother John (who figures in both "Ad Astra" and "All the Dead Pilots"); but the novel makes it clear that Bayard misses the wild tumult of the war at least as much as he misses his brother. Bayard's Aunt Jenny, who draws upon her experiences with the men who returned from the Civil War, sees that war incapacitates not because of its suffering but because of the "helling around with no worry and no responsibility and no limit to all the meanness they can think about wanting to do" (p. 53). She adds that Johnny "at least had consideration enough, after he'd gone and gotten himself into something where he had no business, not to come back and worry everybody to distraction" (p. 54). Bayard tries to replace the violence of war with drunken, reckless driving— during which he manages to bring about the death of his grandfather—with hunting, and finally with a short, fatal stint as test pilot in a hopelessly misengineered biplane. Although the glamorous Southern past of Bayard's family is certainly a contributory factor in his quest for self-destruction, a story like "Victory" helps to emphasize the extent to which the central problems of *Sartoris* are contemporary and circumstantial rather than cultural and hereditary. Even Horace Benbow, who returns from YMCA service with a set of glass-blowing gear and the ennui of a decadent poet, has picked up enough taste for disaster to run away with another man's wife, Belle Mitchell. His sister Narcissa admonishes him: " 'Oh, Horry, she's dirty!' 'I know,' he answered unhappily. 'I know' " (p. 199). The mode of death which Horace has chosen is neither so flashy nor so immediate as Bayard's, but it is equally sure.

The narrator of "All the Dead Pilots" says that those flyers who survived the war, unlike Johnny Sartoris, all really died on November 11, 1918: "they are all dead now. They are thick men now, a little thick about the waist from sitting behind desks, and maybe not so good at it, with wives and children in suburban homes almost paid out, with gardens in which they putter in the long evenings after the 5:15 is in, and perhaps not so good at that either: the hard, lean men who swaggered hard and drank hard because they had found that being dead was not as quiet as they had heard it would be" (p. 512). The flyer's experience is paradoxical: the quality called forth, the "courage, the recklessness, call it what you will, is the flash, the instant of sublimation; then flick! the old darkness again. That's why. It's too strong for a steady diet. And if it were a steady diet, it would not be a flash, a glare" (p. 531). There seems to be an ecstasy of action which is analogous to the ecstasy of mystical contemplation, and the danger of either form of experience is that it may unfit man for ordinary human life and emotion. The civilization to which the flyers return need not actually be flat and sterile, because to them it will necessarily seem so. They carry their wasteland with them.

It wasn't even necessary to have participated in the war in order to be ravaged by it. Cadet Julian Lowe of *Soldier's Pay,* who never made it into combat, is as lost a soul as any. Lowe's first encounter with Donald Mahon crisply defines his emotional problem: "He saw a belt and wings, he rose and met a young face with a dreadful scar across his brow. . . . Had I been old enough or lucky enough, this might have been me, he thought jealously" (p. 25). Lowe's letters to the war-widow Margaret Powers, his unwilling intended, tell a pathetic story: "I told mother last night and of course she thinks we are too young. But I explained to her how times have changed. . .how the war makes you older than they used to. I see fellows my age that did not serve specially flying which is an education in itself and they seem like kids to me because at last I have found the woman I want and my kid days are over" (p. 277). Not only has Lowe's war been stolen from him, his youth has also been stolen: he falls into a comic pose of precocious adulthood, which is all the sadder for its being entirely unearned. Although Faulkner undoubtedly carried himself more gracefully than the callow young man ridiculed in his first novel, their military careers are closely parallel. Faulkner left Mississippi for Canada in July 1918 to begin his training as a pilot in the Royal Air Force. The November armistice found him no nearer France, and he returned to Oxford the following month. (For a concise account of the writer's immediate postwar career, see Carvel Collins, ed., *William Faulkner: Early Poetry and Prose* [Boston, 1962], pp. 3-33.) Whatever allowances one may wish to make, Faulkner's postwar stay in and around the University of Mississippi was hardly the most attractive period of his life. The military flair and weary sophistication which he brought to the campus (trying, among other things, to make Ole Miss safe for French Symbolism) seems to have distinguished without especially endearing him. Indeed, if his portrayal of Lowe contains even a breath of self-satire, Faulkner's life after the war did not particularly endear him to himself.

The fact that Faulkner missed the war is crucial to his early fiction in a number of ways. It accounts in part for his glorification of the aviator and for his relative underemphasis on the war's sheer physical destruction. It also explains the insistence with which Faulkner gauges the waste of the war through the figure of the returned rather than the fallen warrior. For Faulkner the most significant aspect of the war was not that it could kill but that it could somehow be loved. Despite the horrors of war, something about it answers basic human desires in a way that nothing else can. Faulkner does not attempt to analyze the motivations of his warlovers, nor do his characters themselves, few of whom are reflective or even articulate. Johnny Sartoris, who conducts a private war with his commanding officer in "All the Dead Pilots," is said to have "a working vocabulary of perhaps two hundred words" (p. 514). When Alec Gray of "Victory" writes his parents from the front, a typical letter reads in full: "I am well. It has not rained in a fortnight. Love to Jessie and Matthew and John Wesley and Elizabeth" (p. 448). Great patches of *Sartoris* are devoted to young Bayard's moody silences. Within these works love of violence is treated not as a symptom of some deeper-seated psychic disturbance but as a fact of the human condition.

However accurate Faulkner's conjectures about the fascination of violence may be, they posed hazards to his development as a writer. *Soldier's Pay,* the war stories, and *Sartoris* are pervaded by a nearly identical sense of futility, which seems to have three alternating voices—a cosmic giggle, a cosmic whimper, and a cosmic sigh. Since these voices seem generally widespread during the Twenties, it may be that the danger which Faulkner faced was not escaping the decade, becoming a fine subject for literary history and sociological analysis, but certainly not presenting any claim to the title of America's greatest novelist. The dangers are clear in *Sanctuary*

(1931), a work whose position within the canon has been subject to some dispute. In *Faulkner: Myth and Motion* (Princeton, 1968), Richard P. Adams notes that the usual way of considering Faulkner's development is to honor his dates of publication, moving directly from *Sartoris* to *The Sound and the Fury*. Adams suggests, though, that *Sanctuary*, a sequel to *Sartoris* in its continuation of the story of Horace Benbow and his sister Narcissa, is logically the next work in the line of Faulkner's growth.

Adams' recommendation is astute, though for reasons beyond those he offers. *Sanctuary* belongs in the discussion of Faulkner's early work because it is basically a thinly disguised war novel. The novel's primary victim, Temple Drake, is in a position analogous to that of Faulkner's fledgling pilots, feeling herself somewhere on the verge of the real thing. A student at Ole Miss and the daughter of a judge, she divides the favor of her company—but no other favors— among the town boys (who have cars), the college boys (who have dances), and one "man," Gowan Stevens (who has experience, having been to the University of Virginia where, as he never tires of saying, they teach you to drink like a gentleman). Stevens shows up to drive Temple to a baseball game at Starkville—drunk as a gentleman, naturally—and in his quest for good liquor takes her to the moonshine still of Lee Goodwin, whose operations have been taken over by the Memphis mob.

At Goodwin's place Temple's initiation into the world of experience is abrupt. Her first tutor is Goodwin's woman, Ruby, who is harshly contemptuous of Temple's collegiate lovelife: "Man? You've never seen a real man. You don't know what it is to be wanted by a real man. And thank your lucky stars you haven't and never will, for then you'd find just what that little putty face is worth, and all the rest of it you think you are jealous of when you're just scared of it. And if he is just man enough to call you whore, you'll say Yes Yes and you'll crawl naked in the dirt and the mire for him to call you that" (p. 57). When Ruby's attempt to help Temple escape fails, the girl falls into the hands of the gangster Popeye. Popeye shoots Tommy, a Negro who tries to protect her, and then—being impotent—rapes her with a corncob.

Temple moves from nightmare to nightmare. Popeye takes her to Memphis, where he installs her as his captive princess in Miss Reba's whorehouse. When Temple's physical agony turns to frustration within the heavy-breathing atmosphere of the brothel, Popeye recruits a stand-in, Red, to service her while he watches. When her lust for Red becomes obvious and Temple refuses to stop seeing him, Popeye has her lover murdered. Temple's degradation is completed when she lies on the witness stand, thus insuring Lee Goodwin's conviction for Popeye's earlier murder of Tommy and inflaming public opinion to the point where Goodwin is brutally lynched. It is Temple's response to her sordid experience that is the key to the novel: she loved it. She is ravished by sexual violence as thoroughly and hopelessly as Alec Gray of "Victory" is ravished by military violence. Indeed, *Sanctuary* is largely an expanded version of "Victory," in which the brothel replaces the battlefield as the place where man's essential corruptibility is revealed.

It is now generally recognized that *Sanctuary* is an excellent novel. Its superiority to the earlier works I have discussed is primarily a result of Faulkner's having found in brutal sexuality a more compelling metaphor than war for humanity's craving for degradation. In addition, the book's settings are thoroughly functional: both the gutted, run-down mansion where Goodwin runs his still and the shabby, lush decadence of Miss Reba's sporting house provide apt images of the spiritual decay which the work treats. In *Sanctuary* Faulkner's conception of human waste has very nearly found its wasteland (Editor's note: a subject developed in detail in the next article.) What may not be fully recognized, though, is the possibility that *Sanctuary* could have been Faulkner's best novel. It is a logical culmination of his early work and represents a dead end for his characteristic Twenties themes. What saved Faulkner's literary career, of course, was the intervention of *The Sound and the Fury* between his writing of *Sartoris* and *Sanctuary*, an intervention which seems almost as miraculous as it was fortuitous.

The strength of *The Sound and the Fury* is not its total absence of wasteland themes. (Ed. note: these relationships are developed in detail in Lois Gordon's subsequent article.) The wholly inarticulate idiocy of Benjy Compson, through whose eyes the first section of the book is narrated, reflects Faulkner's abiding interest in the random, capricious, and inescapable nature of much of human pain and suffering. Quentin Compson, whose internal monologue forms the second section of the novel, is an even more hopeless embodiment of the character of Horace Benbow in *Sartoris.* Horace's implicitly incestuous feelings for Narcissa become explicit in Quentin's attitudes toward his sister Caddy. Horace's etherialized love for Narcissa leads to a classic case of psychic impotence; his sexual drive is drawn toward the tawdriness of Belle and later (in *Sanctuary*) toward the elemental earthiness of Ruby Goodwin, where it cannot be confused with the "love" which he feels for Narcissa and his stepdaughter Little Belle. Quentin's incestuous longings lead him to a total revulsion for the flesh. Unable to abide the thought of his sister's lost virginity, he lies and tells his father he has committed incest, attempting, as his father puts it, "to sublimate a piece of natural human folly into a horror and then exorcise it with truth" (p. 220). After Caddy, pregnant with another man's child, marries a shallow, pretentious scoundrel, Quentin commits suicide. But if Quentin is an even more severely crippled version of Horace, it is interesting that Faulkner kills him off in June of 1910, before the beginning of the war and some eighteen years before the principal action of the novel. This displacement suggests, at least, that Quentin's problems have been isolated and understood as personal and psychological. They are not presented as symptoms of contemporary malaise. Richard P. Adams argues convincingly that the influence of T. S. Eliot, which he finds running throughout the novel, is "especially visible in Quentin's section" (*Myth and Motion,* p. 231). If so, Faulkner has largely put Eliot behind him: the vision of contemporary civilization as a world from which all value has disappeared, in which everything is sullied and human action is necessarily futile, is the vision of an incipient suicide, not of the writer.

Faulkner's true emergence from the waste land comes in what must seem an unlikely place, the monologue of Caddy's youngest brother, Jason. As late as 1955, Faulkner unhesitatingly named Jason Compson as his "unfavorite" character in all his works (*Lion in the Garden: Interviews with William Faulkner, 1926-1962,* ed. James B. Meriwether and Michael Millgate [New York, 1968], p. 225). Broad as the competition is — one thinks of Popeye and of Percy Grimm of *Light in August* (1932) — Faulkner's designation might even be expanded, because Jason is as nasty an individual as has inhabited any novel. Faulkner's treatment of Jason is markedly different from his depiction of Popeye, a congenitally doomed monster who is almost entirely a victim of circumstance. A child of poverty, so severely retarded that he did not learn to walk and talk until the age of four, Popeye is a profane cosmic joke. Jason's meanness, though — evil would be too dignified a term — is volitional. Jason has willed himself free of those troublesome and inconvenient virtues, compassion, honesty, and courage, which Faulkner was fond of calling verities. Thriving upon ethical and cultural disintegration, he has reduced all human contacts to the level of commercial transactions. Michael Millgate cogently summarizes the volitional alienation which underpins Jason's materialistic philosophy: "his is a willed deracination from the community in which he continues to live. . . . it is this very materialism and deracination which makes Jason the one male Compson with any practical competence" (*The Achievement of William Faulkner* [New York, 1966], p. 99).

Within the verbal context of *The Sound and the Fury* the most striking feature of Jason's monologue is its enormous vitality. Whether Jason is commenting on Quentin's suicide ("at Harvard they teach you how to go for a swim at night

without knowing how to swim. . . . you might send me to the
state university; maybe I'll learn how to stop my clock with a
nose spray" [p. 243]), musing on Benjy's financial prospects
("Rent him out to a sideshow; there must be folks somewhere
that would pay a dime to see him" [p. 243]), speculating in
cotton futures and cursing the New York Jews he believes are
robbing him, or himself robbing his niece of the 200 dollars a
month Caddy has been sending for fifteen years, Jason both
speaks and acts with obvious gusto. If he is Faulkner's most
despicable creation, he is also — to this point, at least — his
most formidable. Jason's is the only fully articulate voice in
the novel; indeed, one of the more frightening things about
him is the virtual identity of his private and public voices.
Whatever forces may be splintering the rest of society, Jason's
is a unified sensibility. Unhampered by the past or by
traditional values, he has freed himself to move in a region
which has hitherto been subordinate in Faulkner's work — the
world of immediate cause and effect, in which people work
and scheme and chisel and hoard.

Of course, Jason's values are not unopposed in the novel.
The final section of the work is largely devoted to Dilsey, the
old Negro servant who has raised the Compson children and
who attempts to interpose herself between Jason and his
intended victims, particularly Benjy and his young niece
Quentin. A major problem of the novel, though, is that
Dilsey's steady diligence, human warmth, and Christian compassion are unequal to Jason's challenge. The day-to-day
struggle of keeping the family together is purely a holding
action, and her religious life is so ecstatically apocalyptic
("I've seed de first en de last" [p. 371]) that it is essentially
valueless in dealing with Jason. Dilsey's faith is addressed to
the ultimate problem of evil, offering in compensation for pain
and suffering the eventual salvation of the soul. It can do little
to save the poor flesh itself from human viciousness. *The
Sound and the Fury* ends with Jason in disarray; his niece has
broken into his room and made a run on his private bank,
stripping him of both his savings and his thievings. But if there

is a certain poetic justice in the fleecing of Jason, there is little real comfort to be taken from it, for he has been accidentally and temporarily stalled rather than defeated. His voice has not been answered.

Jason is the first in a line of Faulknerian varmints, a breed which the writer came to classify generically as Snopeses. (His first character named Snopes, Byron of *Sartoris*, is only a lurking sexual psychopath, a sort of apprentice Popeye.) Apparently Faulkner began work on a Snopes novel in late 1926 or early 1927, contemporaneously with his writing of *Sartoris*. However, the first volume of the Snopes trilogy, *The Hamlet*, was not published until 1940, and Jason's monologue in *The Sound and the Fury* remains Faulkner's first full depiction of unvarnished Snopesism in action. Although Faulkner never abanded the concern with absolutes which permeates his early fiction, his discovery of the thematic possibilities of rapacious and unrepentant varmintry had the salutary effect of freeing his vision from its desparate quietism. One of the problems with a wasteland like that of *Sanctuary* is that its corruption is so overwhelming that it becomes almost an honor to be destroyed by it. Indeed, a certain glorification of failure is symptomatic of much literature of the Twenties. There is no redeeming virtue, though, in losing to a Jason or a Snopes. Faulkner never forgets that there are some evils against which man is powerless, but he has learned that there are some evils which can and must be combatted. Jason's monologue opens a potential ground for ethical decision and meaningful human action — a ground which is essentially absent in *Soldier's Pay, Sartoris,* and *Sanctuary.* The Snopesian voice is answered in the later novels by Faulkner's narrators, Gavin Stevens, V. K. Ratliff, and Charles Mallison; but as early as *As I Lay Dying* (1930) Faulkner begins exploiting his discovery that something indeed can be done. In that work the Bundren family endures fire, flood, a touch or two of madness, and other assorted catastrophes, yet still manages to take the body of the mother, Addie, to Jefferson for burial. As homely as the purpose of their journey is, and as beset by both comedy and horror, its successful completion outweighs in human value the combined achievements of Faulkner's wasteland protagonists, Bayard Sartoris, Horace Benbow, and Quentin Compson.

Faulkner did survive the wasteland, perhaps more successfully than any other writer in the language who came to maturity during the Twenties. He found no cures for its problems, no spiritual anodyne which could make the soul less violable or its corruption less absolute, and certainly no cultural formula which would restore society to a golden age. What he found was a different set of problems which gave a new voice to his fiction, a set of problems which was at once closer to the immediate needs of the human condition and less subject to the vagaries of history. He did not win his way out of the wasteland in order to fall victim to the hysterical pamphleteering of the depression era or to the existential doomstering which attended the holocaust and the bomb. His fiction continued for nearly thirty years to deal boldly with both contemporary and historical issues, but it could never again be dated by its ideological trappings.

18

Sanctuary:
Yoknapatawpha's Waste Land

James E. Miller, Jr.

I

In *The Novels of William Faulkner,* Olga Vickery groups *The Sound and the Fury, As I Lay Dying, Light in August,* and *Absalom, Absalom!* for treatment under the title, "The Achievement of Form." She separates *Sanctuary* for treatment under a later section, "The Pursuit of Theme," in a chapter combining it with *Requiem for a Nun.* In effect, her order of treatment represents her value judgment. And she opens her discussion of *Sanctuary* by referring to the "bizarre and exaggerated brutality" of its events. In his book *William Faulkner,* Irving Howe writes of *Sanctuary:* "Faulkner's occasional clumsiness in handling shock and his failure to provide dimension for his characters, trouble the shape of the book." In *The Achievement of William Faulkner,* Michael Millgate refers to distracting passages in *Sanctuary* that appear "mechanically contrived," to a "certain overstrenuousness" and "extraordinary emphasis on descriptions of the characters' eyes," and to "a slightly arbitrary extravagance about the imagery" throughout the book.

Remarks of this kind, expressing puzzlement and critical reservation, can be found scattered throughout Faulkner's best commentators when they come to *Sanctuary.* And there can be no doubt that these remarks and asides represent an attempt to get at something important and jarring in the novel, and it is that something that should be dealt with at the outset. It is encountered on the opening pages of the work.

Horace Benbow bends over a stream to get a drink of water. "Somewhere, hidden and secret yet nearby, a bird sang three notes and ceased" (3).* As he rises, he sees Popeye's straw hat reflected in the water. He looks across the stream at Popeye: "His face had a queer, bloodless color, as though seen by electric light... he had that vicious depthless quality of stamped tin." Again, "the bird sang...three bars in monotonous repetition." As the encounter deepens in sinister overtones, the two men freeze. "They squatted so, facing one another across the spring, for two hours." Occasionally the bird sounds its single notes, and occasionally the sound of a passing automobile is heard, but still the men squat. Popeye's hands are "little, doll-like hands," and his face like the "face of a wax doll set too near a hot fire and forgotten." His eyes "looked like rubber knobs," and seemed to have the "whorled smudge of the thumb on them." When finally the two men proceed on their way, Popeye in command and in the lead, his "tight suit and stiff hat all angles," he looks like "a modernistic lampstand." And they make their way to the Old Frenchman's Place: "A moment later, above a black, jagged mass of trees, the house lifted its stark square bulk against the failing sky" (pp. 4-7).

In short, the two men walk out of this world into the world of the novel; out of a realistic world into a world bizarre and surrealistic. Indeed, they were already in an unrealistic world as they squatted for two hours by that stream. Two hours? Could real people walk after such a stint of squatting? The critical question that these opening pages fling out is whether Faulkner was trying for reality and misfiring, or whether he was trying for something else — a trans-real

---

*Page numbers in the text refer to the Modern Library edition of *Sanctuary*, which contains Faulkner's 1932 Introduction.

quality, an absurd and nightmarish quality — and actually succeeding superbly well.

The world that Faulkner is creating for his novel in this opening chapter is compounded of many elements, drawn from a variety of sources. Perhaps the most obvious are gangster and detective books and movies. Faulkner grew fond of using such material for serious fiction (as in *Knight's Gambit* and *Intruder in the Dust* and elsewhere). Benbow, following Popeye in the opening scene, sees "the continuous jerking of the hat from side to side as Popeye looked about with a sort of vicious cringing. The hat just reached Benbow's chin" (7). There is here, in this cinematic-like scene, as frequently elsewhere in the novel, a curious mixture of the sinister and the ridiculous, of the grim and the absurd, of the ominous and the funny. But there are, too, other sources and models for Faulkner, and perhaps the one most clearly delineated is the comic strip. As a matter of fact, it is difficult to read the first chapter of *Sanctuary* without seeing the action in a series of frames with occasional balloons containing appropriate dialogue.

Several frames might well be devoted to Horace Benbow and Popeye at the spring. Even the bird, with its three distinct notes, could be portrayed in a frame. Popeye himself is described in the old one-dimensional terms of a comic strip character, and his rubber knob eyes could even, in a close-up, show the thumb whorls. The two-hour squat face to face across the spring could probably achieve its only natural representation in a comic strip. The walk from the spring to the Old Frenchman's Place has the mechanical quality easily adaptable to the frame of a comic strip. And it is difficult not to visualize the house itself as it looms mysteriously up against a "failing sky" in a frame all by itself.

All this is not to say that Faulkner was competing with comic strips as a form, but merely that he was striving for a deliberate distortion of reality not unlike the distortion of the comic strip world. He is drawing the reader into a world where his usual sense of normality and of cause and effect will be jarred and upset, where incongruities will abound, and where the sinister and the absurd will intermingle and meld into one another with imperceptible shifting. In such a world it is pointless to object to one-dimensional characters: it is just such characters that help create and establish the world to begin with.

If the bird with its single distinct notes in the first chapter of *Sanctuary* happens to suggest the nightingale of T. S. Eliot's *The Waste Land,* which sings " 'jug jug' to dirty ears," it might just be a part of Faulkner's intention. It is only the first of a number of echoes of the famous poem in the novel. Faulkner's natural setting has none of the innocence usually associated with the natural scene. On the contrary, Popeye's presence, with all his mechanistic qualities, is profoundly subverting. And even the bird sings his three bars "in monotonous repetition: a sound meaningless and profound out of suspirant and peaceful following silence which seemed to isolate the spot, and out of which a moment later came the sound of an automobile passing along a road and dying away" (4). "Twit twit twit / jug jug jug jug jug jug / so rudely forced." Eliot's nightingale, Philomel, sang of her rape; Faulkner's "fishing-bird" perhaps prophesies one.

There is much in the landscape around the Old Frenchman's Place to evoke Eliot's poem. When, further along in the novel, Temple Drake appears on the scene, one of the characters that unnerves her and finally begins to haunt her is the old blind man. Early in her appearance, in her attempt to escape his "sight," she runs off a porch and ends up "on hands and knees in a litter of ashes and tin cans and bleached bones" (42). But she is soon to discover that this "sanctuary" offers no place to hide, and especially no place to hide from the seeming omnipresence of the old blind man. With his tapping cane, he seems to be following her, and she flees. Cornered in her flight, she darts about erratically in the rooms of the house. At one point on hearing the approach of his "dry tapping," she rushes to the kitchen and clutches the box holding Ruby's baby and tries to pray—in a kind of grotesque rendering of a Madonna and child scene: "...she could not think of a single designation for the heavenly father, so she began to say 'My father's a judge; my father's a judge' " (50).

In the violent rape scene that lies quietly like a time bomb at the heart of *Sanctuary*, Temple finds herself cornered in a crib of the barn, confronting a crouching rat, prevented from escape by Tommy guarding the barn door. The men of the Old Frenchman's Place circle restlessly about the barn, as images blur and recur. But one image that reappears and expands is that of the old blind man sitting on the porch, "his face lifted unto the sun" (89). Indeed, Faulkner's deliberate blurring of the sequence of events seems intended in part to let the old man's presence dominate the scene in which he does not actively participate. Popeye drops from above into the crib with Temple, and begins his perverted assault with the corn cob (the reader, of course, not to discover precisely what is going on until later). Temple's response to her rape is directed to the old blind man who exists for her only as a kind of presiding image and deity: "...she began to say Something is going to happen to me. She was saying it to the old man with the yellow clots for eyes. 'Something is happening to me!' she screamed at him, sitting in his chair in the sunlight, his hands crossed on the top of the stick. 'I told you it was!' she screamed, voiding the words like hot silent bubbles into the bright silence about them until he turned his head and the two phlegm-clots above her where she lay tossing and thrashing on the rough, sunny boards. 'I told you! I told you all the time!' " (99).

It is left to Horace Benbow, in recalling for his sister his experiences at the Old Frenchman's Place, to raise the old blind man to the mythic level of a seer-prophet: "And that blind man, that old man sitting there at the table, waiting for somebody to feed him, with that immobility of blind people, like it was the backs of their eyeballs you looked at while they were hearing music you couldn't hear; that Goodwin led out of the room and completely off the earth, as far as I know. I never saw him again. I never knew who he was, who he was kin to. Maybe not to anybody. Maybe that old Frenchman that built the house a hundred years ago didn't want him either and just left him there when he died or moved away" (105). Mysterious in origin, omnipresent, seeing nothing yet seeing all, suffering for self and others, the old blind man is clearly related in function to Eliot's Tiresias.

At the heart of *The Waste Land,* in the middle of "The Fire Sermon," Tiresias becomes the presiding voice of the poem: "I Tiresias, though blind, throbbing between two lives, / Old man with wrinkled female breasts, can see / At the violet hour, the evening hour that strives / Homeward, and brings the sailor home from sea." What Eliot's Tiresias sees through his transcendent blindness is the tired seduction of the typist by the "young man carbuncular." But of course, Tiresias does more than see: "And I Tiresias have foresuffered all / Enacted on this same divan or bed; I who have sat by Thebes below the wall / And walked among the lowest of the dead." Tiresias is a participant in the young man's assault on the bored typist, but in his male-female identity he obscurely plays both roles, suffers for both seducer and seduced. In his notorious footnotes, Eliot tells us: "What Tiresias *sees,* in fact, is the substance of the poem." Is what the old blind man *sees* in Popeye's "rape" of Temple the meaning of *Sanctuary*? The reader's attention is deflected by the sensationalism of the corn cob, which he will witness later in the courtroom. But perhaps the old man senses the presence of twisted passions that destroy, in contrast to the life-giving sun to which he turns. And of course it is to him that Temple turns as a kind of confessor in the middle of the violation of her body (temple); it is his image she conjures up when in need of someone to share her outrage, however compounded it might be of hidden pleasure.

In drawing on the resources of high culture and low, of modern poetry and comic strips, and in creating a world of highly stylized characters and elements, Faulkner made *Sanctuary* probably his most contemporary book. Like the "realism" of recent American fiction, *Sanctuary's* stylized

realism is a strange mixture of the actual and the semi-
allegorical, the everyday and the extraordinary—all artfully
contrived to convey a more acute sense of the way things
really are than traditional realism can. And the way things
really are is rather horrible. We have become accustomed to
talking about our own time as so intrinsically awful and reality
so unbearable that we have granted the novelist the privilege of
abandoning traditional realistic techniques and of adopting
more stylized as well as more shocking methods and strategies.
In "The Fiction Writer and His Country," Flannery O'Connor
has provided a rationale for these new techniques: "...you have
to make your vision apparent by shock—to the hard of hearing
you shout, and for the almost blind you draw large and
startling figures." Faulkner anticipated and foreshadowed
these techniques in *Sanctuary,* and achieved in the process a
higher or transcendent or an essential reality. What Faulkner
did in *Sanctuary* connects in many fascinating ways with what
Flannery O'Connor does in *Wise Blood,* Joseph Heller in
Catch-22, Thomas Pynchon in *V.,* Ken Kesey in *One Flew
Over the Cuckoo's Nest,* Kurt Vonnegut, Jr., in *Cat's Cradle,*
or Jerzy Kosinski in *The Painted Bird.* All of these novelists at
various points violate our sense of reality, but at these very
points they all, too, give us a transcendent sense of the world
that is so real that it is painful, when it is not hilarious. Often
it is both, simultaneously. Comedy and humor play no small
part in these recent works, and it plays a similar important
part in *Sanctuary*.

II

The comedy of *Sanctuary* not only delights the reader but
also startles him—because of its context of violence, brutality,
degradation. Perhaps because he is startled, the reader is
discomfited by the humor, shamed in the vague realization
that he is laughing where he should be serious, is giggling
where he should be sympathetic, is amused where he should be
repelled. If this novel is, as some critics have claimed,
Faulkner's darkest, why should the reader get a kick out of

reading it? Didn't, indeed, Faulkner make a mistake by inserting comedy in an essentially serious work, thereby diminishing its impact? Lawrance Thompson (in *William Faulkner: An Introduction and Interpretation*) may serve as a typical example of critical reaction. He cites examples of Faulkner's comic scenes and then comments: "Such entertaining lapses into burlesque do obviously constitute artistic faults; but they at least heighten the reader's awareness that Faulkner is consistently employing variants on the comic and satiric mode, as a means of keeping his moral indignation under artistic control" (p. 114). Thompson's charge that Faulkner's satire descends too frequently to burlesque may be admitted — or rather, it may be admitted that much of Faulkner's comedy is a form of burlesque: whether burlesque is a "lapse" from satire is a question that does not seem as critically relevant to *Sanctuary* as the simple question whether the comic scenes, satire or burlesque, destroy the book's serious tone and meaning.

In short, are the comic scenes simply a mistake, a means for Faulkner of keeping his "moral indignation under artistic control" (as Thompson suggests), or do they serve some other purpose? As a matter of fact, *Sanctuary* is not divided neatly into serious and comic scenes, but almost all the episodes are some curious mixture of the two elements. That opening scene is shot through with comic detail, and the very movement of the action hovers precariously on the thin line separating the humorous and the serious. Other scenes, like the confusing and multiple and continuous pursuit of Temple through the night at the Old Frenchman's Place, are implicit with comedy, and there are even comic overtones, however muted, to the novel's central event of horror — Popeye's use of a corn cob to rape Temple (some of these are suggested when Temple tells the story of the rape to Horace Benbow, "with actual pride, a sort of naive and impersonal vanity"). Thus the so-called comic scenes do not represent the introduction of elements generally foreign to the novel. Considered in their context, they appear to be in their natural setting, and represent the surfacing and coming into central focus of an element that runs through all the novel. Indeed, the comedy and horror are so closely intertwined in *Sanctuary* that no single scene is so "pure" as not to posit, at some depth or level, the opposite of its main emotional coloring and impact: the comic has sub-strata of horror, and the horror has its sub-strata of the comic. Perhaps somewhere in this mixed structure lies the novel's ultimate meaning.

The comic scenes that have attracted the most critical attention are those in Chapters XXI and XXV, the first telling the story of Virgil and Fonzo Snopes's puzzled stay at Miss Reba's house in Memphis, the other describing Red's funeral at the roadhouse followed by a small gathering (including the small boy, Uncle Bud) at Miss Reba's to mourn Red's death. In concentrating on these scenes, critics have sometimes forgotten their setting. Fitted neatly in between them, in the long Chapter XXIII, appear the scenes that give the most graphic and repellent descriptions of the corn cob rape (as narrated by Temple to Horace Benbow), and the scenes of intensest nausea experienced by Horace in reaction to what he has witnessed and heard. Thus, two comic highlights are intersected by the novel's grimmest elements, reminders of the terrible event that lies at the center of the novel's action, and they are followed swiftly by the trial and conviction of Lee Goodwin and his lynching by burning (Chapters XXVI-XXIX). It is hard to believe that this structuring was careless on Faulkner's part. Indeed, the back-to-back juxtaposition of the comedy and horror is so striking and deliberate that Faulkner must have been counting on some kind of fused effect.

Virgil and Fonzo rent rooms at a place they take to be a hotel but which turns out to be Miss Reba's. As they lie in bed hearing the mechanical piano and the numerous voices, they speculate on what is going on. First they think Miss Reba must have a big family; then they decide it is a party. Later they wonder what business she is in, and, when they find a woman's undergarment around the wash stand, they decide she is a dressmaker. They count themselves lucky to find a brothel

nearby, but Virgil is cautious of the value: "Aint nothing
worth three dollars you caint tote off with you" (190). The
reader is likely to find all this amusing until he recalls that this
is the same house that houses Temple as prisoner, and until he
remembers that the sexual itch or compulsion moving Virgil
and Fonzo is the same that, in a perverted form, drove Popeye
to his rape of Temple. And the chapter closes with the
entrance of the repulsive "Cla'ence" Snopes who leads his
country kinsmen to a Negro brothel, where they see "a room
filled with coffee-colored women in bright dresses, with ornate
hair and golden smiles" (192).

Following on the heels of this sexual comedy (with its
sinister undertones) comes the full force of the book's sexual
horror. Horace Benbow seeks Temple out at Miss Reba's (he
has bought the information from Cla'ence Snopes) and gets
the full account of her rape in her own irrational narrative
(which in its whimsy has its comic undertones). Horace
Benbow is profoundly shocked by what he hears: "He thought
of her [Temple], Popeye, the woman [Ruby], the child,
Goodwin, all put into a single chamber, bare, lethal, immediate
and profound: a single blotting instant between the indignation and the surprise" (213-14). But even this vision of
"cauterising" all the principal actors in the drama "out of the
old and tragic flank of the world" does not leave Horace in
peace. He has been shaken to the roots of his soul, and he
suddenly identifies the "voice of the night" as "the friction of
the earth on its axis" (215) — a vision that affirms the
inevitability of man's — and woman's — sexuality. He is forced
finally to confront his own deep-down terror at his step-
daughter's sexuality as he identifies her with Temple at the
moment of the rape, hears the corn shucks sounding beneath
her thighs, and rushes in panic, nausea, and dread into the
bathroom to collapse and vomit. This may be for Horace his
lowest moment, his moment of clearest self-knowledge, and
the moment when his defeat by the "evil" he battles is
determined. If his stepdaughter is Temple, can he be — can he
contain — Popeye? Is the murderer of Tommy within? How

sensitive can a sensitive man be and still function in the world? Finally all he hears is the "furious uproar of the shucks" (216).

If the Snopes sexual comedy offers ironic contrast to the horror of the novel's central sexual violence, so the murder of Red and his surrealistic funeral offer ironic contrast to the novel's other murders and their violent consequences. Red's murder, committed off stage, results in nothing more than a grotesque funeral orgy during which, at one point, the body rolls out of the coffin on to the floor, where the bullet hole through his forehead lies exposed to view. The sentimentality, drunkenness, and desire for pleasure and sensation all flow together to form a picture both bizarre and refracted — as though seen through a rain-sheeted window.

In contrast, the earlier murder of the "feeb" Tommy sets in motion the major action of the novel. But the action set in motion is as bizarre in a way as Red's funeral, and as far removed from genuine justice as the funeral from genuine piety. The final consequence, inasmuch as any consequence in Faulkner's universe can be "final," is another murder, that of Lee Goodwin by a lynch mob. Although Lee Goodwin is innocent of any crime, having neither raped Temple nor killed Tommy, his death gives the townspeople great psychic satisfaction: he is their scapegoat for their own furtive desires to rape Temple and commit violence ("I saw her. She was some baby. Jeez. I wouldn't have used no cob" [287].).

Sexuality and death thus offer Faulkner both his comic and serious themes in *Sanctuary.* Looked at one way, they are comic; looked at another way, they are grotesque and horrible. By bringing the two perspectives so close together, Faulkner was implying something about the nature of human experience itself: that it absurdly contains, at one and the same time, the comic alongside the tragic — humor in the horror.

III

Cleanth Brooks, in *William Faulkner: The Yoknapatawpha*

Country, states flatly that *"Sanctuary* is clearly Faulkner's bitterest novel." Why he thinks this is so he does not make entirely clear. But even more puzzling is why he does not analyze this novel in the moral frame with which he opens his work, claiming that there are two moral standards in Faulkner's world (as in his southern heritage) — a sense of community and a "still vital religion with its cult, creed, and basic norms of conduct." Of all Faulkner's novels, *Sanctuary* should have presented Brooks the greatest challenge to his thesis, but he evades the challenge. Perhaps the reason is that *Sanctuary's* intense bitterness lies in its insight into the hypocrisy and hollowness of both the religion and the community presented in the novel.

The very title of this novel, *Sanctuary,* has traditional religious connotations. But as one reads into the novel, he discovers that those connotations are ironic. No one finds genuine sanctuary in the novel, but what little shelter is discovered is found *in spite of* community and religion. The house symbolism is intricate and rich, beginning with the Old Frenchman's Place, including Miss Reba's establishment in Memphis, and running through a variety of institutions and places in Jefferson. It is one of the novel's major ironies that the two places that offer more comfort and shelter, more genuine human communion, than any other are the whore house in Memphis and the jail in Jefferson. One of these is outside the pale of community and religion, the other created to impose punishment on their enemies.

Sanctuary presents one of Faulkner's bleakest accounts of southern religion. Its debased state is summed up best, perhaps, in the symbolism of the heaven-tree (the ailanthus) that stands next to the jail: "The last trumpet-shaped bloom had fallen from the heaven-tree at the corner of the jail yard. They lay thick, viscid underfoot, sweet and oversweet in the nostrils with a sweetness surfeitive and moribund, and at night now the ragged shadow of full-fledged leaves pulsed upon the barred window in shabby rise and fall" (122). This repulsive tree represents the full, dark fruition of a religion that finds its contemporary meaning in the institution of the jail. Like the tree's fallen blooms, the church has become "oversweet" with a "sweetness surfeitive and moribund." There is nothing left but the stench of sentiment and dead dogmas. It is no wonder that in this strange community, the jail offers greater sanctuary than the church. As Horace reports to Miss Jenny: "This morning the Baptist minister took him [Lee Goodwin] for a text, not only as a murderer, but as an adulterer; a polluter of the free Democratico-Protestant atmosphere of Yoknapatawpha county. I gathered that his idea was that Goodwin and the woman should both be burned as a sole example to that child; the child to be reared and taught the English language for the sole end of being taught that it was begot in sin by two people who suffered by fire for having begot it" (123-24).

In Jefferson, it is difficult to separate religion and community, as the community justifies its terrible anti-human behavior in the name of the religion. Ruby and her baby are confronted with the need for sanctuary in Jefferson, as they await the trial of Lee Goodwin, her man and the baby's father. It is the good "church ladies" of the town who pressure the hotel proprietor to evict the mother and child. Horace Benbow asks, "You mean to say you let the Baptist church dictate who your guests will be?" (175). As the proprietor makes excuses, Horace asks where Ruby and her baby have gone. The proprietor does not know, but he says, "I reckon somebody took her in, though." "Yes," Horace replies, "Christians. Christians" (175). Indeed, nobody has taken the woman in — and, on the contrary, the townspeople have seen it as their Christian duty to run her out of town. Horace's sister, Narcissa, proves the most "Christian" of all in betraying her brother to force him to stop supporting Ruby and defending Goodwin (she gives the district attorney, in charge of prosecuting Goodwin, enough information to find Temple and use her to destroy Horace Benbow's case at the trial). Ruby's sanctuary does, finally, turn out to be on the edge of town, in an old shack occupied by "an old half-crazed white woman who was believed to manufacture spells for Negroes" (193). It is a strange place: "All night a dim light burned in the crazy depths of the house . . ." (193). At almost any hour of the day, Negroes could be seen entering or leaving. Although Faulkner leaves this sanctuary in considerable shadow, it appears that the old woman and her establishment represent a vitality that has run out entirely from the institutional Christianity in the community. In many ways, the half-mad woman appears to represent in the novel something of the same nature represented by Madame Sosostris, the "famous clairvoyante" with the "wicked pack of cards" (with which she prophesies the poem) in T. S. Eliot's *The Waste Land.* Both figures represent an energy, integrity, and earnestness (however superstitious) that have disappeared from religious belief.

IV

The concluding chapter of *Sanctuary* presents Popeye's background, describes his hanging for a murder he did not commit, and shows, finally, Temple and her father in Paris, bored, detached, restless. The action of the novel has in a sense already been completed. Lee Goodwin has been lynched by the self-righteous and "Christian" community for a crime he did not commit, and Horace Benbow has returned to the home and wife that, at the opening of the novel, he was trying to escape. He has been soundly defeated in his efforts to cope with an evil he does not fully understand by a community bent on maintaining its myths of innocence and respectability. Horace's return home appears to be a capitulation to those myths, an acknowledgement of defeat and loss of self, and a return to the spiritual and moral paralysis from which he had feebly tried to escape. He has perhaps gained the self-knowledge of his futile psychic involvement with his step-daughter, Little Belle, and recognizes that he must reconcile himself to her loss of sexual innocence.

In trying to come to terms with *Sanctuary's* last chapter,

critics have found themselves either baffled or disapproving. Irving Howe, for example, writes: "Only in the last chapter, a perfunctory summary of Popeye's early life, does Faulkner stumble." Allen Tate, in an Introduction to a paperback edition of *Sanctuary*, writes: "Awkward as the conclusion may be, and anti-climactic as the mere expository account of Popeye and Temple is at the end, it is difficult to imagine a resolution to the violence at the center of the novel. There is nothing to be resolved."

Much of the difficulty with the conclusion springs from the difficulty with coming to terms with the character of Popeye throughout the novel. He is one of the most vivid and memorable of all Faulkner's characters, a creature of horror who seems to be something of a cross between T. S. Eliot's hollow man (headpiece filled with straw) and Sweeney (but because he is impotent, not "Sweeney Erect") — with something thrown in too of *The Waste Land's* fisherking, sexually crippled in a dry and burnt out land. But more than these or any combination of them, Popeye is himself and unique. It is usual for the critics of *Sanctuary* to make some such remark as this by Dorothy Tuck (in *Crowell's Handbook of Faulkner*): "Popeye is a figure of pure evil." What does such a description mean?

Faulkner sheds some light on Popeye in some of the conversations recorded on his work. In *Faulkner in the University:* "Q. In *Sanctuary*, Mr. Faulkner, is the character of Popeye emblematic of evil in a materialistic society? What would he stand for? A. No, he was to me another lost human being. He became a symbol of evil in modern society only by coincidence but I was still writing about people, not about ideas, not about symbols" (p. 74). In *Faulkner at West Point:* "Q. Sir . . . Did you see or do you see Popeye and Joe Christmas as being similar people? A. Not at all. Popeye was the monster . . . Q. Sir, did Popeye have the same problem of not having a society to belong to; A. Now I don't understand Popeye. He, to me, was a monster. He was just there" (p. 83).

If we, with Faulkner, see Popeye as "another lost human

being," or as a "monster," it is difficult at the same time to label him "a figure of pure evil." Such a label, if it means anything, means that he is some kind of satanic villain, deeply motivated and fiercely committed to do evil. Such, of course, is simply not the case. As readers and critics, we have yearned to heap blame on Popeye for all the terrible events of *Sanctuary*, and we have been upset in finding out that his frail figure will not bear the weight of our wrath. Indeed, Faulkner planned it that way as a trick on his audience, a trick designed to bring self awareness and insight.

Did Faulkner fumble in summarizing Popeye's background in the last chapter of *Sanctuary?* There is a little-known account of *Sanctuary's* conclusion by the Englishman Jonathan Cape, one of Faulkner's publishers, in J. Maclaren-Ross's *Memoirs of the Forties:*

> Our New York branch did *Sanctuary*, though Chatto and Windus brought it out over here because they'd a contract as his British publishers. Faulkner wrote it while I said to him "This is all very well, but I'd like to know more about Popeye's background, where he came from and so on, also why he's impotent like this." And Faulkner said: "Why it's all there in the first chapter, all about his parents and childhood." Well I looked back through the first chapter but damned if I could find anything like that except that Popeye was scared of birds, so then Faulkner himself had a look. "By God, he said, "If I haven't forgotten to write it after all!". . . He went off back to his watchman's shack and over a jug of corn liquor got out the missing chapter. But by that time the book was being printed, and we couldn't fit it in at the beginning, so Faulkner said: "Let's put it in last and the hell with them." So that's how the book comes to be constructed like that. Faulkner was most apologetic about it, couldn't think how it had come to slip his mind (p. 19).

This is a fascinating account, but perhaps betrayed by its glibness. It does not square with what Faulkner has said about improving his work in revising *Sanctuary*, nor with what we know about the revision from the preservation of the original proofs. But most important of all, this account presents Faulkner as an ordinary novelist simply concerned about sticking in information about a character's background. We know from Faulkner's other great novels that he simply did not work that way. We can, I think, only assume that in this episode, Faulkner was spoofing Jonathan Cape, or that Cape is misremembering or embroidering an event of the past.

Popeye's background, had it been given early in the novel, would change entirely the way we read *Sanctuary.* There can be no doubt that Faulkner was fully aware of this simple fact. As the novel is now structured, Popeye is the first character to appear in the novel, and he is a sinister presence throughout, his rubber-knob eyes haunting the appalling action as it unfolds (not unlike the eyes of Dr. T. J. Eckleburg haunting *The Great Gatsby,* but of course to different effect). It is Popeye who has committed the rape with a corn cob, who has killed Tommy, who kills Red — who, in short, sets all the events in motion that bring a train of disasters in their wake which disrupts the community and destroys the innocent. Just as we have inflated his image to bear the weight of all his guilt, perhaps even smug in our satisfaction in having a scapegoat to blame for all the novel's evil, we discover in the novel's last chapter that he is indeed a hollow man made of stamped tin and rubber eyes, that he is indeed simply "another lost human being," that he is indeed a "monster." He had no hair until he was five years old, and the doctor told his mother that alcohol would kill him: "And he will never be a man, properly speaking. With care, he will live some time longer. But he will never be any older than he is now" (300). We discover, perhaps to our horror, that we have been heaping our hatred on a child-man, devoid of the normal attributes of a human being, a monster more to be pitied than blamed, a creature simply unworthy of the grandiose role of evil-doer that we want to assign him. His birth on Christmas day perhaps brings to mind, ironically, W. B. Yeats's "The Second Coming": "And what rough beast, its hour come round at last,/ Slouches towards Bethlehem to be born?"

In placing Popeye's background in the last chapter of *Sanctuary* for its most resonant effect, Faulkner was following a method he was to follow in all his great fiction. Faulkner's novels tend to flow backward in time at the same time that they move closer to the present. For example, in *Light in August,* we do not learn of the ambiguity of Joe Christmas's birth until deep into the last half of the novel. In *Absalom, Absalom!* we do not learn of Thomas Sutpen's crucial boyhood experience until long after he has appalled us by his behavior. As I have written in *Quests Surd and Absurd:* "In a sense . . . each one of Faulkner's novels represents a descent into the vortex of time, a vortex created by an event that disturbs, upsets, alarms, or frightens the family or community. In moving frantically back and forth in the search for the causes and consequences of this key and singular event, Faulkner creates the structure of his novels: a whirlpool or circular structure suggesting that the secret of time (or life) is not to be found in the simple, straight chronology of one event following another, but rather in hidden corners . . . of the past, with only remote or oblique or subterranean . . . connections with the event of the present being probed" (p. 53).

Popeye is executed in Birmingham for a crime he did not commit, and he appears to be without ordinary human feelings, indifferent to his life or death. Temple and her father sit in the Luxembourg Gardens in Paris, hearing the music of Massenet, Scriabine, and Berlioz. Temple yawns, and gazes in her compact at a face that is "sullen and discontented and sad": "She closed the compact and from beneath her smart new hat she seemed to follow with her eyes the waves of music, to dissolve into the dying brasses, across the pool and the opposite semi-circle of trees where at sombre intervals the dead tranquil queens in stained marble mused, and on into the sky lying prone and vanquished in the embrace of the season of rain and death" (309). These last, quickly sketched scenes are some of the bleakest in *Sanctuary,* not unlike some of the scenes of sophisticated decadence in *The Waste Land.* Just at the time that we come to some kind of dim understanding of Popeye, he is extinguished in circumstances irrelevant to his deeds and to any definition of justice. Temple, originator of much of the novel's violence and brutality and inhumanity, walks the earth bored with the uneventfulness of her life, prepared for the next, new sensation. The very sky itself, "lying prone and vanquished," appears to proclaim the withdrawal of any God of justice or deity of concern. The season of *Sanctuary* is, indeed, the season of "rain and death."

19

Meaning and Myth in *The Sound and the Fury* and *The Waste Land*

Lois Gordon

Much critical attention has been devoted to philosophical themes and structural devices in *The Sound and the Fury.* My intention is first to explore the novel as a psychological portrait of a family in decline over a number of generations, to analyze in detail the destruction that ungiving parents visit upon their children, then to relate the novel to *The Waste Land* in terms of both theme and aesthetic design.

I.

Who are the Compson family, the inhabitants of Faulkner's infernal arraignment? How can we define, in psychological terms, the nature of their moral vagrancy?

The mother of three sons and a daughter is the socially pretentious, hypochondriacal, and utterly selfish Mrs. Compson, a woman whose clenched embrace to the residual codes of Southern propriety prompt her, on the one hand, to keep her idiot son, Benjy, at home, rather than institutionalize him, but whose egocentrism and self-pity, on the other, override her every good intention. Mrs. Compson is continuously and profoundly ashamed by Benjy's presence, which she considers both boring and God's curse.

So taken with personal pride and family background, Mrs.

Compson often argues with her husband that her family is equal to his, and she defends as a "true gentleman" her brother Maury, a drunk and financial leech, who in fact exploits his idiot nephew in having him (and Caddy) deliver love notes to a neighbor's wife. Mrs. Compson goes so far as to change the boy's name from Maury to Benjy, when he is five, for fear of associating this "humiliation" with her family history.

Caroline Compson is so thoroughly committed to "honor" that she dons a black veil of mourning after she sees her fifteen-year-old daughter, Caddy, kiss a boy. When Caddy's sexual experience becomes more dramatic, the mother would take her youngest and favorite Jason and abandon the rest of the family for, as she says to her husband: "[Caddy] not only drags your name in the dirt but corrupts the very air your children breathe." Years later, when Caddy, now a family castoff, "a fallen woman," sends them much needed money, Mrs. Compson prefers to burn the checks, these "wages of sin," than to acknowledge Caddy's existence. Mrs. Compson either lies about or rationalizes her deplorable acts: She would take Caddy back into her house, were it not for her dead son's and husband's memories.

So consumed with personal pride, she even views her son's (Quentin's) suicide as her shame, and contemplates — Christian that she prides herself on being — whether or not all of these children are God's curse upon her. Throughout, as each son recalls, she locks herself in her house (She leaves it only for funerals), and complains of illness. Her guilt-provoking neuroticism is memorable in the much repeated: "I'll be gone soon. I know I'm just a burden to you."

Defenseless against "Miss Cahline" is her husband, a lawyer and a reciter of Latin poetry. On the one hand, Mr. Compson is always aware of his eventual loss of the Compson Mile, that concrete emblem of Southern aristocracy dating back to the Battle of Culloden. On the other, he is capable of kindness to his children. But he is erratic and essentially irresponsible in his dealings with them. He loves Caddy, but when she, like

Benjy, becomes a test of his affection and trust, he withdraws and takes refuge in alcohol. When Quentin tries to confess his incestuous desires towards Caddy and his suicidal impulses, Mr. Compson is too caught up in his own self-protective, bitter cynicism to realize his son's desperate plea for help. Jason he overlooks almost entirely. Mr. Compson's philosophy seems simple. For one thing, man is a "degenerate beast," and truth consists of "natural events and their causes." Although he and his wife play their game concerning who is the more aristocratic, Mr. Compson does not even hold lip service to the Old Southern values. For him, any ideals, such as honor or chastity, are obsolete or unrealistic because humanly ir-relevant. Purity is a "negative state, contrary to human desire," and honor is an empty word, since acts, if given moral labels, exist within time, and all things change in time. Not only is moral judgment temporary, but even one's personal evaluation of an act (and "conscience") is meaningless, since time modifies even memory.

Although Mr. Compson articulates a cool cynicism, he is nevertheless, an inverse image of his wife. If she bespeaks values, but in fact holds nothing as sacred, he, on the other hand, disclaims any values while his heart hungers for meaning. His cynicism, this disillusioned idealism, is betrayed through-out as he generalizes the human condition:

> Purity is a negative state and therefore contrary to nature. . .
> On the instant when we come to realise that tragedy is second-hand.

> People cannot do anything that dreadful they cannot do anything very dreadful at all they cannot even remember tomorrow what seemed dreadful today.

> A man is the sum of his misfortune. One day you'd think misfortune would get tired, but then time is your misfortune.

> [Man is] a problem in impure properties carried tediously to an unvarying nil: stalemate of [saw] dust and desire.

These, then, are the Compson parents, people driven by pride and a sense of personal loss in a changing social world, people who cannot give, sympathize, or control. As we shall see, their children are a self-fulfilling prophecy and they belie rather than bespeak their parents' morality. As each child tells his tale, or becomes a character in another's, in this series of variations on the theme of death-in-life, there is but one sustaining motif: Each child cries out to his parents for basic compassion and understanding, love and forgiveness, only to be treated by both his father and mother as an emblem of the Compson disgrace.

In his conception of Benjy, Faulkner solves the technical problem of presenting to the reader an objective view of the past. By brilliantly conceiving of an idiot son, who because of his mental level is incapable of subjectively relating or interpreting experience, Faulkner is able to directly relate facts, without speaking in the omniscient author's voice.

With the innocence of a three-year-old, the thirty-three-year-old Benjy has no awareness of time, so past and present mingle. A sense perception may be the only stimulus necessary for him to link present and past experience. Benjy judges no one. He presents objective statements of events — the deaths of his grandmother (Damuddy), father and brother; the branch sequence where the four children played and Caddy muddied her pants; his name change from Maury to Benjy; and Caddy's wedding. He concentrates on his beloved sister Caddy, who smelled like leaves, his "pacifiers," (the jimson weed, his slipper and cushion), the cemetery and fence where he often played, Dilsey's kindness and his relationship to her family, and, of course, the mirror, firelight and trees, which he loved. Faulkner's transcription of Benjy's sense perceptions take on a primitive poetic quality: "[Mother] was lying with the sickness on a cloth on her head . . . Her hair was on the pillow. The fire didn't reach it, but it shone on her hand, where her rings were jumping."

But we perceive that most of Benjy's "recollections" are painful. There is a sense of baffled helplessness about him perhaps unmatched in modern fiction. One recalls, for example, Benjy's laments on the golf course — at one time his pasture — when he confuses a golfer's "caddy" with his dear sister. Also poignant is the day the schoolgirls taunt him at his gate, where he faithfully awaits Caddy's return. There is, in addition, the horrific occasion when Benjy confuses one of the girls with his sister, is accused of molesting her, and is subsequently castrated. The gas mask, colors of the day, and his associations are fused:

> I was trying to say [Caddy], and I caught her ... She screamed and I was trying to say and trying and the bright shapes began to stop and I tried to get out. I tried to get it off my face, but the bright shapes were going again. They were going up the hill to where it fell away and I tried to cry. But when I breathed in, I couldn't breathe out again to cry, and I tried to keep from falling off the hill and I fell off the hill into the bright whirling shapes.

For the rest of his life Benjy would have to say: "I got undressed and I looked at myself, and I began to cry."

Benjy may not understand words, and he may not judge others coherently or verbally, but because he responds to love and honesty, he becomes the moral center of the novel. As Roskus, Caddy, Quentin, and even the neighbor Mrs. Patterson say: "He know lot more than folks think." Benjy feels his mother's falseness; he can "smell the sickness" of the household. And in his own way, he is understood. He alone provides a moral code for Caddy. He cries when she puts on her fancy new hat and perfume, when she and Charlie carouse on the swing, when she later loses her virginity. Caddy understands this censure, and washes her mouth, and repents her deeds. She assures Benjy: "I wont anymore, ever. Benjy. Benjy."

Much of Benjy's commentary has sexual significance, and as we shall see, Faulkner characterizes each of the children in terms of normal or abnormal sexual development. Benjy, for one, objectively relates events which, while intellectually incomprehensible to him, nevertheless affect him sexually. (In mental retardation sexual impulses remain normal.) When, for

example, Dilsey tells him he can no longer sleep in the same
bed with Caddy:

> You a big boy . . . Caddy tired sleeping with you . . . but I
> didn't hush . . . Caddy said "I'm coming." I hushed . . .
> Caddy got in between the spread and blanket. She didn't
> take off her bathrobe.

Of the Branch incident, Benjy recalls:

> Caddy took her dress off . . . Then she didn't have on anything
> but her bodice and drawers, and Quentin slapped her and she
> slipped and fell down in the water . . . Caddy was all wet and
> muddy behind, and I started to cry."

Benjy, like the other children, is profoundly affected by seeing
her muddy bottom as she climbs the pear tree to look in
Damuddy's window.

Chapter I then functions as a mirror of the past, with
Benjy's objective statement of events. Since he cannot
interpret these, since he has no point of view, in a sense his
account is as impersonal and suggestive as Eliot's evocation of
the past in his multiple literary allusions. As we bring to Eliot
our interpretation of the past, we bring to Benjy the Compson
story, which he only names but never interprets. In addition,
as the manifold sense perceptions and events enumerated are
subsequently modified in successive chapters, Benjy's fragments, like Eliot's, grow towards symbolic proportions. These
force us, as do Eliot's, to participate in the drama unfolding,
and, as we shall later discuss in detail, it is we, Faulkner's
reader, who become the narrator of the tales.

By the time we reach Chapter II, in time eighteen years
before, we are not only swept into Quentin's pathetic
soliloquy this last day of his life, but we in a sense reencounter
and reevaluate a society of people already familiar. Chapter
Two presents, in a sense, variations on a few themes:
Damuddy's death, Caddy's loss of virginity, her wedding, the
Branch sequence, the fight with Dalton Ames. Unlike Benjy, in
his factual account, Quentin brings to the events both an
emotional and moral perspective. Quentin is obsessed with
time, with his incestuous desires toward Caddy, her sexual

promiscuity, his father's cynicism, his mother's hypocrisy and hypochondria; and as he thinks about these he provides details to Benjy's bare outline. We are reminded, particularly, of his mother's favoring the youngest child, Jason, at the expense of the others, and her lethal Puritanical mind, in which thought or suspicion is equal to deed: "Done in Mother's mind though. Finished. Finished. Then we were all poisoned." He stresses his father's retaliatory "You are confusing sin and morality women don't do that your mother is thinking of morality whether it be sin or not has not occurred to her."

If the present time of Chapter One was Benjy's birthday, and the section closed with his falling off to sleep, after the keynote: "Mother's sick," Chapter Two is Quentin's death day, his "private celebration," and it begins with his a-wakening and charts the complexion of his diseased mind. Benjy lacks any concept of time, so past and present mingle. But if Benjy lacks logic and the ability to abstract, Quentin finds it difficult to free himself from abstractions, and both the present and past are intolerable. Quentin is not, I think, as many readers have suggested, simply the representative of the Old South, an example of the final destruction of traditional values, nor, more importantly, is he, in his need for ob-literation, in search of Edenic youth, because his childhood was incalculably sad. Quentin seeks an escape in the timeless-ness of death, to some extent, because he cannot tolerate the present and its absence of traditional values. More im-portantly, he cannot tolerate past or future with his lingering guilt from the past. Tearing the hands off his clock cannot help nor can his continuous efforts to avert his shadow or the smell of honeysuckle.

From the time Quentin was very young, he was overly protective of his sister, trying to safeguard her innocence. But throughout, he denies sexuality as a vital human phenomenon. Instead, he associates sex or love with death. Whereas Benjy associates Damuddy's death with the children at play, Quentin more expansively juxtaposes her illness and eventual death with his incestuous desires for Caddy and their childhood play

in the branch, as though the one (love or sex) effected the
other (death). Similarly, Quentin views Caddy's wedding
announcement as a coffin: "It lay on the table a candle
burning at each corner"; and he recalls her honeymoon
preparations as "Bringing empty trunks down the attic stairs
they sounded like coffins French Licks." (Mrs. Compson
would abandon the children to go to French Licks.) Quentin's
sexual identity disturbs him. He is defensive and embarrassed
about his youthful, innocent play with Natalie. In both his
fisticuffs with Dalton Ames and Gerald, he complains that he
"passed out like a girl," and he makes several curiously phallic
associations: He connects his frustration during the branch
episode with his fractured leg, and his inability to actually
commit incest with dropping the suicide weapon, the knife.
Quentin is plagued by his own virginity: "Why couldnt it have
been me and not her who is unvirgin?"

Yet whatever Quentin's childhood experience with his
sister, whether typical or not, his inability to subsequently live
a normal life was due mainly to his relationship with his
parents. The oldest child, Quentin was always given to
formality and academic pursuit, but despite all of his study, he
never considered the possibility that sin and guilt (and hence
forgiveness) might be a part of human experience. Although
his mother often clutched her Bible and mouthed religious
phrases, she herself never accepted the reality of a transcendent faith. Quentin became the victim of his mother's
bogus religiosity and essential superstitiousness. He accepted
her lesson that the thought (of sin) was equal to the deed.
Because he fantasied incest with Caddy, he must be damned in
the eternity of hell's fire. Yet in his distorted mind, which also
connected to his father's notions of time, this hell would be a
pure world, because it would lie outside the boundaries of
time; it would offer a redemptive honor.

But his mother also mouthed empty notions of honor and
chastity, and in his need for a morality, Quentin tragically
sought within reality for the verification of those ideals, only
to discover that the world would not meet his expectations.

Mrs. Compson's influence ultimately was completely negative, an inflated sense of family history, racial and social prejudice and condescension to others, and of course, distorted notions of virtue and honor. Quentin's truest legacy from his mother was pride, in the end his own self-hatred and condemnation, ironically, the inversions of honor.

The fact of the matter is that Quentin never believed his mother loved him, and this is poignantly clear during the last minutes of his life. Among his last words on this day of "celebration," he pitifully says: "If I could say Mother. Mother." and "If I'd just had a mother so I could say Mother Mother."

It would be extravagant, I think, to say that Quentin's death by water is his search for the womb, but a complicating factor in considering his compulsion for death is that because Mrs. Compson was usually "ill" upstairs, and often indifferent to the children, Caddy became a kind of substitute mother. In addition, not only was Quentin torn by guilt and anger toward Caddy and his mother, but he was also guilt-ridden for taking the family money to attend college and not fulfilling his promise to Caddy always to care for Benjy.

If Quentin suffers by confusing Mrs. Compson's morality with a meaningful ethic, his suffering is compounded by his father's cool and contradictory bearing. From him Quentin heard that virginity is only a word, purity "a negative state . . . contrary to nature." Quentin went to his Father (capitalized) for help, but when he spoke of incest and suicide, his father's cynicism served only to undercut the boy's idealism. Quentin wanted to believe in honor, but the fact that he did not, and could not, because he in fact felt natural urges that contradicted his mother's views while coinciding with his father's, thrust him into an intolerable position that would rack him continuously. On the one hand he could plead: "If things just finished themselves," but on the other, he equally believed they did:

> all stable things had become shadowy paradoxical all I had
> done shadows all I had felt suffered taking visible form antic

and perverse *mocking* [Note how Caddy uses this word later]
without relevance inherent themselves with the denial of the
significance they should have affirmed thinking I was I was not
who was not was not who.

Quentin, rootless in Cambridge, as he was rootless in
Jefferson, is, in a sense, the wandering knight, the Platonic
lover imprisoned by his own shadow, as castrated a Christ
figure as Benjy, in search of the New World. It is therefore
fitting that, on this last day of his life, he recall so much about
his parents. In his ritual preparation for eternity, Quentin first
destroys his watch, the "mausoleum of all hope and desire,"
paying attention to which, his father had said, is no more than
a body reflex, "like sweating," "excrement." In addition,
"Christ was not crucified; he was worn away by a minute
clicking of little wheels." As Quentin pursues his own
crucifixion — most poignantly concluded by the very human
act of brushing his teeth — his last thoughts bring his various,
irreconcilable conflicts to the fore. There is a raw beauty
about Quentin's words and a profound sadness as Faulkner
communicates the lack of understanding between parent and
child:

> he we must just stay awake and see evil done for a little while
> its not always and i it doesnt have to be even that long for a
> man of courage . . . i you dont believe i am serious . . . he you
> cannot bear to think that someday it will no longer hurt you
> like this now . . . that who is conceived by accident and whose
> every breath is a fresh cast with dice already loaded against
> him . . . despair or remorse or bereavement is not particularly
> important to the dark diceman.

As we progress to Chapter Three, Jason's tale, we move to
seemingly greater rationality and objectivity. Precisely because
Jason is the most "sane" (Faulkner's comment) of the
brothers, we thereby hold him most responsible for his acts
and demand of him compassion and respect for others. His
profound lack of trust and his loveless nature, however, set
him up to be the most diseased of the children.

Jason is the modern Southern businessman, representative

of the new commercial South (as Faulkner sarcastically complimented him, "a Snopes"), a worthy adversary for what he considers Northern Jewish mercantilism. Jason seems to lack even a nostalgia for fading magnolias and gracious belles, the gentility of the Old South. He is pragmatic, vulgar and bigoted, and his opening and closing statement: "Once a bitch always a bitch" provides not only a fitting contrast to his two brothers but a wonderful insight into his everyday credo.

Although Jason is concerned with the present and future, his tale is filled with memories of the Compson past. Many of the same experiences of the first chapters are retold: Damuddy's, Quentin's and Mr. Compson's deaths, Jason's isolation from the other children, his mother's favoritism ("Since I first held him in my arms I knew then that he was to be my salvation."). As the youngest, however, he was deprived of many material benefits, as well as the erratic affection and misguided advice of his father.

We recall Benjy's and Quentin's comments of Jason's childhood cruelty and business sense, (he hoarded his money, liked to play treasurer), as well as his prudishness and defensiveness toward his sexually maturing sister ("You think you're grown up, dont you . . . better than anybody else.") One is therefore not surprised to encounter in the adult Jason someone for whom time is money and "once a bitch always a bitch." Now he extorts money from his sister and mother and makes clear his distrust of others, particularly women: "I never promise a woman anything not let her know what I'm going to give her. That's the only way to manage them."

His most disquieting trait is his cruelty to others. He sadistically tears up the carnival ticket before Luster's eager eyes. More glaring is his cruelty to Benjy. He not only facetiously considers the family's renting out their "Great American Gelding" to a sideshow, but he also says of Benjy's castration: "They never started soon enough with their cutting and they quit too quick." His solution to family problems is similar: "I know at least two more that needed something like that."

Jason's sexual roles are also of interest. In his maturity he is as unnerved by his niece's pubescent seductiveness as he was by his sister's, and his preoccupation with the shameful body is marked in his continual description of her as "damn near naked." Jason manages his own sexuality in a business-like relationship with his Memphis whore. Yet his mother treats him, quite obviously, like the husband in the house, and Dilsey cryptically says: "You're a cold man, Jason, if man you is." Witnessing Caddy's muddy bottom, as she climbed the pear tree, had its effect no less on Jason than on Benjy and Quentin.

Although Jason says he is "a different breed of cat from Father," he is, in fact, very much like his father. Jason is indifferent to those who look to him for help. To his niece, whom he calls "little whore," he is cold when in effect she pleads for help, wishing she were dead. Jason holds a variation of his father's philosophy, for if morality is a fiction and nothing really counts, then anything goes. As his father might have said: "I don't know why it is I cant seem to learn that a woman'll do anything." But Jason is his mother's offspring as well, in need of camphor for his psychosomatic ills, and mainly concerned with social appearances.

He is, I think, the most complex of the brothers. Though bigoted and rude, he has some sympathy from Faulkner. As desirous as Jason is to maintain his brusque and vulgar manner, this in itself betrays a lonely and suffering man. The combination of his black humor (usually self-deprecating) with his inability to totally repress any kind thoughts toward others, and the details of his childhood, in fact, engage our sympathy for him, the victim of an oppressive world of selfish parents and the youngest child.

As a boy, even as Benjy reports, Jason was teased for his obesity and clumsiness; he was blamed for everything, even opening Benjy's gate, which Benjy admits opening himself; and he was always threatened when he cried: "You want to get whipped?" Jason was an emotional child, but his mother always compared him with Uncle Maury, in fact an irresponsi-

ble, adulterous drunkard. If Benjy and Caddy often shared one
bed, Jason slept with his grandmother. Yet, when after she
died, he wept at each mention of her name or worried she
would be "undressed" by buzzards, he was only mocked by
the other children as a "cry baby." That the grown Jason
should reject emotional displays is surely understandable, as is
his now treating everyone else as scapegoat. That he should
also be resentful of his father's giving a good part of the family
money to Quentin and Caddy and, as he puts it, of drinking up
the rest, is also understandable. Jason is so scarred over in
response to the wounds of his deprived childhood, he can
barely think about it. There is something poignant in his
admitting there was a time he could trust others: "I was a kid
then. I believed folks when they said they'd do things. I've
learned better since. Because, like I say, I guess I don't need
any man's help to get along. I can stand on my own feet like I
always have." One also responds to his bitterness in the often
repeated "What did I ever have?" Benjy at least had his slipper,
Caddy her new dresses, Quentin his expensive Harvard
education. Jason had, of course, his mother's consuming
dotage and the promise of a bank job which never mate-
rialized. We, therefore, feel some compassion for his "I dont
expect much but I do want to eat and sleep without a couple
of women squabbling and crying in the house." Ironically, one
even suspects a degree of sincerity in his "I have as much pride
about my kinfolks as anybody." Because he cannot destroy
the illusory world of his vain and helpless mother − like his
father, he tries to shield her from all unpleasant reality − he
commits himself to an eternity of hell. Quentin may have his
private hell with Caddy, but Jason surely has his own private
and public one with his mother. Jason may extort money from
her, but she extorted his future.

A terrifying reality of the book's end is that, apart from
Benjy, Jason and his mother are the sole survivors of the
Compson house, bound to each other in a malignant sym-
biosis. But Jason understands Mrs. Compson and the punishment each has to endure. He answers, for example, her

complaint that it must be God's will that she suffer for her
children with "Seems to me you go to a lot of unnecessary
trouble doing it."

The great irony of his life is that while he prides himself on
the willful control of his fate, he is ultimately as helpless as his
brothers. As we see in the last scenes of the book, after he has
taken a loss in the stock market, he must finally depend upon
a passively aggressive sheriff and a mocking railway man. The
sheriff confronts him with his greed in extorting Caddy's
money and even accuses him of driving his niece away.
Ironically, as well, it is the emblem of his life, his car, whose
gasoline fumes incapacitate him. In the end, Jason is driven
and ruined by a past no less purposive than Quentin's or the
others'. His final illusion is that he really believes that if he
recovered some money he could go away and finally get his
"even chance": "And once I've done that they can bring all
Beale Street and all bedlam in here and two of them can sleep
in my bed and another one can have my place at the table
too."

Much has been said thus far of Caddy. In Benjy's chapter
we see her as the most vivacious of the children, and even as
substitute mother in the household. Although sometimes
willful and often bossy, she is always patient and loving.
"You're not a poor baby," she reassures Benjy, "Havent you
got your Caddy." She knows how to pacify Mrs. Compson,
and it is she (and Dilsey) who ultimately maintain the family.
Caddy understands everyone, precociously insightful, she
assures Quentin that reality and one's dreams or codes of
honor are not synonymous: "Do you think that if I say it
[that I'm not pregnant] it wont be?" To her mother she says:
"You go upstairs and lay down *so you can be sick* [italics
mine]."

Concerning her sexual promiscuity and so-called dis-
honorable pregnancy, one might say that Caddy in fact
illustrates Mr. Compson's attitude that nature, not morality,
rules, while at the same time she internalizes her mother's
articulated codes of honor. Caddy acted the only way she

knew possible to survive her parents: "There was something terrible in me sometimes at night I could see it grinning at me . . . through their faces it's gone now and I'm sick." For Caddy, the only way, she thought, to flee the death-in-life quality of her home was in sex. But this was not without its terrible cost, for, as Caddy said, sex made her feel dead. Caddy condemned herself for her acts, as her confessionals with Quentin make clear. As a child she thought her actions improper, and as an adolescent she saw herself responsible for her father's alcoholism, and even his death. As the Appendix suggests, Caddy would suffer guilt the rest of her life, and in the end, give herself to a Nazi officer, her ultimate self-punishment. But always, as a girl, Caddy exemplified love and loyalty. And because she was always good to Benjy, we feel for her Faulkner's "To me she was the beautiful one . . . my heart's darling," the reason he wrote the book.

Just as the Compson children provide the yardstick with which to judge the legacy of values from one generation to the next, so does the subsequent generation illustrate the impact of the past on the present. Seventeen-year-old Miss Quentin, Caddy's daughter — in the last two chapters which take place in the present — lives with Mrs. Compson, Benjy and Jason. Sexually promiscuous, stubborn and quick-tempered, Miss Quentin appears to many readers to be a lesser Caddy, a girl who inherited her mother's vices but none of her virtues. It is true that, at times, she is disrespectful to Dilsey and unkind to Benjy. One might consider, however, that unlike her mother, she never knew Benjy when he was a small child, which perhaps mitigates against her impatience. In terms of her sexual promiscuity, moreover, if her mother's was a drive for survival in a house of illness and death, then is not Miss Quentin's need for release even more compelling?

Miss Quentin lives, after all, with her grandmother whose selfishness, self-righteousness, and guilt-provoking are more flagrant than ever. In two powerful scenes with her and Jason, Miss Quentin clarifies a great deal about the Compson family and reinforces the novel's thematic core: "Dilsey . . . Dilsey, I

want my mother," she says, and, "There's a curse on us it's
not our fault." There follows:

> I dont see why I was ever born . . . I dare anybody to know
> everything I do . . . I dont care . . . I'm bad and I'm going to
> hell, . . . I'd rather be in hell than anywhere where you [Jason]
> are.

> He wont let me alone. . .It's his fault. . .He makes me do it.
> . . .Whatever I do, it's your fault. . . . If Im bad, its because I
> had to be. You made me. I wish I was dead. I wish we were all
> dead.

Jason replies: "That's the first sensible thing she ever said."

One cannot listen to this without recalling her uncle's need
for death and hell, as well as his suicide pact with Caddy. One
also recalls Caddy's and Benjy's comforting moments together
when Caddy might have said "I hate rain. I hate everything."
But there followed, in Benjy's words, "her head came into my
lap and she was crying, holding me, and I began to cry." Now,
however, Mrs. Compson is unmoved by her granddaughter's
wish to be dead, for she expects the worst from her, given, as
she puts it, "the heritage she already has." (Once the
grandmother alludes to the girl as the incestuous offspring of
Caddy and Quentin.)

Miss Quentin has grown up hungering for a mother, but
the "arrangement" was that Mrs. Compson would take the
baby ("You will never know the suffering you've caused," she
proclaimed to the infant), with the provision that she could
isolate it forever from her mother. "[Miss Quentin] must
never even learn that name [Caddy]. Dilsey, I forbid you ever
to speak that name in her hearing. If she could grow up never
to know that she had a mother, I could thank God." One
recalls Mrs. Compson's adorning her dress of mourning for
Caddy years before, and her plea to her husband when the
children were young: "Let me have [Jason] . . . and you keep
the others. They're not my *flesh and blood.* [Italics mine]."
Ironically, Caddy has been back in town, begging Jason to
have Miss Quentin back; she has implored her brother, and we
note the phrase, which occurs at least a dozen times in the

novel, to be kind to his "flesh and blood."

Mrs. Compson seems paranoid in her complaint that her husband, Quentin and Caddy united against Jason and her: "They deliberately shut me out of their lives . . . conspiring against [us]." Quentin and Caddy, she still believes, were given too much freedom; Caddy was too vain, Quentin's suicide selfish. Jason's response reflects his solipsistic vision — all human misery derives from the female. Perhaps Quentin killed himself, Jason speculates, because he knew Caddy's child "was going to be a girl . . . one more . . . than he could stand." The sequence closes with Mrs. Compson's censure of the dead Quentin and outcast Caddy for not denying themselves for their family. What more, one wonders, could one do than give up his child or his life for the Compson Code?

It is the black servant Dilsey who provides a degree of stability, comfort, and love to Miss Quentin and the other Compsons. Dilsey held the family together, commented Faulkner, "just because it was the decent and proper thing to do." Dilsey has survived the changes in the Compson house, and throughout, like Benjy, she judges no one. Again, like Benjy, she strengthens the novel's moral core, love. It is significant that after presenting the death-in-life portraits of each of the Compson brothers, which have delineated the suffering imposed upon and felt by each, that Faulkner writes a third person narrative, in great part about Dilsey, whose actions, rather than whose point of view, reinforce our comprehension of the book's human core. It is as if what we have inferred in three chapters is now articulated in the author's omniscent voice.

Dilsey, like Benjy, appeals to our senses. She allows us to see the Compsons for the first time — Jason a caricature of a bartender, Mrs. Compson, "cold and querulous," and Benjy, like a trained bear with pale blue, sweet eyes. Our portrait of Dilsey is at once literally and morally descriptive:

> She had been a big woman once but now her skeleton rose, draped loosely in unpadded skin that tightened again upon a paunch almost dropsical, as though muscle and tissue had been

courage or fortitude which the days or the years had consumed until only the indomitable skeleton was left rising like a ruin or a landmark above the somnolent and imperious guts, and above that the collapsed face that gave the impression of the bones themselves being outside the flesh, lifted into the driving day with an expression at once fatalistic and of a child's astonished disappointment, until she turned and entered the house again and closed the door.

If Benjy gives us the past, Dilsey is the past that has survived. Perhaps, as we shall later discuss, she is a kind of Tiresias figure who, with Benjy, shores up the fragments against final ruin. But for now, just as we have heard that Benjy "know a lot more than folks think," we also hear the same of Dilsey: "[She] raised her face as if her eyes could and did penetrate the walls and ceiling."

To be sure, Dilsey has suffered, but she has also endured. She has lived with a rheumatism-ridden husband and watched him die; she has survived his moods concerning the curse of living with her stoical: "We all got to go"; but she has been truly understanding of him, as she has of each of her children. Dilsey has brought up not only her own and the Compson children, but also the grandchildren. A contrasting figure to Mrs. Compson, who is described as "a mediaeval jailer" carrying keys to all the rooms, Dilsey has a calm about her that is almost saintly. She accepts everything with equanimity. In the face of Jason's cruel treatment of her own grandson, Dilsey is angered but she accepts even this with equipoise, and then is touchingly kind to the boy, always generous within the limits of her means. Perhaps Dilsey's most dazzling quality is her unshakable love for Benjy. Although her funds are surely scarce, she buys him a birthday cake, and she defies her family and friends by escorting the thirty-three-year-old bellowing idiot to church because, as she says, "de good Lawd dont keer whether he smart er not."

Dilsey's attitude is stoical and heroic, in a classical sense. Yet along with this, and her uncompromising love, Dilsey has an unpretentious faith, one that goes beyond convention, one

that accepts simultaneously tragedy and finitude, and redemption and eternity.

Dilsey understands the several dimensions of time — past,
present and future. In both a temporal and transcendent sense,
she has reckoned with death and eternity. On the one hand,
she knows when the clock strikes five times that it is eight
o'clock. But she also says, of herself: "My name been Dilsey
since fore I could remember and it be Dilsey when they's long
forgot me. . . . It'll be in the Book." She knows the pain and
the glory, the sound and the fury; she knows we've all got to
go, but she will do her best until then.

A brief look at the end of Chapter IV brings all the
characters into focus. Miss Quentin has run away with Jason's
money; but since he has extorted it, he cannot press charges.
Half the section involves Jason's racing around town, trying to
locate Quentin and her boyfriend. Jason's headache is overpowering, he cannot drive, and he is slowly capitulating to the
feelings he has devoted his life to suppressing. Faulkner
underscores his sense of impotent masochism: "His sense of
injury and impotence [fed] upon its own sound." He seemed
to "get an actual pleasure out of his outrage and impotence."
Jason is virtually hallucinating; and as he becomes more and
more aware that he can no longer depend upon the order on
which he has built his life — he has even forgotten his hat and
camphor — he feels more and more unmanned.

Juxtaposed to this scene is Dilsey's ritual preparation for
church. Dilsey intuitively senses that things are at an end, and
tying together time and the Compson family, Faulkner writes:
"The clock tick-tocked, solemn and profound. It might have
been the dry pulse of the decaying house itself." Benjy shares
Dilsey's knowledge. He "wailed again, hopeless and prolonged.
It was nothing. Just sound. It might have been all time and
injustice and sorrow become vocal for an instant by a
conjunction of planets."

And to the Chapel (Perilous) they go. At this point, there
is a sudden tonal metamorphosis in the novel. The minister,
whose appearance is totally "insignificant," begins his sermon,

and as he speaks and his intonation and pronunciation become negroid, all are transformed. They appear to awaken from a dream in a moment of communion, transported "beyond the need for words." There is a prayer within and without time, "in and out of the myriad coruscations of immolation and abnegation and time."

Benjy, "serene," becomes our focal point as the minister cries: "I got de ricklickshun en de blood of de Lamb. . . . Look at dem little chillen sittin dar, Jesus was like dat once. His mammy [Dilsey is dressed in purple.] suffered de glory en de pangs." We are reminded of Benjy's name change as the minister cries: "I sees de light en I sees de word, po sinner. Dey passed away in Egypt, de swingin chariots; de generations passed away."

Not only is Jason's wild chase occurring simultaneously, but Faulkner reminds us in numerous details that outside the church the world retains its grotesque actuality. To be sure, the novel does not end here. Indeed, Dilsey and Benjy must return to the "rotting portico" of the Compson house. If the Easter service promised resurrection, reality returns with Mrs. Compson, to whom Jason, had earlier said: "You never resurrected Christ, did you?"

At this point, Mrs. Compson has learned that Miss Quentin has run away, and her response is particularly repugnant. Suspecting that the girl, like her namesake, might have killed herself, she asks if a note has been found: "At least she would have enough consideration to leave a note. Even Quentin did that." And, she continues, "Under God's heaven what reason did he have? It can't be simply to flout and hurt me. Whoever God is, He would not permit that. I'm a lady. You might not believe that from my offspring, but I am."

In the last scene before Luster drives Benjy to the cemetery, Faulkner adds a bitter note. Admittedly, Luster's babysitting job with Benjy is difficult, and one is compassionate with his mixture of duty, sympathy, and frustration in handling it, yet when he taunts Benjy by calling Caddy's name, Benjy's response again undercuts any relief offered by the church sequence: "He bellowed slowly, abjectly, without tears; the grave hopeless sound of all voiceless misery under the sun." Luster then gives him his slipper and the narcissus. His "devilment" returns, however, as he turns the carriage left instead of the accustomed right.

The complex and brilliant irony at the end is that it is Jason who enters the scene to restore Benjy's order. Embarassed that the townspeople are witness to the spectacle of Benjy's bellowing, he screams: "Get to hell on home with him. If you ever cross that gate with him again, I'll kill you."

The novel ends with the line "The broken flower drooped over Ben's fist and his eyes were empty and blue and serene again as cornice and facade flowed smoothly once more from left to right; post and tree, window and doorway, and signboard, each in its ordered place." Has the mindless, habitual order and serenity of the idiot, in fact, been restored? Is the idiot's bellowing a meaningful cry against the atrophy of human values, acted out by Jason? These, and all of our comments about Faulkner's final vision, must be postponed until later, when we discuss the mythic quality of the novel and the participatory role of the reader.

II

That Faulkner intends the Compsons — particularly the sons — to reveal unique perspectives seems to be underscored by the marked formal differences between the chapters. As a result, in analyzing the shape of the novel, many of Faulkner's readers assume that it is structured around the progression, from Chapter One to Four, of different mentalities — i.e. We move from the closed world of the single perspective to the omniscient author; from Benjy, who relates experience through sense perception and who lives outside time, to Quentin and Jason, the one too much within time, the other outside of it, to the Dilsey section, the omniscient recording of human behavior balanced between personal and eternal time, the world of sense and abstraction, reality and obsession.

I would suggest, however, that there are striking similarities in the points of view of these chapters — subtle but vitally noteworthy — which ultimately tend to merge each speaker with his brother, as though Faulkner were working towards a single persona with differing masks.

The greatest paradox, perhaps, is that while Benjy is unconscious of time, and his section is initially the most difficult to follow, he nevertheless presents us with the most honest, factual perception of experience. Benjy may be the idiot, but he gives us the total past without distortions of judgment, without subjective interpretation. Furthermore, he provides the moral core of the novel — the need for human relatedness and love.

Benjy lives in a world free of time, one comprehended through the senses, but Quentin, who is troubled handling the world of the senses, seeks escape in a world free of time. Actually, none of the brothers has a realistic time sense. Neither Benjy nor Quentin allows for change, that is, the future, and Jason will not consciously acknowledge the past. If Quentin hates time because it necessitates change, Benjy, in his own way, demands the same rigid order. Although he cannot understand that time brings change, and so he bellows when Caddy matures to wear her perfume and kiss boys, his need for fixity is not dissimilar from Quentin's, the one immobile in idiocy, the other in abstraction and the commitment to death.

Jason, who thinks his is a sane, logical mind, moreover, is, on the one hand, as imprisoned to time as Quentin and Benjy, always concerned about punctuality at home and work. But he is also as imprisoned by abstractions (in conflict with normal desires) as Quentin. If Quentin in part kills himself for "honor," Jason, in part, commits himself to that frenzied chase, as even *he* admits, for the principle, not the girl or money. At the same time, though he prides himself on freedom from personal commitment and time, he is actually as harrassed by his past and personal relationships as his brothers.

Actually, Dilsey is the only one truly aware (instinctively and rationally) of time, and she is the only one who can love and be loved in return. She alone can balance the world of past, present and future, of sense and thought, of desire and longing. She alone knows that when the clock chimes five times, it is eight o'clock.

Another antithesis exists in the brothers' commitment to a morality. Benjy, in his completely private approach to the world, lacks an articulated moral code, yet he surely has an intuitive, instinctive one; he feels or senses right and wrong, and he acts upon it, if only in bellowing; more importantly, his code is acted upon by others — witness Caddy's behavior. But Quentin, seemingly Benjy's opposite, with his obsessions with honor and chastity, has only abstractions to live with; he neither acts (rationally) upon his ideals nor influences others in their behavior. Jason, who prides himself in lacking any code is, in his relationship with his mother, true to the family honor. Yet, in his treatment of both Caddy and Miss Quentin, and in his contempt towards his Nashville whore, he displays a variation of the Puritanical ethos which, in effect, is also Benjy's and Quentin's. For all the brothers, natural drives are bestial, disgusting, and women destructive.

Such seemingly different children then have much in common. While all of the antitheses remain, each lacks any real sense of time, each is essentially incapable of love, each is victimized by his rigid order, and, as we shall see, that order ultimately gives way to its opposite. As we progress further into the Compson world, we become increasingly aware that each experience is presented through the perspective of a diseased or feeble mind.

Moral decay, and physical and spiritual illness, are underlined not only by obvious plot and characterization, but also by subtle details, until the malaise of one character merges with that of all. Jason's eventual hallucinations bring the cycle full circle from Benjy's feeblemindedness; Miss Quentin's death wish calls forth her uncle's demise; Quentin's and Jason's "impotence" are the shadow of Benjy's castration. At the end, Jason asks the rhetorical:

And there I was without any hat, looking like I was crazy too.

> Like a man would naturally think, one of them is crazy, and
> another one drowned himself and the other one was turned
> out into the street by her husband. What's the reason the rest
> of them are not crazy too?

This is a world of inner and outer disease, the "rotting portico" of the house a reflection of its inhabitants' death-in-life, as well as an emblem of the inevitable destructiveness of time. The present time of the novel may be Good Friday, Holy Saturday, and Easter Sunday, but this is counterpointed by the reality of internal time experienced within that frame. The novel begins and concludes with death (Damuddy's — Benjy's cemetery), and each chapter also begins, ends, and has as its substance, disease and death.

Ultimately, death-in-life, the sound and fury, is told by each of the brothers, and each not only retells the same events, but he often describes them in identical terms. The passage from which Faulkner took his title even unifies the single voice of the "shadow" (Quentin), the "poor player" who "struts" (Jason), and of course "the idiot" (Benjy). Again and again, sense experiences or images associated with one brother echo from the others. It is Quentin, not Benjy, who says: "She ran right out of the mirror [about Caddy's wedding]"; or "We reached the fence she crawled through I crawled through we ran out of the trees the road going on under the twilight." Again, Quentin, not Benjy, lies in his sister's lap and weeps, as Caddy's presence provides the lonely one his necessary solace: "Then I was crying her hand touched me again and I was crying against her damp blouse then she lying on her back looking past my head into the sky."

Not only Quentin, but Jason fears his shadow; yet shadows are Benjy's focus as well: "Our shadows [Luster's and his] were on the grass;" "the windows went black and the dark tall place on the wall came." At the end of the book, Jason, not Benjy, must finally commit his future to the "smell of a red tie;" and Jason, not Quentin, races to beat time, taking Quentin's pleasure in his defiance of it: "He thought about it with a sort of triumph, of the fact that he was going to miss dinner, that by starting now and so serving his compulsion of haste, he would be at the greatest possible distance from both towns when noon came."

Minute details reinforce this merging of voices: Identical comments are uttered by each voice; identical adjectives are used to describe objects. For Benjy the flowers "rasped and rattled"; for Quentin, the honeysuckle was the "rasping darkness of summer"; at the end, Faulkner writes, the pear tree, in bloom, "scraped and rasped against the house." Ultimately, the quarter Luster craves and Jason hoards is the quarter Quentin gives the little Italian girl; the cigar Jason buys Mink is the one Quentin gives a black man in Boston, the same one offered to him by Herbert. Even the bun that Quentin buys the little girl is the cake Dilsey bought for Benjy. This leads to a uniquely complex symbolism where not only birds, bells, flowers, rain, and so forth, build and connect, but also where conversational units, events themselves and characters, modify and metamorphose into poetic values. Because Quentin is haunted by his father's "Time is your misfortune," and he continues, "A gull on an invisible wire attached through space attached," he continually compares human experience or his thoughts to gulls. In Jason's tale it is the sparrows that are offensive (birds used by the gulls), in the last chapter the jaybirds scream. I cannot help but associate the lines in *I Henry IV* where Worcester says: "Being fed by us you used us so/ As that ungentle gull the cuckoo's bird/ Useth the sparrow." The cuckoo, like the gull, hatches its offspring in other birds' nests.

Benjy, who in the end is described as Christ-like, frequently catches himself on a nail, and he also burns his hand; he is, in fact, castrated. Yet, Quentin, who chooses to break his watch, for Christ was worn away by the ticking of little wheels, also cuts his hand. Furthermore, when he describes passing out "like a girl," when his foe for Caddy's love assaults him, he communicates his castration in words that echo Benjy's literal castration with the gas mask: "It was like I was looking at him through a piece of coloured glass. I could hear

my blood and then I could see the sky again." The gasoline
Quentin uses as a cleanser for his stained clothing is the same
gasoline that debilitates Jason, whose headaches have in them
the hand of Blake's Creator at His forge: "It would go into my
head like it would explode any minute, and the sun getting
down to where it could shine straight into my eyes and my
ears ringing so I couldn't hear anything."

At the end of the book, Quentin and Benjy merge with
Jason, and the vision is one of hell. If Benjy, who knows of
Caddy's loss of chastity, acts literally upon her promise that
she will never leave, and so he awaits her daily at his gate and
if Quentin who has suffered for Caddy's loss of virginity and
prefaced his final embrace of honor in hell with his pursuit of
the little Italian sister, then Jason, who also saw his future
through Caddy, ends up pursuing the same phantom as his
brothers. The assault Benjy still re-lives, when T. P. fell upon
him during Caddy's wedding, is the same one, and involves the
same "passing out" that Quentin experiences the last day of
his own "celebration," (a repetition of an earlier one with
Dalton Ames), the same one that Jason will undergo in his
parallel encounter with the authorities and his subsequent
brawl, all because of a young girl.

Jason, in fact, in his final confusion, actually believes that
Miss Quentin *is* Caddy, that he can still get that impressive
bank job. Initially, he says of his niece.

> [She is] the bitch that cost me a job, the one chance I ever had
> to get ahead, that killed my father . . . and made my name a
> laughing stock in the town.

And later:

> I'm Jason Compson. See if you can stop me. . . [The sheriff]
> thinks he can sit with his hands folded and see me lose my job.
> I'll show him about jobs.

Faulkner's commentary continues: "Of his niece he did not
think at all, nor the arbitrary valuation of the money. Neither
of them had had entity or individuality for him for ten years."

There is a brilliant irony in the comments of a bystander,

following Jason's brawl: "What were you trying to do?
Commit suicide? . . . You — her brother?"

Finally, Miss Quentin has escaped the house by climbing
down the pear tree her mother climbed in those muddy pants
years before; the road she takes away from the house is the
road Quentin roamed in Cambridge, the road Jason, in his wild
frenzy, travelled, the road that brought Caddy into town in
her desperate plea that Jason be kind to his "flesh and blood."
This is the circular road of the generations, the path that Benjy
took serenely at the beginning of the novel with T. P. and
Caddy, slipper and flower, when "the bright shapes went
smooth and steady . . . flowing," and at the end of the novel
with Luster and Jason, slipper and flower, after which Benjy's
world "flowed smoothly once more from left to right."

III

This is, however, a volume on *The Waste Land* and the
literature of the Twenties, and it is therefore, of interest, for
the remainder of this essay, to examine whether Faulkner's
novel, published in 1929, shares the spirit of Eliot's great
poem. That Eliot's earlier work had a marked effect upon the
young author of *Soldier's Pay, Mosquitoes,* and *Sartoris,* has
already been noted, but it seems to me that *The Sound and
the Fury* and *The Waste Land* show marked affinities in
theme, as well as aesthetic technique utilized and aesthetic
response demanded.

Thematic similarities are most evident. Although Faulkner
takes as his subject a single family in a small town, and Eliot,
through a collage of allusions, a vast portion of Western
history and culture, their view of the present is much the
same: In the wake of science and capitalism has come moral
and spiritual decay, selfishness and lovelessness — in general,
death-in-life. Both set their works in cold Aprils, in the month
of rebirth and resurrection, and both use the myth of Christ,
of dying and redemption, as the ultimate value against which
to contemplate the disease and solipsism of the present. Man's
plight, in both, is his inability to accept memory and desire.

For both writers, the past contains the present and the present reflects the past, so both fragment linearity to synthesize meaning. Structure and personae illustrate how, as Eliot said, we live in the living moment of the past in the present. Although Faulkner has said "There is no such thing as was only is," and Eliot's modern waste land may be a reflection, indeed a lament, for "was," Faulkner sees the continuity of sadness through the generations. Yet for both Faulkner and Eliot, chronological time is hell, with redemption possible only in a kind of passive, stoical acceptance of the human condition. Dilsey's combination of "endurance," and Christian belief is the *shantih* of *The Waste Land.* Her pose, and the fact that Faulkner's final pronouncement that the Dilseys "endured," is, to me, not unlike the spirit of St. John of the Cross, which I believe informs not only *Four Quartets* but *The Waste Land* as well. Eliot's emphasis may well be more upon the spiritual and Faulkner's upon the earthly, but this combination of stoicism and faith is common to both.

Initially both Eliot and Faulkner describe journeys in search of love and salvation, by knights incapable of love or understanding:

"You gave me hyacinths first a year ago;
"They called me the hyacinth girl."
—Yet when we came back, late from the Hyacinth garden,
Your arms full, and your hair wet, I could not
Speak, and my eyes failed, I was neither
Living nor dead, and I knew nothing,
Looking into the heart of light, the silence.

In each, the knight and scapegoat are one. The Phoenician sailor, the scapegoat god, is Quentin, all the brothers — Prufrock characters essentially incapable of action, who may submerge themselves but who fear drowning and the catharsis it promises. Dreading "the pearls that were his eyes," Quentin worries that the flat-irons may not bury his shadow and that "the eyes will come floating up too out of the deep quiet and the sleep." If one could but submit himself to the realities of personal, external and eternal time, he would not be paralyzed by his "shadow at morning striding behind . . . [or] at evening rising to meet [him] ."

For both Eliot and Faulkner, man is both destroyer and victim, destroyer in the service of false or worn-out values, which he accepts as true, and victim because he accepts those false values. Like Eliot's personae, the carbuncular man, Mme. Sosostris, the mechanical typist, all merging into Tiresias's single consciousness, Faulkner's characters are compelled in the pursuit of values the past has imposed upon them: money, honor, excellence. But they are doomed by the moral and spiritual bankruptcy of history and tradition, whether their present condition reflects the malaise and degeneracy that follows the war between nations or between parents and offspring. If this is the ultimate irony of Eliot's position (his looking toward religion as though it had never, in fact, been tried), it is the tragedy of Faulkner's vision. Eliot may choose to focus on the foul legacy of nationalism, industrialism, materialism, and even the established church, and Faulkner the family, but the resulting atrophy, in both, is the same: man's incapacity to love or take comfort in any type of human relationship, for if he cannot love or find meaning in himself, he cannot believe in anything or anyone outside of himself. He is impotent or castrated in his strivings for human warmth and ultimately dissatisfied with material profit or possession. In his every endeavor he destroys not only others but himself as well. As with Jay Gatsby and Jake Barnes, other forlorn knights of the Twenties, success is possible, but happiness is not. The West may have won the Great War, but it has lost its soul.

Finally, because of their unique form, both Eliot and Faulkner demand enormously of the reader — first of his intellectual resources and knowledge, but mainly of his emotional participation. It seems to me that both *The Waste Land* and *The Sound and the Fury* can be viewed as mythic rites in which the reader serves as the initiate and the author, through the masks of his dramatic personae, the priest-shaman. Appropriate to a rite of initiation, both works demand

tremendous devotion and endurance on the part of the
reader-initiate, a willingness to struggle to understand and a
unique sort of aesthetic participation.

The heart of the mythic rite is the dissolution of the
reality of time in a sequential, objective sense. The past is
reenacted in the present, and the participant (reader) in the
rite exists at one and the same time in the present and past.
There is a suspension of logical reality in search of an
emotional reality which is eternally true and continually
reexperienced by each generation. Both work through symbols
functioning as archetypal images to reach eternal truths which
are experienced in the lifetime of every man throughout
history.

To achieve a timeless quality and to characterize the
present in terms of the past, Eliot relies on allusions to the
literature and culture of the past. These are — or are not —
manipulated within a contemporary context to insinuate the
continuity, absence or metamorphosis of human values and
behavior. To the same ends, Faulkner uses the past of a
particular family which he manipulates in a comparable variety
of ways. The novel concerns a family whose linear history
extends as far back as 1745, the Battle of Culloden, and
indeed through the Compson parents and Quentin the world
of Colonel Sartoris remains palpable. In addition, the continuity of the generations is Faulkner's subject as he focuses
upon the children and grandchildren of a particular family —
living emblems of the impact of the past on the present. But
Faulkner's work is not only historical; it is also prophetic, and
again like Eliot's, it has an open-ended quality. Not only does
Faulkner's Appendix bring the Compsons up to the present
(Benjy is sent to a sanitarium, Jason sells the house, Caddy
becomes a German officer's mistress, the blacks "endured"),
but within the narrative, Quentin, for example, projects his
parents' life after his suicide, and Miss Quentin's escape
suggests her continuing the Compson Experience where the
other children left off. The last scene of the book, furthermore
— Benjy's visit to the cemetery — in paralleling so closely a

sequence at the beginning, with its subsequent "all restored to order," suggests, to me at least, a cyclical movement, a beginning not an end. Even more interesting, Faulkner dissolves chronological time in order to gain his mythic dimension by presenting as his subject matter a specific number of years which, while shared by a particular family, are experienced in totally different yet ultimately similar terms, as we have discussed above. Furthermore, our evaluation of each perspective must always be made against the totally "impersonal" account of Chapter One — Benjy's pure past, like Eliot's "Burial of the Dead," which also provides the substantive core of each of the perspectives that follow. Yet, both initial "chapters" are meaningless until we experience the whole.

Also operating simultaneously with the various perspectives of past and present, and serving as multiple counterpoints, for both *The Waste Land* and *The Sound and the Fury*, are the proclamations of skepticism, nihilism, and superstitiousness set against those of commitment and belief. These separate and blend, antitheses of time and freedom, hope and despair, instinct and ideal. Like plot details, dialogue, sensory experience, and images, also discussed above, virtually every aspect of the novel takes on inexhaustible and antithetical symbolic value, much like Eliot's every detail in his extraordinary poem. The castrated, Christ-like Benjy, in and out of time, lacking reason but possessing truth, takes joy in the magic of fire but experiences the pain of its burn; for Eliot's similarly castrated, aged and ageless persona fire promises salvation in purification while it destroys in lust.

One of the most common of early mythic symbols is the labyrinth, and, indeed, this becomes the method of both Faulkner and Eliot. One is assaulted by the appearance of disorder, of fragments that progress from the confusion of the juxtaposition of the unfamiliar foreign past to the more continuous present. One struggles to find the way, to understand, as he is faced with Benjy's primitive poetry, like the Tarot pack — fragments but clues to the total experience.

It is as if, in beginning both, we must become participants in the process of discovering meaning, first in discerning who is behind the confused voice, and then how the subsequent combination of voices functions. Not until midpoint in both is Tiresias clear, but by that time his voice and ours have merged.

In this, our ritual participation, we internalize the multiple voices, each a part of the whole, each representative of humanity, each living through similar experiences whose meaning, although unknown to him, it is our responsibility to comprehend, to articulate, to feel, and finally to exorcise in the final aesthetic catharsis. It is only in the last sections of *The Waste Land* and *The Sound and the Fury* that we are immersed in the framework of the continuous present, a part of Eliot's "we" or Faulkner's Dilsey, on their journeys to the Chapel, with Christ, the hooded figure, the inarticulate Benjy, also a part of us. Like Dilsey and Tiresias, we have lived through it all and become both Everyman and Seer; we have finally comprehended in the knowledge that passeth understanding.

Ultimately the paradox that unifies both *The Waste Land* and *The Sound and the Fury* is similar to that of the Christian myth and rite of confession. Through the purgation of suffering one may attain eternal joy. Like Eliot, Faulkner takes us on a tortured journey through hell, through the sound and the fury, the madness and terrible lucidity of his speakers. We live through their pain, like Marie's, or the hyacinth girl's, and we endure the mirror of our own hypocrisy and false values, our own pride and shame. Our freedom comes through identification, confession and catharsis, a sort of pre-evangelical preparation for commitment, for *Four Quartets* or *Fable.*

Both works near their conclusion with an image of disintegration, fragments recollecting madness — Benjy's idiotic, chaotic bellowing not unlike the wounded fisher king's on his arid plain. Yet in the same way the *shantih shantih* — barely audible against the alien fragments to be shored up against final ruin — suggests, to me, a faith in the restoration of human values (knowable at least in the myth of historical memory); so too the mere fact that Dilsey endures proffers a similar hope, her faith also modestly articulated against the cacophonous fragments of an idiot's cries. Through both seers, protectors against humanity's ruin, we have seen the beginning and the end, and we acknowledge man's most basic need, love. In the end, as loud as the sounds of the unreal city may persist, that final *shantih shantih shantih* like the whining of the mandoline, will resound deepest, a bulwark against the horror.

Like *The Waste Land*, Faulkner's narrative poem seems to get easier as we reach its last section, because meanings and patterns have clarified. At last all the values filter through the single voice, and movement towards the future is begun. Yet, although seemingly the most straightforward sections, they really provoke our most complex response, for we at last see objectified (and have participated ourselves in) the final, and profoundly simple truth. Love and endurance are salvation. Man *is* responsible for his brother; character and brother are always evaluating each other in human experience, as in the aesthetic experience. We are all our brother's keeper, and this becomes not only theme and structure, but aesthetic responsibility, and our final aesthetic and moral sensibility.

One cannot overlook the profound social pessimism in both *The Waste Land* and *The Sound and the Fury*. Prophetic in this way, as the subsequent decades of the century have shown them to be with the destruction and deepening moral dilemmas of the technological age, one can only wonder at the terrible vision of the artist. But there is also that profound hope, in both works, which is the eternal wellspring of religion and art, and the eternal purpose of the multitudinous mythic rites that man performs to expiate his sin and guilt and propitiate the fates beyond his control. The journey of the knight is no more than every man's every day. Dilsey endures taking care of her family because, as Faulkner put it, it was the "decent and proper thing to do." In *A Fable*, he again writes: "Man is enduring and immortal; enduring not because he is

immortal but immortal because he endures." Eliot says
"Give," "Sympathize," "Control." Are they not both echoing
the deepest and most ancient and most enduring of human
values, which it is the eternal duty of the artist to signify and
retell?

One feels when one comprehends, or perhaps one comprehends when one feels, the deep pleasure — is it aesthetic or
religious — of knowing, or at least of having touched
momentarily, the essentially unknowable, the universal mystery.

20

Renaissance in the Twenties

Blyden Jackson

I hold that all discussions of the Harlem Renaissance which say too much about Harlem and not enough about the whole of Negro America as it was during the period of the Renaissance should be approached with a considerable amount of wariness. The Renaissance has been transmitted to us largely through its literature. That literature, I believe, in keeping with the Renaissance itself, acquired its substantial character, not from the isolated eccentricities of a place, nor from the special programs of a coterie of artists, but, rather, from its relation to the life and the distinctive temper of an entire nationally extensive community, the American Negro world, as I shall call it, of which, I am firmly persuaded, the Renaissance and everything of consequence attributable to it, were ultimately a product and always a faithful and true reflection.

If I am right — if, that is, I judge properly both the written record and the impressions remaining from my own personal recollection — then really to see deeply into this literature of the Harlem Renaissance one is virtually forced to be in adequate possession of a sense of the world from out of which the literature came. It will not do to focus one's attention upon Harlem. Between the turn of the century and the end of

the Renaissance more than twice as many Negroes poured into
Harlem than there are people now in towns like East St. Louis,
Roanoke or Durham. They came from everywhere. The
easiest, closest path led straight up the Atlantic coast. It was
the most heavily traveled. But a goodly number of black
pilgrims filtered in from points of origin scattered across the
continent, and some, like Claude McKay and Marcus Garvey,
for example, were from the islands of the sea. Harlem did
affect all these newcomers. There is, after all, such a thing as
the effect of local custom. But it did not transform them. The
newcomers, the invading host, transformed Harlem. They were
freer in New York than they had ever been at any time or
place before in their whole lives. They were also, therefore, if
for no other reason, more themselves. They could do their
thing. They could be what they had always thought they were.
They could roam up and down Lenox and Seventh Avenues,
and even climb Sugar Hill, and know that they were home.
They could not, of course, completely escape the long,
intrusive shadow of their white man boss. They still lived
somewhat on his sufferance within an enclave of his all-
engulfing larger universe. And it was, moreover, undoubtedly
true that Harlem, during the Renaissance, did constitute rather
deliberately something of a city under glass for white
sightseers from the outside — for monied tourists come to see
the natives in their native habitat. Its consciousness of a white
audience was there, even, to a measure, in its serious art. Yet,
real as was the influence of white patrons, Renaissance Harlem
belonged basically to the world from which its inhabitants
came. Those inhabitants were Negroes who had grown up in a
Negro world, raised by Negro parents or Negro older relatives,
trained in Negro ways, feeling Negro feelings, and thinking
Negro thoughts. They could not but keep Harlem, in the final
analysis, a Negro world, and make of the Harlem Renaissance,
in its final analysis, a Negro Renaissance.

It was my own father's generation, possibly the most
maligned and, conceivably, the finest in inner discipline and
altruistic spirit of any Negro generation that has existed in

America, which in the main did raise and train the Renaissance band of Negroes. It was — this generation of my parents — the first Negro generation born in freedom.

My grandparents' generation, on the other hand, was born in slavery. That meant that it could call nothing its own. Among his other deprivations, a slave had absolutely no privacy which he could protect. For obvious reasons his master insisted on the right to know where he was and what he was doing, if it suited the master's interest, every minute of the day and night. Frederick Douglass remembered of his mother that he saw her only three or four times in his entire life and then only late at night. He was a small boy quartered on one plantation. She worked as a field hand on another. To visit him she had to steal away on foot, after a long day's hard physical labor, walk to where he was and then be sure, unless she was prepared for the lash, to be home, ready to pick up her heavy field-work tools, at the earliest break of day. It is a commonplace of our culture to be sentimental over the relationship between a mother and her offspring. The system of slavery waxed sentimental over nothing that removed the slave from the direct surveillance of his master or his master's deputy. But this is a curious universe. Come freedom, the status of the Negro changed. Now suddenly it served the purpose of the whites not to have Negroes near, but to have them far, to torture them with social distance so that they would know how abominable and impossible they were. Now these Negroes, who were kept so close during slavery, must be segregated and jim-crowed. There must even be an etiquette of race relations. For Negroes, never a title of respect. To them, no common courtesies. They must be made to know that they were creatures doomed to live apart, and when the constant insult was not thought to be sufficient, then it was deemed advisable, often by responsible leaders and pillars of the community, that they be terrorized into not forgetting how essential it was for them to live always, metaphorically at least, if not sometimes in literal fact, on their knees. My father's generation, thus, lived in a very private Negro world. It was in such a world, moreover, that the Renaissance generation achieved maturity.

For the first distinction of Negro life for decades after freedom was the extreme degree to which it was turned in upon itself. The Negro coming home at night from working in a white man's world, crossed a great divide. He re-entered into a private world, shut in from the outside and, in an understandable retaliation, with its own virtually impregnable barriers against the very outsiders whose incivilities had cast it into its general mold. Within this private world, however, the Negro himself roamed, as it were, with exemplary freedom. For this private world was notably compact. It has never been true that all Negroes look alike, or think alike, or act alike. They do differ. And yet it is salutary sometimes to notice relatively, how much they do seem to be cut from exactly the same cloth. In spite of talk about the black bourgeoisie, Negroes, certainly until the latest generation, practically have been classless. It would have been for a long time, if still not now, a most amnesic member of a black elite who presumed that all of his blood kith and kin were similarly elite. Just as moreover, it would have been a truly unique black plebeian who did not have, and know that he had, one or more relatives high in the so-called Negro upper class. The Negro world of the Renaissance was not fragmented by class. Nor was it affected by occupation. Most Negroes, including the professionals, who toiled in Negro professions, held Negro jobs. And as this compact world was saved from inner fissures by its lack of great diversities, just so it was bound closely together by the very scarcity of the institutions which served it. To speak of churches, for example, could give most Negroes almost a sense of intimacy with all other Negroes. Any Negro passing through a strange town who asked another Negro whom he had never seen where the A.M.E. church was situated, so long as he said A.M.E. and not African Methodist Episcopal, could expect to be understood. For Negroes everywhere were familiar with the several shades of Negro Baptists and the only three Negro Methodist denominations. Negroes knew, too, what kind of

Negro businesses to expect in every Negro community. Many Negroes knew the names of just about all the Negro colleges. There were only about a hundred, and the limited number of Negro high schools permitted some of them, like Wendell Phillips in Chicago and Sumner in St. Louis, to be as well-known as the best-known seats of Negro higher learning. There was, too, a Negro press. It was composed of weekly papers, not of dailies. But by the time of the Renaissance three Negro weeklies, much as the big television systems of today in our national community, were national institutions of a sort within the Negro world. One of them, indeed, the *Chicago Defender,* owned by a man who had been born in Georgia, was virtually the equivalent of a Negro bible. There was something scriptural, too, something like the common voice of the Old-Testament prophets, in the zeal with which it preached its gospel of a voluntary Negro exodus from the South. The *Defender* allowed none of its readers to forget how the Negro had suffered solely because he was not white. The lesson, too, was warranted.

The Negro world of the Renaissance was not only private and compact. It was also schooled in adversity and misadventure. Not for nothing had it gone through the years from the eighteen-seventies until the turn of the century, the years which Rayford Logan call the Negro nadir. Negro fortunes in America, indeed, were probably never at a lower ebb than they were in 1900. After all, at the turn of the eighteenth and nineteenth centuries the Negro was legally enslaved. At the turn of the twentieth century in theory he was free. Yet at that date he was in worse shape than he had been when he was only ten years out of slavery. In 1895 Frederick Douglass had died and Booker T. Washington, a few months later, at the Cotton States Exposition in Atlanta, had spoken words of good cheer not to the Negro but to the resurgent reactionary South. At all too nearly the same time the Grandfather Clause was meanly contrived and the Plessy-Ferguson Supreme-Court decision was solemnly handed down. Peonage, often camouflaged as a "cotton tenancy," was rife. The trade of lynching flourished with obscene diligence throughout, especially, the South. The Negro was still virtually illiterate. He owned little property. He was generally cut off from the ballot and barred from politics. The churches disdained him. Respectable people shunned him. Even the old abolitionists largely had abandoned him to his own devices. Yet in the thankless climate of the America they knew from McKinley through Wilson, sans any flourish of trumpets, the generation of Negroes before the Renaissance was to make, as it were, without straw the bricks out of which the Renaissance was built, as well as to begin the engineering of the rearrangements of Negro opportunity which made possible the Charles Houstons, the Thurgood Marshalls, the Martin Luther Kings and all the Black militants of a later time. This generation did it all under the most adverse of conditions and it learned techniques and tactics which it imparted to a whole Negro world. It was composed of Negroes who were tempered by their experience of American life and the quiet virtues which they had thereby acquired at tremendous cost they communicated to every Negro of their time, and not least to the class of Negroes younger than themselves who became sensitive enough to play a leading role in the Harlem Renaissance.

One more thing finally they did, one very strange and beautiful thing. Somehow they set the stage, along the way, for a change in the Negro mood. Somehow they ordained a Negro world which by the onset of the Renasissance had taken into itself from somewhere an almost incredible belief in its own special capacity to enjoy life, to treasure vitality for the very sake of vitality alone. This Negro pride possessed, in its conviction that neither Puritanism nor the love of money nor the dominance of science had wrung out of its soul the joy which one may get from merely being one's own self, a special sense of its own worth. All over the Negro world in the 'twenties, incomprehensible as it may seem to people who never knew it, there was this feeling that Negroes had a special aptitude for living – merely living – which white people either had never had or had lost somewhere along the trail to the modern Babylon which their commerce and their industry was spreading over the land whose might and granite wonder, in Claude McKay's famous phrase, were part of the cultural hell testing the Negro's youth. At Negro gatherings in the 'twenties the Negro audience often opened or closed whatever it did with a song which Negroes call indifferently "The Negro National Anthem" or "Lift Ev'ry Voice and Sing." With apparently no sense of incongruity a black assembly of that time would stand upon its feet and chant with gusto of having its rejoicing rise high as the listening skies, or making that rejoicing sound as loud as the rolling seas. And perhaps the curious behavior of those audiences was justified. If the Negro mood of that day was a-political in comparison with the Negro mood of today, it was also possibly more aesthetic. It did place a premium on its own version of soul and thus, if possibly at too piteous a price, assuage the trauma of an outer world's assaults upon its ego with its own assertion of its superior ability to come to terms with the problem of humane existence.

Here, then, is a subjective view of that Negro world of which the Negro Renaissance was part and parcel. It was the world of *Shuffle Along,* the Negro musical that seemed at the time so marvelous, the world of Charles Gilpin in the *Emperor Jones,* of Negro dancers stomping at the Savoy, of the young Louis Armstrong, descending like a god out of the machine from high in the flies to the stage of the Lafayette Theater mounted on a huge golden trumpet, of Marcus Garvey, with his cry of "Up, You Mighty Race," of thousands of humble wayfarers, come, like black voortrekkers, out of the South to seek the end of their rainbow in the urban environments of the North.

It is also, I wish to argue, the only world in any final terms which really matters in the interpretation of the literature of the Negro Renaissance. Prescriptive criticism, I believe, has little value in the study of what black writers wrote about their Negro world of almost half a century now ago. Nor is sociological data in its pristine form actually a decided help.

Behind the sociology should be the revealed inner state of mind and sentiment of a people, the collective consciousness and sub-consciousness of a world which was neither as articulate nor as introspective as more sophisticated worlds might have been. Because I think a grave injustice has been done by those who dismiss Langston Hughes' sole long piece of fiction written during the Renaissance as a bad book and really, it would seem, an erroneous attempt at the representation of Negro life, I want to take that piece of fiction and test it against this world, of which it should be, if Langston Hughes is any artist at all, actually a revelation and, conceivably, a vindication. I want to put under scrutiny now his novel, *Not Without Laughter*.

* * *

This novel is an account of six years in the life of a Negro boy named James, or Sandy, Rogers, who lived, once upon a time, in the town of Stanton, Kansas, a fictional Kansas town which is really Lawrence, where the University of Kansas is actually located and where, also, Langston Hughes spent some of the years of his own youth. Sandy, when we first meet him, is nine, going on ten. He belongs to a matriarchal clan headed by his aged but still sturdy grandmother, Hager Williams. Aunt Hager remembers slave times in Alabama, where she was born. But she has been in Stanton, in her own words, "fo' nigh on forty years," ever since she and her husband, now dead these ten years, came up from Montgomery. In that time, after seeing two boy children die, she has raised and sent through high school her eldest daughter, Tempy, and educated her second daughter until that daughter, Annjee, married a yellow Negro, Sandy's father, of whom Aunt Hager speaks always most disdainfully and with whom, on those relatively rare occasions when he is around, she loves to bicker. Her third and youngest daughter, Harriett, the one who is occasioning her her greatest heartache and for whom, perhaps, she has the tenderest regard, is still in high school, but already rebellious and sullen and wild.

The three daughters are all, like their mother, dark of hue. But Sandy, a cross between his mother and his father, Jimboy, is brown. Tempy no longer lives under the matriarchal roof. She has wedded well, to Mr. Arkin Siles, a railway clerk who owns houses and attends with Tempy, a true Negro *arriviste,* the local black Episcopal church.

On the head of Tempy, convert to the black bourgeoisie, Hughes heaps throughout the book his withering scorn. It is perhaps the novel's philosophically most questionable motif, though understandable as an over-reaction from a Negro author, like Hughes, whose identification with the Negro masses certainly seemed genuine enough, but who was himself, nevertheless, the nephew of a Negro congressman, from whom, indeed, he got his Christian name of Langston, and the grandson of a woman whose first husband had been one of the free Negroes who accompanied John Brown to Harper's Ferry. Around the figures of Annjee, however, and of adolescent Harriett, Hughes weaves a parable which lifts Gunnar Myrdal's famous dichotomy of Negro leadership, the School of Accommodation versus the School of Protest, out of the cold, forbidding world of academic jargon and scholarly demonstration and, passing it through the sea change of his art, re-incarnates it in the living flesh of the two girls. Annjee is strong-bodied and placid, full of love for her handsome yellow husband, and of grateful wonder that he has found her accpetable as a wife, proud and considerate of her son, and as she once points out, one of the few colored girls in Stanton of a sufficiently equable disposition to have spent, as she has, five years working in the kitchen of the white, and constitutionally querulous, Mrs. J. J. Rice. Harriett, at sixteen, is a slim black beauty, with a satiny skin, a talent for song and dance, and a growing bitterness, which she finds it hard to contain, against both white oppression and Negro toleration of the same. Aunt Hager in her dreams, it would seem, has reconciled the two. She wants Sandy to grow up to be as great as Booker T. Washington *and* Frederick Douglass and to emulate them both. She takes in washing and holds, as best she can, her family together against that day when Sandy will be a man and will have brought honor to himself and credit to his race.

It is this dream of Aunt Hager's, really, which sets the tone and dominates the form of the panoramic view of a Negro family, seen through the ingénu eyes of a boy coming to maturity, which is what the novel actually is. That it should, has seemed greatly to trouble some critics who apparently believe that only accounts like *Native Son* and *Invisible Man*, in which Negroes are futilely angry all of the time and ignominiously defeated in the end, or misty excursions into the poetry of the ineffable such as *Go Tell It On The Mountain*, are honest and worthwhile expressions by Negro writers of the nature of Negro life. *Native Son, Invisible Man, Go Tell It On The Mountain*, deserve all the accolades which can be conferred upon them. They are good books which tell in memorable ways part of the truth. But they do tell only *part*. To some degree, indeed, they have perpetrated a literary fallacy.

Negroes have had their problems in America. Who would dare say otherwise? And the millennium of social justice in America is still, apparently, far in the distant future. And yet, when we look unblinkingly at the facts, the real story of the Negro in America is the story of his success. Against great odds he has not failed. The admission that he has not, seems to displease many people, some of them white, others of them, most unfortunately, colored. But the Black American has never been destined for catastrophe. He has been destined for success. Biological failures die. There are five times as many Negroes in America today as there were when President Lincoln signed the Emancipation Proclamation. The Negro has been, when defined in efficient, rather than conventional terms, a sociological success. As the years advance and the Negro's horizon of opportunity widens he is translating his ability to survive and to live with himself and others into forms of political and economic activity which, even in the standardized terms of our American system, can be recognized as success. It is quite possible, then, for a Negro family to be as poor as the family in which Sandy grows up, to have its differences, as the differences that take Tempy to Mr. Siles, Annjee to Jimboy, and Harriett through a flight from home and a fling at prostitution into top billing in the show world as a queen of the blues, to be limited in its resources, lacking in its connections with the powerful and the affluent, void of a so-called distinguished ancestry and dependent only upon its inner will and strengths, and yet for it, like Sandy's family, to be a rich haven for the human spirit and a place of nurture for very decent human beings.

In *Not Without Laughter*, Langston Hughes, to his eternal credit, faces up to this so far eternal verity of the Negro's existence in America. He goes into the private world of the Williams family, itself as compact as the Negro world from which it takes its character. In that world he finds adversity. But he also finds the strength to meet mischance. And, above all, he finds an ability to sustain a love of life itself. He finds it in Jimboy. He finds it in Annjee. He finds it in Harriett. He finds it being steadily inculcated, in young Sandy. He finds it in the Negroes who file in and out of the four-room frame dwelling on Cypress Street, an alley really, where the Williamses live. He belabors its modification and abasement in Tempy, who has, after all, been corrupted by white ideals. But at the very end of the novel he finds it transported into the new promised land of the North, both in the crowd at the theatre on the South Side which applauds Harriett and her fellow entertainers, and joins them too in their routines when, as is not too infrequent, it is so minded, and in the strains of the spiritual Sandy hears on his way home with Annjee from the show — the spiritual that is drifting out into the night of a black ghetto in the urban North, lifted on to the vehicle of a passing wind by old black Southern voices singing in a Northern store which their possession of the voices has made into a black Southern church.

The people who find unpalatable Langston Hughes' gospel, who prate of his shirking his responsibilities as a social seer to his black constituency, also disapprove of his lack of skill and power as an artist. *Not Without Laughter* is not a pretentious work of art. It is not stuffed with elaborate esoterica that require even more elaborate interpretation, so that both an author and a critic can participate in a precious game which permits their vanities to realize how superior they are to a common reader. It tells its story simply but intelligently. It is a family chronicle as well as, in effect, a voyage from boyhood to the threshold of maturity. It integrates two pictures into one illuminating revelation of the inside of Negro life. And so it is put together like the joint portrait it is supposed to be, not like a play. It is about Negroes and it is full of softly-slurred and very convincingly reproduced Negro speech. But it also takes a lesson from *Huck Finn*. Its style is in itself a subtle reproduction of a Negro idiom. It is, this style, in its own way, a Negro world. *Not Without Laughter* has its faults. The novel contains its share of interpolated tales, although those tales seem to me no more extraneous than the interpolated tales in *Tom Jones* or *Joseph Andrews*. The novel also has more than its share of moments which are overly sentimental. But none of these faults obtrude on the novel's first great virtue. This novel is a tale so well told that it does achieve the impression of making the real world live within its pages. Let me linger a little on this point. Hughes' imagination must have worked at a level of creativity which lesser mortals never know when he created this book. At the beginning of the story a cyclone strikes the Williams' house, wrenching away and bearing into oblivion the Williams' porch, which then must be replaced. Far down into the novel, Sandy wants a sled for Christmas. But his mother has been sick and temporarily laid off from work. Moreover, at this very juncture, Harriett gets stranded in Memphis where she has abandoned the carnival with which she ran off from home. And so one night Sandy sees his mother, who has dragged herself from bed, out behind the house poking in the scraps of wood left by the carpenters who replaced the porch. He knows then that he will not get his sled, and we recognize the strange inconsequence of life, the porch and the sled and the carnival, chance and human passion, and uniting all, in this novel, the talent of an artist who could remember a miniscule effect such as the debris from a cyclone's aftermath. An impressive feature of *Not Without Laughter* is that Hughes' creative powers operate at such a level not once, but constantly. They operate, moreover, in this fashion, not only in the realm of incident, but also in the business of character revelation.

One of the big speeches in the book, if not the biggest, is put into the mouth of Jimboy, Sandy's father. He is upbraiding Sandy for buying candy with the coppers Aunt Hager has entrusted to the boy for Sunday School. "To take money and use it for what it ain't s'posed to be used is stealing," Jimboy says. And he adds, "That's what you done today, and then come home and lie about it. Nobody's ugly as a liar, you know that! . . . I'm not much maybe. Don't mean to say I am. I won't work a lot, but what I do, I do honest. White folks get rich lyin' and stealin' — and some niggers gets rich that way, too — but I don't need money if I got to get it dishonest, with a lot of lies trailing behind me, and can't look folks in the face. It makes you feel dirty! It's no good! . . . Don't I give you nickels for candy whenever you want 'em?" Clearly Jimboy's speech is aimed not only at Sandy, but at posterity. It utters an ethical judgement on the civilization which today has gone to the moon as well as to places nearer home which I need not name. It also reflects on everything which I have tried to say about the Harlem Renaissance and the Negro world which I have argued bred the Renaissance and determined what the Renaissance would be. Such speeches always court the danger of seeming contrived, of not really appearing to belong in the text if the text is supposed to be part of a story that really happened and not merely a sermon or a tract. And perhaps the sense of a little touch of contrivance may attach itself to Jimboy's lecture. But, if it does, as is probably the case, it is still only a very little touch. For the speech is part of a situation that has come alive for us, and it does come as a logical expression from Sandy's father at the time he makes it. Above all, we have come to know

Jimboy. He is a black sheep. But he is not one of Dante's cold-blooded sinners. Nor is he an idiot. In fact, he is, within his limits, the very kind of person in "real life" who should say what he does when he does and precisely as he does.

The speech is in character for him, just as the Hughes' novel is in character for the Renaissance. It is a fable of Negro life in America. It is not a bauble to attract the tourist trade. The Renaissance, the customary legend goes, lasted for less than fifteen years, and then was swept away by the Depression. I prefer to believe that it only disappeared for a while beneath a rush of events that concealed its form and may have even diluted its content. But it is a theory of mine that in Black America a cumulative process is perennially at work. The Bigger Thomases may come and go. The Williams families, in Black America, constitute the equivalent of an eternal verity. They are always there, ready when one New Negro has run his course, to produce another, to denounce, like Jimboy, meanness and duplicity, and to work like Aunt Hager and her children, if in various ways, still with a concerted aim, for a better world, for all the Williamses, of every color and every breed, not only by' and by', but here and now, and in an America, indeed, which the Williamses will have helped to make more what every Williams of good will and bright vision would have it be.

21

Jean Toomer's *Cane:*
An Issue of Genre

Blyden Jackson

with an Introduction and Afternote by the Editor

(No work has benefitted more from the revival of interest
in the Harlem Renaissance as part of a new interest in Black
American writing generally than Jean Toomer's puzzling and
provocative *Cane,* a book of unquestionably great power and
vitality that deserves a place in the front rank of American
literature. A principal cause of the neglect of *Cane* has been
what Professor Jackson calls "an issue of genre"—Is the work a
novel? If critics could not classify it, they seemed unable to
deal with it—a pathetic indication of the paralysis of much
American literary study. In the ensuing essay Professor
Jackson traces the history of the problem of "placing" *Cane*
since its publication half a century ago. More is at issue,
however, than simply "pigeonholing" the major work of a
remarkably original writer. In recent years a number of young
scholars have become intrigued with the problem of identifying the genre of a number of significant American works—from
Sherwood Anderson's *Winesburg, Ohio* to John Barth's *Lost in
the Funhouse*—that have characteristics of both miscellaneous
collections of short pieces (not even necessarily stories) and
dramatically and thematically unified novels. The most comprehensive effort deals with such American (and foreign)
works, Forrest L. Ingram's *Representative Short Story Cycles*

317

of the Twentieth Century, proposes the term "short-story
cycle" to describe these works and facilitate their interpretation. So far *Cane* has not been analyzed in terms of Professor
Ingram's elaborately detailed theories; but a growing number
of critics have proposed reasons for considering *Cane* "a
novel." To Professor Jackson's history, I will append a
summary of eight of these theories along with an account of
my own reasons for regarding *Cane* as a Black "Waste Land"
with a unified structure analogous to that of Eliot's poem. —
Warren French)

* * *

Cane was published as a book first in 1923. It is important
to note that a goodly measure, if not all, of it had appeared in
separate autonomous bits before the appearance of the book.
Arna Bontemps, for example, in his introduction to a
paperback *Cane* issued in 1969 cites *Broom, The Crisis,
Double Dealer, The Liberator, Little Review, Modern Review,
Nomad, Prairie,* and *S4N* as periodicals in which units of *Cane*
had appeared before publication of the book.

When *Cane* did appear, it was organized in three sections,
each section, as well as the whole book—to paraphrase, as well
as quote, an apt observation of Bontemps'—constituting a
melange of poetry and prose whipped together in a "kind of
frappé." In the first section there are six short stories—or
sketches—in prose and twenty interpolations of verse of
varying lengths, probably representing fourteen separate
poems. In the second section there are seven short stories—or
sketches—in prose and nine interpolations of verse representing, apparently, seven separate poems. In the third section
is one story only, the novelette "Kabnis," presented much in
the form of a play—the form in which it had been offered for
the stage and rejected by Kenneth MacGowan for lack of
plot—and the interpolations of verse, three of them repetitions
of the same one-stanza poem and the fourth, a quotation from
a portion of a Negro spiritual. The stories—or sketches—in the
first section are all set in Georgia and associated with the

variety of small-town life which is more agrarian than urban. In the second section the setting shifts to Washington and, in one story called "Bona and Paul," to Chicago. Georgia, of the countryside and small towns, is again the setting in "Kabnis." Clearly it is possible to find a certain unity—or certain unities—of setting in *Cane*. No single character, however, or group of characters appears in more than one story or sketch.

Cane was reviewed in two important Negro journals and house-organs, *Opportunity* (of the National Urban League) and *The Crisis* (of the NAACP), shortly after its publication. A review by Montgomery Gregory, at the time the Director of Dramatic Art and Professor of Public Speaking at Howard University, appeared in *Opportunity* in December, 1923; a review by the founder and editor, W. E. B. DuBois, whose heroic stature in the history of the American Negro here needs no proclamation, appeared in *The Crisis* in February, 1924. DuBois had little to say about the form of *Cane,* except to call it, unequivocally and without hesitancy, a book of stories and poems. He was, as a matter of fact, much more interested in disputing Toomer's knowledge of Georgia, where Toomer had lived for four months and DuBois for thirteen years. He was also interested in recognizing Toomer's knowledge of human beings. Montgomery Gregory, on the other hand, examined the form of *Cane* in some detail. Without ever labeling it a novel, but with evident indebtedness to the "Foreward" supplied by Waldo Frank, Gregory did find in *Cane* verse, fiction and drama "fused into a spiritual unity, an 'aesthetic equivalent' [Waldo Frank's words] of the Southland." Yet a check word by word of Gregory's review discloses that the reviewer was able to sense this spiritual unity without ever alluding to *Cane* as a novel, and the reference to Toomer in an account of an *Opportunity* dinner for writers, given in 1925, is to "Jean Toomer, Poet and Short Story writer, author of 'Cane.' " In *The Negro Caravan,* an anthology first published in 1941 and edited by three Negro scholars highly venerated by their contemporary, and even younger black colleagues, Sterling Brown, Arthur Davis and the late Ulysses Lee, *Cane* is

called "a collection of sketches, short stories, and poems." In
Dark Symphony, an anthology of Negro literature first
published as recently as 1968, with one black editor (James A.
Emanuel) and one white (Theodore L. Gross), *Cane* is called a
"miscellany of Toomer's early work, containing fictional
portraits and poems of life in the villages of Georgia and in
Washington, D.C." It is described in virtually the same way in
Black Voices (1968), edited by Abraham Chapman, an older
white scholar whose attachment to Negro literature may be
much conditioned by the close personal relations he once had
with Richard Wright, as well as by his sympathetic reading of
the older Negro scholars. Quite possibly, the consensus on
Cane as its form appears to Negro scholars of the older
generation affirms itself loudly and clearly in *Negro Voices in
American Fiction,* published in Chapel Hill in 1948 and
written by Hugh Gloster, now President of Morehouse College,
but for most of his professional life a professor or department
head of English at various Negro colleges and, additionally, the
founder and first president of the College Language Association, once, if not still, the Negro facsimile of the Modern
Languages Association. In his book Gloster classifies *Cane* as
"a potpourri of stories, sketches, poetry, and drama." One
deviation from this probable consensus may be observed. Alain
Locke, a Negro scholar of great authority among Negroes—and
some whites—in his day and a catalyst of such power and
magnitude in the Harlem Renaissance as to be sometimes
called its midwife, in the "Who's Who of the Contributors" to
The New Negro (1925), the volume prominently associated
with the Harlem Renaissance and first a special issue of *Survey
Graphic,* which Locke edited, specifically, though rather
cursorily, refers to Toomer as the author of *Cane,* "a novel."

Apparently, therefore, it is conceivable that the current
disposition to call *Cane* a novel may have derived much, if not
all, of its original impetus from a passage in Robert Bone's
now relatively well-known *The Negro Novel in America,* first
published in 1958. Hugh Gloster wrote of Negro *fiction*—all of
Negro fiction; Bone, only of the Negro novel. Darwin Turner

has said, therefore, in the *Negro Digest* (January 1969) of *Cane*, "it is not a novel, not even the experimental novel for which Bone pled to justify including it in his study of novels by Negroes." He could have quoted Bone: "Jean Toomer's *Cane* (1923) is an important American novel. By far the most impressive product of the Negro Renaissance, it ranks with Richard Wright's *Native Son* and Ralph Ellison's *Invisible Man* as a measure of the Negro novelist's highest achievement." Whatever Bone's inducements in dealing with *Cane*, he did nothing by halves. If he made *Cane* a novel—which, of course, it may be—he also made it a good one, which, of course, it may be also. And yet, in the light of most that had been said about *Cane* before Bone published and in the absence of more conclusive evidence than seems to have appeared even yet, Bone's action does seem precipitate, especially in view of some of its consequences.

As not only a Negro novel, but also one of the three best Negro novels, according to the only "old" work dealing with the Negro novel, *Cane* has been acquiring, in the recent years since black literature has become more fashionable than it previously was, what might well be designated as the beginning of a sacred canon. Not unnaturally, when the form and shape of *Cane* is contemplated, the human tendency to exalt *expertise* requires of any explicator at least a little ingenuity to demonstrate that *Cane* is an organic whole. An attractive article of faith in this sacred canon has been the asseveration that *Cane* although *sans* some of the traditional trappings of a unified piece of long fiction—such as a protagonist and a plot—is nevertheless a novel. In one recent issue of the *CLA Journal* (March 1971), for example, Bernard Bell undertakes to show how the poems in *Cane* operate to give the whole book a functional unity and Patricia Chase does likewise with *Cane's* women. Clearly, indeed, that Jean Toomer may have resorted to an unusual means of composing a novel is altogether possible. He may even, for that matter, have resorted to such means without being aware, either in whole or in part, of what he was doing. Art is full of instances in which

an artist accomplishes more, as well as less, than he intended.
Yet, in reference to *Cane* and its form, some of the means
currently in use to argue for its novelistic identity reflect
conceptualizations that can hardly be said to have been even in
existence in the 1920s. There is a theory of the absurd, for
instance, inherent in Patricia Chase's description of *Cane's*
women which, as Miss Chase herself goes to some pains to
insist, relates *Cane* to existentialism. And James Kraft in his
article, "Jean Toomer's *Cane*" (*Markham Review*, October
1970), even as he is specifying that, in his opinion, "the form
of *Cane* suggests the kind of breadth and complexity that is in
the novel" [note the word *novel*] and at the same time also
apparently acceding to Darwin Turner's explanation that *Cane*
grew from "pieces of shorter fiction. . .not originally written
as parts of a novel," so that "emphasis cannot. . .be placed
upon the form as an original conception," is still able (using,
along the way, an allusion to Melvin Dixon's article in the
July, 1969 issue of *Negro Digest* viewing favorably a black
aesthetic that demands "an organic, self-creating unity of
forms") to say, "if it is thought that in the black aesthetic
unity is organic, or self-creating, then the formal unity of *Cane*
as a novel is not affected by Toomer's not originally
conceiving of the parts as forming a whole."

Fifty years ago when *Cane* was composed, Toomer,
whatever his intentions, could not have been thinking—at least
not in doctrinaire terms—of an existentialist theory of the
absurd or a black aesthetic. Two of his far from obscure
contemporaries—Waldo Frank and Gorham Munson—both of
whom happened to be white, as well as friends of his, and
neither of whom was apparently insensitive to the form of
Cane, whether it was the result of a deliberate design or an
organic growth, did comment, however, on the total effect of
the book. Neither of them, incidentally, ever refers explicitly
to *Cane* as a novel. Waldo Frank, as has already been indicated,
wrote a "Foreword" for *Cane,* in which he conceives of it as a
"chaos" of verse, tale, and drama, but also does detect in the
book a "rhythmic rolling shift" from lyricism to narrative, as

from mystery to infinite pathos. It was his view that, carefully read, in *Cane* a "complex and significant form" does take substance from the chaos, a form which—to repeat his phrase that Montgomery Gregory quoted—he saw as an "aesthetic equivalent" for the South. For, actually, Frank was more concerned in his "Foreward" to emancipate Toomer from a race and a region than to do anything else. He insisted that Toomer was primarily a poet, even a poet in prose, and he clearly thought of Toomer's poetic gift as lyric, not epic—not, that is, as the equipment of an artist with a novelist's sense of life or of aesthetic forms. But, still, it was against the possible idea that *Cane* was just a Negro book, or merely a bit of the South in exclusively parochial terms, that Frank was inveighing.

Gorham Munson's appraisal of *Cane* appeared in *Opportunity* in September, 1925, in an article entitled "The Significance of Jean Toomer":

> *Cane* is, from one point of view, the record of [Toomer's] search for suitable literary forms. We can see him seeking guidance and in several of the stories, notably *Fern* and *Avey,* it is the hand of Sherwood Anderson that takes hold. But Anderson leads toward formlessness and Toomer shakes him off for Waldo Frank in such pieces as *Theatre* [sic] where the design becomes clear and the parts are held in a vital aesthetic union. Finally he breaks through in a free dramatic form of his own, the play *Kabnis* which still awaits production by an American theatre that cries for good native drama and yet lacks the wit to perceive the talent of Toomer.

It cannot be persuasively argued, therefore, that Munson thought of *Cane* as a novel. Indeed, it would seem rather clear that he thought of it quite otherwise, as a work of which the separate parts displayed a variety of forms. But it can be argued—and this of some moment—when all of Munson's appraisal of *Cane* is taken into account, that, like Waldo Frank, he is much more interested in demonstrating that Toomer had transcended race than in making any other point. Munson's references to Sherwood Anderson and Waldo Frank, or to a native drama for an American theatre, are, in

themselves, incompatible with a black aesthetic. But in his
concluding statement (not quoted above) about *Cane*—and
therefore about Toomer—Munson arrives at the contention
which is truly his prime concern. Here he argues that Toomer
has divined the chaos of the modern world and understood
that the great categorical imperative for the modern artist is to
determine his own proper reaction to that chaos. For Munson,
that is, as for Frank, Toomer was supremely, as well as
superbly, the artist, universally so, using whatever might be the
particularities of his accidental identifications with time and
space only to render less abstract the abstractions of all human
kind.

Jean Toomer cannot be dismissed as a writer of no
relevance to Negro literature. *Cane,* certainly at this moment,
should hardly be dismissed as a work that is clearly not a
novel. Nor should any of the present critical activity in
connection with *Cane* necessarily be either discouraged or
summarily decided. Much of it, I would readily contend, adds
to our enjoyment, and our fuller comprehension, of a work
well worth the time and effort which a host of explicators may
elect to spend upon it. But it may well be all too apparent that
the present relation of critical scholarship to *Cane* but
illustrates a state of affairs still too endemic in the treatment
of Negro literature. For the serious study of literature
demands always a due regard for the services of literary
history.

Everything, for example, about the form of *Cane* would
not be necessarily altogether settled if we could speak with
reasonable assurance of Toomer's own declared intentions. But
knowing these intentions would help. It has been rumored that
Toomer once indicated to his publishers that *Cane* was a novel.
If he did so, it does not yet appear from a search, supervised
by Mrs. Ann Allen Shockley, Associate Librarian and Head of
Special Collections for the Fisk University Library, of the
more than thirty-thousand manuscript pages of Toomer
material in the Toomer Collection at the library. It does
appear that Toomer did write at least three works which he

presented explicitly as novels: "The Gallonwerps" (1927), "Transatlantic" (1930), and "Eight-Day World" (1932). None of them was ever published, apparently because he found no publisher willing to accept any of them. There is at least a suggestion in this probable circumstance that Toomer may have lacked the very sense of form which some publishers or publishers' agents believed a novelist should have.

To start apodictically, with the presumption that *Cane* is a novel, and then to proceed to show how, through the use of symbolisms, or of characters, or of themes, or of progressions in mood, or of the continuous presence of a poet-observer, Toomer imparted to *Cane* perhaps a higher unity than can normally be found in the conventional novelistic ligatures may, in the end, have no untoward consequences. And it is still too early to begin to say too conclusively that *Cane* is not a novel. But it is also, probably even more, too early to say that it is, and surely much too early to pass on from such an exposed position to some of the larger claims, either about the nature of Toomer's art or the relation of that art to the Negro in America, which already, howsoever in the name of sweetness and light, have been made.

* * *

Afternote: Despite Robert Bone's acclamation in *The Negro Novel in America* as early as 1958 of *Cane* as one of the three "highest achievements" of the Negro novelist, not until 1969, when the paperback edition introduced by Arna Bontemps made the book generally available were any critical explications limited to the novel published. The next five years saw, however, the publication of at a dozen and a half analyses of the novel as a whole or of the relation of individual parts to the whole. Such highly regarded black scholars as Darwin Turner and W. Edward Farrison have emphatically rejected the idea of considering the book as a "novel"; nevertheless at least eight other analysts have insisted on focusing their efforts on finding some "unifying" device in the work. (A number of other critics have mentioned the "unity" of the work, but have concentrated on some other aspect of it.)

The most satisfying of these discussions remains Todd M. Lieber's "Design and Movement in *Cane*," which appeared in the *CLA Journal* in 1969, the same year that the paperback *Cane* became generally available. Lieber finds the book more than just "thematically unified"; he argues that it also possesses a comprehensive design that encompasses its separate parts into a sustained progression. Part One, he finds, portrays the inherent beauty, mixed with pathos, of the black culture that "must be embraced if the black man is to attain spiritual life." Part Two, he continues, presents the consequences of the spiritual death that occurs when the black rejects his heritage; and Part Three shows the spiritual rebirth that a return to the South and an acceptance of blackness makes possible. This interpretation makes of the book at least as much of a novel as Herman Melville's *The Confidence Man* is, by presenting the protagonist not as one individual, but as "the black man," possessing, rejecting, and at last accepting his black identity through a variety of physically different, but spiritually similar individuals. Not all blacks—or whites—are willing, of course, to accept this transcendental notion of all men possessing parts of a single soul; and the generic classification of *The Confidence Man* remains after a century at least as controversial as that of *Cane*.

Donald G. Ackley's "Theme and Vision in Jean Toomer's *Cane*" (*Studies in Black Literature*, 1970) makes of the book a kind of triptych, with the first section "primarily an effort to catch the parting soul of slavery and pour it into song"; the second, a clarification of the "vague specter" of the dominant but dead white society that "haunted" the early stories; and the third as a dramatic presentation of the major themes of the earlier sections. It is difficult to determine from this account, however, what aesthetic principle might turn Toomer's collection into more than a kind of sociological slide-lecture.

Two analyses in *Studies in the Novel* (a general journal; the two just previously mentioned are largely confined to black scholarship or criticism of black literature) expound contrasting optimistic and pessimistic theories that warrant treating the work as a unified novel. John M. Reilly's "The Search for Black Redemption: Jean Toomer's *Cane*" argues that in the first section Toomer establishes the conditions for black redemption, but in the second part shows the increased inhibition of spontaneous life, and in the third part has Ralph Kabnis emerge as a horrible example, the victim of the sin of racial oppression, who has become like the sin itself "a foe of life." William C. Fischer's "The Aggregate Man in Jean Toomer's *Cane*," on the other hand, concludes that while many of the male characters are egotistically isolated and emotionally paralyzed by "the reality of racial bloodletting," they are counterbalanced by others whose strength and sensitivity permit them "to survive as an ongoing inspiration."

Patricia Watkins answers her own question "Is There a Unifying Theme in *Cane*?" by explaining in an article in the *CLA Journal* in 1971 that throughout the book Toomer is saying "that man is a creature alone and apart, unable to share and commit himself with another, and after many abortive attempts to do so, he finds that nothing has happened and nothing has changed." The critic evades, however, the question of whether the work is a "novel" or not and might have pointed out that the same theme unifies many collections of poems like Edwin Arlington Robinson's about Tilbury Town and E. A. Houseman's *A Shropshire Lad*. In a companion piece, "The Unity of Jean Toomer's *Cane*," Catherine L. Innes takes on the most extraordinarily difficult and almost thankless task of demonstrating that this unity can be found in the book's consistent portrayal of the failure of a philosophical premise to be realized if social conditions are not propitious for its fulfilment (that is, she portrays Toomer not as rejecting the philosophy, but lamenting the absence of a social situation in which it might be fulfilled). The theory is that expounded by P. D. Ouspensky in *Tertium Organum*, a continuation of Bacon's *New Atlantis* that influenced such friends of Toomer's as Hart Crane, Waldo Frank, and Gorham

Munson, and that envisioned, through the development of
"cosmic consciousness," the hidden meaning of all things
being realized. The problem about this reading is why — if
Toomer wished to propagandize for Ouspensky's theories as a
solution to the world's ills instead of rejecting them — he never
even mentions them as an overlooked possibility in a book
that contains a great many religious speculations.

These religious speculations are doubtless the reasons for
the authors of two of the most intriguing articles about *Cane*
regarding the book as "oracular." Benjamin McKeever's early
and brief *"Cane* as Blues" *(Negro American Literature Forum,*
1970) explores the relationship of the book to this popular
form of Negro music and interprets it as an "oracular" attempt
to bear witness to the idea that "the Negro is not an
apprentice to equality but a journeyman to suffering." In a
much more complex study, "Jean Toomer's *Cane:* A Modern
Black Oracle" *(College Language Association Journal,* 1972),
Bowie Duncan first views the book as "a definite break with
traditional linear thought about composition" (like Joyce's
contemporary experiments and the later efforts of writers like
Kurt Vonnegut, Jr.) and compares it to an elaborate jazz
composition that lays down themes and performs variations
upon them "without defining a rigid progression," thus
producing "a composition that is continually in process."
Thus, Duncan goes on, "it seems that in the book as a whole
the variations on the theme and its relationships between the
past and the present, the ideal and the real, are infinite, and
there seems to be no resting place for the composition or the
audience. . . Thus the composition continues without specific
direction, though somewhat guided by the themes. *Cane* is
multifaceted, like an onion or a Chinese puzzle, and as an
oracle, it speaks of a reality like itself, something to be
experienced without absolute finality."

The only problem that these two intriguing interpretations
— which seem to me, especially in their finding a close
relationship between *Cane* and black American music, to get
closest to the spirit that infuses the work — pose is that while

they argue for its unity, they remove it far from the tradition of the novel, because the oracle has traditionally been a poetic, a lyric form — that might manifest itself, for example, in the wailing words that could accompany a blues or the cryptic language appropriate to an elaborate jazz composition. We are carried back at last to the apprehension that Professor Jackson cites of Waldo Frank's that "Toomer was primarily a poet, even a poet in prose" and that his "poetic gift" was "lyric, not epic." The many interpolated lyrics in *Cane,* then, are not out of place; it is the prose pieces rather that strain to become — and often succeed in becoming — poems.

This perception of *Cane* as essentially lyric and oracular compels a comparison with Eliot's *The Waste Land* that had appeared only a year before. Certainly no one can deny that the South, the America that Toomer depicts is a "waste land" as fearful as that which Eliot conjures up. Curiously, however, close as many of the analysts of *Cane* have come to suggesting similarities between the two works, none that I can discover has specified them. Perhaps they feared — with good reason — that they might be seeming to say that Eliot "influenced" Toomer. Before proceeding, I must make it explicit that I perceive no such "influence." Even where Toomer's work parallels Eliot's, it does not echo it. What I wish to call attention to is the remarkably similar way in which a black American writer looking at the plight of his people and a white writer, equally despairingly familiar with the United States and Europe, looking at the decay of Western culture generally, articulated their visions.

Despite *Cane's* being divided into only three parts and *The Waste Land* into five, the two works may be seen to be strikingly similar — yet imaginatively varied — in structure if we compare the first two parts of *The Waste Land* with the first part of *Cane,* the third part of Eliot's poem with the second part of Toomer's work, and the last two parts of *The Waste Land* with "Kabnis."

The first of these equations is warranted, I believe, by the kinds of materials encompassed in the opening sections of the works. As I have argued in the introductory essay to this volume, the first two sections of *The Waste Land* present us with first a panoramic, "long-shot" view and then several close-up scenes of life in a sterile, decaying society. Toomer does the same thing in the first part of *Cane*, but instead of moving in cinematic fashion from a long-shot to a close-up, he alternates — in the manner of a later novel like John Steinbeck's *The Grapes of Wrath* — panoramic and dramatic views of the plight of the Southern blacks, using poems (as Steinbeck uses "inter-calary chapters") to present the general scene and using a series of vignettes of individual black women to illustrate the effect of the general conditions upon individuals (as Steinbeck uses the chapters in the story of the Joad family — it is noteworthy, in passing, that Toomer's women experience disappointments and disruptions in their lives similar to those experienced by Steinbeck's Ma Joad and her daughter Rosasharn). Throughout the first two sections of *The Waste Land* and the first section of *Cane*, emphasis falls upon both the failure of either exploiters or exploited to achieve any really meaningful human relationships, or to find — as in Toomer's "Esther" — any redemptive hope in a holy man. Esther's "sudden thought" that "conception with a drunken man must be a mighty sin" recalls the sordid conversation about child-bearing in the pub in *The Waste Land*. "Blood-Burning Moon" perhaps goes even further than any of Eliot's visions in depicting the way in which the hostile groups destroying each other will ultimately destroy themselves, but both works reach, before moving into their middle sections, an utter despair about the possibility of any future in traditional social orders.

Both the third part of *The Waste Land* and the second part of *Cane* explore — alternating songs with sketches — the prospects that cities offer for the salvation of the individual and the society and both come up with totally negative answers. As pointed out in the introductory essay, the third section of Eliot's poem asks the question, "After such knowledge, what forgiveness?" The second part of *Cane* poses precisely the same question. In the final episode, "Bona and Paul," the vacillating black youth Paul leaves his white date to offer an incredible apology for his behavior to a skeptical doorman at the "Crimson Gardens" ("a body whose blood flows to a clot upon the dance floor"). Then when he tries to go back and reaches the spot where he and the girl had been standing outside "the gilded exit door," she is gone. Since Paul cannot accomodate himself to either black or white worlds or establish some place between them for himself, he finds himself rejected and abandoned, like Eliot's passionless typist after her encounter with "the young man carbuncular."

So far the parallels between the two works have required the most careful scrutiny of the structuring of seemingly vastly different materials. The similarity of "Kabnis" to the last two parts of Eliot's poem — despite a great philosophical difference between their conclusions — is, I believe, more readily apparent. I have earlier commented that the fourth part of Eliot's poem corrects an unbalance by suggesting that too much water may be as dangerous as too much drought. Similarly Ralph Kabnis's situation in Georgia suggests that the young black man's "coming home" to the cane-fields of the rural South may be as fraught with pitfalls as his flight to the cities.

The specific inter-link between the works occurs, however, in the conversation of Kabnis's black employer, Hanby, a Puritanical "Uncle Tom," whom white tradesmen tolerated "because he spends money with them." When Hanby finds Kabnis drinking with some riff-raff, he lectures the young teacher "with a full consciousness of . . . moral superiority":

> ". . . the progress of the Negro race is jeopardized whenever the personal habits and examples set by its guides and mentors fall below the acknowledged and hard-won standard of its average member. This institution, of which I am the humble president, was founded, and has been maintained at a cost of great labor and untold sacrifice . . . To prove to the world that the Negro race can be just like any other race."

What Eliot has shown in his poem is what these "other races"

are like. Through Hanby, Toomer presents the supreme irony
of racial representatives laboring and sacrificing in order to win
the respect and imitate the manners of a corrupted and
decaying culture.

Neither *The Waste Land* nor *Cane* ends, however, on this
over-whelming note of irony; both suggest a possibility of
finding a way out of "the waste land," though these tentative
suggestions mark the major divergence between Eliot's and
Toomer's visions. Eliot — as explained in the introductory
essay — sees hope for the future in the Hindu Upanishads — a
movement into a rigorously intellectual and ascetic discipline.
Toomer suggests rather that this hope resides in a return to the
rhythm of natural cycles of birth, death, and rebirth that have
been frustrated by the institutionalization and communization
of society. After Kabnis removes a ceremonial robe and leaves
the ceremonial chamber, "Light streaks through the iron-
barred cellar window . . . The sun arises. Gold-glowing child, it
steps into the sky and sends a birth-song slanting down gray
dust streets and sleepy windows of the southern town."

This ending comes closer to the ending of Faulkner's later
Light in August than to the ending of *The Waste Land.* The
"cane" itself plays in Toomer's work a role like that of the
wheat in Frank Norris's *The Octopus* — the WHEAT that
remains, while men, "motes in the sunshine," perish.

Despite this final difference, however, the movement of
both *The Waste Land* and *Cane* is similar enough to suggest,
first, that the ultimate value of *Cane* lies in its providing the
junction point at which two traditions intersect — the
tradition of the sensitive blacks' protest against oppression and
dehumanization, the tradition of the sensitive post-industrial
revolution white artists' disaffection and disaffiliation from
"Establishment" institutions. Both works grow out of a
weltanschauung in which the artist, rooted in nature, despairs
over materialistic man's becoming the enemy of his environment. Second, the analogies between the works suggest that
the agitation over the question of whether *Cane* is a "novel"
may only distract attention from a full appreciation of this

assemblage of fragments of verse and prose. *The Waste Land* is also — though stylistically more coherent — an assemblage of fragments about a culture that has been shattered into fragments. The form of the work is itself part of the bitter comment that the work makes. But we have long been aware that *The Waste Land* is not simply a disarray of fragments, because the parts are inter-related in a whole that means more than the sum of the parts. *Cane* can be most satisfactorily viewed, I believe, as the same kind of montage. If we must have a label for such works, let us use Bowie Duncan's "Oracles" and avoid fruitless rewritings of books and redefinitions of genres to accomodate them to each other.

I have attempted to suggest only a few of many provocative similarities and differences between *Cane* and *The Waste Land*. This note provides neither the time nor place for undertaking a comparative study of such enormously complex works with such broad social implications. I have hoped here only to suggest that it is very likely that *Cane* originated — as *The Waste Land* is said to have — as "the relief of a personal and wholly insignificant grouse against life" that went on to express — to quote my words about *The Waste Land* in the "Postscript" to the opening essay in this volume — "feelings [that] correspond closely enough to those of the artistically receptive members of [the artist-grumbler's] contemporary or some subsequent society to establish his reputation as a spokesman." Further analysis of the dramatic, ideational, and symbolic parallels between *Cane* and *The Waste Land* and their psychological and social implications will reinforce, I believe, the arguments of those who have claimed a unique artistic value for this long neglected work. Some discomforting speculations about the relationship between the 1920s Literary Establishment and concepts of social justice may also arise from pondering the reasons why *Cane* had to wait so long for that kind of recognition that *The Waste Land* was almost immediately accorded.

22

How To Read a Canto

Max Halperen

By 1920, Ezra Pound — the stormiest literary hurricane of the twentieth century — had already led many lives: he had passed through a number of poetic phases; he had criticized art, music, literature, and society; he had been and was a "foreign correspondent" for little magazines like *Poetry* and *The Little Review;* he had helped Yeats redirect his poetry and had beaten the drums for Eliot and Joyce; he had translated Provencal and Chinese poetry and Japanese No plays; he had started or touted literary movements like imagism and free verse, and had passed beyond them. And he had a number of other lives to go, several of which would culminate in a decade in St. Elizabeth's — where he continued writing, criticizing, contributing, translating, touting — and trying to help any young poet who would listen.

As a poet, however, this one-man world had already committed himself to the poem that would take the rest of his life and that would integrate or at least incorporate the entire skein of experience and idea that is Ezra Pound. When he began *The Cantos* in 1917, he described it in a letter as a "new long poem (really L O N G, endless, leviathanic)." He could scarcely have known just where his life, and therefore the poem, would lead him, but he certainly was aware of the ambitiousness of his project. It was and remains his major bid for poetic immortality. No wonder, then, that Pound, far from wrapping himself in a cloak of assumed indifference, expressed concern more than once that his poem be properly understood, and lashed out bitterly when he felt he was being misunderstood. Yeats thought he was being helpful when, in *A Packet for Ezra Pound,* he repeated what Pound had told him about the fugal nature of the poem. "If Yeats knew a fugue from a frog," Pound told one of his correspondents, "he might have transmitted what I told him in some way that would have helped rather than obfuscated *his* readers." Two years later, Pound was even more exasperated: "God damn Yeats' bloody paragraph. Done more to prevent people from reading Cantos for what is *on the page* than any other smoke screen."

"Reading . . . for what is *on the page.*" Is it possible to do so? The smoke screen created by both attackers and defenders of the poem seems thick indeed. "Doubtless," wrote one critic,

> the reader will already have observed that one of the things I have asked of Mr. Watts is that he should be familiar with page 38 of the *ABC of Reading;* for unless the critic happens to know that page, he can scarcely be asked to understand Canto LXXV (though with the hint in line 9 a writer with the ability to read music and a knowledge of fifteenth-century musical symbology might possibly puzzle it out alone).

Thick indeed. And is it possible to read for what is on the page despite the inherent difficulties of the poem itself, seeing it neither as "rambling talk" (Allen Tate) nor as a set of obscure statements that can be understood only in relation to their sources?

I think with a minimum of help — the sort of help provided by very occasional reference to the *Annotated Index to the Cantos of Ezra Pound* — it is quite possible to read the poem as a poem, provided one gives it the same attention one gives any difficult poem, being alive to the tone of each line, awake to its implications, aware of its context. If that is done,

one will find, I think, that documents, translations, descriptions, personal comments — all may be read as images, directly reflecting the poet's state of mind or implying his attitude toward what he is presenting.

The following, then, is an experiment in reading, concentrating on the opening cantos. If the poem is at all ascertainable on its own merits, then surely these cantos are acid tests. Rewritten and reshuffled, they can scarcely be read as part of a narrative design. Canto I appeared at the end of Canto III in the first published draft. Canto II, with a different opening, was published originally as Canto VIII. Canto VI has been cut to half its original size. Comment that might have explained some of the material has been cut away. Pound himself admitted privately that some of the early material was presented in a manner "perhaps too enigmatically and abreviatedly. I hope, heaven help me, to bring them into some sort of design and architecture later."

As far back as 1912, Pound wrote: "One wants to find out what sort of things endure, and what sort of things are transient; what sort of things recur. . . ." We may take *The Cantos* as the record of Pound's attempt to "find out." It is, then, a quest. And Pound, wishing to indicate something of his own long poetic journey, begins Canto I with a translation from the *Odyssey* that runs for two pages:

> And then went down to the ship,
> Set keel to breakers, forth on the godly sea. . .

It is a long journey. Through dark fog and over "deepest water," the ship moves on its strange voyage, coming at last to the dread shores of Hades. Odysseus and his men need advice on how to get home, and they have been told that only the ghost of the prophet Tiresias can help them. On the shores of Hades they pray, pour libations, sacrifice sheep. At last Tiresias arrives, drinks the sheep's blood, and tells Odysseus what lies in store for him. Then come the rest of the "impotent dead" to drink the blood, be momentarily revived, and tell their tales.

Suggesting an artistic continuity from Homer's time until
now, the ancient epic serves as a gateway to Pound's modern
epic, for Pound also is about to set out on a journey through
mist and over deep water — though his will be an intellectual
journey; and Pound also will attempt to inject blood into the
ghosts of the past so that they may speak to and comment on
the present. "Nothing is new," Pound wrote in the thirties,
"and all good is renewal." In fact, Canto I may be taken as an
example of such renewal, for Pound has translated, not
directly from the Greek, but from a Renaissance Latin pony
by the Andreas Divus cited at the end of the Canto, and has
employed, not modern English, but the " 'Seafarer' metre, or
something like it." The implication is that despite (or because
of) these transformations, Homer's book of the dead retains its
muscle.

But to read the Canto as though it already incorporated or
even implied much about the rest of the long poem is, I think,
to miss what is on the page. For the moment, the Homeric
vision has renewed itself in Pound's mind, as, presumably, it
did in Divus'. But after Tiresias speaks, the vision fades,
perhaps because of limitations inherent in the material itself —
the translation does, after all, suggest a certain remoteness
from our own time; or because of limitations in the experience
of the poet himself — he does, after all, have a long journey to
make. In the *Odyssey*, the prophet's advice is quite detailed,
but in Pound's version it is cut to a very brief statement that
provides no advice at all. In his search for what is recurrent
and what is permanent, this new Odysseus will have no Tiresias
to guide him. "Lie quiet Divus," says Pound toward the end of
the Canto to the Latin translator of the *Odyssey*. "I mean,
that is, Andreas Divus." The spell is broken. The excitement of
those primitive rituals on the shores of hell has given way to a
matter-of-fact comment. And Odysseus ceases to speak in the
first person:

And he sailed, by Sirens and thence outward. . .

There are, then, to be no guides to the realm of the

permanent. But there are many Scyllas and Charybdises —
several of which are singled out in Cantos II and III.

Though sailing into the past over "deepest water," Pound
has always denied any sentimental yearning for the bygone:
"It may suit some of my friends to go about with their young
noses pointing skyward, decrying the age and comparing us
unfavorably to the dead men of Hellas or of Hesperian
Italy. . . . But I, for one, have no intention of decreasing my
enjoyment of this vale of tears by under-estimating my own
generation." As far as he is concerned, he seeks only what is
permanently alive, or what can be made to live. But that is
scarcely the only concern; there is also the problem of
presenting the past in such a way that it, like Tiresias, speaks
directly to the living. For living ideas may easily be stifled by
dead forms, by outmoded styles and methods, by words that
do not quite suit the material, by minds unable to absorb a
new viewpoint. Thus, the need to break old forms and to
disrupt old mental grooves, and thus Pound's concern with it.
Precisely that need lies at the heart of Canto II.

The point is made rather simply in the opening lines of the
Canto:

> Hang it all, Robert Browning,
> there can be but the one "Sordello."
> But Sordello, and my Sordello?
> Lo Sordels si fo di Mantovana.

The direct address to Browning suggests a sense of kinship and
implies something of an internal struggle — as though Pound
had toyed with the possibility of adapting Browning's method
and had, regretfully, discarded it. It suggests also, I think,
something of the joyous energy flowing into the young poet as
he finds it possible — even necessary — to strike out on his
own. Much as he might admire *Sordello* — and we have
evidence aplenty that he did — Pound cannot simply rewrite
the earlier poem either in form or in content. But Sordello as a
person — no longer within quotation marks, and thus no
longer a literary character — can, of course, be used again;
there can be more than one version of the thirteenth-century

Italian troubador, and Pound's version, "my Sordello," will
necessarily be different from Browning's. Now, as though
beginning a fresh appraisal, Pound records the biographical
snippet: "the Sordellos came from Mantua."

These lines take us, then, from a fixed form, *Sordello*, to a
new form and a fresh look at the source materials. The
following lines reverse the order: an ancient image of life and
life's energies, the elemental sea itself, is stirred up; however,
the result is nothing but a wave running in a beach-groove,
reanimating an ancient theme:

> So-shu churned in the sea.
> Seal sports in the spray-whited circles of cliff-wash,
> Sleek head, daughter of Lir,
>   eyes of Picasso
> Under black fur-hood, lithe daughter of Ocean;
> And the wave runs in the beach-groove:
> "Eleanor, ελεναυς and ελεπτολις!"

The meaning of these lines is probably clearer in the first
version of this Canto, which was prefaced by a rather heavily
ironic image of passion and inspiration in bondage to the past:

> Dido chocked up with tears for dead
>   Sichaeus;
> And the weeping Muse, weeping, widowed,
>   and willing,
> The weeping Muse
>   Mourns Homer,
> Mourns the days of long song.

Several lines later Pound tells us that

> Tyro to shoreward lies lithe with
>   Neptunus
> And the glass-clear wave arches over
>   them;
> Seal sports in the spray-whited circles
>   of cliff-wash,
> Sleek head, daughter of Lir,
>   eyes of Picasso

and the rest follows.

Three stages seem to be indicated in the earlier version:

farthest out to sea, the sea-god; closer, the circles of cliff-wash; finally, the beach-groove. After the images of weeping Dido and the widowed Muse, the appearance of Neptune indicates a new infusion of elemental energy, possibly a new vision. The present tense implies that such energy is always present, always recreative. As we move closer to the shore-line, we see evidence of the creative energies of the sea, first in a physical embodiment: "Seal sports . . ." But those energies are also mental ("sleek head") and artistic ("eyes of Picasso/ Under black fur-hood"); these too are creatures, "daughters," of the elemental natural forces represented by the sea god, whether he is named Lir (Irish) or Ocean (Greek).

And yet, when the fresh spurt of energy comes ashore, when the creative impulse spends itself, it may well result in nothing more than the repetition of an old idea, it may move in an old groove — the theme of destructive beauty. There is renewal here, but of a sort that deadens instead of enlivening. The Greek epithets describe Helen as ship- and city-destroying (derived from Aeschylus' *Agamemnon* — a fact which may content some but which is quite beside the point). Eleanor, however, is not simply another Helen; she is, as Canto VI describes her, also "domna jauzionda," the joyous lady capable of attracting and encouraging the troubador elite. Thus Pound restates the need to break old forms and to look at materials afresh. The beach groove ignores differences; it would lose whatever is unique in Eleanor.

In the present version of the Canto, So-shu (whose identity has never been settled) clearly replaces Neptune as the instigator of fresh power. The shift from Mantua to China in itself suggests an infusion of new materials and forms. Churning in the sea, So-shu is in touch with the infinite and the elemental; by stirring, he creates new combinations. But even his Oriental waves slip into the old Occidental groove. It is difficult to break an old habit of mind.

The problem is scarcely a new one; it was discerned and described by Homer. He might have been blind, but his ear was precise, his technique certain:

> And poor old Homer blind, as a bat,
> Ear, ear for the sea-surge, murmur of old men's voices.

> And doom goes with her in walking,
> Let her go back to the ships.

He could fix both the surge of new energies already noted in the Canto and the fears of old men. We are given the speech of the elders of Troy as they watch Helen on the wall:

> Moves, yes she moves like a goddess
> And has the face of a god
> . . . . . .
> And doom goes with her in walking,
> let her go back to the ships.

This, of course, is another version of the beach-groove. Beyond, the sea's energies forever enter man:

> And by the beach-run, Tyro
>   Twisted arms of the sea-god,
> Lithe sinews of water . . .

But on the beach no new groove is carved; there is only a "Quiet sun-tawny sand-stretch."

Even the assurance and energy provided by the vision of a god may be lost. It is possible to be certain of an immortal truth, yet be unable to convince others. In fact, a group faced with the same experience may see it quite differently from the one perceptive visionary. In Canto II, the god Bacchus appears to a sea-captain. Far more than does Ovid, the source of the tale, Pound stresses the certainty of the vision. Twice the repeats:

> I have seen what I have seen.

He insists:

> Aye, I, Acoetes, stood there,
>   and the god stood by me,

and again:

> When they brought the boy I said:
> "He has a god in him,
>   though I do not know which god."
> And they kicked me into the fore-stays.

The last line quoted indicates the connection between this episode and the rest of the Canto. Acoetes sees the god, but none of his men do. King Pentheus of Thebes, to whom Acoetes tells his story, refuses to believe it. And the Canto fades out into a world, not of certainty, but of instability:

> The tower like a one-eyed great goose
> cranes up out of the olive-grove.

The instability of the world in which the poet seeks the recurrent and the permanent — this seems to be the central theme of Canto III. On the slither of time the poet must seek the eternal — the gods. In an early draft of the first Canto, Pound wrote:

> And shall I claim;
> Confuse my own phantastikon,
> Or say the filmy shell that circumscribes me
> Contains the actual sun;
>   Confuse the thing I see
> With actual gods behind me?

At the opening of Canto III, Pound describes himself as a young and impecunious aesthete, alone and idle in Venice:

> I sat on the Dogana's steps
> For the gondolas cost too much, that year,
> And there were not "those girls," there was one face,
> And the Buccentoro twenty yards off, howling "Stretti,"
> And the lit cross-beams, that year, in the Morosini.

The repetition of "that year" calls attention, here as elsewhere, to the temporal and impermanent nature of these experiences, while the third line suggests their personal accidental quality (if one is diligent and devoted to such matters, one may trace "those girls" to Browning; but Pound expunged Browning from the passage and I see little reason to insist on writing him back in; the line stands as a statement about two different experiences and that is what matters). But against these fragmentary experiences, Pound places an image of the gods, who — representing immortal truth and immortal vigor — are ever-present:

> Gods float in the azure air,
> Bright gods and Tuscan, back before dew was shed.
> Light: and the first light, before ever dew was fallen.

They are presented as an idle young aesthete might see them or intuit them: beautiful but unrelated to the world of men. Upon entering that active world — as Pound does through the tale of the Cid —

> My Cid rode up to Burgos,
> Up to the studded gate between two towers,

one finds it difficult to engage the gods; one finds not eternity but death and destruction:

> Ignez da Castro murdered, and a wall
> Here stripped, here made to stand.
> Drear waste . . .

In Canto IV Pound asserts the method, already implied in a number of places, by which he hopes to overcome time and change. Joining and juxtaposing images, he outlines, in a tentative way, several recurrent attitudes. He also asserts — and this too has been implied — that it is not enough for the poet to discover what recurs and what endures. Odysseus may return with the wisdom of the prophet, but loses all companions. Acoetes is firm — "I have seen what I have seen" — but he is the only one to see it and is destroyed. The artist's knowledge must somehow be related to the active world of men. Otherwise, as Pound has never tired of insisting, such knowledge is useless.

Recalling the end of Canto III, Canto IV opens with the destructive vision that animated Homer's pen:

> Palace in smoky light,
> Troy but a heap of smouldering boundary stones.

But as the artist who would preserve rather than destroy, and who is concerned with the vision and the spirit that can animate an entire community, Pound appeals:

> ANAXIFORMINGES! Aurunculeia!
> Hear me. Cadmus of Golden Prows!

> The silver mirrors catch the bright stones and flare,
> Dawn, to our waking, drifts in the green cool light;
> Dew-haze blurs, in the grass, pale ankles moving.
> Beat, beat, whirr, thud, in the soft turf
>   under the apple trees,
> Choros nympharum, goat-foot, with the
>   pale foot alternate.

"Anaxiforminges" — "ruling the lyre" — opens Pindar's second Olympian Ode, and suggests a community event in celebration of the gods; Aurunculeia is the bride in whose honor Catullus wrote his wedding song, another ceremonial at whose center is the god of marriage; Cadmus is, of course, the legendary founder of Thebes. All suggest communal enterprise centered in communal belief. They are presented too cryptically, perhaps, but the very brevity of these allusions indicates, I should think, that Pound has not discovered in these earlier suggestions very useful guides for his purpose. His mind slips from these fragments to the reality of an ever-present dawn alight with creative vigour; and in the dance of nymphs and fauns there is a suggestion of joy and freedom expressed, though not confined by, the pattern of the dance. The pattern implied by Pindar can be but a pallid reflection of this dance.

In sharp contrast to the imagery of "green cool light" and "pale ankles moving," we are shown an old man "by the curved, carved foot of the couch." Like the old men of Troy, he will speak of doom, and we may expect the "beach-groove" of Canto II to be explored, as indeed it is, with allusions to the dark stories of Tereus' passion and the destruction of Acteon, and with suggestions of their Provencal counterparts: the wave of renewal and recurrence runs in the beach-groove. The first half of the canto focuses on a vision of Diana at her bath, a vision that includes both a sense of ecstasy and a sense of mystery:

> Not a ray, not a sliver, not a spare disc of sunlight
> Flaking the black, soft water;
> Bathing the body of nymphs, of nymphs, and Diana,
> Nymphs, white-gathered about her, and the air, air,
> Shaking, air alight with the goddess,
>   fanning their hair in the dark.

Nymphs, white-gathered about her, and
    the air, air,
Shaking, air alight with the goddess,
    fanning their hair in the dark.

Out of such a vision emerges poetic energy and productivity,
but, for the community at large, the will to secrecy may be
destructive of whatever is fine and innocent:

And she went toward the window,
    the slim white stone bar
Making a double arch;
Firm even fingers held to the firm pale stone;
Swung for a moment. . .

But there is another way in which the gods may manifest
themselves: publicly and communally, by the light of the sun:

The liquid and rushing crystal
    beneath the knees of the gods.
Ply over ply, thin glitter of water;
Brook film bearing white petals.
The pines at Takasago
    grow with the pines of Ise!

"Ply over ply" indicates Pound's attempt to see through
cultural levels for what recurs. In reaching around the globe
for his imagery of order Pound is, of course, preparing the way
for the Confucian and Chinese Cantos, and he is suggesting as
well that the East provides a necessary counterpart or
corrective for the basic patterns of the West. He returns briefly
to Catullus' wedding song and makes it a reflection of the
"Choros nympharum": "Blue agate casing the sky" recalling
"the green cool light"; "saffron sandal so petals the narrow
foot" recalling the "pale ankles moving." Here is recurrence,
though scarcely a very exact one.

But between what the artist perceives — such perceptions
as Pound is currently piecing together — and the spirit that
drives the community, there ought, Pound insists, to be some
correlation. That is the note on which the Canto closes.

Canto VI restates the problem in a new guise. A group,
"we," is opposed to the one, "you." The many may know

what the one has done, for action is readily perceivable. "We" may also know what Guillaume, one of the founders of the troubador tradition, has done. These are fairly public matters:

What you have done, Odysseus,
    We know what you have done. . .
And that Guillaume sold out his ground rents
(Seventh of Poitiers, Ninth of Aquitain).
"Tant las fotei com auzirets
"Cen e quatre vingt et veit vetz. . ."
The stone is alive in my hand, the crops
    will be thick in my death-year. . .

But as the following lines indicate, there are mysteries to which the many, though having access to common knowledge, do not possess the key — that of language, for example, and that of sensitivity. The Provencal couplet stands for precisely what it is — something most of us will not understand and a sense of pagan joy our society has dispensed with ("I copulated with them as you shall hear/ One hundred and eight-eight times"). The next two lines suggest the perception of the one, the artist perhaps, capable of sensing the spirit in what otherwise would be dead matter. Like the Greek gods, the spirit is universal and immortal, and the artist to whom the stone is alive may, like an ancient demigod, bring the wasteland to life. The line also suggests that there is a connection between the artist's perception and the health of the land — a point Pound will make time and again in the course of *The Cantos* — and it suggests further the possibility of combining perception and power in one man — another idea that Pound will harp on in the course of his long poem.

The transmission of such perception depends, as the poem has already suggested, on receptive mentalities. They are not easy to find. Eleanor is of the line of Guillaume, and we meet her later in the Canto as the "joyous lady" of the troubadors. But then "Louis is wed with Eleanor," and a new, unperceiving mentality is introduced. To Louis, the line of Guillaume has nothing to do with the poetic and the spiritual; it is purely political:

And had (He, Guillaume) a son that had to wife
The Duchess of Normandia whose daughter
Was wife to King Henry e maire del rei jove. . .

The spirit of the Odyssean voyage, as Pound defined it in
Canto I, has nothing to do with Louis' crusade:

Went over sea till day's end (he, Louis,
    with Eleanor).

The first half of the line is derived from the translation in
Canto I, while the second half recalls the foolishly pedantic
"He, Guillaume." We are in different mental worlds, though in
the same physical ambience.

The spirit in the stone is a mystery. But even public
documents may hide the truth to the artist who is not willing
to play the part of historian. After taking us through the
divorce between Louis and Eleanor and the marriage of
Eleanor and Henry II, Pound presents a wedding agreement:

Nauphal, Vexis, Harry joven
In pledge for all his life and life of all
    his heirs

Shall have Gisors, and Vexis, Neufchastel
But if no issue Gisors shall revert . . .

Here as elsewhere the ellipsis is intended to suggest a good deal
that remains unstated — for, as an earlier version of Canto VI
reports at great length, Harry joven, Henry II's heir, died
before the wedding, but Henry steadfastly refused to return
Gisors. Another agreement follows, one between Richard III
and Philip of France:

"Need not wed Alix . . . in the name
Trinity holy indivisible . . . Richard our
    brother.

Again, the dots hide a good deal; the simple fact that
something has been left out is all that Pound wishes to indicate
here; it is not terribly important to note that the agreement
was signed in an atmosphere of ungodly hate that scarcely
warrants the references to the Trinity and to "our brother."

But when one has all the facts, both documents and poems

may, if properly aligned, prove useful in shaping the form of a recurrent mood or idea. At long last the fact that Sordello came from around Mantua is to be given a place in the story — as part of an emerging idea or spirit, linked to another fact and thus suggesting that Pound may have something solid to work with. Bernart de Ventadorn sings of his lady as one who, like Diana, "sheds such light in the air." But, concerned with the spirit, not with private possession of the beloved, Bernart asks:

> "Send word I ask you to Eblis
>   you have seen that maker
> "And finder of songs so far afield as this
> "That he may free her,
>   who sheds such light in the air."

It is now that Pound returns us to Sordello:

> E lo Sordels si fo di Mantovana,
> Son of a poor knight, Sier Escort,
> And he delighted himself in chancons
> And mixed with the men of the court
> And went to the court of Richard Saint Boniface
> And was there taken with love for his wife
>   Cunizza, da Romano,
> That freed her slaves on a Wednesday
> Masnatas et servos, witness.

This Sordello is one who recognizes in others such as Cunizza the same freedom of spirit he possesses himself; Sordello's biography and Cunizza's testament reveal the same order of mind as Bernart's. A new groove begins to be shaped.

*　　*　　*

The discussion above is scarcely designed to prove that everything in Pound's long poem is self-evident. That cryptic passage at the opening of Canto IV is enough to bury any such nonsense, and it takes only a glance at the rest of the poem to discern many such passages. But whatever source-hunting is needed to clarify an allusion, the reader's first task is to ascertain its force and meaning in *The Cantos,* not its position in the source. In fact, anyone who has read carefully both *The Cantos* and Pound's major sources — Pére de Mailla's multi-volume history of China, for example, or the collected works of John Adams — must conclude, I think, that the sources are often beside the point, and often misleading. Only "on the page" can we discover Pound's intentions. Only "on the page" do we find, if we look closely, a carefully designed set of themes and variations for each Canto — themes and variations usually announced at the opening of the Canto.

Perhaps — and one must confess to a certain wistfulness at this point — if the poem acquires enough readers who are willing to read the poem, not poetry-substitutes, it may become possible to assess it sanely and meaningfully, saving it from both the Pound cult and the anti-Pound cult.

23

Robert Frost and *The Waste Land*

Guy Owen

The question of Frost's reaction to *The Waste Land* can be easily answered. Predictably, he was underwhelmed by the poem. And if Eliot's work had any influence on Frost's verse, it was negative, confirming the New England poet's determination to perservere doggedly in his own Yankee manner. George W. Nitchie has suggested that the notes to *Steeple Bush* were a belated parody of Eliot's notes to the book edition of the poem. If so, Frost had second thoughts and later dropped them.

Now that his letters have been published and the second volume of Lawrance Thompson's invaluable *Robert Frost* is out, Frost's attitude toward *The Waste Land* becomes unequivocal and can be clearly documented. As soon as the poem appeared in 1922, Frost recognized Eliot as a formidable threat, and as Thompson wrote, ". . .he quickly sided with those who found ways of trying to dismiss both Eliot and Joyce [*Ulysses* was published in the same year] as pretentious fakers." Such a reaction comes as a surprise to no one who understands Frost's character and his conservative (sometimes anti-intellectual) stance, now that the spurious image of "the good grey poet" has been exploded. As his letters to Louis Untermeyer reveal, he spent an inordinate amount of creative

energy sniping at poets he considered a threat to his
reputation: E. A. Robinson, Amy Lowell, Carl Sandburg,
Wallace Stevens and Edgar Lee Masters, to name only a few.
At the same time, he lavished praise on minor talents, "his
boys," like Untermeyer, when they were in a position to
promote him with reviews and articles or find space in
anthologies for his poetry. Such a circumstance is perhaps only
human. On the other side, it must be remembered that Ezra
Pound and Eliot were not always beyond reproach in the ways
they promoted each other. Frost, naturally, preferred to do his
sniping at Eliot under cover; but quite early his attack on *The
Waste Land* surfaced, causing him considerable embarrassment.
In the end, a number of Eliot's admirers, such as Rolfe
Humphries and Horace Gregory, counterattacked with acid
reviews of Frost's later books.

Unfortunately, Frost, always jealous of a newcomer's
fame, repeated the usual trite arguments against taking *The
Waste Land* and *Ulysses* seriously at a literary gathering in New
York — actually at a cocktail party in a magazine office,
during which Christopher Morley read his notorious parody of
The Waste Land. Frost felt out of place (the office was that of
Snappy Stories). Obviously disgusted by the gathering of
"New York-alecs," he allowed himself to get into a heated
argument with the journalist Burton Rascoe. Later he was
enraged when he discovered that Rascoe had devoted his
weekly column in the New York *Tribune* to attacking both his
traditional poetry and his disparaging comments on Eliot.
Observing that Frost agreed with John Livingston Lowes'
contemptuous dismissal of Eliot, the columnist continued,
"Frost himself has little sympathy with Eliot's work, but then
he wouldn't naturally; his own aesthetic problem is radically
different from that of Eliot's." The Yankee poet responded
with a vitriolic letter, calling Rascoe, "You little rascal"; but
Louis Untermeyer dissuaded him and the letter was never sent.
Though the feud with Rascoe ended at that point, Frost's
antipathy for Eliot had now become public knowledge. No
doubt Frost's letters would have had more to say about Eliot,

but perhaps Frost felt that he was safely out of the way in England, especially after he became a British citizen in 1929. However, Frost continued attacking Eliot as a "charlatan" on college campuses and around his academic cronies. As late as 1934 he was writing his daughter Lesley that he regretted attacking Eliot in public. But even here he could not resist a jibe at *The Waste Land:* "Eliot has written in the throes of getting religion and forswearing a world gone bad with war. That seems deep. But I don't know. Waste Lands — your great grandmother or the grandmother on your mothers [sic] side! I doubt if anything was laid waste by war that was not laid waste by peace before" (*Family Letters of Robert and Elinor Frost*).

No doubt Frost's dislike for *The Waste Land* was intensified after he met Eliot. Their initial two meetings, in fact, were disasters, and Frost came to loathe Eliot as a snobbish upstart. They first met in 1928 in London when Frost and his wife returned to England to revisit old haunts. They were brought together by Harold Monro, who sponsored a successful Frost reading at his Poetry Book Shop. At the dinner Frost was anything but easy with his young rival and secretly pleased that Monro had earlier refused to publish "The Love Song of J. Alfred Prufrock." It was clear, too, that Eliot had no interest in Frost's poetry. As Lawrance Thompson wrote, the occasion was strained from the start: "What annoyed Frost most was the way in which this native of St. Louis affected an English accent. Long before the evening was over, Frost decided to go on disliking Eliot as a tricky poet — and as a mealy-mouthed snob."

In 1932, the second meeting of the two poets at a banquet in Boston given in honor of Eliot was even more of a disaster. Eliot's pontifications (and accent) disgusted Frost so much that he wanted to leave the table and not return. However, he did stay, and was pleased when Eliot was asked to read his "The Hippopotamus," since the poet had already repudiated the anti-religious satire in the poem. When asked to read a poem himself, Frost was driven to what can only be called a dishonest act: pretending to compose a poem on the spot (while Eliot was intoning his), he then read "My Olympic Record Stride," which he had actually completed months earlier. Frost later felt guilty about this dishonest effort to upstage Eliot, but he apparently did not regret his choice of poems. By choosing it he seemed to imply that Eliot had succumbed to foreign influences:

> And I hope they're going to forgive me
> For being as over-elated
> As if I had measured the country
> And got the United States stated.

Eliot, obviously, had not stated much about his native land. On the contrary, he has spurned his country, not only becoming an English citizen but even a declared monarchist.

All the evidence is not yet in on Eliot's attitude toward Robert Frost, for there are only scattered letters, and Robert Sencourt's *Memoir* refers to Frost only once. But Eliot's attitude is clear enough. He once remarked that Frost was the most ego-centered man he had ever met. He politely declined to attend the Frost reading in London, though he did accept Harold Monro's dinner invitation to meet his fellow American. Eliot's reference to Frost in "American Literature and Language" labeled him "The last of the pure New Englanders"; that is, a provincial poet of merely local interest. And he found it easy to lump Frost with Edward Thomas and the other Georgians with whom Frost had been identified during his stay in England before World War I. In "To Criticize the Critic" Eliot wrote: "I was in reaction, not only against Georgian poetry, but against Georgian criticism. . ." Of course, he could have felt only contempt for the Bergsonian elements in Frost's poetry, just as Frost must have scoffed at the Indian ideas in *The Waste Land.* Clearly Eliot looked on Frost, like E. A. Robinson, as a minor, even "negligible," talent.

It need hardly be pointed out that Frost and Eliot held many things in common. They were both Harvard men, steeped in tradition and the classics; they were both profoundly conservative in politics and economics, with very real reservations about democracy; they shared the aloofness of the elite and were skeptical about any idea of progress. Each of them spent the 20's groping for religious values — though Frost, the disciple of Thoreau, would never take Eliot's step of joining a church. On the more personal side, both of them had unhappy marriages and struggled with mental problems. Finally, in matters of technique, both poets emphasized objectivity, were skeptical of *vers libre,* rebellious against Victorian poetic diction and themes, and each was obsessed with getting the rhythm and tones of actual speech into his poetic line. Nor should it be forgotten that both men were interested in reviving poetic drama. John Robert Doyle's *The Poetry of Robert Frost* suggests other similarities. A good deal to hold in common — yet the poets were poles apart in their art.

Why, then, Frost's unswerving antipathy toward *The Waste Land,* the most influential poem of the 1920's? First, let me return to what he told Burton Rascoe, then elaborate briefly by touching upon more speculative points. The subject needs to be pursued, for it has only been touched on previously. In the process one should become aware of the major differences between the two main streams of post-war poetry: the "experimental" on one hand and the "traditional" on the other, keeping in mind the simplistic nature of these labels.

"I don't like obscurity in poetry," Frost told Rascoe. "I don't think a thing ought to be obvious before it's said, but it ought to be obvious when it's said." Here is Frost's declared reason for dismissing *The Waste Land.* He had spent a generation writing poems that occasionally achieved a classic purity, lyrics as clear as the spring with the leaves raked away in "The Pasture." "I myself would rather not be misunderstood by so much as a policeman," he told Sidney Cox. "I am in favor of being understood." Little wonder he was baffled, even angered, by a poem written in over half a dozen languages, with its sudden cinematic shifts without logical transitions and multiple allusions to arcane works — all shored up by notes that often muddied the water of the text. Robert

Frost stressed clarity in his poems (there are obvious excep-
tions like "The Lovely Shall Be Choosers" and "All Revelation"), and he distrusted literary allusions and borrowings. He
told Daniel Smyth, in *Robert Frost Speaks,* that he understood only one sentence of *Finnegans Wake.* Frost might have
had poets like Eliot in mind when he wrote his satiric poem on
John Livingston Lowes' *Road to Xanadu:*

> To entertain the critic pack
> The poet has to leave a track
> Of torn up scraps of prior poets.

Unquestionably, Robert Frost would have distrusted the
very roots of Eliot's aesthetics. *The Waste Land* is, of course, a
product of Imagism and the French Symbolists. During the
20's, and earlier, Eliot had repudiated the unusable past, going
back to John Donne, grafting Laforgue and Baudelaire on to
the flexible blank verse of Webster and other Jacobean
dramatists in such poems as "Prufrock" and "Gerontion." As
already indicated, as a part of a program to clear the way for
his and Ezra Pound's poetry, Eliot had spurned all that the
Georgians stood for. Frost, on the other hand, would have
little to do with Imagism or the Symbolists. His poetry goes
back ultimately to Wordsworth, not Donne. Corbierre and
Baudelaire would have only disgusted him. After all, one of his
favorite poems was Walter de la Mare's "The Listeners," and
during his readings he tried to interest his college audiences in
Longfellow's poems, always careful to read the poems without
providing the poet's name.

Eliot has been referred to as a French poet. No doubt
Frost would have approved. He stressed the Yankee quality of
his own poetry and more and more distrusted "foreign"
influences. Instead of succumbing to European influences, as
Eliot had done, Frost returned home in 1915 determined to
"get Yankier and Yankier." In fact, shortly before *The Waste
Land* appeared, bristling with Sanskrit and French quotations,
Frost was writing to Hamlin Garland, "I wonder if you think
as I do it is time for consolidating our resources a little against

outside influences on our literature and particularly against those among us who would like nothing better than to help us lose our identity."

Unquestionably, too, Frost would have found the poem formless, or nearly so. "Art strips life to form," he wrote, and in "Pertinax":

> Let chaos storm!
> Let cloud shapes swarm!
> I wait for form.

He tried to write poems that had the shape of a beautiful Greek vase; thus no doubt Eliot's "sprawling" work would have struck him very much like uncooked clay, lacking direction and order. He would not be the first to recognize the repeated motifs, the myth of the Fisher King that subsumes the poem, and its logic of the emotions. For him the poem would have lacked a center.

In defense of Frost, one may recall that others also dismissed *The Waste Land* as obscure and formless. Louis Untermeyer was one of these, though he later modified his criticism. But even so perceptive a critic as John Crowe Ransom had serious misgivings about the poem's unity, and quarreled publicly with Allen Tate about its merits. (Incidentally, one gathers from Valerie Eliot's recent facsimile edition of *The Waste Land* that Eliot did not "wait for form"; he waited for Ezra Pound to excise the extraneous sections and help give the poem a sense of design. Pound's editing improved *The Waste Land* immensely, though it is difficult to believe that Eliot would have printed the manuscript that is now available for the first time.)

Ezra Pound wrote in the Mauberly sequence, one of the greatest poems to come out of World War I and the 20's: "The age demanded an image/ Of its accelerated grimace." As Warren French has observed, T. S. Eliot provided that image in *The Waste Land.* Though Frost was launched in England by Pound, who wrote two reviews of *A Boy's Will,* he did nothing to fill in the outlines of such an image, nor would he have wanted to. His sensibilities and training were rooted in an

earlier tradition; if he ever read Laforgue or Baudelaire, one
imagines that he would have been revolted, for he felt that
misery and ugliness should play only a minor role in art. In
fact, Frost distrusted too much misery and horror in poetry;
these emotions did not intrigue him or open up much poetry
for him. Somewhere he observed that there were all kinds of
beauty, but "vile beauty" he could never attempt. Eliot, of
course, proclaimed that the modern poet must look beneath
the beauty and glory of the Twentieth Century to its horror
and boredom. But not for Frost the slimy rat's belly and
sterile landscape, the whore of the "Preludes" or the "merdes"
of "Gerontion." Can anyone imagine him writing the parody
of Pope which was dropped from *The Waste Land?*

> Leaving the bubbling beverage to cool
> Fresca slips softly to the needful stool,
> Where the pathetic tale of Richardson
> Eases her labour till the deed is done.

Perhaps it is just as well that Frost did not see the original
manuscript before Pound blue penciled whole sections. Such
lines as the following would have disgusted him:

> And at the corner where the stable is,
> Delays only to urinate, and spit.

Or in Part IV of the original manuscript:

> Even the drunken ruffian who descends
> Illicit backstreet stairs, to reappear,
> For the diversion of his sober friends,
> Staggering, or limping with a comic gonorrhea . . .

Yet Robert Frost did not entirely turn his back on what he
called "vile beauty." For example "Out, Out" is one of the
most painful poems written in the Twentieth Century, and
there is enough horror in the murder recounted in "The
Vanishing Red" to satisfy the tastes of Eliot's disciples. The
mental anguish of the speaker in "A Servant to Servants" is
almost unbearable, as is the tension between husband and wife
(obviously autobiographical) in "Home Burial," a poem so
painful to the poet that he never dared read it in public.

In addition to this are Frost's anti-war poems and the "anti-poetic" content of such atypical poems as "The Discovery of the Madeiras" and "The Subverted Flower," where the young girl, like Prufrock, is frightened by sex, and reduces the boy to a bestial level. The unusual animal images here — the girl becomes a spitting cat and the poor boy a dog — are particularly effective. Furthermore, Frost provides his own kind of images of sterility in the 20's in such poems as "The Census-Taker," where the setting is a hundred mile waste of cut-over timber, "An emptiness flayed to the very stone." There are numerous images here of decay, bones, and ruin — but it would be a mistake to assume that Frost was echoing *The Waste Land.*

Frost, of course, shared Eliot's deep distrust of the city and the world of technology, though he wrote nothing comparable to Eliot's "Preludes," nor would he have been guilty of the disgusting images and vignettes that pervade *The Waste Land.* He is not, however, the New England provincial that Eliot made him out to be, not was he Eliot's typical Georgian poet, object of so much scorn. Perhaps smarting under the label of nature poet, Frost told Sidney Cox that he knew more about the city than the country. One doubts this, in spite of the fact that Frost had lived in London and knew New York well. Certainly the poet did not know the city in his bones; it did not not loom large in his "felt experience" or grip his imagination in the same way as his New England countryside and village folk. For example, in "New Hampshire" New York is simply a place to escape from. Confronted with "a New York-alec" who belongs to "the new school of the pseudo-phallic," Frost is driven to exclaim: "Me for the hills where I don't have to choose."

Still, one must not brush aside Frost's claim that he has not really ignored the city in his poetry. After all, he did write "The Lone Striker," about a factory worker turning his back on his job, and there is his one frankly Freudian poem, "A Brook in the City." Industry and technology enter into other poems, and usually Frost takes a dim view of such progress:

for instance, the telephone in "The Line Gang" and the train in the Thoreauvian "The Egg and the Machine." Of course, the urban world plays a role in the later masques, and machines play sinister roles in such poems as "The Self-Seeker" and "Out, Out." But in spite of his claims, Frost did not know the city or the industrial world at all well. When he made use of them in his poems, he was as likely as Eliot to be severely critical.

Mention of Freud, one of Frost's special hates, brings us to the question of sex in *The Waste Land.* Once again, this is mere speculation, but it is likely that Frost would have found the preoccupation with sex — homosexual and heterosexual — unpalatable. Of course, Eliot was suggesting that without the love of God, all acts of love are diminished to the bestial. Frost might agree; still he would not have sympathized with the piling up of such scenes as those with the typist and carbuncular clerk, Mr. Eugenides, and the daughters of the Thames. Frost relished all kinds of gossip and was not above meddling in the sexual affairs of his friends, but he had a wide streak of prudishness in him, which he readily admitted. He often reacted against writing that to him exhibited the kind of thinking "endemic to the brothel." He could have had Eliot in mind when he complained to Sidney Cox about modern writers who "pule out faint shames and fears and oh-dear-me's in occult verse. Their manner is someone else's — in France or England. Perhaps they go and tell a psychiatrist their dreams and run back their sewage to their reservoir."

"There are two types of realists," Frost said. "There's the one who offers a good deal of dirt with his potato to show that it is a real potato. And there is the one who is satisfied with the potato brushed clean. I am inclined to the second kind." Art, that is, not only strips life to form, but also cleans it up. In addition, he told Graham Gorham Munson (*Robert Frost: A Study in Sensibility and Good Sense*) that he liked Longfellow because he felt no need to "fill his soul with sick and miserable experiences, self-imposed and self-inflicted, and greatly enjoyed, before he can sit down and write a lyric of strange and compelling beauty. . ." In any case, Frost shied away from direct treatment of sex in his own work, though some of the characters in his dramatic poems know what it is to be gripped by passion. Among the few poems that do face up to sex are "The Subverted Flower," "The Discovery of the Madeiras," and "The Witch of Grafton," but they are atypical.

There are other themes that Frost and Eliot share, and they must be touched on briefly. *The Waste Land,* of course, made despair the most fashionable stance of the 1920's. Innumerable disciples, as different as W. H. Auden, Allen Tate, and Archibald Macleish put on "the illusion of disillusionment" like a cloak. Needless to say, despair and disillusionment permeate Robert Frost's *Collected Poems*, though in this respect he owes nothing to Eliot; they are simply part of his "felt experience." His despair is grounded in his own neurotic childhood, the death of his father, the poverty of his youth, his difficulties with Elinor White — before and after their marriage — the insanity and ill-health in his family and his prolonged struggle to find an audience for his poetry. There are other reasons, too. If there is any "literary" basis for this theme in his poetry, perhaps it can be attributed to the bankruptcy of New England transcendentalism. Though Frost always fought shy of literary influences, he doubtless felt the impact of some of Robinson's and Hardy's poems, perhaps even Housman's. Once again, there is no evidence that Eliot exerted an influence; the general disillusionment of the era helped shape the sensibilities of both poets. For example, as early as "Stars" in *A Boy's Will* Frost had voiced a cosmic despair like that of Hardy:

> And yet with neither love nor hate,
> Those stars like some snow-white
> Minerva's snow-white marble eyes
> Without the gift of sight.

There are also poems in *North of Boston,* such as "A Servant to Servants" and "Home Burial," that will match the despair of "Prufrock" or "Gerontion." And the despair continues throughout Frost's career, for, unlike Eliot, he underwent no

dramatic conversion, lifting him out of the waste land of the
Twentieth Century. Unquestionably, the pessimism in his
poetry deepened during the 20's, especially in poems that
reflect the war, the death of Edward Thomas and the growing
encroachment of technology on his pastoral world. Long after
Eliot's happy conversion Frost was writing poems like "Design," "Acquainted with the Night" and "The Lovely Shall Be
Choosers."

One of the main themes of *The Waste Land* is man's
alienation — alienation from God, from nature, and from other
humans — and Frost was concerned with all of these during
the 1920's. Especially interesting here is the abyss that exists
between married couples. Eliot divorced his first wife, and it is
now assumed that the neurotic wife in "A Game of Chess" and
the exchanges with her husband are autobiographical:

> "What shall I do now? What shall I do?. . ."
> "What shall I ever do?"
>   The hot water at ten.
>   And if it rains, a closed car at four.

The facts of Frost's unhappy marriage have only recently
become public, though the theme of alienation in marriage
obviously haunted him. It is given its greatest treatment in
"Home Burial," perhaps his finest dramatic poem; but it also
appears in other poems, notably "The Fear" and "The Hill
Wife." Frost, also like Eliot, was obsessed with man's ultimate
loneliness, in or out of marriage, as "Bereft" and "An Old
Man's Winter Night" testify. This concern is established in his
first two books, *A Boy's Will* (1913) and *North of Boston*
(1914); there is no apparent change in the poems written after
1922.

Like Pound's "Mauberly," *The Waste Land* is colored by
the horrors of World War I. Valerie Eliot has written about her
husband's frustrating attempts to join the Navy during the
war. Frost, too, thought of joining the army, though he was
too old. Perhaps he used the threat merely to torture Elinor
during a time when their relationship was unusually strained.
In any case, he was not oblivious to the war. (One of his most

heartless comments was that he hoped that it would kill off all the pacifists.) He believed that apathy was worse than war and thought only fools believed that wars would end. In *Mountain Interval* "Bonfire," a weak poem, reveals his concern during the 1920's. In the same volume "Range-Finding" shows that life goes on — beautiful and sinister — after the battle is over.

However, the death of his friend Edward Thomas brought the war home to Frost as nothing else possibly could. Thomas was the closest friend he ever had — so close that he was once asked about a possible homosexual relationship. Frost had persuaded his friend to turn from prose to poetry, with the result that Thomas wrote some of the most memorable poems to come out of the Georgian movement. (*The Times Literary Supplement* recently allowed itself to claim that Thomas was a far greater poet than Frost!) "For E. T." and "A Soldier" are memorable anti-war poems; both of them spring from the death of his English friend.

To conclude, then, Frost and Eliot shared many of the same themes during the 1920's, but beyond this their paths diverged. Eliot went on from triumph to triumph during a decade whose taste he helped to mold, while Frost retreated into a stubborn Yankee stoicism where his mind seemed to lose its capaciousness and flexibility. Tragically, at the end of the 20's his greatest work was behind him (his best book appeared before 1922), so that his *A Further Range* (1936) could be reviewed, fairly, as "a further shrinkage." His sensibilities had already been fixed by 1922, and *The Waste Land* had nothing to teach him. His only reaction to it was a negative one. As Frost told Burton Rascoe, "I like to read Eliot [this is doubtful!] because it is fun seeing the way he does things, but I am always glad it is his way and not mine."

24

E.E. Cummings in the Twenties

Bethany K. Dumas

E. E. Cummings? Or should it be e. e. cummings? Or maybe e e cummings, all lower case no caps? The poet's name appears in all these forms. So closely associated is he, in the minds of most readers, with unusual typography, erratic punctuation, and the use of lower case letters where convention demands capital letters that the conventional capitalization and punctuation of his name is certain to cause the metaphorical raising of an eyebrow on the part of many readers. I shall never forget my experience with an Iowa high school student who wrote me several years ago wanting to know where she could "find out all the information on e e cummings." I replied that perhaps I could help her best if I knew which sorts of information she particularly wanted; in my reply I gently admonished her that it was a politeness to accord even poets the usual niceties, and that she might want to use the form "E. E. Cummings" when she was writing about him, and, further, that subsequent references might well be to "Cummings" or to "Mr. Cummings" rather than to "e e." I never heard from her again. I have always suspected it was because my suggestions about the form of the poet's name constituted heresy to her mind. Statements have been made to the effect that Cummings had his name legally changed during his lifetime, and that the "correct" form is, indeed, e. e. cummings. Harry T. Moore wrote in his "Preface" to Norman Friedman's fine study, *e. e. cummings: THE GROWTH OF A WRITER:*

> FIRST: if I don't use capitals for e. e. cummings, it isn't just a stunt. He had his name put legally into lower case, and in his later books the titles and his name were always lower case. And I have a weakness for Edmund Wilson's rendition of cummings, in his *Finnegans Wake* parody, as hee hee cummings. So be it — all this goes with the iconoclasm of the twenties, with its unpunctuated, uncapitalized poetry. The lower case is a kind of continuing talisman of cummings, though it doesn't embed him in the twenties.

I myself have never seen any evidence that Cummings legally changed his name; Mr. Moore's point is well taken, however, and *talisman* is a good word for Cummings' use of lower case. The word itself comes from the Greek verb *telein,* meaning to initiate into the mysteries, or to complete (from *telos,* end), and I think Cummings would very much have enjoyed the notion that his use of lower case was a vehicle for initiation. Mr. Moore is also right, I think, in suggesting that it does somehow go with the iconoclasm of the twenties, but that it does not at all embed Cummings in that period.

The truth is that Cummings the artist was largely formed during the twenties, and that the directions of his growth in later decades were pointed by experiences he had during the twenties. The published works of the decade are the evidence of this. They consist of four volumes of poems (though most of the poems in the first three volumes actually come from the same manuscript), one book-length prose work, a double handful of essays, and one play. At the beginning of the 1920's, Cummings was still very much a spectator (in Malcolm Cowley's sense of the word), a "gentleman volunteer" — albeit a very well informed one. He had given his Commencement Address on "The New Art" in 1913, when he graduated from Harvard, but it was well into the 1920's before he began making the important transition that was so directly the result of his experiences during World War I and his subsequent examination of American society from a stance of his own. By the end of the decade he was firmly in the tradition of those who, in Lawrence Durrell's words, were striving "to persuade people to become their own contemporaries." In making the transition, he moved through a period of being regarded by many as a Peck's bad boy of letters. To many readers, he has remained that, a linguistic puzzle or even a curiosity. It is interesting to note that many of his readers in the twenties regarded him in that same light.

Like other writers of his generation, Cummings watched much of the war as an ambulance driver. As such, he was in good company; the list of his contemporaries who were ambulance or camion drivers in 1917 also included Dos Passos, Hemingway, Julian Green, William Seabrook, Slater Brown, Harry Crosby, John Howard Lawson, Sidney Howard, Louis Bromfield, Robert Hillyer, and Dashiell Hammett. Unlike the others, however, Cummings was forced to become personally involved in the war, for he spent several months in a French concentration camp, *La Ferté Macé*. The incarceration was the result of minor indiscretions on his part — indiscretions compounded by his close friendship with Slater Brown, who not only objected to a certain pettiness he claimed to have encountered in his immediate superiors, but who also voiced those objections in letters to such notorious persons as Emma Goldman, the internationally known anarchist. Cummings was released from prison later in 1917; he spent the next three years (save for a brief period at Camp Devens, Massachusetts, when he was drafted) in New York City, where he had moved from Cambridge in 1916.

That move probably reinforced the spectatorial attitude on Cummings' part; some of his early New York poems are highly spectatorial in tone, as is his first full-length prose work, *The Enormous Room* (1922). That book deals with the prison experience itself and is most important stylistically for its successful evocation of a sense of immediacy on the part of the reader. The immediacy, however, pertains primarily to

Cummings the individual, not to Cummings (nor to any one else, for that matter) as an integral part of the curious society in which he moves for the few months he is in prison. The very model for the work, *The Pilgrim's Progress,* suggests the highly personal nature of the experience. Unlike its model, though, *The Enormous Room* does not suggest a way of salvation for Everyman. Of course, Cummings never suggested that there is a single path to whatever salvation is possible, but in later works he does explore more fully the nature of the moral relationship of the artist to society, partly as a result of his experiences in Europe during the war and his reaction to both America and Europe in the twenties. My emphasis on the events of the war years and the following decade is not meant to diminish the importance of Cummings' earlier years. It was, I am sure, the stability of his early family life that kept him from the state of *deracination* into which so many of his contemporaries slipped. In some ways, Cummings grew closer to his origins as he grew older. John Dos Passos once commented on the effect of that growth:

> A phase we had in common of this same private cult was an offhand downunderneath reverence toward the idiosyncrasy of the divergent, various, incalculable men, women, and children who make up the human race. As Cummings grew older he narrowed it down. Tolerance is not a New England vice. I never shared his intolerance. He had the brahmin's disdain for anyone who didn't live up to certain specifications. *(The Best Times.* New York, 1966. p. 152)

However, the influence of his early life on his life in the twenties was a negative one. His move from Cambridge to Greenwich Village was highly significant, for it paralleled a move away from traditional values, such as the work ethic, to the bohemian life symbolic of the artist's quest for freedom.

Stylistically, Cummings' greatest achievement during the twenties was his growth away from the literary influences which are so clear in his earliest publications of the decade, those of the nineteenth-century poets generally, and the Pre-Raphaelite Brotherhood in particular — I think of "EPITH-

ALAMION," "OF NICOLETTE," and "PUELLA MEA" from
Tulips and Chimneys (1923). Some of Cummings' earliest
poems sound quite Georgian in their pre-occupations and his
technical methods of treating them. His poems have the
general characteristics of Georgian poetry, with its archaic
vocabulary, its subject matter, its strict forms, and its
dependence on vowel sounds for its music. One important
difference is that Cummings' poems are never in the least
bucolic. I have said elsewhere that it is impossible to imagine
his having lived anywhere except in New York, finally. For all
his romanticism, he is in many ways a very urban poet.

The "spectatorial" nature of his attitude toward the world
around him is so marked in some of his early poems of the
twenties that we have almost the impression of being at a
side-show when we read the poems; we read of "Doll's boy"
and "the Cambridge ladies who live in furnished souls" and
little Effie, "whose brains are made of gingerbread," and they
are in some ways very curious exhibits. On the street we see
the "FIVE AMERICANS," who exist primarily as great greedy
globs of flesh. There is a kind of toughness in all this that
probably helped Cummings grow out of the early romanticism
that so pervaded the earliest poems. They are important for
another reason, also. They indicate on his part an attitude of
acceptance that is in sharp contrast with the rejection
practiced by someone like Eliot, whose disgust with the
twentieth century was so pervasive that he turned to the past
for his consolation. Cummings always objected strenuously to
certain aspects of American life, but he did not turn from it in
disgust. He pretty much took it on its own terms, reserving to
himself, of course, the privilege of disdaining certain aspects of
it.

Much of his criticism of the United States extended to
include the entire western world. But on one point his attacks
were clearly directed at what was then an almost exclusively
American institution. His poems directed against American
advertising practices are vitriolic at times. To Cummings,
America was a waste land of the particular sort dominated by

the early stages of rising *consumerism*. It was something of a
shock, I think, to someone like Cummings, having successfully
shed the work ethic (production) of his parents and their
generation generally, to then find himself caught in the midst
of rising consumerism. I think particularly of poems from *is 5*
(1926), one of which, "POEM, OR BEAUTY HURTS MR.
VINAL," begins thus:

> Take it from me kiddo
> believe me
> my country, 'tis of
>
>
> you, land of the Cluett
> Shirt Boston Garter and Spearmint
> Girl With The Wrigley Eyes(of you
> land of the Arrow Ide
> and Earl &
> Wilson
> Collars)of you i
> sing:land of Abraham Lincoln and Lydia E. Pinkham,
> land above all of Just Add Hot Water And Serve—
> from every B.V.D.
>
> let freedom ring

The poem is also important as an early example of
Cummings' use of scatalogical metaphor as a vehicle for his
criticism of society. The concluding lines provide a classic
portrait of the Regular (at any price) American:

> littleliverpill—
> hearted-Nujolneeding-There's-A-Reason
> americans(who tensetendoned and with
> upward vacant eyes,painfully
> perpetually crouched, quivering, upon the
> sternly allotted sandpile
> —how silently
> emit a tiny violetflavoured nuisance: Odor?
>
> ono.
> comes out like a ribbon lies flat on the brush
> (*Complete Poems*, pp. 230-31).

The politicians come in for their share of criticism, and

never so much as when they are behaving like super salesmen. The same volume of poems contained a fine example of demagoguery debunked:

> "next to of course god america i
> love you land of the pilgrims' and so forth oh
> say can you see by the dawn's early my
> country 'tis of centuries come and go
> and are no more what of it we should worry
> in every language even deafanddumb
> thy sons acclaim your glorious name by gorry
> by jingo by gee by gosh by gum
> why talk of beauty what could be more beaut-
> iful than these heroic happy dead
> who rushed like lions to the roaring slaughter
> they did not stop to think they died instead
> then shall the voice of liberty be mute?"
>
> He spoke. And drank rapidly a glass of water
> (*Complete Poems*, p. 268)

It was not only in his poems that Cummings dealt with the problems of capitalism and consumerism and their threat to individualism. Throughout the decade, he wrote essays for *The Dial* and *Vanity Fair*. These essays are available in *A Miscellany Revised* (New York, 1965), a collection of almost all Cummings' previously unpublished short works. The most interesting are satires, each of which explores in brief an aspect of life in the western world. Of particular interest to us today is the one entitled "Why I Like America," originally published in *Vanity Fair*, in May, 1927. It is in some ways an uncharacteristically optimistic essay, for in it Cummings reaches the conclusion that America is a much more exciting and interesting country than, say, France, the fashionable favorite of many intellectuals during the twenties. The reason for his decision, he says, is that France lives in and on her past, while America is a "happening" nation, one on the move. Here is his summary:

> America makes prodigious mistakes, America has colossal faults, but one thing cannot be denied: America is always on the move. She may be going to Hell, of course, but at least she

isn't standing still. The same cannot be said of *la République français*. Nor can France's immobility be excused on temperamental grounds; the fact being, that France's past has undermined her present. More and more, indeed, the world realizes that France does not move because she is sick. Yet, sick though France is, she cannot hold a candle to your fashionably brained American who would have us believe that the land of Coolidge is a snare and a delusion, that Greenwich Village is boring while Montparnasse is inspiring, etc. – but who, in reality, is using *la République française* as a wooden horse to enter the Troy of his own past. (*A Miscellany Revised*, pp. 196-197)

Now this is partly tongue-in-cheek. But it is largely serious; its seriousness should be examined in the light of Cummings' often professed preference for movement over stasis. The best-known of his rare comments about his own poetic technique, from the "Foreword" to *is 5*, suggests its importance:

> At least my theory of technique, if I have one, is very far from original; nor is it complicated. I can express it in fifteen words, by quoting The Eternal Question and Immortal Answer of burlesk, viz. "Would you hit a woman with a child?' 'No, I'd hit her with a brick." Like the burlesk comedian, I am abnormally fond of that precision which creates movement. (*Complete Poems*, [223])

In some of the essays Cummings comments on our collective shortcomings, frequently symbolized by our political leaders. The prose picture of the results of Calvin Coolidge's having laughed one day remind us that if artists did not always take politicians seriously, it was often because they felt such contempt for them. One thinks of Dorothy Parker's comment about Coolidge. When told he had died, she queried: "How can they tell?" And in "How I Do Not Love Italy," Cummings concludes that what is *really* wrong with Italy is that she is "up to America's tricks of 'progress' and 'morality'." The "tricks" add up to "civilization," of course, and Cummings' opinion of "civilization" may be deduced from a work written during the very late twenties. Entitled "An

Imaginary Dialogue between ALMOST Any Publisher And A *certain* Author A. D. 1930," the work forms the first part of *[No Title]* (1930). It is reproduced in its entirety in *A Miscellany Revised:*

> AUTHOR: If this book makes you laugh heartily, you are intelligent—
> PUBLISHER: And if this BABYISH NONSENSE BORES ME STIFF?
> AUTHOR: If this babyish nonsense bores you stiff, you have "civilization"—
> PUBLISHER: "CIVILIZATION"?!
> AUTHOR: And a very serious disease it is, too—
> PUBLISHER: "DISEASE"?
> AUTHOR: Invariably characterized by purely infantile delusions—
> PUBLISHER: "DELUSIONS"—such as WHICH?
> AUTHOR: Such as the negatively fantastic delusion that something with a title on the outside and a great many closely printed pages in the inside is a book — and the positively monstrous delusion that a book is what anybody can write and nobody can't publish and somebody won't go to jail for and everybody will understand.
> PUBLISHER: Well, if THAT'S not A BOOK, what IS?
> AUTHOR: A new way of being alive.
> PUBLISHER (swallowing his chequebook and dropping dead): No thanks. . .
> *(A Miscellany Revised, p. 216)*

In his first play, *Him* (published 1927, produced 1928), Cummings dealt with the relationship between art and life, more specifically between the artist and the rest of society, by examining the difficulties suffered by a "would-be" artist unable to write and aware that his inability to write springs from an inability to love. The *impasse* springs ultimately from a lack of a sense of identity. In the play the artist is married (to Me), and his problems stem directly from his inability to integrate his husband-self with his artist-self. At the time it would have been quite fair to say that marriage was the ultimate commitment to society on the part of the individual. It is thus quite understandable that Cummings sees a crisis arising from the marriage of an artist, by definition needing freedom. Him's problem is mirrored in Me's dilemma; she is unable to integrate her wife-self with her mistress self. There is no resolution, but there is a particularly interesting conclusion. At the end of the play Him and Me have a child. Him is terrified by the occurrence. One interpretation of the conclusion is that since creation is the result of the union of Him and Me, shocked awareness of the terrors attendant upon creation may help Him to integrate his social self (i.e., his role as husband and father) with his individual self (i.e., his role as artist). At any rate, the play is, among other things, a serious and responsible examination of the problems attendant upon the artist, who must also function as a member of society. Here also we find a description of the artist as a person in motion; early in the play Him explains to Me his conception of himself:

> This: I feel only one thing, I have only one conviction; it sits on three chairs in Heaven. Sometimes I look at it, with terror: it is such a perfect acrobat! The three chairs are three facts — it will quickly kick them out from under itself and will stand on air; and in that moment (because everyone will be disappointed) everyone will applaud. Meanwhile, some thousands of miles over everyone's head, over a billion empty faces, it rocks carefully and smilingly on three things, on three facts, on: I am an Artist, I am a Man, I am a Failure — it rocks and it swings and it smiles and it does not collapse tumble or die because it pays no attention to anything except itself. *(Passionately)* I feel, I am aware — every minute, every instant, I watch this trick, I am this trick, I sway — selfish and smiling and careful — above all the people. *(To himself)* And always I am repeating a simple and dark and little formula . . . always myself mutters and remutters a trivial colourless microscopic idiom — I breathe, and I swing; and I whisper: "An artist, a man, a failure, MUST PROCEED."
> *(Three Plays and a Ballet,* p. 11)

It is appropriate to conclude our very brief look at Cummings in the twenties in the light of that statement about the artist. By the end of the decade, Cummings had firmly established himself as an artist. He had produced significant works in poetry, prose, and drama; he was also a painter of some renown. And he had come to terms with the society in which he lived and begun the long period in which he would successfully live on his own terms, terms very different from those of most Americans. He had begun the enlargement of the boundaries of the lyric poem, particularly the sonnet, and he had begun discovering ways whereby he might more fully bend language to his will. He had established himself as something more than an American *enfant terrible,* playing with shapes and forms. He had, indeed, moved so surely into control of form that he could afford to reject it in some of its conventionalities. He could, for instance, safely announce to a beloved that "since feeling is first/ who pays any attention/ to the syntax of things/ will never wholly kiss you" (*Complete Poems,* p. 290). But he did such things in such exquisitely wrought forms that we knew better than not to pay attention to the fact that form implies meaning. We knew better than to try to take such statements at their face value. We were shown very early, by the rich and joyous intricacy of the "grass-hopper" poem and by the vital sense of play in "Buffalo Bill's" that E. E. Cummings was no diletante, no dabbler. He was eventually to emerge as one of the foremost lyric talents of the twentieth century. His finest lyrics spring from twin sources: his absolute commitment to his art and his ability to pursue that commitment while he lived in a society whose values were often quite different from his own. Many Americans would have judged him a failure, because he was so unsuccessful financially. But that is part of the paradigm; he was an artist, a man, a failure — and he did proceed, so much that progress and becoming became really his *raison d'etre.* One can ask no more of an artist.

25

Eliot as Enemy: William Carlos Williams and *The Waste Land*

Kenneth Johnson

When *The Waste Land* was published, William Carlos Williams was instantly incensed. During the succeeding years he angrily criticized T. S. Eliot many times. In his auto-biography, written almost thirty years after the appearance of Eliot's poem, Williams offers this explanation of his anger: "Eliot returned us to the classroom just at the moment when I felt that we were on the point of an escape to . . . a new art form . . . rooted in the locality which should give it fruit." Williams goes on to say that Eliot did contribute indirectly to "the next step in metrical construction," but, by turning away "from the direct attack," he prevented a more rapid advance to this next step.

As in so many of Williams' other comments on Eliot, this explanation puts the primary stress on form. Williams does speak of "locality," but he quickly returns to the matter of a new "metrical construction." Actually, though quite signifi-cant, Eliot's relative indifference to such a "construction" does not wholly account for the rift between Williams and Eliot caused by *The Waste Land*. The sources and ramifica-tions of that rift are even more fundamental and complex.

Curiously enough, the first thing to be noted is that in the 1920's Eliot and Williams were alike in one important way.

Williams, like Eliot, was often bitterly disgusted with con-
temporary society. Both the prose and the poetry that
Williams wrote in the 1920's (and earlier) make this clear. In *A
Voyage To Pagany,* Williams' autobiographical hero says:
"Darkness and despair: These are my home." In this same
novel, Williams more than once vehemently criticizes western
civilization. *The Great American Novel* emphasizes the preva-
lence of failure, on all levels, in America. The brilliant "The
Destruction Of Tenochtitlan," a chapter in *In The American
Grain,* dramatizes a point returned to several times in that
book — namely, that in the American experience the thoughtless destruction of beauty occurs again and again. This work
also attacks the lingering elements of repressive Puritanism in
our culture; while the poem "To Elsie" is a diatribe aimed at
many features of the American scene.

What becomes clear is that, along with many other artists
during the 1920's, Williams assumed that Eliot and he, because
of their mutual dissatisfaction with contemporary society,
were quite close in spirit. Hence Williams' feeling, after *The
Waste Land* appeared, of having been betrayed by Eliot. As a
focal point of this betrayal, Williams cited the matter of form.
Eliot's poem did lead to a severe decline in the kinds of
metrical experiments that Williams believed crucial. But a
mature writer's form is basically the reflection of his world-
view. Thus, the rock-bottom source of the rift between Eliot
and Williams lies in the two poets' fundamentally different
views of what constitutes basic reality. Inextricably inter-
woven with their differing world-views is their equally different evaluations of the temporal world.

Although both Williams and Eliot were disgusted with
contemporary society, Eliot's disgust gained almost complete
mastery of him — and nothing like this was ever the case with
Williams. What gave Eliot's disgust such power in his early life
was his obsessive awareness of the impurities in himself and in
the rest of the temporal world, impurities which he found
intolerable. He had no firm belief in the existence of purity.
He knew, however, what a theoretical purity consisted of; and

he did vaguely believe that some past epochs attained
ephemeral isolated states of near-purity. In *The Waste Land*
(and, previously, in "Gerontion") he proceeded to compare
the contemporary world to these past epochs. The result was
his despair-filled outcry that everything on earth is inevitably
adulterated and contemptible. Later in the decade, Eliot's
preoccupation with purity climaxed in his acceptance of the
Christian cosmic view. For Eliot, Christianity's Platonic-
influenced realm of timeless purity became the central fact of
reality.

As much as Williams railed against contemporary flaws, he
always gave his allegiance to the temporal world. Although
well aware that many others worshipped the Ideal, the realm
of purity, he aligned himself solely with physical reality. His
extraordinary poem "The Yachts" vividly reveals his preference. The yachts, white, rare, filled with grace, free, and, so,
symbols of the Ideal, are at first admired by a bemused
Williams. The waves through which the yachts streak come to
symbolize mankind — weak, easily broken, desolate. Yet it is
mankind, the temporal world that Williams ultimately sides
with in the poem. As the nightmarish final sequence of the
poem makes clear, he abhors the idea of sacrificing a human
being, sacrificing anything in the impure physical world on
behalf of a metaphysical realm.

Williams never sought an Ideal purity. He never celebrated
a "pure" love between a man and a woman — a love
"untainted" by sex. In a book review of *The Human Body*,
Williams italicizes the last word in a quote from the book:
"Love is lovelier for its *lust*." In his poem "The Raper From
Passenack," he admires the victim of the rape because she
worries only about have been infected, not about the loss of
her virginity. For Williams, virginity, another symbol of purity,
is not to be preferred. In "Queen-Anne's-Lace" he praises a
woman who surrenders her "pious wish to whiteness" — her
desire for virginity, for purity — on behalf of the passionate
love she feels for a man whose hands have grasped her so

fiercely during their love-making that her once flawlessly white body is now blemished with purple marks.

This is not to say that Williams reveled in impurities. Nor did he prettify reality. In "Tract" he reprimands his fellow-townspeople for trying to soften the impact of the harshest of all human experiences, death. What Williams did do was to perceive within the temporal world — despite all its flaws — a richness beyond measure. In his autobiography, he speaks directly about this priceless treasure: it is a dazzling "rare element which may appear at any time, at any place, at a glance . . . It is actually there, in the life before us . . . not in our imaginations but there, there in fact." It is also in ourselves. Thus, Williams gave the impure temporal world a consummate importance and value which Eliot could never countenance.

It was only when Williams ruminated on this point that he came closest to defining the crux of the conflict between Eliot and himself. As James Guimond points out in *The Art Of William Carlos Williams,* Williams' best analysis of the conflict is contained in a letter published by *The Golden Goose* in 1952. In this letter Williams states: "Our age is rich, not poor. It is rich in its inheritances for the mind, for the spirit . . . That is why I have battled T. S. Eliot . . . [Eliot] has vitiated the good and emphasized the stereotype and the dead."

At their best, Eliot's poem-portraits present not insipid stereotypes, but dynamic archetypes. Prufrock and the speaker in "Gerontion" are complex, richly representative characters. It can be argued, however, that although these characters are inclusive twentieth-century figures, they are not *all*-inclusive. Williams, through his gallery of poem-portraits and fiction-portraits, shows that there are other contemporary characters equally representative of other vital aspects of contemporary society. Furthermore, Eliot's characters tend to elicit a narrow range of responses from the reader. Williams' characters stir a variety of responses, for his view of the temporal world was so much broader and more varied than Eliot's. It is also true that Eliot's portraits of lower-class characters, such as the two pub-sitters in *The Waste Land* and Sweeney, are stereotypes. Here, Eliot was, quite simply, out of his depth. He studied his subjects from so great a distance, and with such a closed mind, that his characters convey only his prejudices.

Williams' lower-class portraits are clearly superior to Eliot's. His characters, whether rape-victims or peddlers, hoboes or prostitutes, are vibrant individuals. It was, of couse, easier for Williams to portray such people. Far from being at too great a distance from them, he — as a doctor — literally saw naked humanity right in front of his eyes. More than this, he could sympathize, even empathize with his patients.

As he declares in his poem "Smell!" Williams, in fact, wanted to "know everything . . . have a part in everything" around him. Nothing was automatically excluded as a possible source for a poem. In *Kora In Hell: Improvisations,* Williams writes: "A poem can be made of anything." For that "rare element" permeates all of quotidian reality. Perhaps his most famous declaration of this is found in "The Red Wheelbarrow." Here that element is discovered in "a red wheel/ barrow/ glazed with rain/ water/ beside the white/ chickens." It is upon this element, suddenly perceived in these physical properties, that "so much depends."

Thus, Williams could focus on temporal beauty in a way that Eliot's obsession with adulteration prevented him from doing. Even more significant, Williams, unlike Eliot, could perceive saving values directly in drab or sordid or grim features of quotidian reality, values existing wholly within the context of the temporal world. In *A Novelette* Williams declares there is even a positive value in a flu epidemic; for during an epidemic, he points out, the extraneous drops away, the better values stand out, life is keener, and there "is no time not to notice." The poem "Spring and All" presents a scene that, at first, is a literal — and symbolic — waste land. The "blue mottled clouds" are driven by a "cold wind." The landscape is filled with a "waste of broad, muddy fields/ brown with dried weeds." The bushes and trees have "dead, brown leaves under them/ leafless vines." Yet, though the scene appears totally sterile, the landscape is fed by a life-force. In the midst of the bleakness, "dazed spring approaches." Life "quickens" because — a primary point for Williams — it is "rooted" in the fertile earth. Life perseveres.

Having dealt directly with many dying people, Williams well knew that this life-force does not always carry the day. Nonetheless, he believed that this force does enable some people to persevere. *The Knife Of The Times,* Williams' first collection of stories (written during the 1920's), contains many portraits of people who do just that. This is the main point in such stories as "A Visit To The Fair," "A Descendant Of Kings," "Pink and Blue," and "Old Doc Rivers." Some of his poem-portraits underscore the same point. The woman described in "To Waken An Old Lady," although old and shriveled (like the speaker in "Gerontion"), is not totally sterile. Even the woman in "The Widow's Lament In Springtime," a woman who contemplates suicide, is filled with quiet passion — she would die violently, not with a whimper. And she contemplates suicide not because she lives in a waste land, but because she is painfully aware that the rest of the world is so much more fertile than her aged body and mind are.

It was Williams' allegiance to physical reality that led to his lifelong experiments in free verse and accentual verse. Williams, inspired by concrete particulars, would naturally tend to write such verse. If the core of a poem is, or involves, a description of certain concrete particulars, the poem's rhythms must fit themselves to that key-description; the words used in that description cannot be discarded or even seriously altered because of the demands of a tight rhythmical pattern (or rime pattern). The form of the poem must be quite flexible. On the other hand, any poet writing a poem in which descriptions of physical objects are of secondary importance can establish and maintain a traditional rhythmical pattern comparatively easily. He can discard whole sets of phrases referring to concrete particulars and replace them with analogous references in order to satisfy the rhythmical pattern.

In the early 1920's, Eliot's usual starting point for a poem was an intense, negative emotion, such as disgust or despair, bred by his preoccupation with purity. He tried to find an objective correlative to convey that emotion. In doing so, he was free to describe any of a large number of concrete particulars. Later in his career, he strove to find an objective correlative to express either a more positive emotion or Christian truths. This search still left him great latitude in the matter of choosing images. By no coincidence, then, throughout his writing career Eliot employed traditional rhythmical forms almost exclusively.

I am not trying to set up some kind of stark stylistic dichotomy here. The image-centered poet can — and does — use abstract language; and traditionalists have packed many images into blank verse, for instance. What I am emphasizing is that a poet's world-view inevitably determines which aspect of reality will be his primary subject matter. This decision, in turn, dictates what particular verse-forms can best present that subject matter. Williams' world-view directed him toward radically flexible verse-forms. Eliot's disdain for contemporary society and his hunger for purity led him to write a poem in which the central motif is the speaker's journey through a waste land in search of the Holy Grail. And the choice of this motif, plus the way he wished to present it, naturally led him to utilize traditional forms.

When *The Waste Land* appeared, Williams instantly foresaw and protested against the poem's adverse influence on the experimental rhythmical forms that he employed — and hoped the main stream of American poetry would employ. Williams also sensed — though it took him longer to articulate this point — that the poem's influence concerning both form and point of view would inevitably simultaneously steer other poets away from a primary focus on the temporal world. He feared that these poets would construct a set of beliefs based on a metaphysical foundation, not a temporal one. Until the 1960's, this was exactly what happened in many, many cases.

What Williams proceeded to do was to offer an opposing credo. His credo's base was the "local" environment, the concrete particulars of one's native environment. Building on this foundation, Williams emphasized, as implied in "Spring And All," the cyclical process of nature. Many poems declare that, on earth, decay and death do not prevent — and sometimes even nurture — new life. There is endless renewal. In *William Carlos Williams: An American Artist,* James E. Breslin, discussing this point, stresses that in Williams' worldview the focus is not just on physical objects, but on the flow of experience. Breslin states that what Williams suggests each of us should do is be "a man, unlike the inhabitants of Eliot's 'unreal city,' " — be a man who "fears neither birth nor death, but makes his life a continual process of renewal."

Because of his emphasis on cyclical recurrence, Williams did not endorse Ernest Hemingway's disdain for the past, for history. Williams had no use for dead or outmoded traditions. Nor did he want people to be intimidated by the weight of the past. In contrast to Eliot, Williams, in *The Great American Novel,* states: "The danger is in forgetting that the good of the past is the same good of the present." But this statement also shows that Williams believed the past did contain much that was valuable. Thus, one could learn from the past. Indeed, the main motivation behind his historical study *In The American Grain* was his search for (in Van Wyck Brooks' phrase) a "usable past" — knowledge of the past that could offer principles to help guide contemporary man.

In the research he did in order to write *In The American Grain,* Williams — quite typically — focused his reading not on secondary sources of history, but on the original writings of famous men connected with American history. It is also typical that one of the primary truths he learned was that the finest men of the past, such as Columbus, Washington, Boone, and Poe, did not let themselves be intimidated by decaying or dead Old World traditions. In Williams' opinion, Poe, for instance, could better gain what Europe had to offer precisely because Poe "had a sense within him of a locality of his own."

In Williams' credo, then, physical reality, and the vitalistic "rare element" present in it, and one's awareness of cyclical recurrence — all are sources of strength; and so is history, if studied correctly. Two other powerful positive sources of strength have already been indicated. One is the love between a man and a woman — a love that features, though does not pivot on, sex. The second is the stirring examples of perseverance offered by other people, especially those of the lower class.

There is one other fountainhead of strength to be cited: the imagination, art. Pound states that change breaks down all things "save Beauty alone." Williams, in *A Voyage To Pagany*, says: "Art kills time." Williams, however, qualifies this position. He points out that art can die. A vivid metaphor can become a dead metaphor; inferior art dies more quickly. The creation of new metaphors, new art is always necessary. Still, the greatest artistic works do retain power and can give sustenance to later generations.

Williams believed that the artist, along with the rest of humanity, must seek the beauty contained in physical reality. Once he detects its presence, the artist, Williams states, must also strive "to lift, by use of his imagination and the language he hears, the material conditions and appearances of his environment to the sphere of the intelligence where they will have new currency." When this is achieved, the physical world, "warmed by the arts," will "surpass the very Elysian Fields."

Williams' credo, though different from Eliot's, does point to Williams' agreement with Eliot on a fundamental point: man can live a rich life only if he has a carefully constructed set of beliefs. The lives of many 1920's writers foundered because, although they rejected what they considered to be the false or outdated beliefs of their elders, they tried to live without developing any new firm beliefs. Both Williams and Eliot knew better than this.

It was, then, not only the form of *The Waste Land*, but the world-view dictating that form that triggered Williams' hostility to this enormously influential poem. Williams' continued stylistic experiments constituted one prong of his counterattack on that influence. The credo he evolved was

another. It is true, however, that the creedal differences
between the two men were not totally disparate in all features.
Although Williams centered on physical reality, he did talk
about an ultimately indefinable "rare element," and about the
concept of cyclical recurrence, and about enduring truths and
historical patterns, and standards of love and beauty that
individual human beings should try to emulate. That is to say,
he repeatedly moved beyond the concrete to the conceptual,
the abstract. Conversely, by the time Eliot wrote *Four
Quartets,* he came to value physical reality much more highly
than he did during his earlier years, for Christianity had taught
him that physical reality is permeated by the eternally pure.
Nevertheless, in essence, the world-views held by these writers
were antipodal. Eliot believed in the existence of a metaphysical realm, and Williams did not.

26

The Bridge: Emotional Dynamics of an Epic of Consciousness

Donald Pease

> And I have been able to give freedom and life which was acknowledged in the ecstasy of walking hand in hand across the most beautiful bridge in the world. . . (4/21/24)[1]

When *The Bridge* first appeared, most readers betrayed an attitude towards it similar to that T. S. Eliot had for Walt Whitman. They had to overcome an aversion for both its subject matter and its form before they could begin to read the poetry at all. In the 1950's, critics began to argue for the unity of the poem (most convincingly Bernice Slote), but Eliot's cult of impersonality cast a shadow over most of these efforts. Eliot's attitudes spawned a criticism that assumed detached assent by the reader to attitudes embodied in a poem. Crane's poetry comes from an entirely different direction.

What Crane intended to create was an "epic of modern consciousness" motivated by and organized through the "emotional dynamics" of individual lyrics. It is a critical commonplace that Crane conceived the poem as being vitally

---

[1] All quotations are from *The Letters of Hart Crane 1916-1932*, edited by Brom Weber (Univ. of California Press; Berkeley and Los Angeles, 1966).

connected to the traditional epic. What seems virtually
unknown is that Crane saw the very process of the poem
required the reader to become a participant in the action
through these emotional dynamics.

Crane strives for "...an assimilation of this (American)
experience, a more organic panorama, showing the continuous
and living evidence of the past in the inmost vital substance of
the present" (9/12/27). In order to achieve this, his poetry
must be based on "the articulation of the contemporary
human consciousness *sub specie aeternitatis* and inclusive of all
readjustments incident to science and other shifting factors
related to that consciousness" ("Modern Poetry"). How can
Crane make a "past" that is *sub specie aeternitatis* available to
readers in the present who do not even possess a central source
of values? Clearly Crane wanted the work to have a profound
effect on his audience. He has written:

> The validity of a work of art is situated in contemporary
> reality to the extent that the artist must honestly anticipate
> the realization of his vision in "action" (as an actively
> operating principle of communal works and faith) ...
> (6/20/26).

In order to realize these aims, Crane had to fully engage
the reader by creating a form combining the intensity of the
lyric with the inclusiveness of the epic. Crane had to enact
situations wherein the reader could experience and realize the
values the situations demanded. Crane could not just assume
the reader had prior knowledge. The poem became the very
source and field of knowledge. "It can give you a *ratio* of fact
and experience, and in this sense it is both perception and
thing perceived...poetry...may well give you the real connective experience, the very 'sign manifest' on which rests the
assumption of a godhead" (3/17/26).

He believed poetry supplied a complementary pole to
science. Whereas science provided objective categories of
knowledge, poetry facilitated the subjective experience whereby those categories became alive for each man. He further felt
that as science uncovered more and more complex realms of

energy, the subjective consciousness had to be cultivated in order to uphold these new discoveries. In the present age, objective knowledge had outdistanced subjective awareness and poetry was to bridge the gap.

> . . . But my poetry, even then, — in so far as it was truly poetic, — would avoid the employment of abstract tags, formulations of experience in factual terms, etc. — it would necessarily express its concepts in the more direct terms of physical-psychic experience. If not, it must by so much lose its impact and become simply categorical (3/17/26).

In *The Bridge,* Crane must educate and expand the consciousness of the reader to the point where he can perceive his place *sub specie aeternitatis,* for

> The audience is one half of Humanity, . . . and the poet the other. ALSO, the poet sees himself in the audience as in a mirror. ALSO, the audience sees itself, in part, in the poet. Against this paradoxical DUALITY is posed the UNITY . . . (3/1/24)

The very title of the poem prepares the reader. A bridge introduces a new relationship among earth, sky, and water. As means of connection, bridges emphasize boundaries and barriers. Individual lyrics form pediments of the energy field of *The Bridge* and build towards connective experiences with physical and spiritual frontiers.

In *The Book of Job,* God asks Satan where he has been. Satan replies in words that serve as the epigraph. This epigraph suggests that the twentieth century seems Satan's territory but by walking to and from and up and down it through the medium of *The Bridge,* the reader may be in a position to reclaim it.

In the poem, a typical office worker wonders at the rippling freedom of a seagull. "With inviolate curve" the bird disappears into the same dimension as the worker's daydream of sails. He speculates that both bird and sails are "flashing scenes" from a world that co-exists with his but unavailable to him. What does remain as permanent evidence of this other world is that other "inviolate curve," the Brooklyn Bridge. So he addresses the Bridge as holy, organic and ordering presence for all of nature.

A fellow worker "scuttles" to the parapets and falls like a jest. He has no matching freedom, vitality or word. Mere man appears a joke compared with this man-made spiritual presence whose workings regulate the rhythm of the day. The office worker's humble sense of wonder bridges the gap between himself and this Bridge that exists at the limits of human consciousness, "Terrific threshold of the prophet's pledge/ prayer of pariah, and the lover's cry." This Brooklyn Bridge does not merely join Brooklyn with Manhattan, but night with day, earth with heaven, past with present. Now this modern day Job stands in the shadow of the Bridge, perceives its vast potential and asks, "Unto us lowliest sometimes sweep, descend/ And of the curveship lend a myth to God." The speaker as lowliest asking for help from the highest stands in a position of great potential energy. This basic situation of questing figure under the shade of some form of the Bridge repeats itself throughout the first half of the poem. Worker and reader are now ready for the Bridge to make its potential energy dynamic, to disengage itself from its moorings and become by turns curveship, dream woman, memory, train, river, rainbow, covered wagon, sailing ship, cape, constellation, mansion, and Atlantis in its process of lending a myth to God. For Crane the only way God can become present will involve man's recognition of his "sign manifest" in everyday reality. "Myth" is the sign or word of God apprehended in this world.

In "Ave Maria" Crane shifts suddenly from the world of the present back to the time when Columbus sighted the New World of America in all of its possibilities. The office worker finds himself as Christopher Columbus on the curveship *Santa Maria* in mid-ocean. Columbus, having been proved true in his vision, and his quest, finds himself in mid-ocean struggling to take them home. Columbus' emotions match the stormy waves of the sea. From this point of maximum energy, Columbus keeps constant watch over the waves. His keen-eyed vigilance results in a vision of "this turning rondure whole." While in this state of global awareness, he perceives the need to be mindful of the Divine Love displayed in the New World. Explorers must not exploit her riches.

He now addresses God more familiary, for God has blessed his voyage with his guardianship in the form of the "corposant." With the scientific accuracy of the compass complemented by faith and a sense of his destiny ("true appointment"), Columbus missed the dangerous reefs. Now he perceives cosmic beginnings when God danced the universe into being. "From Moon to Saturn in one sapphire wheel:/ The orbic wake of thy once whirling feet,/ Elohim, still I hear thy sounding heel!"

Columbus as visionary dedicated to extending the frontiers of human knowledge finds himself tenoned "of heavens cordons." God reveals to him his crowned glory in this world while granting Columbus the divine mission to discover the eternal fields of knowledge. Now the world becomes visible as God's "Kingdoms naked in the trembling heart *Te Deum Laudamus* O Thou Hand of Fire" — these visions do not punctuate, for the remainder of *The Bridge* completes them. The remainder of the poem builds to a revelation of this exact situation in the present. There is only one consciousness throughout this poem — the consciousness of Columbus at various levels of awareness. The process is to heighten this consciousness through the dynamics of the emotions. Emotions are the means to knowledge and must build to a peak in the key lyrics so that the consciousness of Columbus voyager/ poet/reader can re-apprehend and uphold eternal knowledge in the present.

The action of the poem describes a circle. A circle directly joins the end with the beginning, the past with the present and serves as the ideal figure for a poem bent on "showing the continuous and living evidence of the past in the inmost vital substance of the present" (9/12/27). For Crane a cycle of human life unites directly with other circles in the universe. This "salver of infinity becomes a gateway to new dimensions.

The cycle of *The Bridge* might be diagrammed as:

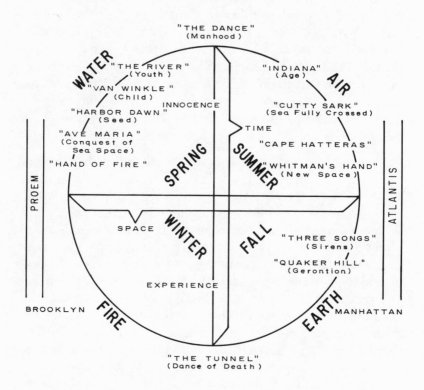

FIGURE—"The Tunnel" (Dance of Death)

In "Harbor Dawn" the consciousness suddenly shifts four
centuries in time, but it still floats mid-ocean. This time the
voyager struggles between waking and dreaming states. "White
surplices", "beshrouded wails" "signals dispersed in veils"
continue the ritual mystery of "Ave Maria." But noises of the
twentieth century street dissipate the vision. Now the hands of

a dream woman perform as deep an activity as that "Hand of Fire." Her cool arms and prayerful hands contrast sharply with the snowy hands of the window panes and the Brooklyn sirens that weave all of us into the diminished dimensions of Cyclopean towers and winch engines. The morning star, that final connective between night and day, seems to pledge another meeting for the dreamer and his lady.

Columbus begins unfulfilled. He must find that presence, that woman who disappeared with the dawn.

In "Van Winkle" and all the other sections up to "Cape Hatteras" the voyager will discover the past in the present. The daily routine of walking to the subway becomes an opportunity to remember childhood identification with conquistadors and other figures in the childhood of America. The voyager like Van Winkle finds himself awake in a time he feels no part of, and through memory he begins to see the co-existence of the past, "he'd seen Broadway/ a Catskill daisy chain in May." These childhood memories also prefigure his confrontation with the airplane, the transformation of the snake of time, and his need for the maternal fulfilling smile.

Rip Van Winkle was like one of those hoboes in "The River" who carry the traveller on Bridge-become-subway back into days of the western frontier. The disconnected, meaningless slogans passed by the fast moving train counterpoint the organic language of these lost pioneers whose words "like the elemental gist of unwalled winds" have some of the original power of breath and spirit. These hoboes are living remnants of those woodsmen who treated the young continent like a beautiful young woman. They lead us to a vision of "Time like a serpent down her shoulders, dark, / And Space, an eaglet's wing, laid on her hair." The continent embodies the unity of Space and Time. The crawling snake dictates the motion of the stalking eagle so the Indians felt the snake of Time was a living aspect or dimension of the eagle of Space.

The train now becomes a part of the iron that disconnected space and time. It upset the continental harmony. Here hoboes humming "Deep River" transform train into a long serpent and finally into the river. Now the rivers of the continent connect her with the two oceans, but the river we reach seems "lost within this tideless spell." However, on flowing farther, the River gathers its magnificence to become a "quarrying passion." Its movement across space offers a torturous memory of the greatness of its past until finally the River achieves a level of emotional intensity equivalent to that of Columbus as it "flows within itself, heaps itself free." It goes into itself and confronts all the impurities that have occurred in its motion from its source towards its "biding place," the Gulf, a source as well as a goal of rivers. When River joins Gulf, the poem magically opens.

The River connecting with the Gulf constitutes a Passion, a continental ecstasy. The River, Time and bloodstream of the continent, has magnificently flowed into its Timeless goal and source — the Gulf of vast space. The dimensions of land and sea, Space and Time are now at one as they are in the setting of "The Dance."

The action of "The River" has built to such intense passion that the voyager experiencing that emotion can remember his graceful insight into the transformation of winter into spring. That morning star of "Harbor Dawn" emerges as a winter king whose heated love rites with a glacier woman loosen the waters and urge the growth of crops in "The Dance."

Through this memory, the savage world coexists with the present as its source and fulfillment. Here all of nature has a hand in the mating dance of Maquokeeta, the Sky God whose throne emanates as the morning star. As Sky God he has the power of the eagle and needs the snake for his dance with Pocahontas, "the torrent and the singing tree," who appears as the glacier woman. Their dance establishes the continental rhythms. This moment shares a resounding place with that of Columbus when he heard Elohim's whirling heel — Above and Below, Heaven and Earth, Time and Space merge as "The serpent with the eagle in the boughs."

"Indiana" begins the transition to the present through

enacting the white man's dissolution of the land in the gold rush. Pocahontas has become the mother. This woman has a great feeling for this land, but she and her husband were prodigal. They broke Columbus' covenant with the continent by rushing "down the plenitude" for an Eldorado and ended up "counting famine on this lee." But this mother remains vital enough to establish a new pact with an Indian mother through a smile and a gaze.

Now that covered wagons have crossed the space of the continent, her son Larry takes off for the sea. His mother's smiling face and extended arms form a gestural bridge between the conquest of the land and the further conquest of the sea.

Such turreted sprites as appear in "Cutty Sark" completed that conquest. Significantly, "Indiana" ends with a dash that carries the reader over into "Cutty Sark." Here a drunken sailor — some modern equivalent of Larry — wanders around South Street in New York. The sailor has no love and seems as unstuck in time and place as Van Winkle and the hoboes, "that damned white Arctic killed my time. . ." "No — I can't live on land — !" His drunken disjointed conversation counterpointed by the song "Stamboul Nights" seems a variation of the theme of cultural confusion displayed in the collage of slogans at the beginning of "The River." This drunken sailor gives the voyager/poet knowledge of the sea in the same way the hoboes gave him the land. When the poet sees "The frontiers gleaming of his mind, "the sands upholding those frontiers loosen and run down so fast the frontiers disappear, a singing "while machine" appears whose melody leads the voyager into an ecstatic dance around an axletree reminiscent of that on Columbus' *Santa Maria.* This supernal jukebox transforms "Stamboul Nights" into the eternal tune of the lost island of Atlantis. Atlantis was for a long time considered the bridge between the New World and the Old, and many considered America to be Atlantis. America once again has been seen in her full potential.

Elated by this vision, the poet begins to walk across Brooklyn Bridge. Midway, he spots in the water the ghosts of the great clipper ships. These ships, like Atlantis, were a means of bridging the space between East and West. They brought Cathay to America in the form of tea and spices. Their very names suggest a world where a *Leander* could indeed sink in its pursuit of a dream. *Thermopylae, Black Prince, Flying Cloud, Rainbow* call to mind a period whose sense of life was closer to a mythic center — where ships were "skillful savage sea-girls that bloomed in the spring" and winked round the Horn with Yankee dreams — a time now almost as extinct as Indians or "old and oaken" navies.

If "Indiana" carries us from the continent to the surrounding space of the sea, "Cutty Sark" completes the conquest of that space. The two wrecked racing ships *Taeping* and *Ariel* carry us to the ships' ghoul mound "Cape Hatteras."

This section begins in the distant past with the subterranean, geological formation of Hatteras, the "saurian ghoul." The age of dinosaurs seems alive again with pterodactyl-like airplanes ruling the skies. The poet/voyager sails home to his hearth to eat an apple (familiar feast in a fallen world) and read Walt Whitman. Here on Cape Hatteras many of the problems of the Iron Age confront the poet. Crane has called "Cape Hatteras" the center of the poem. It begins what I would call Crane's songs of experience — contrary states of consciousness to the preceding songs of innocence. In the previous lyrics the voyager remembered periods past when the spiritual vision was close to the surface. Here in "Cape Hatteras", derricks, chimneys and tunnels violate the deep "red, eternal flesh of Pocahontas." "Thin squeaks of radio static" interfere with the messages of the winds and the waves. And "now the eagle dominates our days." Space, a new space — a space unconquered by Columbus and not yet traversed by clipper ships rules over man. Science also presents an obstacle by causing man to see himself as "an atom in a shroud" and through aeronautics hear "himself an engine in a cloud." This world and man's actions within it seem to be dreams, for man does not have a sense of being in control of his destiny.

The voyager must begin to experience this world in all of

its contingencies until the present discloses the essence of the past. He invokes Walt Whitman's aid for the ability to see into the world of the machine. Whitman, the "Great Navigator without ship" must conquer space in the way Columbus did. For the remainder of the section, Whitman's eyes, "bright with myth" aid the protagonist in his vision of the modern.

On this saurian ghoul mound, Whitman and the voyager spot the saurian denizens of the space age — airplanes "giggling in the girth of steely gizzards" then returning to their "dragon's covey." They see the Wright Brothers prophetic biplane transform itself into a doomed machine as "hell's belt springs wider into heaven's plumed side." Through Whitman's eyes, the poet has seen these planes as means of establishing the prophesied relationship between man and infinite space. But man does not use the planes to make Heaven a part of earth. Instead, through the air battles of World War I, he extends the rule of Satan. We witness an air battle become a process of destiny. Small planes take off to shoot a "Corsair of the typhoon." Intoxicated with space, the pilot, unaware of his pursuers, "sowest doom thou hast nor time nor chance to reckon." This doom results from misunderstanding man's relationship with space. The poet urges, "Remember Falcon-Ace, Thou hast there in thy wrist a Sanskrit charge to conjugate infinity's dim marge — Anew. . .!" The Sanskrit Vedas state that man's birthright includes awareness of all space. With this perspective in mind, we see the shells that destroy the pilot as a "reprieve" from a more dangerous undertaking.

Now at this juncture between life and death, on this Cape that relates earth, air and sky, the voyager fully realizes Whitman's inspiration. Whitman "at junctions elegiac . . . with vast eternity . . . bringest . . . new bound of living brother-hood." He has mastery over Time and Space and Life and Death, for he has realized all of these in himself. In his poetry he responded to the "deepest soundings" of the universe and here becomes identical with the source of all life as wielder of "the rebound seed." Whitman also suffered through a fraternal massacre like World War I, but for him the dead spring forth luxuriantly as newer leaves. Just as his *Leaves of Grass* enabled the poet to hear the glory of nature when he first read them ("Cowship and shad . . . flaked like tethered foam/ Around bared teeth of stallions"), Whitman now brings the poet into harmony with a prophetic purpose — to establish a new bond among men.

Whitman becomes *Panis Angelicus,* for his *Leaves* made a communal bread of knowledge from those wheat fields sighted by Columbus in "Ave Maria." Whitman replaces the whirling dervish Elohim whose "sounding heel" Columbus heard in "Ave Maria" and here "sets breath in steel" to animate with spirit the skyscrapers and monoplanes of the twentieth century. As Whitman stands up to fling "the span of that great Bridge, our Myth," the voyagers see the planes as corsairs of that "span of consciousness" Whitman called the open road. Whitman passed Death, "that Barrier none escapes" and stands here on this new frontier of consciousness to guide us in our quest. The "Hand of Fire" of "Ave Maria" gets in touch with the protagonist through Walt who will remain through the remainder of the poem.

> Not soon nor suddenly — no never to let go
> My hand in yours Walt Whitman so —

Here we have reached the "teriffic threshold of the prophet's pledge as foreseen in the poem. In "The Dance" the voyager was the "lover." From "Three Songs" through "The Tunnel," he is "pariah." The most immediate roadblock to the prophetic vision is a consciousness supplied by T. S. Eliot. Throughout his career, Crane was obsessed with the dangers Eliot's poetry presented to his imagination.

> I have been facing him (Eliot) for four years, — and. . .I have discovered a safe tangent to strike which, if I can possibly explain the position, — goes *through* him toward a *different goal.* (6/12/22).

> . . .I think, that my work for the past two years . . . has been more influenced by Eliot than any other modern . . . However, I take Eliot as a point of departure toward an almost complete

reverse of direction . . . I feel that Eliot ignores certain spiritual
events and possiblities as real and powerful now as, say, in the
time of Blake. (1/5/23)

"Three Songs," "Quaker Hill" and "The Tunnel" have echoes
of "Gerontion," "The Love Song of J. Alfred Prufrock,"
"Portrait of a Lady" and *The Waste Land.* But Crane
completely reverses Eliot's aesthetic. Whereas Eliot insisted on
an impersonal poem, Crane presents a personal imagination
which sees into quotidian experience and transforms it into its
dynamic reality. In the "Three Songs" (the "Thames Daughters" of *The Bridge*), the poet's visionary power itself comes
under attack.

In "Cape Hatteras" the voyager has moved across the
Bridge to Manhattan to receive Manhatta's son's prophecy.
Now he begins his task to propagate a new bond among men.
He needs a lover in order to create this "living brotherhood."
The woman he needs should have all the spiritual qualities of
Eve, Magdalene and Mary. But such a woman does not
materialize. His experiences only reveal a cheapened woman of
the night, a gardenless Eve of the Iron Age. The sea reflects the
Southern Cross to emblematize the new bond between sky and
water, but even the Cross turns "phantom." By extension, the
readers who are to partake of the new pact become lithic
trillions of Leanders drowning in their quest for Hero.

In "National Winter Garden," the closest the poet can get
to a dance with Pocahontas consists of leering at a belly dancer
whose "silly snake rings" and "lewd trounce" sadly travesty
the dance of the "Tribal Morn." Instead of spiritual brother-
hood, "to the empty trapeze of your flesh, O Magdalene, each
comes back to die alone." Not even sex gives a sense of
manhood or renewal as *post coitus* she must "lug us back
lifeward — bone by infant bone."

In "Virginia", the singer gets past the sirens and finds his
love. With echoes of a popular song, blue-eyed and Saturday
Mary with claret scarf and office job in the Woolworth tower
transfigures the experience of the twentieth century street.
When she arrives, the Fall of the world becomes Spring on

Prince Street, and those nickel-dime towers house a Rapunzel
with golden hair. Mary has done what neither of the two
women could do. She keeps the faith shining in spite of the
iron dealt cleavage — and wins the admiration of all mankind.
In so doing she recalls *Santa Maria,* Pocahontas and the
Indiana mother while prefiguring Isadora Duncan and Emily
Dickinson of "Quaker Hill."

"Quaker Hill" enacts the downward movement of the
poet's psyche from "Three Songs" to "The Tunnel." Here the
poet reflects on the bovine constituency who do not even
recognize the change of seasons. Behind him lies a house like
the house in "Gerontion" gone dry in a dry season. This house
formerly served as a watch-tower as it gave vista across the
borders of three states. Presently, its windows seem eyes like
the poet's "that still uphold some dream . . . cancelled
reservations." This area once called "The Promised Land" now
sees a Quaker Meeting House transformed into the "New
Avalon Hotel," a bootleg gin mill for week-end golfers. The
spirit the Quakers so cherished and waited for no longer finds
a demand among these factions of the dead. He needs a
spiritual scout, "I must ask slain Iroquois to guide me farther
than scalped Yankees knew to go." The Yankees have been
scalped of their spirit. Only the Indian knows the original
potential of the land. At this point the difficulty of writing
The Bridge becomes the subject matter, "Quaker Hill" begins
the poet's passion wherein he will assume the heavy burden of
the contemporary world and try to break through. His
"birthright by blackmail" demands that he relinquish his
all-encompassing vision ("far stemming view") and accept the
radically diminished "worm's eye" sensibility of modern man.
In this dark night of the poem, the poet becomes a less than
human consciousness so that he might break through and
expand this consciousness for himself and the reader. This
autumn and still song of pain "breaks the heart, yet yields that
patience that is armour and that shields love from despair."
"Quaker Hill" itself chants a song that patiently prepares for
the terrible winter of "The Tunnel."

In "The Tunnel" we discover that the diminished sensibility the voyager has decided to become is that neurotic, self-consciousness of J. Alfred Prufrock. After a miserable night at the theatre, he delivers a praise that with the subscription. After all, the spectacle has killed some of the troops of his enemy, Time. Afterwards, his life or death decision will be whether to take the "L" or walk. Then he must remember to "be minimum" with his gestures to survive the swarms in Columbus Circle, and above all avoid those revolving doors that might cage him like a frightened rat. Subways are like the scattered streams of the Mississippi — they are the dispersed language of the cities. The subway dwellers' monotone keeps up a confused drone that recalls the dim slogans of "The River." The people here feedback the nonsense they perceive in silent sounds of disjointed dialogue. Whereas Prufrock's hell seems rather harmless — the artful stage effects of a self-conscious dandy — this one's real. The hideous tunnel echoes of the train seems an eternally playing phonograph in hell, "and love a burnt match skating in a urinal." Human consciousness in the 20th Century has become an extension of the city subway system.

A benison soon appears from the unconscious as out of the underground tunnels there comes a burnt match of a man who "bursts from the smouldering bundle." Edgar, that dandy who best understood the borders of death and the nations' impulse for destruction, offers an alternative to Prufrock. Poe felt totally oppressed by his sense of place in America but out of this very sense he created an original vision that he maintained even as Death stared "gigantically down."

This apparition prepares the voyager for the spastic and demented Dance of Death the subway executes in its dive under the river. A Genoese washer woman accompanies the voyager on this trip. "Eyes and hands" concretely connect her with all the other women in the poem and link this trip with the voyage of Columbus in "Ave Maria." Now the roaring sounds and lurching humps of the trains replace the dangerous waves of mid-ocean. The poet must weather the storms of the demonic tunnel that would snatch away his last stronghold, his conscience that was from birth "navelled in the plunging wind." He does persevere as far as his neurotic sensibility can go to become "shrill ganglia impassioned with some song we fail to keep." At this extremity, anguish bottoms out to become ecstasy as like Lazarus, he returns from the hold of Death to hear "a sound of waters bending astride the sky unceasing with some word that will not die . . .!" The voyager and reader here directly connect with the same "incognizable Word" of the "Ave Maria" section. Unlike Eliot who would transcend *The Waste Land* by requiring the reader to surrender to a pattern of fragments that call to mind the energy of their sources, Crane discovers the spirit in and through the machinery of the modern age. He experiences the world in all of its fragmentedness and through powerful emotion rides the experience to its limits until frustration becomes ecstasy. Like Blake he knew that any experience can become its contrary if taken far enough. So in "The Tunnel" he found the "Western Path right thro' the Gates of Wrath," transformed the way down of tragedy into the way up of divine comedy, went "through him (Eliot) toward a different goal."

Meanwhile, the poem has come full circle. By the "River that is East," the "kiss of our agony" gathers not the speaker of "The Tunnel" but Christopher Columbus and all of us who have travelled with him. At this moment the poem functions at exactly the same emotional level as at the end of the "Ave Maria" section. That highest moment of the past when Columbus saw America in all its glory coexists in the present. Memory which served as a bridge, a reminder of the intervening experiences between then and now, disappears into the river. All of those experiences have reached their fulfillment as the voyager remembers he is of one consciousness with Columbus. All past becomes present and all Space finds its center here as "Kiss of our agony Thou gatherest, O Hand of Fire gatherest —." The "Hand of Fire" of "Ave Maria" which has remained extended throughout the poem now clasps the "Hand of Fire" in "The Tunnel" to complete the circle, send waves of energy coursing throughout the cycle of the poem's destiny and gather voyager and reader. This migration had to "void memory," for if past exists in the present, there remains nothing to remember.

At this point of energy, the reader who has experienced the fullness of the poem can hear the pure music of "Atlantis." Columbus himself sings this section (that is why he asks "Is it Cathay . . ."). The "we" refers to the readers. We are his crew. By past becoming present, Time has been conquered. All Time is this Time, a dimension of the Space of "Atlantis."

Since the Bridge as Atlantis is synoptic of all Time and all Space, all mythic voyagers exist here, and we may address any of them. At this point, human consciousness functions *sub specie aeternitatis* and utters only the procreant verb of Love. Love serves as that attractive force that connects the circle of *The Bridge* with all circles in the cosmos. The poem has led voyager and reader to a "steeled cognizance," and we experience the Truth of the universe. Columbus returns us home to that field of pure knowledge and source of all values as fulfilled as "The serpent with the eagle in the leaves."

The Bridge has not merely celebrated America's possibilities, but has presented the "connective experience" necessary for the realization of those possibilities. Through the emotional dynamics of the individual lyrics, Crane hoped to catch the reader up in the cycle of the entire poem. The inclusive quality of the epic form weaves together all the poem's lyrics; as the poet/voyager through his confrontation with Time and Space, history and society, finds a context for them in "Atlantis." In the process, he establishes the reader in an awareness of that true spiritual home of which Atlantis and American are types. By so doing he has renewed the original potential of the epic. According to the oral tradition, an epic was not merely a long and entertaining heroic narrative, but a "Word" (*epos*) that had the power to totally transform both teller and listener — it was in the past and is in *The Bridge* an epic of consciousness.

27

Robinson Jeffers' "Tamar"

Robert DeMott

In *Flagons and Apples* (1912) and *Californians* (1916) Robinson Jeffers wrote little memorable poetry. Where his later, mature poetry is unremittingly pessimistic, the poetry of his earlier years was often sentimental and optimistic, reflecting his own youth and early manhood growing up and being educated in the optimistic, illusory era of pre-World War I America.

In *Robinson Jeffers,* Frederic Carpenter writes that in "Human Destinies" Jeffers announced "his belief in the infinite potentialities of man, in man's power of endurance despite recurrent wars, and — most of all — in the mission of the poet to worship 'Beauty' " (p. 35). Jeffers never abandoned the quest for beauty in his lifetime, though he severely modulated the methods by which he sought it. His belief in man's progress and endurance underwent a radical change so that, beginning with his poetry of the 1920s, his work represented a conscious castigation and a prophetic denunciation of American society. In books like *Such Counsels You Gave Me* (1937) and *Be Angry at the Sun* (1941) Jeffers prophesied the cataclysmic events of World War II, though his warnings were not heeded.

During the eight years from 1916 to 1924 when *Tamar*

and Other Poems was privately printed, Jeffers experienced one of those remarkable poetic and personal metamorphoses (like those that marked the careers of Whitman and Melville) after which his poetic vision, themes and style assumed an indomitably individualistic and recognizable signature. A felicitous combination of personal, domestic and psychological events occurred during those years that wrought a profound change in Jeffers' lifestyle, his temperment and his art. His awakening, Frederic Carpenter notes,

> involved two experiences: the first was a long period of indecision and a questioning of the idealisms of the past; the second was a dedication to the actual earth and boulders of the new home which he was laboring to build with his own hands. The first of these experiences was an ambivalent one, which led through confusion and disillusion to a practice of personal isolation and to an eventual preaching of national isolation. The second experience was a positive one; it led away from the romantic aestheticism of his youth toward the practice of manual labor and to the celebration of the active life of the ranchers and sheepherders of his Carmel coast (p. 36)

Jeffers died out of his early life as a romantic poetaster, and he was reborn as a mature poet of consistent thematic and stylistic achievement.

When Melville (writing to Hawthorne in 1851) dated his artistic life from his 25th year, he demonstrated an awareness of the mysterious yet wonderful breaching of his creative talents. Jeffers was no less aware of his own evolvement as a serious writer. His "Tamar" is a unique record of the dimensions and energy of his rebirth. It is equally useful as a barometer for measuring Jeffers' emerging poetic preoccupations, which are sometimes antithetical to, and sometimes similar to, those of other modernist poets.

In any retrospective appraisal of the poets of the first fifty or sixty years of the 20th century, Jeffers seems to be the most *sui generis.* He is, to use Henry James Sr's comment on Emerson, a "man without a handle." Ultimately, Jeffers' quest for poetic and metaphysical answers became the most radically individualistic and isolated of any modern poet. Where the

Eliotic tradition gained adherents in John Crowe Ransom, Allen Tate and Robert Lowell, other giants of the modernist era had their followers, too. William Carlos Williams has been considered a founding father with an entire generation of poets since 1945, and Wallace Stevens stood behind poets like Robert Duncan, Denise Levertov and Theodore Roethke. But Jeffers has inspired only one. His avowed disciple, William Everson (Brother Antoninus), himself a poet of magnificant force and power, wrote *Robinson Jeffers: Fragments of an Older Fury* (1968), which is at once a dynamic testimony to Jeffers' singular achievement and to the exclusiveness of that achievement.

The problem, then, remains Jeffers' relationship to the poetry of modernist America. From the very beginning he eschewed the direction the new poetry was taking. In the "Foreword" to the *Selected Poetry* he spoke with the voice of a poet whose way promised to be different than that of his peers.

> Long ago, before anything here was written it became evident to me that poetry — if it was to survive at all — must reclaim some of the power and reality that it was so hastily surrendering to prose. The modern French poetry of that time, and the most "modern" of the English poetry, seemed to me thoroughly defeatist, as if poetry were in terror of prose, and desperately trying to save its soul from the victor by giving up its body . . . It must reclaim substance and sense, and physical and psychological reality. This feeling has been basic in my mind since then. It led me to write narrative poetry, and to draw subjects from contemporary life; to present aspects of life that modern poetry had generally avoided; and to attempt the expression of philosophic and scientific ideas in verse. It was not in my mind to open new fields for poetry, only to reclaim old freedom (p. xiv — subsequent page references will be preceded by the abbreviation sp).

In Jeffers' credo we can recognize some of the diverse elements which occupied other poets of his age. Pound's demand that poetry be as well written as prose, and his holding up Flaubert and James as models, reflects Jeffers'

ROBERT DeMOTT

belief. The focus on contemporary life and the attention to the physical reality which Jeffers called for are among the hallmarks of the work of the Imagists, as well as of Wallace Stevens and William Carlos Williams. Earlier, Edgar Lee Masters (whom Jeffers met in 1926) hinted at the efficacy of psychological themes in his *Spoon River Anthology* (1915), as well as E. A. Robinson in his Tilbury Town poems. Similarly, the long narrative poem has already found a practitioner in E. A. Robinson, whose *Merlin* (1917) and *Lancelot* (1920) were prominent examples of that genre.

Of course, it is quite possible that Jeffers was not aware of these diverse developments in modern poetry, and so it is rather easy to accuse him of provincialism. Certainly, his comment to James Rorty in 1927 that he considered Edwin Markham to be the most admirable American writer of the time lends support to that contention. So does his involvement with, and loyalty to, a number of minor local California writers like Genevieve Taggard, George Sterling and Rorty. Finally, however, accusing Jeffers of provinciality seems belittling and contemptuous. To say, rather, that he possessed a single-mindedness of intent and purpose that would not allow the developments of other poets to deter him from his own artistic program seems somehow closer to the truth. His understanding of significant characteristics of modern poetry and of the direction those characteristics pointed, is sufficient proof of his awareness of contemporary developments. His not specifically naming the poets who practiced new trends (though that Eliot and Pound are meant seems obvious) stems from his reticence rather than his ignorance. Nevertheless, there was a shared sense of participation in, and engagement with, the cultural matrix of the post World War I 1920s that created an overlapping in the aims and methods of the poets writing during that era. Jeffers cannot be faulted for reiterating some of the poetic concerns of others, especially when he came to a realization about those values by himself and on his own. For instance, Jeffers' kinship with Eliot is predicated on their use of the long poem, their belief in the decline of the west, and their use of mythic elements. His kinship with, say, William Carlos Williams is based on their decision to see life without the intermediary obstructions of religious belief, the importance of nature as a constant force in human life, and a utilization of the principle of decreation. Thematically, all three poets differ wildly, yet they are all marked by a readily recognizable style. What Jeffers has done with his legacy is entirely of his own making, so that it is more accurate to speak here of kinship with some aspects of other poets rather than influence.

Coincidentally, "Tamar" was begun in 1922, the year Eliot's *The Waste Land* was published. Jeffers' awareness of the immediate impact of Eliot's monumental piece was subsumed in his comment that the most "modern" English poetry represented a direction of development he could not accept. Indeed, by 1923, Jeffers had formulated a strong reaction to the "superfluousness of imitative poetry" (his phrase for the new poetry). In an unpublished preface which Jeffers wrote in August of that year, and which he intended to include in *Tamar*, he wrote:

> a second-rate mind is sure to confuse eccentricity with originality; its one way of saying something is new is to deform what it has to say . . . Here, I believe, is the origin of those extraordinary affectations which distinguish so much of what is called modern poetry . . . If we alter thought or expression for any of the hundred reasons: in order to seem original, or to seem sophisticated, or to conform to a fashion, or to startle the citizenry, or because we fancy ourselves decadent, or merely to avoid commonplace: for whatever reason we alter them, for that reason they are made false. They have fled from reality (Quoted in Melba Bennett, *The Stone Mason of Tor House*, p. 107).

The "higher form of poetry" which Jeffers intended to write was characterized by three laws he considered lacking in modern poetry: It "must be rhythmic," he wrote, "and must deal with permanent things, and must avoid affectation."

The variety of technical elements at work in Jeffers' poetry to underscore his poetic concerns may be illuminated

by a brief look at his language and style in "Tamar." There is
none of the compression, juxtaposition and technical wizardry
we have come to associate with the new poetry of Eliot,
Pound and the Imagists. Even the ambiguity and convoluted-
ness of Stevens, Frost and Crane is missing. Instead Jeffers
preferred the direct statement and immediate encounter with
reality he saw in the best prose. Yet even prose had a
drawback. "Prose can discuss matters of the moment," he
wrote in the "Foreword" of *Selected Poetry,* while "poetry
must deal with things that a reader two thousand years away
could understand and be moved by" (p. xiv). Investing his line
with an organic, rhythmic beat he gave his poetry the solid
palpability and motion of the natural world. In the lines

> O swiftness of the swallow and strength
> Of the stone shore, brave beauty of falcons,
> Beauty of the blue heron that flies
> Opposite the color of evening
> From the Carmel River's reed-grown mouth
> To her nest in the deep wood of the deer

Jeffers captures the inherent rhythm of nature at the same
time he deals unaffectedly with "permanent things" (sp, 15).

The oral characteristic of Jeffers' narrative poetry does not
depend on the selective juxtaposition of fragmented statements. Rather, his characters speak with an orotund fullness
and depth. He portrayed the direct involvement of the
speaking voice, and he was particularly concerned with the
heightened quality of speech by characters in tension.

Questioned by David Cauldwell, Tamar's father, who has
learned that she and her brother Lee have committed incest,
Tamar replies:

> "I have swum too deep into the mud
> For this to sicken me; and as you say, there are neither
> Brother nor sister, daughter nor father, nor any love
> This side the doorways of the damnable house.
> But I have a wildbeast of a secret hidden
> Under the uncovered breast will eat us all up
> Before Lee goes" (sp 40).

The "talk of genius" Jeffers called poetry like this "The great hawk's cry line or passage . . . the more unforgettable because it comes naturally, in conversation, like the star's image in the lift of a wave" (*Letters*, p. 41).

In "Tamar" Jeffers' lyricism joins with descriptive power to create a sensitive and poetic rendering of reality. In his narrative poem description is essential for setting the scene — "A night the half-moon was like a dancing-girl,/ No, like a drunkard's last half-dollar/ Shoved on the polished bar of the eastern hill-range" (sp. 3) — as well as for describing human actions — "Young Cauldwell rode his pony along the sea-cliff;/ When she stopped, spurred; when she trembled, drove/ The teeth of the little jagged wheels so deep/ They tasted blood" (sp. 3). Occasionally it provided Jeffers with an opportunity to inject a warning: "Ah Tamar,/ It was not good, not wise, not safe, not provident,/ Not even, for custom creates nature, natural,/ Though all other license were" (sp. 9). The effect of his verse, five beats to the line, quickened and sometimes doubled in others, creates a long and intensive line which manifests a basic harmony, wholeness and comprehensiveness Jeffers perceives in the natural world.

In America the tradition of the long poem is a rich and varied one. Its 300-year history dates from Michael Wigglesworth's *Day of Doom* (1662) to a vast number of contemporary long poems, many of them still in progress, like Robert Kelly's *The Common Shore*, Diane Wakoski's *Greed*, and Robert Duncan's "Passages." Jeffers' particular version of the genre denies the overt centrality of the artistic self as speaker, protagonist and creator that Whitman had accomplished in "Song of Myself." Neither did Jeffers employ the multiple persona and masks essential to Eliot's *Waste Land.* Instead he chose the narrative technique and dramatic development employed in fiction and drama. The narrative structure provided Jeffers a means of preventing the lapsing intensity and abatement of lyricism which often besets the long poem. In 1928 he told Herbert Klein, (a student writing a Master's thesis on Jeffers' prosody) that he wanted to make his narrative poetry

> rhythmic and not rhymed, moulded more closely to the subject than older English poetry is, but as formed as alcaics if that were possible too . . . I like to avoid arbitrary form and capricious lack or disruption of form. My feeling is for the number of beats to the line. There is a quantitive [sic] element too in which the unstressed syllables have a part. The rhythm comes from many sources — physics, biology, beat of blood, the tidal environments of life, desire for singing emphasis that prose does not have.

In "Tamar" Jeffers sustained the total movement of the poem by injecting his lines with the weight of both physical and psychological reality. The result was a combination of penetrative vision, surging elemental power and heightened dramatic tension characterized by what Jeffers termed a "detached and inclusive view-point" (Letters, p. 117).

In his criticism of the evolving dominance of the new poetry Jeffers was not alone. In the reactions of other poets, especially William Carlos Williams and Hart Crane — examined in the preceding essays by Donald Pease and Kenneth Johnson — the ambiguous legacy which Eliot created and defined was being challenged even while it was being acknowledged. In his bitter condemnation of Eliot, Williams also realized his strengths: "Eliot had turned his back on the possibility of reviving my world. And being an accomplished craftsman, better skilled in some ways than I could ever hope to be, I had to watch him carry my world off with him, the fool, to the enemy."

"Tamar" demonstrates Jeffers' determination to chart a course through the wasted land of post World War I society that was as distinctive as any of the great moderns'. He was not part of any tradition, nor of any poetic orthodoxy, and he discouraged followers or disciples of any kind. Living a relatively isolated life at his own hand-built Tor House in Carmel, California, he worked diligently at producing radically honest poetry based upon elemental strife, mythic patterns, passionate longing, annihilative force, and geographic confinement. Jeffers repudiated the naive sentimentality of his first two books and replaced it with a poetic vision of naturalistic proportions.

"Tamar" was Jeffers' first important long poem of his prolific career. Frederic Carpenter has called it one of the "most 'singular' of his poems, and one of the strangest in literature" (p. 59). A free verse narrative, it was suggested by a passage in II Samuel 13. An incestuous strain in the Cauldwell family, farmers on the rugged California coast, began years ago with the intercourse of David and his sister Helen. Helen died but her spiritual presence lives on through the medium of Stella Moreland, David's sister-in-law:

> Tamar with her back
>   bent like a bow and the hair fallen forward
> Crouched naked at old Stella's feet, and shortly
>   heard the voice she had cried for. "I am your Helen.
> I would have wished you choose another place to meet
>   me and milder ceremonies to summon me.
> We dead have traded power for wisdom, yet it is hard
>   for us to wait on the maniac living. . .
> (sp. 27).

David Cauldwell's son and daughter, Lee and Tamar, prove the Nietzschean concept of eternal recurrence of history, when they too commit incest. At a mountain pool Tamar offers herself to Lee and they have intercourse. Lee is guilty and ashamed. " 'It was my fault' he says, " 'I never shall be ashamed again' " he added. " 'What/ shall I do? Go away?/ Kill myself, Tamar?' " (sp. 11). Tamar is far less perturbed than Lee. She has tasted sexual freedom, the first act in her attempt to change the drab life she is confined to in the Cauldwell household. Their intercourse, a figurative act of "dying" for Tamar, becomes an early symbol of her rebellion against traditional values. With her bold act she has initiated a long process of assertion to fulfill her desire for trans-human superiority. After five months of sexual abandon with Lee, Tamar becomes pregnant: "To the fifth moon, when the moon's mark on women/ Died out of Tamar" (sp. 16).

Frightened by the destruction of her dream of a "sterile and sacred" love, and fearing the biological determinism of her condition, which will mitigate against her desire for power and freedom: "Her soul walked back and forth like a new prisoner/ Feeling the plant of unescapable fate/ Root in her body (sp. 16), Tamar seeks some way to purify her body. Meanwhile she decides she will need an excuse for her condition so she tries to conceal her sin by taking Will Anderson, a former suitor who is naive and innocent, as her lover. In a re-enactment of her incest with Lee, Tamar seduces Will in much the same manner and place, telling him " 'This is our marriage' " (sp. 21).

Meanwhile Tamar grows increasingly dissatisfied with the stifling human relationships of the Cauldwell house. She tells Aunt Stella, the psychic medium, that " 'I think I am going mad, I must talk to the dead; Aunt Stella/ will you help me?' " Tamar, who is by now "in the darkness/ Already, a fiery darkness' " (sp. 23), enacts a strange ritual late one night on the coast beach. Stella raises the voices of the dead who command Tamar to strip naked and perform a wild dance. The ghosts of the ancient Indian tribe which once ruled that area will not "come walking" unless Tamar obeys their dictates. During her dance she is raped by those male spirits, her fetus is miraculously aborted, and she is able to commune with the spirit of the deceased Helen, whose arguments cannot dissuade Tamar from her reckless plans for her new power. Thematically and psychologically, the experience on the beach is the center of the poem — a cataclysmic nadir in Tamar's psychological and physical descent. A sort of withdrawal, it presages her return and her eventual ascent toward a position of unquestionable power. The beach scene, then, fraught as it is with images of "dying," "death," "pain," and "passion," represents Tamar's descent into the symbolic nether world of demonic knowledge. When she emerges from the night's terror she has fully destroyed her ties to moral and ethical norms of traditional society. She has been reborn in what Arthur Coffin, echoing Nietzsche, calls a "transvaluation of values" (*Robin-*

son Jeffers: Poet of Inhumanism, p. 77).

In the final scenes of the poem Tamar becomes jealous of Lee's impending departure for France and his commitment to fight with the Allies in World War I. In a wanton attempt to escalate her own will to power, Tamar even seduces her aged, Bible-quoting father in her bed where she is recuperating from the effects of her rape. Powerless to defend against her taunts: " 'You/ thought it was your house? It is me they obey./ It is mine, I shall destroy it. Poor old man I have earned/ authority' " (sp. 40), David gives in to her at the same time he quotes Scripture. In a final paroxysm of contempt and desire, Tamar brings her three "lovers," David, Lee and Will, together in her bedroom. By tantalizing them and taunting them she sets them to fighting, particularly Lee and Will Anderson. The final moment of the drama is given over to an annihilative vision. During the violent encounter in Tamar's bedroom, an idiot aunt, Jinny, sets fire to the house and destroys everyone. To the very end Tamar is defiant. Blocking their route of escape through the bedroom window, Tamar cries out " 'I have my three lovers/ Here in one room, none of them will go out,/ How can I help being happy?' " (sp. 63).

This brief description of the plot of "Tamar" hardly does justice to the power and intensity of Jeffers' poem. It deserves to be read through with particular attention to the cyclical presence of the seasons and their relationship to the visionary experiences which occur in the poem. It also deserves a careful investigation as a self-reflexive poem of Jeffers' own artistic struggle, particularly the paradigmatic relationship of the artist's own process of creation, based on withdrawal and return, or decreation and emergence, with Tamar's pattern of descent and ascent. I will comment briefly on that aspect of the poem later, but what I say there is intended to stimulate further speculation of the matter, not to end it.

Besides the Biblical overtones in the poem, the relationship of Enceladus to "Tamar" is apparent. Jeffers has utilized the fabric of an ancient myth and rewoven it in modern garments. Where Eliot employed myth structurally, as well as thematically, Jeffers used it only thematically. In liberating the Enceladus tale he reclaimed some old freedom for it. Frederic Carpenter says that "Tamar's" plot "retells an ancient and archetypal myth" and "may be described as a modern myth about myth" (p. 60).

Jeffers cast his version of the myth in a modern quasi-naturalistic framework. The Cauldwell family's demise is worked out against the prominent natural background of the California coast. The physical presence of the Point Lobos area is so strong, in fact, that Jeffers asks early in the poem

> Was it the wild rock coast
> Of her Tamar's breeding, and the reckless wind
> In the beaten trees and the gaunt booming crashes
> Of breakers under the rocks, or rather the amplitude
> And wing-subduing immense earth-ending water
> That moves all the west taught her this freedom?
> (sp. 9)

Naturalism, particularly in Jeffers' use of environmental force, and the burden of the hereditary sin of incest in the Cauldwell family, who have "utterly despised/ The bonds of blood," still does not adequately account for "Tamar." The picture of humanity Jeffers created was based also on the presence of the nether world of demons and spirits. The phantoms of the protagonist's unconscious (the artist's as well) are loosed upon the world in such scenes as when Tamar, dancing naked on the beach, is raped by the Indian spirits of the place:

> It seemed to her that all her body
> Was touched and troubled with polluting presences
> Invisible, and whatever had happened to her from
>   her two lovers
> She had been until that hour inviolately a virgin,
> Whom now the desires of dead men and dead Gods
>   and a dead tribe
> Used for their common prey. . . (sp. 26)

The implications of the entire scene point to the limitations Jeffers saw in the use of naturalism as a literary mode. Naturalism was reductionist and constricting in its denial of supra-human presences and could not properly explain, for example, the visitations which Aunt Stella experienced.

Jeffers created an illusion of comprehensiveness in "Tamar" by, first, incorporating the entire range of human emotions from "delight and passion" to "disgust and loathing," emblematic of the movement from the awakening of sensual pleasure between Lee and Tamar, through the sadistic pleasures and post-incestuous guilt of their intercourse; and secondly, by giving some indication of the depth of the inner world of reality through the use of psychological aberations in his minor characters, as well as his admission of a nether world of spirits and ghosts. Jinny and Stella symbolize the breadth and depth of psychological abnormality manifested in their frequent dreams, nightmares, psychic transcendences, and visions. Jeffers accepted their roles as necessary:

> Though it is not thought
> That the dead intervene between the minds
> And deeds of the living, that they are witnesses,
> If anything of their spirits with any memory
> Survive and not in prison, would seem as likely
> As that an exile should look longingly home
> (sp. 61)

If Eliot constructed a world in The Waste Land based on a fragmented assimilation of knowable reality (Madam Sosostoris, "the famous clairvoyant," is an exemplar of bogus knowledge), Jeffers constructed a world in which the unknowable portions often exercised a greater influence on man than anything else. In "Tamar" being in touch with the hermetical world is a valuable source of experience and a means by which humans can become integrated with the greater, potentially harmonious patterns of natural processes. Following Tamar's rape she is exhausted, yet she is also dignified because of the knowledge she has gained:

> She in the starlight
> And little noises of the rising tide
> Naked and not ashamed bore a third part
> With the ocean and keen stars in the consistence
> And dignity of the world (sp. 29)

In "Tamar" Jeffers wrote an early approximation of his
doctrine of Inhumanism, voiced more prominently and explicitly in 1925 in "Roan Stallion" ("Humanity is/ the start of
the race; I say/ Humanity is the mold to break away from, the
crust to break/ through"), and developed in other works from
The Woman at Point Sur (1927) to the famous Inhumanist
section of *The Double Axe* (1948). Two major influences
stand behind Jeffers' articulation of a unified doctrine of
Inhumanism. The first is Nietzsche, whose remark "The Poets
lie too much," struck Jeffers forcibly at the age of 19. "I
decided not to tell lies in verse," he wrote in the "Foreword"
to *Selected Poetry:*

> "Not to feign any emotion that I did not feel; not to pretend
> to believe in optimism or pessimism, or unreversible progress;
> not to say anything because it was popular, or generally
> accepted, or fashionable in intellectual circles, unless I myself
> believed it; and not to believe easily. These negatives limit the
> field; I am not recommending them but for my own
> occasions" (p. xv).

The second is Lucretius, whose *De Rerum Natura* was
instrumental in providing Jeffers with a sense of the presence
and force of nature. Arthur B. Coffin has explored these
matters exhaustively. He concludes that Jeffers "used the
various concepts of Nietzsche's philosophy to clear away
outworn intellectual traditions and religious preconceptions in
order to develop his own doctrine of Inhumanism. That
Nietzscheanism was a useful — though sometimes limited —
tool for Jeffers is now obvious. That his Lucretian-derived
Inhumanism and its insistence upon transhuman mangificence
flourished from inception is equally clear" (p. 257).

Further background on "Tamar" can be gained by noting
its kinship with Shelley's "The Cenci," especially their similar
uses of the incest symbol. Incest served, Robert Brophy writes
in *"Tamar, The Cenci,* and Incest," (*American Literature*,
42:244) as a metaphor "partly for what civilization has
wrought in terms of self-regarding, inverted values and

institutions, partly for the mold-breaking, transcendent reper-
cussions precipitated by the act."

Brophy's and Coffin's findings, as well as those of
Radcliffe Squires in *The Loyalties of Robinson Jeffers*, help
identify Jeffers' intellectual influences and validate his own
admission that he wanted to put some "philosophic and
scientific ideas in verse." Yet "Tamar" forgets a unique vision
that surpasses mere philosophic and scientific approximations.
It explodes off the page with a savagery, power and subject
matter that is no where presaged in Jeffers' early work and was
unmatched among the poetry of his peers in the 1920s.
"Tamar" was Jeffers' public pronouncement of the depths to
which his creative fires had been stirred during his eight year
quietus since *Californians*. A new Jeffers emerged in "Tamar"
who ripped the veil from reality only to realize that the vision
he created was potentially demonic and self-defeating. In order
to correct himself, he wrote "Roan Stallion," but again he
knew he had to compensate for *that* vision too. So *The
Woman at Point Sur* (1927) was the result, and yet that too
needed further amplification in *Cawdor* (1928). The nature of
Jeffers' dilemma may be glimpsed in his comment to James
Rorty in 1927:

> "Tamar" seemed to my later thought to have a tendency to
> romanticize unmoral freedom, and it was evident a good many
> people took it that way. That way lies destruction of course,
> often for the individual but always for the social organism, and
> one of the later intentions of this "Point Sur" was to indicate
> the destruction, and strip everything but its natural ugliness
> from the unmorality. . .
>
> Another intention . . . was to show in action the danger of that
> "Roan Stallion" idea of "breaking out of humanity," mis-
> interpreted in the mind of a fool or a lunatic (*Letters*, pp.
> 115-116).

On and on Jeffers wrote to articulate a cosmic view of nature,
and to place man, however insignificantly, in the scheme of
things. He meant to warn mankind "that there is no health for
the society that is always introverted on its own members"

(*Letters,* p. 116). To establish the effectiveness of this point conclusively, Jeffers populated his narratives with protagonists of superhuman aspirations who struggle toward personal transcendence and self perfection. Like Melville's Ahab they represent the apotheosis of individualized quests for satisfaction, as well as the potential for self-destruction. If, like Tamar, these heroic protagonists are finally defeated, their grapplings have been meaningful enough to become the matter of poetry. In the enormous struggle of a Tamar, we may also view the artist's own condition.

Technically and metaphysically Jeffers departed from Eliot's position in the early 1920s, although like Eliot he accepted the imminence of the decline of the West. Jeffers' way out included a stern, unremitting, often bitter, warning to mankind that he must re-establish a living kinship with the earth and nature. Man must break the mold of inwardness, narcissism and self-praise in order to regain what Jeffers called living "outward." He once wrote James Rorty that he did not "think industrial civilization is worth the distortion of human nature and the meanness and the loss of contact with the earth, that it entails" (Bennett, pp. 149-150).

In exploring the universal interpenetration of mind and world, self and object, Me and Not-Me, which also pervaded the poetic quests of his modernist peers, Jeffers, unlike them, and unlike Emerson before them, found solace, justification and salvation in the world instead of the self. In so doing he was continually able to fulfill his requirement that poetry deal with permanence. At the conclusion of "Tamar," after fire has consumed the Cauldwells, Jeffers wrote:

> Grass grows where the flame flowered;
> A hollowed lawn strewn with a few black stones
> And the brick of broken chimneys; all about there
> The old trees, some of them scarred with fire,
> endure the sea wind. (sp., p. 64).

His sentiment reminds one more of Williams' "Spring and All" ("By the road to the contagious hospital") than it does of Eliot. Furthermore, it helps place in perspective the enormous significance of nature and natural processes in the work of later American poets like Theodore Roethke, Gary Snyder and Wendell Berry. Jeffers' lifelong quest for beauty was repeatedly realized in his adoration of the cosmic order of nature which formed the backdrop for man's own actions. Paradoxically, beauty was often attained through death or destruction. It is, Arthur Coffin writes, the clue "of escaping from the mold of humanity in order to mingle one's own atoms with the greater splendor" of nature (p. 249). For Jeffers (and for Lucretius, his intellectual mentor in this matter) death was not to be feared.

The Waste Land provided Western man with an image of society based upon conspicuous waste and corruption. Everywhere dryness and sterility, manifested in images of burning, are symbolic of the spiritual and cultural aridity of early 20th century life. The Waste Land was the first great poetic statement of the conservator's tradition. Temperamentally Eliot was unable to envision, much less accept, that the destruction he saw everywhere about him was a forerunner of a new age.

Where there is a tendency to accumulate on Eliot's part, another branch of poetic tradition is less miserly. I think particularly of Williams' statement in Spring and All (1923) that "destruction and creation/ are simultaneous" helps substantiate Jeffers' ideas on decreation. In Williams, the image of fire, especially the great fire which destroys the library in Book III of Paterson, is a necessary and positive force because it is the means by which the avatars of an old and outworn tradition can be entirely eliminated in order to make way for new growth, expansion and change. Similarly, in "Tamar," Jeffers' encompassing use of fire and concomitant imagery of death and destruction (embodied figuratively in Tamar's admission " 'I am the fire,' " as well as the literal conflagration which destroys the house) are metaphoric announcements that there is really nothing worthy of preservation in the realm of social and personal values except the expression of revolutionary individuality. Far from being a

statement in the conservator's tradition, "Tamar" entertains
the efficacy of a vision based on complete annihilation.
Tamar's fight against the archaic and corrupt traditionalism of
the social and religious structure (represented most effecitvely
by her father, David Cauldwell) is a metaphoric rendering of
Jeffers' own resistance to the potentially limiting closure of
the new poetry. In "Tamar" Jeffers proclaimed the death of
that tradition against which his heroine fought so violently.
" 'O believe me I hate you dead . . ." (sp., p. 29), she says. In
her condemnation of orthodoxy we may read something of
Jeffers' own rebellion against the dead weight of the historical
past, conventional morality and outmoded values. He invested
his heroine with qualities of full blooded life that bespoke his
fascination for her strength and power. Tamar has "more hot
and blind, wild-blooded/ And passionate life than any other
creature" (sp., p. 31), and she contrasts markedly with the
moribund members of her family.

Jeffers created a Tamar who creates herself. In her
circumspection of morality, in her evolution to prominent
authority in the Cauldwell household, Jeffers created a picture
of unfettered egoism, which is equally the expression of the
artist's supreme desire for mastery and control. After seducing
her father and transcending the limitations of the cyclical
recurrence of history, Tamar says:

> I told you I have authority.
> You obey me like the others, we pure have power.
>   Perhaps there are other ways, but I was plunged
> In the dirt of the world to win it, and, O father,
>   so I will call you this last time, dear father
> You cannot think what freedom and what pleasure
>   live in having abjured laws . . . (sp. 41)

In her brutal and honest triumph over her father and his values
(" 'There is no peace, there/ is none, there is none, there is no
peace/ But His,' he stammered, 'but God's' ") Tamar becomes
a character who lives beyond the laws of moral convention and
religious stricture. In fact it is possible to see in Tamar's
struggle, the struggle of Jeffers as artist. Strictly speaking, of

course, Tamar is not an artist, but she does represent the dimensions of psychic unrest and rebellion which characterize the artist's condition. In the world Jeffers created, Tamar, like the artist, exists beyond morality. Her attainment of power over her family is symbolic of Jeffers' newly discovered subject matter and his control over his materials; her transcendence of ethics and morality is symbolic of the committed artists's denunciations of "imitative" formal conventions; her candor and honesty are symbolic of Jeffers' agreement with Nietzsche's warning that the poets lie too much. In "Tamar" Jeffers announced, rather violently, his own creation as a reborn poet who underwent a psychic and artistic metamorphosis of profound significance. To a certain degree, the entire poem, I think, may be read as a self-reflexive expression of Jeffers' transmogrification.

Yet while art and life exist side by side and some similar organic rules apply to both, the artist will not let us forget his own hand is everywhere apparent in his work. The freedom which Tamar achieved is finally ambivalent and potentially destructive because it asks too much of the artist. Jeffers realized that the freedom Tamar gained was not only at the expense of traditional values, which he despised, but also at the expense of nature and art, which he adored. Tamar's "rise," if one were to chart her development, is to a position so highly exalted that she replaces God in the Cauldwell household. Jeffers saw nothing wrong with her deification, but inherent in her divinity was a denial of nature as well. " 'I have so passed nature,' she tells Helen, 'That God himself, who's dead or all these devils/ Would never have broken hell, might speak out of you/ Last season thunder and not scare me' " (sp., p. 30). Tamar's titanic transcendence of nature was more than Jeffers could allow. The creation of Tamar as a thoroughly honest heroine, whose apocalyptic actions Jeffers later considered as romanticizing "unmoral freedom," is an important step in recognizing the significance Jeffers placed, not in the preservation of the values of a society which he considered decadent, but in the opening out of humanity to a scale co-equal with nature's. He wrote to James Rorty that "some of you think that you can save society; I think it is impossible, and that you only hasten the process of decadence. Of course as a matter of right and justice I sympathize with radicalism . . . from an abstract viewpoint there is no reason that I know of for propping and prolonging the period of decadence. Perhaps the more rapid it is, the sooner comes a new start" (*Letters,* p. 117).

A radical vision of descent, ascent, transvaluation and annihilation, "Tamar" was Jeffers' initial effort at creating a deified character who lived beyond morality, law, nature and art. Tamar embodied the demonic urge, inherent in many artists, to obliterate the past in a paradoxically self-creative yet personally consuming drive toward psychological individuation and formal fulfillment. "Tamar" was Jeffers' primary statement, in radically metaphoric terms, of the necessity for a new human and artistic vision. Yet for Jeffers the burden of Tamar's experience, knowledge and development was that finally she transcended the human sphere so completely as to become a denial of artistic creation itself. Perhaps Tamar's surpassing both nature and art, the twin poles of meaning in Jeffers' own life, was more freedom that he could allow his heroine. William Everson has written that as a poet Jeffers could "only *create* the condition of his beatitude, and when he calls it Annihilation he is thinking of the canceling *in itself* of that appetitive need within him which is the aesthetic impulse and whose mode is the creative act" (p. 159). It is not coincidental, then, that in his next major narrative poem, "Roan Stallion," California, the heroine, accepted the limits of the human condition rather than surpass them. By killing the stallion she rejected what Jeffers probably had come to consider as impossible — a future of wild, lawless rapture and primitive, sodomized pleasure that denied both art and nature.

From 1922 to 1925, the early years of Jeffers' growth to mature consciousness, he wrestled with the nature of freedom in its formal, aesthetic, cultural and moral manifestations. His peculiar investigation of a defiant female heroine, Tamar, and the subsequent questions he raised and the solutions he sought in her poem marked his poetic and philosophic quest with as much gravity, commitment and attention as the quests of his better known modernist peers. Whether his later work became a "monotonous litany of doom," as Arthur Coffin has said, does not mitigate against the startling freshness and vitality of vision which characterized his first mature work. In "Tamar" Jeffers' recorded his artistic struggle to define and delineate the varied dimensions of his own highly individual response to the decadence of the post World War I era. That he departs from Eliot in technical and metaphysical ways should encourage our evaluation of Jeffers as an unaffectedly honest poet who judged his own work on the basis of Milton's criteria for poetry, that it be "simple, sensuous and impassioned," not as a minor poet who refused, through ignorance or stubbornness, to follow the voice of poetic orthodoxy. Perhaps a recognition of these differences prompted Jeffers to inform Harriet Monroe in 1932 that Eliot was not an "American poet, but almost the only interesting English one" (*Letters*, p. 191). The inference of "interesting" is clear — one uses that adjective when there is no other critical appraisal to make.

28

"Archy Jumps Over the Moon"

Dan Jaffe

archy leaps over the moon
hey diddle diddle
let mehitabel fiddle
while archy leaps over the moon. . .

drawing by robin gale jaffe

Preface

I like to reread the poems of don marquis when the world seems too much with me, which is almost always directly after the 10 p.m. news. And although I am hardly profound then, having been pretty thoroughly worked over, I keep getting clear intimations that don marquis, or should I say archy, not only cheers me up but also has a lot to say. This has been the judgment made for more than 50 years by American readers despite the fact that courses in American literature, influential textbooks, and intellectual historians generally ignore don marquis and his friends. That's more than I'm willing to do for the following reasons:

Archy the cockroach has his own voice, fashioned out of the total language; he captures the American idiom but remains distinctly himself.

Archy is a compassionate realist. He faces the hardness of
the world and still cares about the hurts of others.

Archy plays the game of poetry, making strengths out of
limitations. Archy writes in lower case because he can't
operate the capital lever. But his lower case turns, in addition
to other things, into symbolic, class commentary.

Archy presents us with a wide range of concerns, locales,
characters, and feelings.

Archy loves disguises. Only disguised could an American
epic so full of cynicism, criticism of the culture, reminders of
our pretentiousness and silliness not only be published in the
commercial press but become widely successful.

Archy can dance to other people's music, mimic other
people's gestures. Often his allusions, stylistic and referential,
have ironic bite. How we love his satire and parody.

At times he even gets metaphysical.

Archy is the only cockroach I know who is a hero.

i

art for recoverys sake

archy i have been trying to write
to you for a long time but havent
been able to find your address youre
not listed in the phone book and
neither is the new york evening sun
or the herald tribune you may
wonder why i thought about writing
well its because the journalist you
called boss put all your correspondance
first in the papers then
in a book and let us human beans know all
about you and mehitabel some people
would consider that a breach of confidence
but i for one am glad because it made me

one of your fans these days
its awful hard to find a writer
to read when youre sick and your stories
about mehitabel the cat warty
bliggens the toad your maxims your
account of the heroic end of freddy the rat
tragic full of pathos as it was
brought me many hours of forgetting my aches and pains
and the attendant philosphical uneasiness that
comes when you lie in a bed too long

ii
down home style

archy i guess theres not much
chance youll get this letter i
thought i would put it in a bottle
and set it adrift in the main stream
but a poet friend of mine says that goes
right down the sewer these days
so instead ill put it in a book
the way don marquis did your jottings
youre probably wondering why since
im a human bean im not capitalizing
or putting in punctuation its much
easier for me to work the typewriter
than it was for you i dont
have to bounce up and down on my head
and lift weights in between times
to keep in sufficient shape to juggle words
its my egalitarian instincts thats why
i figure why shouldnt we be equals
considering your genius
and the lack

of periods and commas
is my signal to you
that im not some patronizing slummer
i always thought you had found
not only the quickest most expedient way
to send your message to the world but also
a style that was the direct reflection of
your philophical and class position
take away commas periods dashes and
capitals and the whole structure
comes tumbling down the
world is a typewriter and
in the beginning was
the word

                              iii
                    critics arent so bright

a critic i know says
he knows why im so hung up
on the writing of a cockroach
your enthusiasm says he
takes you right out of the
main stream there must be an answer
and hes sure he has it
in an earlier life dj says he
you must have been one too
and that explains why you like
to view life from the underside
so much why you enjoy the unrespectable
and hardly intellectual babble that don marquis
collected from the typewriter the morning
after all of which goes to show
that critics arent so bright archy
this one doesnt even know hes

accepted your whole transmigration
explanation of genius
so now how can he say
mehitabel the cat wasnt cleopatra
or archy a true vers libre bard
but what i really wonder is
what that critic was
in his earlier lives

iv
heehaw heehaw

one thing that the critic
never seems to understand
is that critics
seem just as useless to poets
as poets to critics
these days its getting harder
and harder to tell whos who
but archy i just want to know
why you waited to be a cockroach
before you dropped your poems on us
i mean you must have known
the abstract theys would put
you down no matter what
now if you could have roared or
trumpeted them out swashbuckled
across the landscape
instead of just leaving a trail of crumbs
ah the impact
but no matter what you say
this way they just laugh heehaw
point out the scurilous nature
of political discourse they heehaw

announce the anthropomorphical mess they
heehaw heehaw note the comic foibles of the day
they heehaw allude beyond their
heehaw heehaw and they just
heehaw so much heehaw they start to hurt
down in the belly
down near the essentials
which may be the point

RJAFFE

you dropped your poems on us ...

v
backbiting

listen the other day i heard
some professorial types talking
about the world the university
capitol hill and tv
and i thought of you archy
because you said all the same
things in different words
and that so long ago
maybe poets are prophetic after all
its all a matter of perspective
said one regal looking dean
and even the writer in residence
agreed with that
but none of them rhymed very well
or really saw things from the under side

vi
sympathy

dear archy ive decided
not to feel sorry for you
and mehitabel any more
sure youve had your lumps
and some of them self willed
but you had your fun too
prancing around in the manner
of kipling and homer
and all sorts of others
you tickled and poked and
even sipped booze out of
saucers without ever going
to the hoosegow

and mehitabel always did
get around to yodel her
toujour gai toujour gai
which is more than i can
say for lots of folks i know
who stay kicked all their lives
i do not blame you archy
for your bitterness against mankind
but behind your hard words
theres always a soft joke
and i know archy the cockroach
would never bait a hook with a boy

vii
archys true colors

dear archy i was talking
with a speech teacher
the other day and he suddenly
says what happened to your voice
you dont sound like yourself
you sound like something that
came out of a book written by
a cockroach then he looked at
me as if he wanted to prescribe something
for my consonants and vowels
its all archys fault
i said and don marquis should bear
some of the blame but once they
get into you its hard to get them out
which i guess is why im writing
these notes in the way i am
well he said thats too bad
you could have been milton or

will shakespeare or even wallace
stevens they each had their own voices
i mean its all a matter of touchstones
all of which showed his bias

viii
MAKING IT IN THE BIG TIME

THE TIME HAS COME FOR ME TO SAY
IN THE MOST INSISTENT WAY
THAT ARCHY AND MEHITABEL
ARE REALLY PHILOSOPHICAL
THAT THEY'RE THE VICTIMS OF A PLOT
THAT SAYS NON HUMAN BEANS CAN NOT
ON THE WINGS OF POESY FLY
AND THAT IT'S UPPITY TO TRY
NO ONE SINCE AND NONE BEFORE
GAVE SUCH PROOF THE PRESS COULD SOAR
DESPITE THE BIAS OF THE HUMAN RACE
THEY BOTH DESERVE THE UPPER CASE

ix
telling them off

archy the other night
i heard a yodeling in the back yard
i thought mehitabel was with us
but it was just my critic acquaintance
fresh from a new triumph over literature
says he the epic spirit is dead
where is our homer now our
virgil who can speak with the voice of the age
that is ageless and grand
and then he twirled his phi beta chain

and scratched the protuberance of his vest
there are times archy to be tactful
and silent and let the insipidity
about us echo on the air
but i for one have never learned
such restraint i have declared war
on the critics who close the doors
of their anthologies on cockroaches
and who will not listen
archy you have ranged across
the landscape and through time
from barstool to city room
from alley to meeting hall from
pennsylvania station to mars
the green planet from olympus to
the oasis behind the radiator
and your lingo is ours in all our
stages for a cockroach youve got a
hell of a good ear you
are not only an american vers libre bard but
a veritable sam johnson who gives us the
words of shakespeare and bacon
along with toujour gai toujour gai
you never got stuck in a poetic diction archy
you just kept junketing
around from level to level like
mehibabel through her lives sipping
the cream and chewing fishheads
from the garbage can
such polyphony a lesson
for poetic runts who can only
play one instrument
a fellow named rod hereabouts
keeps beating the triangle with his head
more anon
    dj

ARCHY JUMPS OVER THE MOON"   437

X
justice at last

well archy i think ive figured out
why you have not announced yourself
recently through some new means
i know of course that by this
time youve probably transmigrated again
maybe youre our cat gatto but shes
certainly not letting on
anyway youve disappeared about
as completely as weldon kees off
the golden gate or hart crane
into the dark and thats sad
but not really surprising when
i think about the artists sensitive soul
oh its sad to be so ignored by
all the types who put the stamp
of approval and legitimacy on
things so what if people keep reading
those notes you wrote fifty years ago
its not enough archy you ought to
be in the canon of american lit
so sophomores could learn
about democratic vistas and
equality and the cockroach view of things
instead of henry adams
who i dont think
you would have got along with at all
but i wouldnt really grieve because
we will overcome and theyll have
to let you in after all because
readers insist

29

Expressionism: The Waste Land Enacted

Jordan Miller

Expressionism is an artistic style as clearly identified with the twentieth century as classicism with fifth century B. C. Greece or sentimentality and romanticism with eighteenth and nineteenth century England or Europe. But expressionism, in its short history as a distinct dramatic and theatrical style, is unique in its simultaneous existence with the more dominant style of its time, realism, from which it originally sprang. For the first time within a given theatrical era two separate and distinct "styles" — that is, two modes of writing, thematic development, and staging — existed side by side, each demanding extensive use of the same technical facilities of the theatre, each producing an end result of considerable difference from the other.

Interestingly enough, some of the earliest practioners of expressionism were at first noted for their intense realism. This fact is not so strange, however, when one realizes that the two most important changes in the art of the theatre during the nineteenth century served both styles equally well, and the creator of one could often, with comparatively little difficulty, make equally effective use of the other. The first was the shift in emphasis to the portrayal of the common man functioning within contemporary society as a legitimate subject for

JORDAN MILLER

invention in the history of the theatre, the development of
practical electric illumination. The theatre artist was thus
provided with both the impetus and the means to place before
his audience a highly illusionistic picture of the day to day
aspects of "reality," while at the very same time, this creator
of representational "realistic" stage literature, using the same
subject matter or theme, was also provided with the tools he
needed to depart into the broadly presentational, virtually
limitless possibilities of "stylization," the non-realism or
supra-realism which we have come to call "expressionism."

August Strindberg of Sweden, writer of naturalistic plays
portraying the violent and everlasting battle of the sexes,
turned in 1902 to the creation of *The Dream Play,* one of the
greatest of the stylized dramas bearing the name of expressionism. This vivid, often baffling picture of the nightmare of
human existence released the stage from its previous restrictions of showing life "as it is," permitting the artist instead to
command the stage to express his own view of life as it *seems*
to be. Unlike the realist, held to the closely literal interpretation of reality, and the impressionist, who conveys a fairly
subjective and emotional interpretation of the outward appearances of reality, the expressionist turns inward to portray
the sense and the feel of things below the surface. The
expressionistic play, said Strindberg, in explaining this highly
personal approach to "reality," is a place "where anything
may happen; everything is possible and probable. Time and
space do not exist." The physical properties which he places
on stage, the doors, windows, hand props, and the setting
itself, shift visibly before the audience, increasing in size,
changing in function, appearing and disappearing, while
characters enter and leave with no relation to reality,
plausibility, or any sequence of time or place. Strindberg's
expressionism in *The Dream Play* is the prototype, and very
nearly the epitome, of a dramatized human wasteland, full of
frustrations, confusing paradoxes, terror, oppression, foulness
and filth — all the product or by-product of the pitiful

situation of being human — with but a glimmering of hope at the end. What emerges as one reads the play today is an overwhelming expression of a very specific, wholly subjective point of view toward reality that is personal, intimate, and ultimately terrifying.

The expressionist does not merely discuss nor explain the aspects of life as a wasteland; he demands their enactment. Through costume, makeup, decor, the entire *mise en scene* becomes a way of expressing the artist's view of the truth in a highly graphic form, unlimited by conventional technical boundaries. It abandons literal representation, but turns to a kind of symbolism, often allegorical, found not only in dreams and nightmares, but also in creations as simple as the political cartoon or comic strip. Scenes can be deliberately short and abrupt, with dialogue often delivered in sharp staccato. The expressionist is attracted to displaying the individual lost in the great mass of men, influenced and driven by the crowd that often appears on stage moving and speaking in orchestrated, choric effect. The expressionist sees a mechanistic civilization, at which he stands aghast, deploring the imposition upon society of the machines that mankind has invented.

The expressionist, witnessing man's marvelous gifts which permit him to create the gear-driven monsters that in the end can destroy him, seems to be writing a drama of intense fear and despair. At the same time, he recognizes that man has within him an awareness of his doom and the ability to avoid it if he so wishes. Having made the machine, he can destroy it. There is very little to do with fate, the gods, or the lack of free will. If he wants to, the expressionist can be made somewhat of an optimist, pointing out to man that the robots cannot reproduce themselves, for they are soulless machines. The end of the world will be the end of man and of the machine as well. Hal, the computer of *2001*, begging for mercy, cannot prevent having his brains disassembled, but unless man sees his own problems and reverses the trend, he, like the occupants of Hal's spaceship, will find it is too late. Aware of what he is doing, man *can*, if he tries, avoid the catastrophe.

JORDAN MILLER

Thus the expressionist is a product of a particular time. The writers of Europe in the nineteen teens and twenties, followed by their American counterparts, saw evolving before them a social wasteland of fantastic proportions, but as seen in the image of Eliot's unreal city, it was almost purely a human creation from which faith and the gods had fled in horror.

Eugene O'Neill, America's acknowledged first expressionist, like Strindberg, whom he admired and often emulated, was first received as an intense realist. But he was also an experimenter throughout his life, and very early in his career he established himself as a dominant artistic figure in the more highly imaginative aspects of the drama with the appearance in 1920 of *The Emperor Jones,* one of the true landmarks of American drama.

Hailed as the first genuinely expressionistic play in this country, *The Emperor Jones* makes use of a considerable number of expressionistic stage techniques, but thematically its emphasis upon mysticism and loss of faith is some distance from the European approach, particularly as practiced in Germany. It is, however, in the Strindbergian sense, the expressionistic enactment of a frightening and deadly nightmare world, limited as it is to the experience of a single individual. O'Neill was always deeply preoccupied with the problems of the lost soul, not so much in the midst of a mechanistic society as in a world without faith. As a result, the Emperor Jones becomes the victim of a consciously racist system which has relegated him to shining shoes in the white quality Pullman cars and thence to a penal chain gang, rather than a mechanistic and impersonal society that renders him a faceless member of the crowd. Moreover, Jones rises by his own cunning, as well as a lot of luck, to his summit of power, enabling him to achieve a kind of personal identity which Elmer Rice's Mr. Zero never possesses and which O'Neill's own Yank loses very quickly. Jones himself, Smithers, and the natives lack expressionistic distortions in costume, movement, or speech. Appearing somewhat greater than life, they remain throughout the play very life*like.* On the other hand, Jones does become an expressionistic protagonist in his status as an allegorical Everyman lost in the jungle of existence, retrogressing, through lack of faith, into the primitive beginnings common to us all. Though the victim of a particular social attitude, Jones rises above the simple blacks and whites of racial antagonism to represent all lost souls.

The Emperor Jones in production emerges essentially as a one-man *tour de force,* a prolonged monologue, with considerable risk of becoming tiresome or even ridiculous, for it demands a kind of heroic performance that rises above the uninspired and stereotyped speech patterns and the constant danger of lapsing into a tasteless cliché of the white man's stage version of the Southern black. Properly executed, under effective directorial control, however, this play can be overwhelming in its use of expressionistic stage techniques. O'Neill is able to strike directly at the nerves of his audience, visibly and audibly, in order to create for those who watch the same shattering experience facing the rapidly collapsing emperor. Foremost, of course, is the harrowing beat of the native drums. Beginning at the rate of the normal human pulse, it continues throughout the play with relentless, unceasing force, building in tempo toward the hysterical climax. It is a brilliantly calculated effect.

Add to the drumbeats O'Neill's projection upon the stage of the hallucinations of Jones' disintegrating mind. From the entrance of the Little Formless Fears to the final emergence of the witch doctor and the crocodile god, the audience shares with the fleeing monarch every moment of his accelerating hysteria. Even in the more even-tempered opening scene, O'Neill conveys the palpable unreality and foreboding with the glaring reds and whites of the grossly inappropriate jungle throne room. Then as Jones sheds piece by piece the trappings of his "civilization" the twisted shadows of his racial past, essentially the past of all humanity at one time or another, carry protagonist and audience rapidly into the hellmouth of mental breakdown and death.

In 1923 Elmer Rice wrote what is probably the single best

American expressionistic play. His first play, *On Trial*, produced in 1914, had experimented successfully with the techniques of flashback, new to the stage at the time but now so familiar, especially in motion pictures, but until his venture into all-out stylization, Rice had been devoted to fairly straightforward realism in his one-act plays and in the longer ones, often in collaboration. As expressionism, both thematically and theatrically, everything in *The Adding Machine* (no pun intended) adds up. The play's vision of men and women functioning within the debilitating routines of contemporary society as no more than digits on a page is squarely in the European expressionistic tradition. Mr. Zero, the cipher of a hero, eternally caught in the enervating routines of daily work and a totally deadening home life, is frustrated in his job, in his sex life, and in every way he turns to seek some sort of emotional well being. Unnoticed and unrewarded, he is the product of the machine that creates him, uses him, destroys him, and then remakes him. All of this, Rice clearly shows, is the predictable result of what men are doing to themselves and to each other. Though the encounter of Eliot's impassive stenographer and her boy friend carbuncular may display variations, the theme is the same. Rice has formulated an equally dismal picture of stultifying forces which reduce the level of human performance to unvarying mechanical functions.

Who has placed Zero on his high stool, endlessly adding figures for pittance a week? Other men. Who has locked him into his frustrations with a jealous, shrewish nag for a mate, and who has declared that the few moments of release which he has been able to seize in gazing at the scantily clad strumpet next door are illicit, immoral, and even illegal? Other men, and, of course, Zero himself, for Zero, all his wishes to seek freedom for his imprisoned urges notwithstanding, is as highly "moral" as the rest. The possibility of even limited momentary relief with the drab and fortyish Daisy Diana Dorothea Devore is forbidden, and she, too, must deny herself to the pitiful Zero who, blank card that he is, could probably have saved her life. She is equally trapped.

In the heaven that is hell, who is responsible for the fate of the Zeros who arrive there? Surely not the "angels," or "god," for, such as they are, they seem totally detached from what is going on, save to regroup and return the Zeros to the real hell that is life. In fact, whoever is "in charge" is so disinterested as to permit Dean Swift and Abbé Rabelais access to the Elysian Fields, along with the puzzled murderer Zero, the baffled matricide Shrdlu, and the pursuing suicide Devore. Just as on earth, it is ordinary men, the Zeros and the Shrdlus, who "rule" heaven. Totally unable to recognize what heaven and hell really are, they will eternally punish themselves for having strayed so far from the rules of the "good" and "righteous" life which they and their own kind have designed. And of course the Daisy D. D. Devores will never be able to have what they want, either. Though arriving in a desperately sought paradise, they discover that "life" there is as empty as ever, because the Zeros and the Shrdlus will forever attempt to figure out what's wrong and will turn in horror from enjoying the everlasting and well-deserved reward that eternity offers them.

On the technical side, Rice knows well how to use the mechanical and electronic devices of expressionism to best advantage. The settings of *The Adding Machine* provide an instantly effective picture of the mad world in which Zero is trapped from the dominating foolscap wallpaper scribbled with figures to the wildly distorted courtroom, prison, and after life. In costume and behavior, particularly in speech, the characters who surround Zero during his lifetime present a grim but highly amusing expressionistic interpretation of the meaningless behavior and the deadening boredom of those caught up in the crushing impersonality of the society that destroys. Mrs. Zero's opening monologue continues through the first scene curtain, a never-ending stream of complaint and invective delivered to the listening but unhearing spouse, who finds it still continuing as he returns from work, spewing forth unstoppable. The non-dialogue exchanged between Zero and the faded Miss Devore as they wrestle simultaneously with a flood of figures and their own thoughts reveals the mounting problems that stir within their two pitiful souls. Thereupon the whistle blast sends them automatically, robot-like, off their stools and homeward. The break with the routine, the intrusion of the Boss, begins one of the most effective and terrifying scenes of expressionism in all American drama. As Zero's world explodes the stage disintegrates with him. The Boss utters words that cannot be comprehended, then turns into a grotesque mechanical doll whose jaws keep working as long as the spring is wound up. The world whirls, the noises compound. The end of things is at hand, arriving in a flood of brilliant crimson and then black silence.

Hardly less theatrically effective is the visit of the families of digits who represent with Zero the nonentities of the little man's world. Though of different shapes and sizes, they are virtually indistinguishable otherwise, enthralled with the trashy movies, the latest shady stories, the most recent surgery of mutual acquaintances, the superficiality of everyday politics, performing a fine parody of the banal idiocies that so often make up such group conversation. Other scenes — Zero's long and pitiful harangue to the jury, the grotesque visiting scene in prison, the eeriness of the graveyard and its skull-throwing corpses, and the "pleasant place" of the hereafter — all maintain the face and the force of highly effective expressionistic techniques.

In the end, the question must be answered: Is *The Adding Machine* a dirge for the little man who can never rise and must sink deeper into the oblivion that is his eternal fate, with no way out, no salvation, no redemption? So long as we remain human, yes. Still, Rice offers escape even to Zero, into the willing embrace of poor Daisy Diana, the most sensible and sensitive of all. Desperately wanting, desperately needing her willing offer of the experiences of the flesh, he refuses the rescue she could provide and fights her off to run his course in heaven right into the hands of the angels who will send his useless self back into the world, kicking and screaming, where he will be more useless than ever.

The Adding Machine in its beautifully stylized form remains a singularly depressing play. Even the laughter of the comic scenes is based upon the sense of terror that dwells on the futility of it all, on either side of the grave. The presence of the impersonal giant of a social machine, together with the man-made mechanical devices which it spawns, that destroys Zero and all his acquaintainces, is overpowering, and certainly the awareness of the wasteland thus created, sterile and unproductive, renders *The Adding Machine* a marvellously effective expressionistic play.

Eugene O'Neill's *The Hairy Ape* of 1924 is better expressionism than his *Emperor Jones* for it is conceived with considerably more unity of style. Surprisingly, however, audiences first viewing it were more than a little bewildered, assuming as they did that the "realist" O'Neill was presenting a literal picture of life in the bowels of an ocean liner. As O'Neill himself pointed out, no ship ever designed included space for its men in the manner conceived for Yank Smith and his fellow beasts. They are, in O'Neill's picture of men serving the never-satisfied machine, caged apes, stooping under incredibly low ceilings, shovelling tons of coal to the screaming blast of the engineer's whistle. The words they speak, the metallic hollow ring of their voices, the echoing choral effects and the phonograph horn quality of their responses all should suggest to the audience that they are witnessing something far beyond the pale of real life. In contrast, and equally unreal, O'Neill paints the white-clad, icily virginal do-gooder in Mildred and the equally detestable elderly aunt, sitting on the ship's deck enjoying the voyage at the expense of the creatures below. Into their purgatory Mildred will, in her proper social responsibility, venture a visit, carrying her twisted ideas of learning how the other half exists. Her demands are pre-posterous, as she herself is preposterous, and the clash between Mildred and the apish Yank becomes a situation contrived solely for effect. Likewise preposterous but effective is the result, which sends the hitherto satisfied Yank, relishing his fare of coal dust, grime, and sweat, into an incurable traumatic shock.

Like Rice's spectacular demonstration of Zero's exploding world at the moment of dismissal, O'Neill's picture of Fifth Avenue is one of the highlights of American expressionism. Monstrous objects are for sale at monstrous prices in monstrous store windows. Painted and calcimined promenaders, described by O'Neill as "gaudy marionettes," ignore Yank as if he, and all he represents, never existed as they strut and simper in their detached unawareness. The desperate Yank will fight them, but his fists will land like an iron pile driver in the midst of a ton of cotton candy. The instant arrest by a mob of whistle blowing policemen, the prison, IWW hall, and ultimately the ape's cage, where Yank finds his place and exchanges himself, one ape for another, continue the uniformly excellent expressionistic style. The theme, as well, holds true to more "traditional" expressionism, for Yank is the product of a very definite kind of society which expects things of him (making the ship go), takes them (enjoying the fresh sea air on deck), and casts him aside (calling him a "filthy beast"). We are in a world more specific and precise than the abstractions of Jones' jungle. Yank's wasteland is no product of nature, but is something that men themselves have created and attempt to live in. It is the Foulstrand of Strindberg's *Dream Play*, or the smoke clogged fogginess of Eliot's refuse-strewn London. Yank, furthermore, is not at war with himself in the manner of Jones, and the battle which Yank fights in his man-made wasteland is consistently portrayed in sight and sound not as the projection of one man's hysteria, but as an expression of an entire society in which both Yank and the Frankenstein monsters who walk Fifth Avenue must exist at one and the same time.

For all the overt social implications in the play, O'Neill avoids direct social criticism in *The Hairy Ape*, for he refuses to make choices between the forecastle and Fifth Avenue. He will condemn neither outright, except to show that both have combined in their own peculiar ways to render the physically mangificent Yank an emotional wreck, happy to be crushed to death by his beastly brother. Like Zero in heaven, Yank suddenly finds he is unable to adjust. Zero, pursued by his "values" of morality, must flee from heaven to repeat his futile circle. Yank, shocked to find his own values can't hold up as he had assumed they must, ends in the ape's cage, crushed and mangled, instead of in the ship where his function has had some limited meaning at least. O'Neill solves the problem for his protagonist no more than does Rice. There seem to be no reasonable answers. Wherever one turns, the wasteland remains inescapable, and though both Zero and Yank have the means of escape within themselves, neither is able to do so. God, the fates, the angels, are no more concerned about Yank than they are about Zero. What man hath put in motion, only he can put asunder, and the expressionistic artists within Rice and O'Neill don't see much chance of that taking place.

The combined efforts of George S. Kaufman and Marc Connelly produced the fourth and last of the great American expressionistic plays of the 1920s in *Beggar on Horseback*, also in 1924. The title was taken from a work of 1588 by Robert Greene called *Card of Fancie*, a line of which reads: "Set a beggar on horseback and he will never alight," which may or may not be relevant to the play. The theme was adapted very freely from a German comedy called *Hans Sonnenstössers Höllenfahrt*, involving a journey to hell by the central character. With the "hero" changed to a struggling young American composer and hell changed into a nightmare vision of contemporary business and a family that is part of it, this hilarious comment on society run, machine-like, by the book, producing endless goods of uniformly tasteless quality while piling up riches of material worth but absolutely lacking in any recognizable spiritual value, is a devastating indictment.

The dream as a framework is certainly nothing new. Men have learned about themselves and the universe in this manner since Jacob dreamed his ladder. *Beggar on Horseback*, how-

ever, holds to the tradition of the European expressionists in
its portrayal of society's maddening sterility and the irrational
pattern of behavior which it fosters. Scenes intrude quickly,
almost violently, upon one another. People, such as the
butlers, multiply without reason. Characters who die revive to
judge their murderer; their costumes include telephones or
rocking chairs attached as if ingrown. The auditorium and the
stage combine as acting areas at one time or another. Nothing
stands still; everything changes. It is difficult at any one time
to say precisely what is happening or precisely where one is.

Beggar in many ways is a closer relative of The Adding
Machine than of O'Neill's two plays mainly because each of its
dream-sequence scenes grasps a concept of "reality" and
develops it along many of the same lines which Rice explored
in the story of Zero's fall. With Yank and Jones being
destroyed by their individual inability to come to terms with
themselves as much as with the society that pursues and
persecutes them, O'Neill turns to the more mystic approach.
Zero in his world and Neil in his are functioning, or attempting
to function, within an incomprehensible universe. Zero falls
before something decidedly malelovent. Neil moves within a
group that displays the lunacy of most human behavior that
can be quickly recognized and grasped by anyone who has ever
encountered the endless mazes of business or government.
Though the computer and the punched card of the 1970s were
unknown in 1924, the result of trying to secure definitive
information, or even a pencil "to do some work with," was the
same then as now, and the universal quality of the Kaufman-
Connelly satire is still meaningful. Neil fights a machine-like
system as much as today's private citizen fights the electronic
monsters which refuse to cancel his subscription or to
acknowledge that his bill is paid.

Nor do Kaufman and Connelly stick solely with the
business world, turning as they do to the vulgarities of a
society wedding on the one hand, or to the vaudeville of the
trial. Zero is condemned in similar manner, but his trial bears
precious little resemblance to the half circus sideshow, half

movie performance, and, not illogically, for this is an expressionistic world, half political campaign that Neil must endure to receive "justice." Zero in jail may be experiencing a travesty of "justice" and "just punishment," but Neil in his cell in the art factory is part of a system that is all too close to reality for comfort with "art" reduced to the lowest level of human effort, lacking even a semblance of imagination or original invention.

Beggar on Horseback, unlike its three companion pieces, emphasizes the comic, and it means to point its ridicule through laughter, rather than through serious viewing with alarm. The happily-ever-after conclusion is as much fantasy as anything else, but it is nice romantic fantasy, the proper awakening from a bad dream. Kaufman and Connelly are in a wacky world where the jungle or clanking machine convey no threat. Whatever our faults, they say, we can, if we try, laugh them to death, and we need not fear annihilation because the nightmare will end when the Neils and Cynthias raise little brown cows and little red hens in their little white cottage. Nobody "wakes up" in the world that Rice and O'Neill present their "dreamers," whose reality is nightmare, and whose nightmare ends only in death.

To say that these four plays constitute the full limit of American expressionism *per se* is, of course, patently absurd. American dramatic expressionism in one way or another continued throughout the decade. There were other writers, and, in the case of O'Neill, other plays that continued the stylistic experimentation which expressionism fostered. Somehow, none had quite the power, nor demonstrated the skilled artistry, of the four we have discussed. John Howard Lawson's *Processional* of 1925, using a jazz background and obviously much concerned with the struggle between the haves and have-nots of miners and owners, was, as critics have pointed out, crude and often absurd. Sophie Treadwell's *Machinal* of 1928 was in the tradition, but less dramatically effective. But most of all, it was O'Neill who continued to command greatest attention in his constant experiments.

Some will say that O'Neill's later plays are even better expressionism than the earlier two, but O'Neill seldom again devoted the same consistent effort to the style throughout a single play as he had in *The Hairy Ape* and to lesser extent in *The Emperor Jones. Gold* of 1921 made use of a mad sea captain's hallucinations, but there was more fantasy than expressionism in the limited number of scenes involved, and the old man's belief in lost treasure was far removed from the social implications of expressionism. *All God's Chillun Got Wings,* in 1924, a tragedy of miscegenation and domestic strife, made use of strikingly stylized settings, but the theme and the characters who developed it were thoroughly realistic. *The Great God Brown* of 1926 made tremendously effective use of masks, but they had been one of the most important devices of the Greek theatre two millenia before. O'Neill's use of his masks was fascinating and intriguing, as well as frequently confusing, but his mystic exploration of lost souls was closer to poetic tragedy than to expressionism, even though the subject matter did involve the business success-failure syndrome of common expressionistic themes. The break-away houses of *Desire Under the Elms,* also 1924, and *Dynamo,* 1929, were impressive stylized backgrounds, but each play turned far more to the analytical explorations of naturalism than to the mechanistic problems of expressionism. O'Neill's insistence on reproducing a humming power house in the latter play was far more Belasco realism than it was expressionism. In *Marco Millions* of 1928 O'Neill sent his Marco Polo through scenes of imaginative fantasy, but his seriocomic observations of Babbitry opposed to the inscrutable East ended up more as a romantic tale of exotic adventure upon which expressionistic techniques were superimposed. The extended monologue-soliloquy-asides of the monster *Strange Interlude* in the same year were no more inventive than the masks of *Brown* had been, and the story they told in nine long acts was essentially soap opera realism. Perhaps O'Neill's brilliant failure with *Lazarus Laughed,* produced in California in the spring of 1928, featuring its Dionysiac central figure of the risen Lazarus and its multiple masks and choreographed crowds was, as some hold, his best expressionistic play. Yet its picture of a laughing god and its combination of pagan and Christian myth seems remote from the contemporary immediacy of the expressionist's concern with lost men such as Yank or Zero.

The expressionists of the 1920's, best exemplified by far by the four works which have occupied our time here, opened many doors in the following decades as it freed the stage from past restrictions in its demonstration to the artist of the theatre how well he could combine his writing with the newest in stage techniques to create an effective new style with an impact of considerable substance. Into the 1930's the effects of expressionism were clear and important, providing the impetus for such outstanding socially oriented creations as Clifford Odets' *Waiting for Lefty* in 1935, Marc Blitzstein's *The Cradle Will Rock* in 1937, Paul Green's *Johnny Johnson* in 1936, Irwin Shaw's *Bury the Dead* of the same year, and so on. Before the thirties were over, however, expressionism as a style in its own right had fairly well burned out. The great Depression turned the socially conscious dramatist into more of a propagandist than an artist, and the coming of the second half of the global war that had ceased momentarily in 1918 seemed to complete the process of rendering what the expressionist had to say in the 1920's obsolete. But the effects of what the expressionists of the 1920s did to the great benefit of theatricality remain, visible in such diverse accomplishments as Tennessee Williams' *A Streetcar Named Desire* of 1947 and his nearly purely expressionistic *Camino Real* of 1953, Arthur Miller's *Death of a Salesman* in 1949, and, of course, the modern tradition found in Albee, Kopit and others.

Suffice it to say, then, that Elmer Rice, Eugene O'Neill, and George Kaufman with his friend Marc Connelly gave to the decade of the 1920's four views of man in his contemporary world which we can claim as American drama's best expressionistic plays. In the quality of their writing and their use of what the stage technician had to offer, they have probably not been excelled. Equalled here and there, perhaps, but not excelled. Each of these plays can still be performed with good effect, for they remain almost as relevant as ever. The wasteland which their creators saw, even in the midst of what seemed to be a lasting era of prosperity and social "progress" and painted so well in Eliot's portrait of an often very disgusting world, has not disappeared. In fact, it may permanently engulf us yet, and the loud warnings from the 1920's remain worth the heeding.

30

The Other O'Neill

Jordan Miller

When Eugene O'Neill wrote his application for admission to George Pierce Baker's English 47 playwriting class at Harvard he stated his goal specificallly and simply: "I want to be an artist or nothing." From the one time waterfront bum, ex-sailor, college dropout with no credentials except a thin volume of badly written one-act melodramas that fell stillborn from a vanity press, this was at best naive, at worst a preposterous presumption, but it was above all things honest. The earnest, dark and brooding young man meant what he said, and throughout his lifetime pursued that goal with an intensity unequalled by any other modern dramatist. The decade of the 1920's served as O'Neill's journeyman years, a time during which the only demonstrated consistency in that artistic pursuit was his total and often infuriating inconsistency in theatrical style and dramatic integrity of the product which he fed to the Greenwich Village experimenters and to the uptown Broadway sophisticates. Averaging two plays a year, O'Neill baffled and confused his audiences and his critics by undertaking such a variety of form and subject as to drive his most faithful followers to distraction. The 1920's, while witnessing some of the playwright's greatest lifetime triumphs, was also forced to cringe before some of his most abject failures.

O'Neill was, and still remains, one of America's foremost expressionists, but his full fledged use of expressionism's free-wheeling theatricality was limited in the 1920's to only two plays, *The Emperor Jones* and *The Hairy Ape*. * It is the "other" O'Neill, the writer of predominantly realistic drama of tragic temperament who is to emerge from the decade as the more important theatre artist. Fascinated by men and women trapped in loveless marriages and sterile sex, insisting that the old gods were dead and that new ones had to be found, in frequently harrowing stage pictures far closer to "reality" than the stylistic manners of expressionism permitted, he displayed emotional and spiritual wastelands of a terrifying nature. The results ranged from dismal artistic catastrophes to remarkable, even sensational, successes, while underneath everything there persisted the determination to be an artist or nothing.

In many respects the 1920's were O'Neill's years of crying in the wilderness. Sometimes listened to, often unheeded and rejected, the artist he strove to be remained isolated, wandering about in his own personal desert. Carried around as an infant with his father's roving troups, boarded out to a series of private institutions, often deprived of making any kind of permanent friends, and with a brother ten years his senior, O'Neill could never put down roots himself in an actual home, not excepting the "cottage" that is the New London setting of *Long Day's Journey*. As an adult he moved restlessly from Cape Cod shack to Connecticut farm to Bermuda manor house to French chateau to Georgia estate to California valley mansion to New York flat, removed from old friends, rejecting his children, like Yank of *The Hairy Ape* never to discover his own place in the world where he could successfully "belong."

Particularly within the decade this "nomadic" aspect is apparent in O'Neill's inability to come to grips with his own artistic capabilities. Had his self-imposed isolation resulted in consistently acceptable dramatic themes or had the "purity of

---

*See chapter on "Expressionism: The Wasteland Enacted."

thought" which he strove to achieve by keeping himself as far
as possible from the theatrical commercialism of the Broadway
of his day brought him and his plays the understanding he
sought, his personal distance might not have been of much
concern. But the isolation of the artist, as well as the man,
often came through in the blurred message or the mystic
obscurities which constantly intruded between O'Neill and his
audiences, particularly in the first half of the decade. However
carefully planned his message might be, however devoted his
artistry, he continually found himself unable to formulate and
maintain a uniform dramatic approach that would identify his
own artistic style or bring some message of significance to his
viewers. Increasingly digging at the roots of the "sickness of
today" which he found dried and lifeless in the unreceptive
sands of the wastelands his characters inhabited, he constantly
surprised and shocked his audiences and inspired his critics to
call down the wrath of heaven upon his head for his artistic
ineptness, then drove them to praise him as one after whom all
conventional dramatic forms would pale to insignificance. But
praised or damned, as an artist he remained essentially alone.

Looking back from our present vantage point with O'Neill
as an established literary figure, the endurance of both
playwright and audiences as they fought this battle of getting
O'Neill established must be termed admirable. There must also
have been in existence some sort of benign spirit which made
sure that the playwright would propitiously space his successes
among the horrors of his feebler efforts in order to keep his
audiences and critics attracted and patiently hopeful. It was a
highly useful decade for O'Neill as artist and for the American
theatre as well, for it was the time during which O'Neill
sought, tried out, and refined the elements of later, triumphs
now recognized as masterpieces — specifically the most
devastating wasteland of his entire canon, the last chance, end
of the line, bottom of the sea refuge of Harry Hope's bar in
The Iceman Cometh.

Even if James O'Neill did not actually ask his son, upon
viewing *Beyond the Horizon*, if he was "trying to send the

audience home to commit suicide" the question would be a pertinent one for the old romantic actor who regarded the theatre as a place for pleasurable amusement and adventure. To young Eugene it was meant for the conscious expression of art. He accepted the criterion that great serious drama, to become great art, must seek meaning in the passions and troubled lives of human beings, and with a recklessness of youthful fervor which seemed to many a prodigious and wasteful expenditure of talent, he waded through the dunes of Provincetown and Cape Cod to write of the figurative sands of the sterile atmosphere and arid unproductivity of lives that have not been able to gain nor to hold the ability to love, to dream, and to share. However, resist as he would the gratuitous excitement of contrived events that typified so much of his father's theatre, O'Neill's signal flaw in his search for his true artistic vein was his adherence to what one noted critic called "the path of sensationalism." O'Neill seemed at times unable to resist an almost morbid attraction to the abnormal and the repulsive in order to make an obvious dramatic point. By today's standards much of O'Neill's subject matter was mild indeed, but to the audiences of the 1920's it is not hard to see how at least six of the twelve plays he produced between 1920 and 1925 could raise the fear that he would soon become mired in this enervating slough of despond. Each of the six places heavy emphasis upon personal debilitation either physical, mental, emotional, or spiritual, and they are not a particularly pretty collection.

O'Neill maintained that his primary concern as an artist was not with human relationships man to man but with the relationship of man to God. The distinction is not always as well delineated as O'Neill might have wished, and a great deal of the failure of these six plays can be attributed to their stress on very human and not particularly stimulating man-to-man (or more precisely man-to-woman) relationships from which "god" is mostly excluded. In this crowded five-year span of experimentation O'Neill seemed incapable of creating an artistically viable relationship between men and women on any

ordinary human basis. Confusing and perplexing as his mystic
explorations may have been, he was throughout the 20's on far
firmer ground when his protagonists questioned their gods or
the forces within their own souls. Responsiblities of one man
toward another, and of man toward himself, are successfully if
agonizingly analyzed in the later masterpieces of *The Iceman
Cometh* and *Long Day's Journey Into Night,* or in the lesser
and more greatly flawed *A Moon for the Misbegotten* and *A
Touch of the Poet,* but they are the product of another, later
age in O'Neill's development, and they are inhabited by people
with whom O'Neill himself was more intimately acquainted,
many of them drawn from his own life. The early failures tried
too hard to expose the thoughts and lay bare the love lives of
those with whom his familiarity was too limited, and in all of
them any look at the relationship with the spirits beyond was
hardly considered at all.

How many of these plays ring a bell for the "average"
person with reasonable knowledge of O'Neill — *Diff'rent* of
1920? *The Straw, Gold, Anna Christie* of 1921? *The First
Man,* 1922? or *Welded,* 1924? Only *Anna Christie,* I am sure.
The others have remained firmly and happily buried. Unable
to proceed beyond the assertion that men and women are
regularly trapped in snares of their own design, O'Neill
brought no original idea to mark him a thinker of consequence. Except for *Anna Christie* they had no commercial
success, and critics, along with O'Neill, rejected them. O'Neill
even refused to recognize the prize-winning *Anna Christie* as
one of his best, declining to permit its inclusion in printed
collections over which he had any control.

Their subjects? Hark to the catalogue of human desolation,
the wastelands that O'Neill placed around and within his
protagonists.

Diff'rent, in two acts separated by a time span of no less
than thirty years, examines with little result and a lot of
foolish posturing on the part of the protagonist, Emma
Crosby, the effects of a single-minded devotion to being
"diff'rent" — *i.e.,* pure, unstained, untouched by the world's

nastiness. In other words, sex. Emma's ideal is Caleb Williams, a good man, an excellent New England sea captain, devoted to his fiancée. But Caleb is human, and he is subject to the temptations of the flesh provided by dark-skinned beauties who loll in the antithesis of a wasteland, the idyllic South Seas into which he sails. Emma finds out. Instantly, her life is laid waste. Caleb is no longer like her, that is, no longer "diff'rent," for he has succumbed to earthly pleasures and has sinned. "Diff'rent" Emma can no longer tolerate him. He is ordered out of her sight. But Emma, clinging to her Puritanical code, placing the idea of love above love itself, has saved, and simultaneously destroyed, her own soul. Refusing to forgive the good captain who still, three decades later, loves and wants her, she descends in an irony so gross as to be atrocious even by O'Neill's worst standards into a sexually frustrated old maid, twisted in her perversions of "love" to such a point that she desperately plays for the worst young punk O'Neill could conceive. The result? Faithful Caleb, finding that being human, rather than "diff'rent," has no payoff, viewing the outlandishly garbed and painted shell of the Emma he had once thought worth waiting for, hangs himself. As this sordid, unlikely tale ends, Emma, so much the better for her, is preparing to do likewise.

We can brush aside *Gold* with its extravagances of a mad sea captain, hallucinations of the walking dead, and sunken treasure. Isaiah Bartlett, crazed and maundering, destroys himself and his family in a grisly fantasy of risen corpses. It is not a pleasant household to observe. A more important play is *The Straw,* set in a tuberculosis sanitorium, complete with clinical details of life and death among the consumptive. The critics yelped, imploring O'Neill to get out of the pest house and into the fresh air (what would they say today about *Medical Center,* or *Marcus Welby?*), but there was some notice that O'Neill had begun to create a semblance of sympathetic character interaction between the dying protagonist, Eileen Carmody, and the more healthy and sophisticated Stephen Murray. Unhappily, the critics were mostly right, for the world portrayed inside and out of the white sterility of the sanitorium is sickly and decayed. Beyond the hospital doors live the cruel and selfish family which has so thanklessly cast off its loyal member as unclean in the affliction that is none of her fault. "The world" has little to offer the sensitive Eileen whom it has thrown away to die, for the Carmodys, and all like them and the bratty families they produce, will inhabit and run it to their own ends. Inside the hospital is some hope, but mostly a resigned expectation of death. O'Neill permits genuine affection, even love, to develop within these unlikely surroundings, but he offers it to his protagonists as the last straw to grasp in desperation as a possible life-saving miracle. The gesture, of course, is futile. Throughout the play it is difficult to move beyond the desolation of the death-watch — no Magic Mountain here — and *The Straw* remains yet another of O'Neill's cracked milestones along the way.

Anna Christie, successful prize winner that it was, remains in the O'Neill vein of exposing the sickly pale underside of life. As in his earliest short plays, the desert is the sea, source of life, eternal mother, desolate, threatening, murderous. Into the seamy waterfront bar, onto the coal barge, into the sinister envelopment of fog, fog, fog all the bloody time comes Anna, a hopeful breath of youthful life and vigor, but, alas, a prostitute. Make that, for Anna's sake, ex-prostitute. To be sure, the prospects for the reformed Anna and the sea-creature Matt Burke, washed up *Tempest*-fashion from the treacherous waves right into the laps of Chris and his daughter, are apparently good. Apparently. For there is always the threat of the evil old devil itself, the sea, the strongest character on stage, the only one who really "knows," and what it knows, fog enshrouded as it is, it will not tell. Perhaps it will redeem Anna, bring genuine love and happiness, wash away her sins and the stains of her fall. And perhaps not. For all the seeming optimism, *Anna Christie* never permits its audience to escape the brooding menace, the misted wasteland of water. *The Ole Davil* O'Neill once called this play. Was it more appropriate than he realized?

Finally, *The First Man* and *Welded,* as depressing and hopeless a pair of plays as anything O'Neill ever created. The suffering which the characters endure to no particular end represents the nadir of O'Neill's 1920's venture into the human wasteland. In the one, Curtis Jayson, having lost two young daughters, refuses to have another child and insists, for "love" of her, that his wife accompany him on his anthropological expedition into the Himalayan plateau in search of the first man. Martha Jayson, in the natural consequence of her husband's professed "love," conceives again. Instantly that "love" is turned to hate, as vicious and violent as that of any primordial beast lurking ready to pounce in jungle or mountain. Jayson attacks his wife as a thankless, thoughtless, selfish creature who has now wrecked everything. Her death in screaming childbed agony and the survival of the male infant — the "first man" — bring Jayson to his senses, but it is too late. O'Neill had created no sympathetic or meaningful character with whom audience empathy might conceivably develop. In the other, a four-character verbal marathon that threatens to out-Strindberg Strindberg, O'Neill is at his most tedious in determining to scrape every frayed nerve in the love-hate syndrome that he held to be the basis of marital sex. Unable to live together, unable to live apart, Eleanor and Michael Cape fight, wound each other, flee, seek their respective sources of emotional succor — the other man and the respectful prostitute — and return to each other, unsatisfied, to resume the loving and hating, wounding and healing that are the permanent weld of the marriage relationship.

In less than four years O'Neill had bombarded his audiences with a half-dozen "realistic" plays, for the most part badly written ill-conceived slice-of-life attempts to focus his unsettled, and unsettling, thoughts about the intimate relationships of men and women as creatures of passion. They were strained, over-simplified, embarrassingly exaggerated portrayals of lust, greed and selfishness delivered in earthy melodramatics, the product of O'Neill's rough and heavy-handed attempt to break the stranglehold of dramatic conventionality. He succeeded only in creating a tubercular heroine of some sympathy, a mad sea captain of none at all, a sexually frustrated and disgusting old maid, and a dubiously romantic reformed prostitute, among other assorted creatures of small appeal, each of whom have had literary ancestors of much higher quality and none of whom had anything to say worth the trouble of their creation. If these had been the total result of Eugene O'Neill's quest to be an artist, the audacity of that blunt communication to Prof. Baker would have been proven. For almost anybody else such a dismal collection of rant and blather in some thirty-nine months of effort would surely have been the end of the road. There is, one assumes, an absolute limit to what the public will put up with.

Happily for his future and for those who faithfully prayed for him, O'Neill was simultaneously proceeding with an equal number of plays more clearly articulating his affirmed interest in the theme of man and god. The "god," of course, cannot be specified; O'Neill never intended any concrete identification. Different for each play, the deity in question maintains a semblance of uniformity as an abstract quality of spirituality involving the characters' relationship to an essence which dwells within themselves or within the universe in which the characters move. The universe is hardly less bleak, and O'Neill scarcely strays from his vision of men and women in frequent moral struggle against the grips of enervating, debilitating natural forces. Desolation, compounded if anything, still prevails, but the emphasis is different. The actions of the protagonists are not so much involved with their personal responsibilities toward others in society as with themselves and their makeup as human beings. The dark powers within are worthy of greater attention than the superficialities of the battle of the sexes that mark the other plays. Now the challenges of the wasteland can raise the conflict much closer to dramatic tragedy. Styles become less "realistic," while the protagonists become more interesting as human beings. Further, the grotesque for its own sake is markedly absent.

Again six plays, but the ratio is reversed. Only *The*

Fountain of 1925, buried in scenery and bad poetry, remains unsuccessful and forgotten. The others, *Beyond the Horizon* and *The Emperor Jones* of 1920, *The Hairy Ape,* 1922, *All God's Chillun Got Wings* and *Desire Under the Elms* of 1924, are vintage early O'Neill, at least three now recognized as minor classics.

 Beyond the Horizon may or may not be a valid tragedy. It probably isn't. We can leave the debate on that point to another time; what is significant with this first long play, his initiation to the professional Broadway stage, is that O'Neill is closer to his best artistic abilities than he would be for another four years. Robert Mayo, the doomed protagonist, would not be given a comparably sympathetic counterpart in a "realistic" O'Neill play until the appearance of the tragic naturalism of *Desire Under the Elms.*

 Robert's decision to remain home has little to do with his responsibilities toward others. True, he quickly disillusions Ruth, for whom he foregoes his long-anticipated voyage, but she will survive, better without than with him. His eventual fate results from his failure to respond to what is within his own soul. Instead, his brother Andrew, equally against his better self, ventures beyond the horizon; both men are then destroyed, Robert physically and Andrew spiritually, as one man's paradise becomes the other's hell. The sights, sounds, and odors that repulse Andrew in his visits to "exotic" ports around the world would without doubt have been beautiful to Robert's romantic spirit. On the other hand, the summer's heat and backbreaking farm toil which Robert must face would, we know, have been successfully challenged by Andrew the born farmer. In this often plodding humorless drama O'Neill knew better than he seems to have realized at the time the potential tragic, and hence artistic, value of revealing the truth about what happens when one fails to respond to the call within. The gods are pitiless if ignored, and Robert Mayo pays the fatal price. It would take a lot more "experimenting" in style and theme before O'Neill would hit this proper vein again.

Brutus Jones, placed within a milieu of startling difference, madly circling within the forest, looks straight at Brutus Jones in each succeeding hallucination. Destruction is his own making as he struts, then runs, and finally stumbles and collpases in the jungle wasteland that strips him of all the trappings of "civilization." The allegory is plain, for it was "civilization" at its exploitive worst which taught the boot-polishing lackey in the plush smoky decadence of the white quality Pullman cars how to fight in any jungle, be it rain forest or built of bricks, asphalt, smoke, and soot. The flaw within Jones, however, has little to do with anyone but himself. Taking his lesson from the civilized jungle of the white man's cut-throat world, he has become his own god; the "real" one stays on the shelf where he put it long ago. He frantically calls to it, seeks to remove it from its resting place, but it has long been rendered ineffective. Brutus Jones is totally alone and he is doomed. Yank, of *The Hairy Ape*, also abandons his old god of force, fire, coal, and sweat, and, like Jones, he is left helpless. The new and strange world of Fifth Avenue is a jungle that becomes a greater wasteland to him than the animal cage hell of the stokehole ever was. "Society," into which Yank forces his way kicking and screaming, is hostile, barren, and unsupportive. And it is fatal. In reality, the mannikins that walk the streets are as dead as Yank himself, but they have their own god to whom the good Dr. Caiphus prays for them. Yank dies, like Jones, a wasted man, stripped of the last of whatever dignity he had been able to bring himself. Jones had built himself his empire in the midst of a hostile nature; Yank, the natural man, built an inner "empire" of brute strength, incapable of saving him in the midst of a hostile society. Both abandoned at the end, and the best that Yank can do is to release an inarticulate gorilla into the world to replace him, one jungle animal for another. One feels it is, at worst, an even trade.

The overstuffed atmosphere of Ponce de Leon's search for youth in *The Fountain* is atypical O'Neill that merits little heed. Its reliance on the force of dreams and the power of illusion is, of course, an O'Neill staple, but the attempt at historic romance does not come off. The playwright ventured onto his weakest ground in this pseudo-poetic fantasy, and although it provided yet another avenue for the venturesome artist to travel in his search for theme and form, it proved a dead end which nobody regretted abandoning.

The realism of character and incident of *All God's Chillun Got Wings*, though staged in expressionistic overtones, returns us square into the middle of O'Neill's world of isolated human beings driven inward by a hostile society, incapable of finding salvation within themselves short of complete surrender of cherished dreams and madness. In the style of his least successful efforts, O'Neill hands Jim and Ella Harris a ready-made plan for disaster in a situation so daring for its time as to shake the foundations of New York law and order: miscegenation. Yes, a white woman was shown married to a black man, whose hand she not only dared to hold but, monstrous to relate, deigned even to kiss. But the playwright is able to extricate from out the surface antagonisms and threats of violence a more meaningful dramatic conflict than he gained from his sanitorium inmates or his more orthodoxly welded couples. *All God's Chillun* is not about miscegentation, nor about a racist theme at all. While decades ahead of his time in creating blacks with a consciousness of their own ethnic integrity, dignified and jealous of their own heritage and more believable than any of their race yet seen on stage, O'Neill is not aiming at socially oriented preachments to nor indictments against one side or the other. What he is doing is placing his desperately searching rejected protagonists into a world that is literally closing in on them. It is Brutus Jones' jungle world to Ella, symbolized by the ritual mask; it is the black man's ghetto world to Jim whose valiant efforts to escape into the white man's haven of education and equal opportunity is repeatedly thwarted not by the white man, but by Jim's fear of him. Each is out of his element, going counter to "nature," at least as seen by a society which designates the proper place for each. Hence, the "proper" gods whether those of Jim's own proud family, or those of Ella's prejudiced universe, are as abandoned as Jones' or Yank's. Neither Ella nor Jim can recognize, and hence neither can overcome, the forces that are destroying them, being as they are the forces carried within themselves forever as an inheritance from the society which tells one of them, however far she has sunk, that being white, she is superior to any black, husband or no; and which tells the other, no matter how hard he tries, no matter how superior an intellect he may possess, that he is still black and will remain a servant, a poor Jim Crow, to any white, even though it may be his own wife.

The wings of the chillun cannot carry them flying all over god's hebbin. God, be it white or black, has closed off paradise and has deserted the ever-narrowing world, which O'Neill demonstrates in a constantly constricting stage setting, of Jim and Ella, who must play out their children's game into eternity, cursing god for what has happened and wondering how he can forgive himself for what he has done.

The climactic effort of O'Neill's five-year output of good and ill came in 1924 with the appearance of *Desire Under the Elms*. This drama of primitive passions leashed and then unleashed on the rock-hard desert of a lonely, cruel New England farm brought O'Neill his earliest critical recognition as potentially Greek in tragic concept. Here, in individuals the scale of Ephraim Cabot or in crimes as monstrous as infanticide, rests classic tragic potential. Even the atmosphere portends a tragic fate: brooding elms, stone fences, the sense of something evil in the corners and crevices of the old house. There are ghosts of the past which reach out from the grave to control the living, and there are lust and greed from the present which the living use to combat them. It may be a "purty" farm, even to those whose doom it seals, but it is as unresponsive and as deadly to those who fight it as were Robert Mayo's sunbaked fields. Only the exceptional and almost superhuman Cabot can command it to respond and yield to his wishes, for he can be equally grim and terrible in exercising his will upon it.

The development of the tragic characters in this broad
adaptation of the Phaedra theme shows the progress O'Neill
had made since *Beyond the Horizon*. He was not yet
absolutely sure of his grounds; the sands were shifty enough to
yield further disasters along with further acclaim in the
decade's last two years, but the strength of Eben Cabot and
the tortures of his soul attempting to assert its own rights
against the human antagonism of old Ephraim and the more
natural, tragically fateful opposition to the farm are delineated
on the stage with infinitely greater skill. The earth-mother
sensuous strumpet and seductress Abbie Putnam is a far cry
from Ruth Atkins of *Beyond the Horizon*. Abbie joins her
stepson-lover in succumbing to elemental passions and to a
fate inevitably determined for them both once the wheels are
set in motion, but in becoming partner to it all she acquires a
dignity and stature which O'Neill had constantly sought
without success for earlier feminine protagonists. The hys-
terically irrational act of child murder, fortunately kept at
proper esthetic distance, is a natural consequence of these
passions, and the full realization of its horrors succeeds in
bringing Eben and Abbie together in a tragic catastrophe more
convincing than anything he had invented before in his natural
jungles or human-built wastelands.

By the mid-1920's O'Neill still seemed bent on being that
"artist or nothing" with the temperament to proceed toward
becoming the greatest playwright in the language. Never
lacking in inspiration or material, and able to attract a public,
he still failed to achieve the greatness that serious critics
prayed he might and which O'Neill himself must surely have
desired. In 1925 he expressed his discouragement to drama
critic and historian Arthur Hobson Quinn, stating that he was
convinced that "most of my critics don't want to see what I'm
trying to do or how I'm trying to do it." Joseph Wood Krutch,
nearly always an O'Neill champion, made a pertinent observation on this subject of O'Neill's communication with his
audiences when he wrote that men like Poe, James, Adams,
Thoreau, Melville, and Hawthorne were great literary artists

but were also lonely men whose public did not readily welcome what they wrote because of their failure to "participate in the spirit of the age." O'Neill was introducing tragedy with a capital T, and audiences were afraid. He, like Eliot, saw things which the rest of the world did not like to see and professed not to understand.

From 1925 to 1929 the entire nation was exhilarated by a booming propserity of seemingly unquestioned permanence. It was a time of mounting riches, Fords by the million, Rotarians by the clubful, and God blessing the manufacturer. The best subject for attack, if you simply *had* to attack anything, was Main Street and Babbitry. Any person who doubted the prosperous life of the future and wrote tragedy with a capital T would certainly not be understood. Writers might worry about the decline of morals, the racketeering of the bootleggers, and the irresponsible young generation in coonskin coats and flapper styles, but nobody was really interested in primitive passions and dark gods. To O'Neill, however, mankind was in serious trouble. In four plays, three of them successful in one way or another and the fourth, alas, still another unredeemed failure, O'Neill tore into the sickness of modern society and led his audiences through spiritual wastelands never previously explored by an American dramatic artist.

At the height of this era when money conquered all and dollars flowed from stocks, bonds, and John D. Rockefeller, O'Neill, the isolated prophet in his lonely cave, cried out in one of his more fascinating experiments that The Great God Business was faulty, destroying alike the souls of the artistic sensitive dreamer and the hard-headed businessman. He called the play *The Great God Brown,* and he peopled it with men and women carrying masks of "outward reality" with which they constantly covered or revealed as occasion demanded the "inner reality" of their true selves. Confusing, baffling, disturbing, even infuriating to those who refused to play O'Neill's elaborate game, this modern morality portrayed a world unreceptive to the artist who would create beauty for the sake of beauty, but whose prostitution of talents in the structure of the First Supernatural Bank it will accept. It is a world where the uninspired will welcome the talents of the genius, exploiting and selling it as his own; where love is so inverted that solace and understanding can come only from the woman of the streets; where the selfless and devotedly romantic wife succeeds only in killing, albeit with kindness, the husband who needs her and whom she cannot understand nor, without his mask, recognize. It is a mad world, my masters, within which men are, like the parts in Henry Ford's assembly line, interchangeable. Dion Anthony becomes Billy Brown, Billy Brown becomes Dion Anthony, and nobody knows the difference. Lost in the shuffle is Man, and the local representative of law and order who comes to view the body can't even spell it without help.

The obscurities of *Brown's* masked complexities have held the play to a level of *success d'estime* with every performance since it first appeared, never quite acceptable to critics or audiences as really good O'Neill, but always regarded as a challenge to performers and to audiences, constantly worth a visit. The case of *Dynamo,* O'Neill's answer to Henry Adams and his last play of the decade, fared not nearly so well. The old god was replaced by a new one, not a true spirit but a false prophet called electricity, spawned by sensuously humming generators. Presented in February 1929 when the stock market began its last lurch for the top, it showed several mentally unstable men and women — atheist, unbending Puritan, sensual daughter, monomaniac son — assembled in a sort of rogue's gallery of the worst types that O'Neill had expended so much time on during the first half of the 20's, all clashing in a furious encounter involving murder, beating, dynamo worship, and electrical suicide. The result was nothingness. Those who lasted it out were hard put to discover the salvation that the protagonists so fiercely sought. "Frequently raving, unconscionable bunk, pretentious rant" they said. O'Neill regarded it as one of his most misunderstood plays, insisting that his ideas "stood out like red paint," but nobody saw any paint, let alone red. It was a frightening world peopled by madmen, living in breakaway houses, spouting a great deal of raillery in monologue soliloquies, far from the best of O'Neill's many fascinating wastelands.

In January of 1928, before *Dynamo*, O'Neill did finally achieve the level of recognition his supporters long felt he deserved with his first production by the prestigious Theatre Guild, to remain his producers the rest of his life. They chose *Marco Millions*, O'Neill's belated exposé of Babbitry in the person of Marco Polo facing the legendary Kublai Khan. It may be passed by for many of the same reasons that *The Fountain* is forgotten. Its rather charming satire shows a playful, if no less serious, O'Neill, hitherto relatively unknown, but the playwright was again out of his element, overdoing the staging, overplaying the romantic, and laying too heavy a hand on the subtleties of character and incident. Successful to a degree far beyond *The Fountain*, it was soon lost amid the rush to see the display of agonies and ecstacies of Nina Leeds in a nine-act multi-hour marathon called *Strange Interlude*. *

Matters of style, the length and the famous spoken thoughts, are not valid concerns for a contemporary study of *Strange Interlude*. Despite the sometimes hysterical praise it received for its theatrical experimentation nothing much came of this particular innovation except a realization, as O'Neill discovered very quickly with *Dynamo*, that nobody, not even O'Neill, could do anything like it again. The play by any account is a monster. The chances are, had it not been by O'Neill, it would have collapsed of its own weight before it got started. It did not, and its success became one of the great theatrical phenomena of the decade.

No other O'Neill play would do quite what this one did in its shattering look at the spiritual afflictions of a single soul

---

*Lazarus Laughed, O'Neill's Dionysiac interpretation of the New Testament miracle called "A Play for an Imaginative Theatre" received 28 performances by the Pasadena, California, Community Playhouse in April 1928 and has never been commercially produced.

bent on creating a world to its own pattern, destroying all in its path, including itself, in a human wasteland of epic size. Nina Leeds is, obviously, quite quite mad. Those around her, save her own offspring who literally flies the contaminated nest, must certainly realize that her obsession for the dead Gordon is cause enough to put her away, but they are as hypnotized into executing her will as if the deadly cobra were playing the pipe for its master. It is, on the basis of rational believability, a preposterous soap opera, a tedious biography of a nymphomaniac. By the time it is all over and Nina chooses at forty-five or thereabouts to sit in the cool shadows of cool evenings in cool gardens to rot in peace with dear old Charlie we can do little but applaud the end of it and judge that everybody from top to bottom got just what he deserved.

But that's not the point. Nina is O'Neill's creation of Woman. Like the play itself, she is monstrous, representing every aspect of the female human animal in its utmost capacity and rapacity. She is all things of her sex — daughter, adored virgin, whore, wife, mother, mistress — name it and she fits. Men are her objects of manipulation and she prides herself in being a vital living part of each of them, so integral that none can function without her, save the escaping son, who is a reincarnation of the beloved Gordon and a kind of superman anyway. John and Eleanor Cape may have been welded each to each, but their problem was nothing compared to the iron bands that Nina Leeds forges to hold Sam, Darrell, Marsden, and even the ghost of Gordon Shaw, unto herself. Nina Leeds carries within her psyche O'Neill's greatest inner wasteland. She has lost her faith, questioned god, abandoned him (or her) and has herself become the primordial female force. Proclaiming the ability to offer undying and boundless love, she fastens it upon a ghost and thereupon proceeds, in the name of love, to get from the living beings around her everything she wants, drains their lifeblood, and gains at last the final hollow nothingness of an emotionally empty, sexless world. The bang is gone. The whimper is all.

For the ten years of the 1920's Eugene O'Neill pursued a

career in the American theatre which nobody has ever come close to equalling before or since. There was only one other modern dramatist who could demand his will be done, and who was equally praised and scorned, but George Bernard Shaw kept his pixie image before his public for his entire life, and he wrote some of the finest comedies in English. Eugene O'Neill, whom Shaw once called a "banshee Shakespeare," remained the artist in the wilderness, refusing to become a public figure, refusing to compromise his tragic bent, an intensely private individual whose public stance, compared to Shaw's, was a hermit's isolation. Far more than Shaw, who covered half a century, O'Neill was the genuine product of the decade of the 1920's. Eliot, the poet-mystic, gazed into the heart of society and found it arid, sterile, and disgustingly unproductive. O'Neill, the mystic-tragedian, who would have been a poet but, as he admitted, too often merely stammered, also saw and was dismayed. Heeded or not, the stammering was heard, and the 1920's, horrors and all, were O'Neill's proving ground. The makings were there, but the goal of the artist had not been reached and the masterworks were yet to come.

31

The Waste Land and the American Breakdown

Kingsley Widmer

One of the most powerful yokings of "broken images" in Eliot's poem puts together the modern city and the traditional spiritual "waste land" in an ironic fusion of fragmented quest mythology and our fractured urban sensibility. These connected disconnections, these associated disassociations, not only provide the primary experience of the poem but much of *The Waste Land's* significance for the Twenties, and beyond. Such break-down of sensibility became not only aesthetically influential but morally prophetic. And, as so many of the essays in this collection persuasively suggest, *The Waste Land's* disconnections often provide the connections of our culture.

The most essential order of disconnection, I suggest, does not come from the Alexandrian fracturing and fusing of myths, which properly end up rather mocked, but in the modern sensibility which suffers, and even oddly exalts, its sense of disconnection. The allusive literary and mythological mosaic must be viewed with irony, as the dry mock of a superior sensibility which perceives its alienation and fragmentation as an aesthetic and moral discipline. The "unreal city" with the crowd flowing under the "brown fog" is, of course, inadequately real because the poet, unlike the crowd and the characters in the poem, has a literary vision of the great damned Western capitols, such as Webster's bloody-Elizabethan Rome, Baudelaire's swarming-ant-hill Paris, and Dante's eternally sighing Limbo. Yet simultaneously this self-conscious and cultured awareness rends Eliot's actual London of the Twenties into the unreality of learned literary cityscape. "Eliot is our culture-hero," said Delmore Schwartz, who made our realities feel like "a foreign country."

Thus of the very mundane crowds in London the poet can make the Dantean sigh, "I had not thought death had undone so many," though only he knows how undone. The sexual, social and religious undoings we see in the poem's kaleidoscopic scenes and futilely damned souls include the breakdown of redemptive possibilities. "Shall I at least set my lands in order?" The only "yes" seems to be by setting them in disorder, by artfully stylizing the despair. "The Peace which passeth understanding" is that of the necropolis, of not only the collapse of the ideal of the great polis as redeeming civilization, but of affirmation as refined negation.

The varied and large implications of the poem rest on a quite individual and peculiar state of self-consciousness. I see *The Waste Land* as in considerable part a willfully eccentric poem and a personal lament, a confessional work even, of the disenchanted American poet abroad in the great city. The late-romantic disguise in literary and mythological pastiche is not to be taken literally; rather, it tends to confirm the poem as a statement of the break-down of an individual sensibility. After due adjustment for understatement, I suggest we accept Eliot's claim (as quoted by Theodore Spencer) that *The Waste Land* was "rhythmical grumbling," a personal "grouse against life." The much touted Eliotic "impersonality" is mere gesture, and the famous "objective correlative" an ornate way of cauterizing the self-pity that motivates so much modern art, as it must, because this is not the culture of an authentic community. The poem presents the painful and disassociating and self-breaking unreality of the great city and civilization for Tom Eliot in 1922. Partly because it was so responsive, partly because it pointed in the right direction of prophetic pertinence, and partly because of its own history in creating the consciousness it decried, the individual fragmentation acquired a far larger significance.

The early Eliot repeatedly sang of the break-down of urban sensibility. In the negative lyricism of "Preludes," the concern was with the "thousand sordid images," within as well as without, of urban marginality and the perverted power of the "conscience of a blackened street" which demands while yet denying aesthetic and moral coherence. No wonder that J. Alfred Prufrock's city evening is "etherized upon a table" in an urbanely impotent pattern of "insidious intent." And no wonder that in *The Waste Land* the "unreal city" breaks down at many levels, from the nursery rhyme loss of innocence in "London bridge is falling down falling down falling down" to, as Warren French points up in his essay, the decline of the West and its great city images of redemption in the "Falling towers/ Jerusalem Athens Alexandria/ Vienna London/ Unreal." At both the levels of innocence and cultivation, the poet cannot hope to restore the reality, only resign himself to the fragments. In spite of the ironic detachment—rather reduced here, as in Eliot's other urban scenes, by the obsessive sexual falling downs—the crux of the poem is the inadequacy and break-down of cultivated sensibility.

In his suggestively erratic ruminations on the literature of the early Twenties, *Anni Mirabiles,* the late R. P. Blackmur admiringly spoke of *The Waste Land* as "a sane art almost insane in its predicament." Part of that extreme predicament was undoubtedly personal for the sick Eliot who wrote much of the poem in several months of therapeutic flight from his demanding job, his invalid wife, and his depressing London. Of course the predicament may be stated with ostensible impersonality as horror over modern urban facts and feelings and as an extension of the profound modernist insight that cultivated sensibility will neither redeem the self nor the society. "Unreal city" in the poem was at one time the more bald "terrible city" (according to Valerie Eliot's 1971 edition of *The Waste Land* manuscript). Other unpublished lines of the original, before Ezra Pound's probably excessive deletions, emphatically further the raging negative sense of the city scene with its "swarming creatures" and "phantasmal gnomes, burrowing in brick and stone and steel," those incomprehensible urban masses "Knowing neither how to think, nor how to feel." Eliot's attitude is far more contemptuous than compassionate — no real Christianity here — though no figure in the poem moves exempt from the malaise. (To give the poem a hero, or an heroic author, somehow beyond the negation, seems to miss the essential point; to take androgynous prophet Tiresias as hero is merely running a *jeu d'esprit* into the sands.) All redemptive ideals, whether of affectionate love or of the civilizing polis or of the cultural heritage, sink down in sordid images and noises of megapolitan proliferation and impotence and meaninglessness.

Half a century after *The Waste Land,* and in recognition that it took on an epochal role in our culture, we may be tempted to add "ecological readings" to the poem, not only seeing the "brown fog" as killer-smog and the literal falling-down of London Bridge (as Warren French mockingly notes, appropriately reassembled as a realtor's tourist attraction in the American commercial waste land), but also a larger sense of pollution and wasting of life-systems.

In sociological paraphrase, if you will, our unbalanced urbanization, our megalomania for a fradulent and fragmenting megapolitan disorder, provides much of the point we are prepared to find in *The Waste Land.* The response seems historically valid. The America of Eliot's youth — and of the generation that first responded intensely to the poem as prophecy — was more than eighty percent puritan-toned rural and smalltown; in two short generations, not only has there been an exponential rise in people and wastage, in the undone crowds, but the country has become more than eighty percent decadent-toned city and suburb, in one of the most drastic mass-urbanizing revolutions in all history. Inevitably *The Waste Land* serves as predictive document and social symptom, regardless of Eliot's intention, as well as personal denouncement and poetic symbol. Social and cultural dialectics made this willful personal poem more broadly prophetic of our "unreal" conglomerates which lack so much in aesthetic civility and moral community.

As I interpret Eliot's literary career — in a somewhat more drastic view than that proposed by Professor French in his introduction to this volume — *The Waste Land* seems its culmination. Not only does it peak the urban exacerbation of the early poems, it provides the major achievement of his aesthetic experimentation, far more than the conventional forms and parochial views of his later meditations and plays. Certainly the very subject, the break-up of the cultural heritage and its urban denouement, provides part of the poem's significance. There are, of course, poetic forerunners to Eliot's sense of the wasting city scene: Swift's harsh little verses on London, Smollet's Matt Bramble's distaste for the city, Blake's indictment of its "chartered streets" and other "mind-forged manacles," through the filthy-fogged labyrinth of the late-Dickens and the urban revulsions of the Pre– Raphaelites (their aesthetics lie much closer to Eliot's than is usually acknowledged), even if we don't go abroad into Baudelaire's and Corbièrre's mortuary Paris (and their re- bellions and ironies which Eliot so importantly helped bring into the viable heritage of twentieth century American literature). Yet the city-as-waste-land, so antithetical to the Western tradition's ideal of the city as the ultimate image of civilization, may also reveal a peculiarly American impetus. Certainly the effects of Eliot's poems on our literature and understanding must be felt as filtered through American responses to the cityfying after-war wasting world.

The informing sense of urban disconnection and the mocking distaste for it may be most directly related, indeed indebted, to the immediate predecessor of *The Waste Land*, the linked "Mauberley" poems of Ezra Pound, mentor and editor (and later dedicatee) of Eliot's poem. Pound had much of the "American smalltown crank" in him (in Kenneth Rexroth's words), and one pattern of the fine Mauberley fragments is his doubly mocking aesthete's farewell to London. Pound's view of the great megalopolis more simply than Eliot's emphasized sensation and contempt. But with this, Pound brought into American poetry what Eliot was to practice in The Waste Land and what Randall Jarrell was to later describe as the crucial "mosaic" style of modernism. Quite likely, Pound could do little other than the pastiche of association and dissociation, which he later ran into near final incoherence in The Cantos. No matter, for he gave fragmented sensibility one of its distinctive styles, the tight verbal forms for disconnection and alienation so intimately part of modern megapolitan experience, even if, as one of the great poetic junk collectors, he could not put it all together.

Pound seems to be serving as well as mocking his times when he acknowledges in the Mauberley poems, as French notes, that "The Age Demanded an image/ Of its accelerated grimace" − and which Eliot was to help give it. The first version of Pound's repeated line seems to have been in response to World War I and its "wastage as never before." In the waste land of myriad deaths, the artifacts of culture can only, if one has any honesty, appear to be irrelevant fragments. The Great War was fought, as the totally specious political rhetoric had it, to save Western civilization. Pound appropriately reduces this, in sardonic images, to murder done "For two gross of broken statues,/ For a few thousand battered books." That is the voice of an outsider; Eliot was to take the artifacts of civilization a bit more seriously.

The disconnections, then, come as style refracting reality, an incoherently breaking and brutal war which can only predicate a larger disillusionment − "For an old bitch gone in the teeth/ For a botched civilization." True, Pound's disillusionment and bitterness has, in contrast, say, to the misanthropy of Robinson Jeffers, a kind of detachment, an almost flaneur-at-the-apocalypse tone, which shows his personal disconnection. Yet he responds to the crucial experience, and with style. As Gertrude Stein once noted, in one of her less tiresomely quaint moments, the twentieth century only really started with the war and its meaning. Certainly this is true of our literature of the Twenties where the war-awareness — and the end of a culture and break-down of sensibility which goes with it — becomes a watershed point. The dissociated styles of modernism got their first full American development in response to what was then naively called The Great War. While Eliot's Waste Land is not directly that created by World War I (though it is glancingly present, as in the Pound added word "demobbed" in Part II), the war break-down of the old order provides unmistakeable context for the more fastidious poet's sense of spiritual break-up. The "civilized" West, ignoring its own colonial and class violence (and endless "minor" wars), could optimistically yoke its culture to the supposed "century of peace" between the international post-Napoleonic reactionary ordering and its obvious collapse following Sarajevo. But the sense of the past as fragile fragments and devalued pieces seems appropriate data of consciousness resulting from the war.

It should be noted that the most usual emphasis of Eliotic commentators rides upon the difficulty, and loss, of religious and cultural belief, with academic-Alexandrian pietists adding some promise of reaffirmed cultural and religious faith by an over-reading of the mythological fragments or by the imposition of the later Christian Eliot upon the earlier one. To the contrary, *The Waste Land* may be viewed as primarily an affirmation of the break-down, a therapeutic systematizing of the fragmentation. Eliot, as it were, makes a poetic metaphysics of dissociation. Thus I suggest reading quite literally the crucial line in the ending — the only line which is not an allusion to something else — "These fragments I have shored against my ruins."

My suggestions, then, are to see the significance of *The Waste Land* in the break-down of individual sensibility, in the break-down of human community and order in the expanding megalopolis, and in the break-up of the claims to bourgeois civilization after the Great War. While *The Waste Land* may suggest all sorts of cultural, social, and religious responses, its major coherence remains peculiarly aesthetic, and that aesthetic must do for a politics and a religion as well. The ironies of shoring the fragments (further played upon in Eliot's Notes), the Poundian insistence on the poet committed only to his poetics (even on major themes and narrative coherence one modifies or disposes of lines purely on a stylistic basis), the highly mannered Eliotic images (such as "bats with baby faces in the violet light") — all exalt the aesthetic of break-down as a kind of homeopathy.

To claim the largest art, to insist on the discipline and even exaltation, of "a heap of broken images," becomes both poignant and arrogant — an ultimate faith in an aesthetic strategy. We may find the early Eliot exemplary here, though surely he, and Pound, were not alone in this faith, this untoward obeisance to fractured art. Joyce's *Ulysses,* also a self-exalting pastiched and mosaiced monument, was published the same year as *The Waste Land* (Eliot had earlier read parts of it, approvingly). Crane, Cummings, Stevens, Moore, among American poets, reveal their proximities, and probably some stylistic indebtedness. Related qualities can be traced in the work of many another writer, for *The Waste Land* seems central to what was to become the major modernist heritage out of the Twenties. Expressionism, Dadaism and Surrealism were creating related styles based in fragmentation and dissociation, and, often, bumptious re-connection. One could go on, both more specifically and more broadly, to body out the argument that here we have the special quality of the culture we identify with the Twenties: break-down and artistic exaltation.

Some of the distinctive tone of Twenties sensibility may have less to do with the "boom" times and "new freedoms" made so much of in nostalgic accounts of the time, and the arts, than with the liberating effects of the sense of break-down. The war and the urbanizing and the loss of tradition and the other fragmentations provided an unburdening which at first often seemed positive, even exhilarating, in some of its effects. Despair as well as post-war expansion encouraged a sense of desperate elan, the freedom of disconnection, which the cliches attempt to enshrine as the "roaring" and "jazzy" Twenties. Stock American optimism, and our pathology of "positiveness," which Eliot and others clearly reacted against, was replaced with a negativeness beyond the "loss of innocence" and the once-trumpeted American cultural "coming of age" (Brooks). But the negativeness came out oddly energetic. Iconclasm was no doubt crucial to this. Even such regionalists as William Faulkner ran, in his early and somewhat callow novels, the changes: arch-aestheticism, war-despair, the grotesque jubuliation with broken tradition and myth. Only, I would argue, when Faulkner achieved a harsh poetic fusion with a particularistic, even naturalistic, reality — perhaps encouraged by the Depression? — did he reach his more incisive art, as in *Light in August.* But there, too, we can see the energetic iconoclasm of the preparatory Twenties which helped encourage the most savage portrait of the Protestant ethos to appear in our literature.

The pessimism of the Twenties must often strike us as oddly lively, not only victorious in its sense of past-breaking and ebullient in its sense of defeat, but almost a blues ecstacy. As Aldous Huxley once commented upon the American literature of the period, "high spirits and heroic vitality are put into the expression of despair." There were more ominous qualities, of course, which time was to light up. D. H. Lawrence, commenting on American literature in the Twenties, was also more than half-right in insisting that the essential "soul of the American" was "stoic, isolate, and a killer."

But let us return to the literary image of the city. When, for example, we look at novels concerned with it in the Twenties, we also find the mixture of excited energy and bitter loss. John Dos Passos moved from pre-war aestheticism to harshly disillusioned war novels (especially the destruction of the artist in *Three Soldiers*) to more home-disillusionments for this dour latter-day Jeffersonian in his portrayal of the post-war city. (Jefferson, in some famous comments on his hopes for the new country, inveighed against our developing

large and corrupting cities — such as little eighteenth century
London!) Dos Passos was, as A. S. Knowles, Jr., points out in
his discussion in this volume of *Streets of Night*, "an
inhabitant of the same milieu that produced T. S. Eliot."
There may also be some direct influence of *The Waste Land* on
Dos Passos' unreal city, a New York labeled Nineveh in the last
chapter of *Manhatten Transfer*, his most important work of
the Twenties. There Dos Passos presents a montage of
fragmented and sordid and despairing lives in a series of
fractured narratives (themselves rather old fashioned, as are
the author's moral revulsions). His defeated urbanites only
relate by the mechanical transfer point of the title. The
intellectual and emotional levels of the naturalistic novelist's
characters are mostly banal, the language tritely colloquial, the
images urban-grim, the perspective deterministic. But so are
those of the similar "naturalistic" sections of *The Waste Land*,
such as the pub dialogue of the working class women. The
juxtaposition of self-conscious artistry and naturalistic urban
detailing link the two works in the cultural schizophrenia of
the times. The novelist's New York is as wastingly, though
more sociologically and less lyrically, undone as the poet's
London since both write out of similar revulsions. Dos Passos
notably switches the artisic mosaic from the materials of high
culture to those of popular culture, though Eliot had done a
bit of this with popular songs in *The Waste Land*. In
Manhattan Transfer Dos Passos gives the preliminary development of the song fragments, headlines, historical anecdotes,
and other bits and pieces he was later to massively use in his
three-volume documentation of the early decades of the
American Century, *U. S. A.*, which logically ends with the
Great Depression and the social despair that had always been
implicit in the waste-landish cultural fragmentation.

There were of course many other novelists responsive to
the city-as-waste-land. American intelligence has generally
been anti-urban, or supposedly so. Yet many of the novels of
the Twenties center, realistically enough, on inchoate flight to
the city, in desperate rejection of, and by, the Middle-

American smalltown. Usually the crux in the ambiguous populist expressionism of Sherwood Anderson, for example, includes flight to the city, as with George Willard's inchoate search for manhood and sophistication, misdescribed as art, in the conclusion to *Winesburg, Ohio.* However, earlier scenes showed the desperately lonely and defeated returning to the smalltown. Anderson's personal ambivalence shows the same uncertainties as did his poignantly awkward art. And so do the expatriations and other restless alienations of the Twenties. Even those born to it, as we see in, say, Henry Miller's later accounts of urban life in the Twenties, found it fragmenting and frenzied to the state of insanity — and desperately sought a parallel artistry. Such responses, the social historians blandly note, show an America in drastic urban transition and moral change; more pertinently, they suggest that America never created sensitively acceptable social forms of community, and so we get the flight from Waste Land to what will become new Waste Lands.

The city-as-waste-land pervades our better literature of the period. Even Fitzgerald, fascinated with the "inexhaustible variety" and "promised gayety" of the Twenties urban scene, presents, with his usual doubleness, the images — "simultaneously enchanted and repelled," he wrote with that split sensibility which gave him much of his art. Warren French — as well as James E. Miller, Jr. — appropriately quotes the famous "valley of ashes" description in *The Great Gatsby.* With its "foul river" and eyeless signboard deity, possibly influenced by Eliot's images of the befouled "Sweet Thames" (carrying "cigarette ends" and "other testimony of summer nights") and phantasmal lost gods, it may be the best-known American trope of the dismalness at the edge of the gaudy time. Wasting, of course, of innocence, of time, of their collosal illusion, runs through the novel. I would suggest, also, a related theme: disconnection. Recall the pathetic-comic scene in which Gatsby, after one of his incoherent demi-monde brawls of celebrities and other bored parasites, stands on the steps of his mansion in a formal gesture of farewell, quite ignored by the caterwauling crowd around a smashed-up car whose spectral drunk driver can't seem to understand that he has lost a wheel. Disconnection, as also repeatedly with Gatsby's irrelevantly romantic-chivalric gestures, may be a major informing notion of *The Great Gatsby*, as it is of *The Waste Land*.

Certainly the wasting disconnections, perhaps a bit more than Fitzgerald consciously realized, provide much of the issue of the prose-poem conclusion to *The Great Gatsby*, the meditation by Nick Carraway on the awesomely meretricious American Dream of success. With proper incongruity, we see the wondrous moonlight evening, the promising green light of the wealthy Buchanan's across the bay, the scrawled obscenity on the steps of the late Gatsby's pretentious empty mansion, and partake of a sense of the loss of "the greatest of all human dreams," the American promise, yet only personified in the naive remembrance of a mawkish con-man. As in Eliot's poem, present disconnections carry us "back ceaselessly into the past" history and myth which provide Fitzgerald's ironies about a new-world dream long gone, an unrecoverable myth still spastically operating in the present for a hero and a success not really worth admiring. Only our nostalgic enchantment, fragmentarily raised by the poet and the novelist, gives the momentary richness to a lost and befouled myth, and even that in only literally charmed-up and fractured lines and images.

It should not be surprising that personal fragmentation and breakdown later caught up with a good many of the noted writers of the Twenties who, after all, had made that not only their subject but their aesthetic. The self-destructiveness of Fitzgerald, who was to write but little more of style and insight (some scenes in *Tender Is the Night* and a story or two such as "Crazy Sunday"), was only more neatly brigaded than most with the decade, as his *Crack-Up* pieces of the Depression and his identification of his own "gaudy spree" with that more generally of the American Twenties confirms. No doubt the recurrent American phenomena of writers who go nowhere, who develop no late-style, must be part of it. The Twenties invented the "celebrity" — and "fandom" and much else that was to become the short-circuiting cultural electricity of the mass media — and artists, too, were encouraged, even driven, to fulfilling cardboard and celluloid roles, including artistic self-parody, as is all too evident in the broken down later work of not only Fitzgerald but Hemingway and Faulkner and many others. Fitzgerald foreshadowed the self-defeating one-dimensionality that became the standard price of cultural "success" in America.

Hemingway, creator of a distinctive if narrow style of sensibility in the Twenties, perceptively presented here by C. W. E. Bigsby as a process of disillusioned recoil and saving stylization, provides another literary example of the exhilaration and then break-down, ending in sheer self-parody. It has reasonably been suggested that *The Sun Also Rises* owes much to *The Waste Land.* While we need not be seriously concerned with postivistic scholarship's reduction of culture to influences and other mechanical relationships, the consequent ironic reading of that novel is not inappropriate. There, and elsewhere, we find Hemingway's extreme ritualization of experience, including despair, which has its similarities to Eliot's turning despair into sheer incantation in the later sections of *The Waste Land* as well as in such following poems as "The Hollow Men."

The narrow ritualistic art of Hemingway — he is usually downright embarassing on women, family, society, politics, culture, and ideas — provides a stoic stylization of the "separate peace" of the war generation and the impotence of the following "lost generation." Some of this derives, as Bigsby argues, from fearfully freezing experience and an adolescent refusal of complexity. In futile flight from the waste land of civilized wars and cities, Hemingway's characters search for a "clean, well-lighted place" — most often represented by purificatory mountains and seas — and for morally simplified roles, such as sportsman and fighter and gambler, which they can then protectively ritualize. This presupposes that the rest of the world is a moral and metaphysical waste land.

Perhaps the simplest way of summarizing its Hemingwayesque version is with the animal fable in the last chapter of *Farewell to Arms,* written towards the end of the decade with a detached consideration of the war break-down of possibilities. As beloved Catherine and child are dying, Fredrick Henry reflects on the generally hostile world in which the only certainty seems to be that "they would kill you."

> Once in camp I put a log on top of the fire and it was full of ants. As it commenced to burn, the ants swarmed out and went first toward the centre where the fire was; then turned back and ran toward the end. When there were enough on the end they fell off into the fire. Some got out, their bodies burnt and flattened, and went off not knowing where they were going. But most of them went toward the fire and then back toward the end and swarmed on the cool end and finally fell back into the fire. I remember thinking at the time that it was the end of the world and a splendid chance to be a messiah and lift the log off the fire and throw it out where the ants could get off onto the ground. But I did not do anything but throw a tin cup of water on the log, so that I would have the cup empty to put whiskey in before I added water to it. I think the cup of water on the burning log only steamed the ants.

This is vintage Hemingway in the carefully additive concrete style, the understatement of metaphysical dilemma, the woodsy locale (disenchanted American pastoral), the adaption of classical fable to post-war morality, and the "end of the world" nihilism. "As flies to wanton boys . . ." are the ants to Hemingway, but without Shakespearean tragic proportions in this fated world which has become a chaotic and gratuitous wasting unto death, in and out of war. It's a nearly malicious cosmos, with the paranoic "they," in which the choices are to be burned, steamed or crippled into idiocy. The messiah impulse is there but, as in the early Eliot, is inoperative and dryly irrelevant. And our hero maintains himself by his compulsive little he-man rituals out of the past (whiskey before water) and his coolly discriminating despair. This lacks the pyrotechnical erudition of Eliot, but not the tone and the moral.

One could no doubt make a collection of such negative metaphysical analogies, mosaiced into all sorts of works, in the literature of the Twenties. In some senses, I suppose, they express Eliot's self-descriptive phrase in *The Waste Land* of "voices singing out of empty cisterns and exhausted wells." Yet they also sing with considerable verve, with an energy of disillusionment which is more than world-weariness — the power, perhaps, of a *new* despair, a defiance of old gods and an aesthetic liberation, which seems so essential to the best literature of the Twenties.

Disassociating despair, too, grows old, conventional, and its mannered self-pity became cliche and the hallmark of second-rate modernist imitators. Even in the Twenties, of course, there were strong reactions against it. Some — such as we are shown with Edith Wharton — hold, at their best to an ironic intelligence looking towards the past. Others, such as the vociferous denunciations of the "new literature" by the Neohumanists (academic pietists such as Babbitt, More, Forester, etc.) remain of only antiquarian interest. After all, the Waste Lands and ant-like fates were appropriate to the history that followed of Great Depression, totalitarianism, great-great war, and the futher fragmenting of sensibility into the passivity required by the bureaucratic-technological order. As Warren French notes, the "classical cultural tradition" was rather thoroughly shattered into quite different sorts of fragments by twentieth century experience. More broadly yet, bourgeois humanism was undoubtedly broken up, often from within, by the imaginative fracturings of post-war literature and thought.

Rather more interesting than the conservative responses were the attempts at counter-statement to *The Waste Land* within modernist literature. Kenneth Johnson points out in an essay in this volume that for more than thirty years William Carlos Williams battled what he took to be Eliot's negative, that is, learnedly past-haunted and guiltily purity-seeking, view of contemporary experience as well as poetry. This resulted in an antithetical modernist tradition and iconoclasm, still with us, emphasizing the sensible image rather than the intellectual conceit, the fervently colloquial rather than the ironically mandarin language, the direct affirmative emotion rather than the involuted metaphysical despair. As Williams said of his own poetics, "No ideas but in things." This concentration on the "object" and the "image" produced some fine small poems — and a heritage that more often than not poeticizes trivial and banal things. Even when, a generation later, Williams made his fullest counter-statement to *The Waste Land*, elaborating his "localism" into a long city-poem, *Paterson*, the limitations often seem to be the quality as well as the point.

Other counterings of *The Waste Land* more directly drew upon intellectual passion and broken urban sensibility and images with a similar, desperate exaltation of the aesthetic. The poetry of Hart Crane seems more central than ever here, not least in its large failures. I want to add a critical argument to Donald Pease's explication of *The Bridge* in this volume. Crane announced, in discussing his proposed long poem, that he was reacting against "Eliotic pessimists." He intended, he said in a letter quoted by Pease, to use the poetics of *The Waste Land* as a point of departure but in a "reverse of direction." In his desperate search for what he elsewhere aptly called "intensities," Crane tried heightenedly to fuse the fragments of American experience and posit a new consciousness, create a "mystical synthesis" and overcome the dominant disconnections of our sensibility, or what Pease calls "an epic of consciousness." Brooklyn Bridge was to be the "steeled Cognisance" and "Paradigm" to a visionary image of, somehow, the prophetic and redemptive word.

Characteristic of the times, the ambition, though curiously confined to the aesthetics of marginal urban sensibility, looms large in the willed effort to link the personal anguish with mythic possibilities and megapolitan sensations. The description of New York, especially in "The Tunnel" section of *The Bridge*, which is fairly direct adaption of *The Waste Land*, comes out quite grim (as does also "National Winter Garden" and other pieces) in spite of some rhetoric of ecstacy. As in Eliot's poem, Crane emphasizes the burden of mechanical and threatening time as one of the dominant qualities of modern urban life. Crane, perhaps more directly than Eliot, apprehends city fracturing and frenzy, with his insistence on the mechanical sundering of life ("the iron dealt cleavage"). Inevitably, the American connections are disconnections, less the over-arching bridges and myths of Atlantis, Eldorado, organic primal America (the body of Pocahontas), and Whitmanesque merging *en masse* than the instruments (bridges, rails, wires, subways, trains, planes) which "Bind town to town and dream to ticking dream." Crane tries to transcend the technological age and "iron year" by exalting it rather than lamenting it, not only making the bridge, in its curveship, "lend a myth to God" but by such pressured anagogy as the motors' "oilrinsed circles of blind ecstacy!"

But the circles of the poetry lead back to the hell of "O my City" which still, like *The Waste Land*, leaves one overwhelmed with banalities and fragments, with urban "nerviosities" and "shrill ganglia," with emotional degradation ("love/ a burnt match skating in a urinal"), loneliness, alienation and suicide (after all, the "bedlamite" jumps from *the* bridge). There is no escape of the Eliotic death by internal fire and external water. Even the modernizing romanticism of flight leads nowhere (planes become instruments of war, that in "Cape Hatteras" crashes, and later we hear "The conscience navelled in the plunging wind,/ Umbilical to call — and straightway die!"). There is no escape, only the hope given disconnected and broken shape in frenzied efforts at mosaiced myth and magnified metaphors that there will be "some word that will not die . . .!"

Yet the visionary words become arbitrary in their very forcing and fracturing, which leaves no firm reality; in Crane's unreal city "Dream cancels dream in this new realm of fact/ From which we wake into the dream of act." The longing for an ultimate purpose and shape to things — the "shore beyond desire" — is, in pathetic conception as well as pastiched execution, a forced reach and rhetoric. After all, the poet demands of the shaman-self not the truth of our disrelations but an imposed and admittedly false ecstasy: "Lie to us, dance us back the tribal morn!" As with D. H. Lawrence in the same years, the poet knows that the return to neolithic consciousness within our conditions cannot be, and that to "lend a myth to God" is beyond the credit of the individual poet responsive to modern experience.

Hart Crane wanted to transform the compulsive and grim and fragmented actuality of America in the post-war world into regenerative words, a myth of a myth, an aesthetic ecstacy substituting for a communal order. As one of the more commonsensical recent studies of Crane (R. W. Butterfield's *The Broken Arc*) argues, in contrast to Donald Pease's hopeful synthesis, the whole effort shows "intellectual schizophrenia," with the mystical intent and the naturalistic perceptions, the affirmative myths and the tormented personal details, pervasively contradicting each other. One can't so easily go beyond the ironies of *The Waste Land* (as we might also remind some recent post-Waste Land prophets). Crane's over-reaching produced some brilliant fragments, though just as often incoherently mawkish and forced pieces. Long before finishing the sequence of *The Bridge*, Crane had lost faith in it and the salvational sense of America-become-Atlantis.

With more pathos than lucidity, he wanted an ideal realm — "Where gold is true!" — and thought he could force-forge "something like a key" (as he says of the hobo-outcasts he identified himself with in "The River" section of the poem) to a new wholeness and affirmation of American life. But the real key and metal Crane arrived at is not the iron-cum-gold bridge; it appears, instead, in the self-steeled "Key West." This usually ignored fine lead-poem to the last collection Crane was preparing before his suicide in 1932 — another appropriate sign of the post-Twenties break-down — may bear the limitations of a poetry of invective but also shows Crane's greatest lucidity. The outcast poet-speaker stands off-shore from America, at Key West, and rejects its over-arching aspirations and entanglements, accepting the break-down of the visionary dream. The steel and stone that made the cities and the bridge and the machined dreams now appear as "apish nightmares" that lead not to a god-like myth but to a "dead conclusion." Accepting the hard self of disillusionment ("my salient faith annealed me") in a universe indifferent to meaning ("skies impartial"), he has a more precise, if negative, illumination ("frugal noon") than the over-done dawn of ascension with *The Bridge*. He rejects such Eldorado-Atlantis magic hopes and lies, and comes to the bitter conclusion that it is all wastage: "There is no more breadth of friends and no more shore/ Where gold has not been sold and conscience tinned."

America, a culture as well as a society long committed to machined exploitation and tin deities (Pound, too, used the "tin" image), had to be accepted as a Waste Land in the Eliotic sense. While the initial reports on that were in large part confined to the aesthetic, to the breaking of myths and the tinning of dreams and the break-down of sensibility, more was to come. In *The Bridge* Hart Crane attempted to give temporary aesthetic exaltation to the data of consciousness provided by *The Waste Land,* but with more lucid invective in "Key West" acknowledged a failure which was far more than individual. For the Twenties literary exaltations over the break-down were curiously limited. Though sensitive to urban anguish and outcast suffering, Crane quite lacks a social morality and a political side to his vision. He is more representative than not here in an art of aesthetic exaltation and despair. Anti-politics characterizes most of the writers we identify with the Twenties. Some of this no doubt was, as Fredrick Hoffman argued at length in *The Twenties,* a moral as well as aesthetic "release from nineteenth century restraints." Some of it, and some of the gaiety of the time, was the Americanization, Hoffman also notes, of *epater le bourgeois* in the disaffection from previously dominant conventions, ideologies and forms; the literary movement was to aesthetic experimentation, the personal movement was to "unregenerate bohemianism" (and the cult of youth which went with it and which continued later in Beat-hippy-counter-culture ways); and a larger change of consciousness was implicit.

As I see it, part of the aesthetic change in consciousness carried into Twenties American literature the modernism developing on the European continent from about the middle of the nineteenth century. The "bourgeois-humanist culture," as it has been described (by Blackmur and others) became increasingly anti-bourgeois, and its humanism, as well as humaneness, was sometimes in question. Aesthetics-as-politics points in peculiar, even perverse, ways, not only in a-political poets such as Crane but in the anachronistic reactionary gestures of Pound and Eliot (and in Tate, Ransom, and the other literateurs of the American South), even in the charming rightist-anarchism of E. E. Cummings. Twenties American literature played a fervent anti-bourgeois role, even in the decorous Eliot who, following Pound's early example, expansively mocks the upper-middle class lady in *The Waste Land* (as well as giving a savage portrayal of "the typist"). Even Crane has a rather out-of-key imitation mockery of the middleclass in the "Quaker Hill" section of *The Bridge.* Granted, this aesthetic warfare against bourgeois sensibility was often purely bourgeois in its refinement, as in the hedonistic aesthetic of Wallace Stevens. It is now easy to argue (as does a recent study of Twenties literature, John McCormick's *The Middle Distance*) that the Twenties gave undue place to the often ignorantly cantankerous and elitist attacks on the "boobosie" by H. L. Mencken and the brittle and sentimental carricatures of stock-Americana by Sinclair Lewis. But they were carrying forth an essential (though bumptiously done) function of the culture of the time, the rough-hewing of the aesthetic breaking down of the old sensibility.

More desperate senses of the break-down, no longer maintainable with a purely aesthetic elan, were inevitably to follow. The Great War, of course, was recognized as a political break-down, the brutal fatuities of *real politik* which have never since had quite the same ideological cover though they still be with us. The social and economic break-down of the Great Depression and the spread of fascism can, in retrospect, be read in the cultural manifestations as well as the social forces of the Twenties: almost all the given order has lost its traditional sanctions and its aura of legitimacy.

That Eliot would suborn his own Waste Land awareness into a parochial Christianity which that earlier awareness had shown as quite inadequate, or that intellectual fashionmongers of the Thirties would reject the aestheticism of the Twenties for a "social consciousness" which may have been considerably its disillusioned result, seems now only mildly ironic. After all, to perceive the break-down as social and political reality was rather different than to perceive it as a problem of sensibility and culture, though the one probably comes much out of the other.

Not that change in sensibility should be reduced only to its prophetic political significance — it is important in itself, and continues so. The break-down in the forms of thought and feeling — as with fragmentation as style in modes of mosaic, pastiche, dissociation, etc. — found expression in high-art in the Twenties but took a generation and more to become common cultural currency, not only in such genres as the anti-novel and pop and post-pop art but in advertising, mass media fare and, indeed, much of the general organization of sensibility. In ways which seemed only exciting and peculiar possibilities in the Twenties, ours may be really a culture-of-break-down. That may be why in the *zeitgeist* of the Seventies there are repeated calls to go "beyond the Waste Land culture." We may have some reservations in that bourgeois-humanist culture achieved its glories and its break-down together. We still considerably live amongst those "broken images" exalted by the aesthetic revolts of the Twenties, and may still admire the heroism of shoring these fragments against our ruin. Of course our Waste Land has taken on other dimensions in the mass-technological post-bourgeois order, or disorder, and threatens far more drastic break-downs, leaving us almost nostalgic for the earlier Waste Lands and their aesthetic ecstasies.

Bibliography

The Twenties

The age of jazz, ballyhoo, and deceptive prosperity that no one at the time would have thought of labeling "The Gatsby Era" has always fascinated cultural historians. A general history of the period is William E. Leuchtenberg's *The Perils of Prosperity* (1958), which should be read in conjunction with a collection of documents, *The Twenties: Fords, Flappers, and Fanatics*, edited by George Mowry (1963). Frederick Lewis Allen wrote an entertaining, informal history, emphasizing the follies and foibles of the period, *Only Yesterday* (1931) and discussed the era in a larger context in *The Big Change: America Transforms Itself 1900-1950* (1952). Robert and Helen Lynd's *Middletown* (1929) is the renowned sociological picture of a supposedly average American community of the decade, based on research in Muncie, Indiana. A recent effort to suggest from a literary point of view something of the characteristic tone of the individual American's life during the decade is Robert H. Elias's *"Entangling Alliances with None": An Essay on the Individual in the American Twenties* (1973). Charles Merz's *The Dry Decade* readably illuminates the appalling effects of the "Great Experiment" on American society. Although the third volume of John Dos Passos's trilogy *U.S.A.*. *The Big Money* (1936) is fiction, no factual work gives such a sense of the preoccupations and frustrations of the period, just as F. Scott Fitzgerald's *The Great Gatsby* and T. S. Eliot's *The Waste Land* — whatever the authors' intentions — capture the prevailing *weltanschauung* of the decade.

The Literature of the 1920s

No other single critic has attempted a book of anything like the magnitude of Frederick J. Hoffman's *The Twenties: American Writing in the Postwar Decade* (1949). Building his study around major works of the period by Hemingway, Fitzgerald, Eliot, Gertrude Stein and others, Hoffman relates to these epochal literary creations the characteristic social, political, and especially psychological phenomena of the decade. Although colored by Hoffman's own strong interest in psychiatry and his own very marked literary preferences, this monumental study remains the starting point for any study of this period.

More strictly and conventionally literary in their approach are three classic studies largely limited to some of the major writers of the decade: Maxwell Geismar's *Writers in Crisis: The American Novel between Two Wars* (1942, part of a multi-volumed critique of major twentieth-century American writers), Alfred Kazin's *On Native Grounds* (1942), and *After the Genteel Tradition,* a waspish survey edited by Malcolm Cowley (1937). In the single year of 1973, curiously, all three of these critics returned to reminisce about the 1920s, Cowley in the somewhat fragmentary *A Second Flowering: Works and Days of the Lost Generation,* which is limited largely to recollections of Hemingway, Faulkner, Dos Passos, Wilder, and Thomas Wolfe; Kazin in *Bright Book of Life: American Novelists and Storytellers from Hemingway to Mailer,* which deals principally with post-World-War-II writing, and Geismar in *Ring Lardner and the Portrait of Folly,* an appreciation of one writer as a characteristic voice of the decade.

The predecessor of the present volume, *The Twenties: Poetry and Prose,* edited by Richard E. Langford and William E. Taylor (1966) contains eighteen essays not reproduced in this collection, most of which are of continuing value. Especially interesting is the late William Van O'Connor's "Faulkner, Hemingway, and the 1920's." A more ambitious collection along somewhat similar lines is *The American Novel and the Nineteen Twenties,* edited by Malcolm Bradbury and David Palmer (London, 1971), which contains four long general studies of the decade by Bradbury, Lawrence W. Levine, Henry Dan Piper, and Eric Mottram, and studies of seven individual writers: Sherwood Anderson (by Brian Way), Sinclair Lewis (by Howell Daniels), F. Scott Fitzgerald (by C.W. E. Bigsby), Ernest Hemingway (by Brom Weber), Faulkner (by Arnold Goldman), Dos Passos (by Brian Lee) and Nathanael West — not really a writer of the 1920s — by Jonathan Raban.

The poetry and drama of the period have not received the separate attention that the novel has. Except for the enormous concentration on *The Waste Land* and Hart Crane's *The Bridge* as emblematic statements of the period, most books like *Modern American Poetry,* edited by Guy Owen (1972), deal with longer periods in the twentieth century. Except for the best of Eugene O'Neill's plays, the dramatic literature of the 1920s has been slighted and is generally looked down upon as evidence of the flightiness and superficiality of New York "taste makers" of the times. Arthur Hobson Quinn's *A History of the American Drama from the Civil War to the Present Day* (revised 1955) provides an exhaustive but pedestrian and uncritical guide. Better organized and more discerning is the long introductory historical account in Jordan Y. Miller's anthology *American Dramatic Literature* (1961).

Unquestionably the most important specialized literary development during the 1920s was the Harlem Renaissance, which marked the first really notable demonstration of the racial consciousness of black American artists. Although the merit of the works produced and even the very nature of the "Renaissance" itself remain a subject of debate, Nathan Irvin Huggins has produced a detailed and competent history of the phenomenon in *Harlem Renaissance* (1971). Robert H. Elias's *"Entangling Alliances with None"* also includes an important critical chapter on the Renaissance. The principal white patron of the movement and the great popularizer of the Harlem jazz scene in the 1920s is well presented in Bruce Kellner's *Carl Van Vechten and the Irreverent Decade* (1968).

SHERWOOD ANDERSON (1876-1941) is the subject of a survey of scholarship by Walter Rideout in *Sixteen Modern American Authors* (1974). Professor Rideout is also at work on a biography of Anderson. Anderson told the story of his own career in the not entirely reliable *A Story Teller's Story* (1924). Rideout also finds more valuable than several book-length studies of Anderson, Maxwell Giesmar's long essay in *The Last of the Provincials* (1947). Criticism of Anderson has concentrated on *Winesburg, Ohio.* Many of the most useful articles are collected in *The Achievement of Sherwood Anderson: Essays in Criticism*, edited by Ray Lewis White (1966). Professor White has also produced a series of meticulously edited reissues of some of Anderson's fiction, non-fiction and correspondence, that provide useful supplements to *The Portable Sherwood Anderson,* edited by Horace Gregory (1949) and *The Sherwood Anderson Reader,* edited by Paul Rosenfeld (1947), collections of Anderson's major writings.

JAMES BRANCH CABELL (1879-1958) is the creator in his tales of Poictesme of one of the great conscious mythologies of twentieth century literature. Those parts of the mythology he wished preserved are ordered in the eighteen-volume Storisende Edition (1927-30). Subsequently he wrote several addition novels signed Branch Cabell and two autobiographical works, *Quiet, Please* (1952) and *As I Remember It* (1955). Frances Joan Brewer and Matthew J. Bruccoli prepared a two-volume bibliography of writings by and about him and of the materials in the Cabell collection at the University of Virginia (1957). Recent book-length studies of his work

include Joe Lee Davis's *James Branch Cabell* (1962) and Desmond
Tarrant's *James Branch Cabell: The Dream and the Reality* (1965).
Much material of value about Cabell is collected in the four volumes
of *The Cabellian*, edited by Julius Rothman between 1968 and
1972.

WILLA CATHER (1873-1947), after falling into some obscurity in the
1940s and 1950s because of a provision in her will against the
issuance of inexpensive paperbound editions of her novels, has re-
gained her place in the sun through the unremitting efforts of one of
the most devoted groups of admirers among American critics. The
standard account of her life is E. K. Brown's *Willa Cather: A Critical
Biography*, completed by Leon Edel (1953). Her early writings have
been gathered in two imposing two-volume collections, *The Kingdom of Art: Willa Cather's First Principles and Critical Statements,
1893-1896* (1966), edited by Bernice Slote, and *The World and the
Parish: Willa Cather's Articles and Reviews, 1893-1902* (1970),
edited by William M. Curtin. Books and articles about Willa Cather
are surveyed by Bernice Slote in her essay for *Sixteen Modern American Authors*. Appraisals of her whole career are found in David
Daiches's pioneering *Willa Cather: A Critical Introduction* (1951),
Edward A. and Lillian D. Bloom's *Willa Cather's Gift of Sympathy*
(1962), and James Woodress's *Willa Cather: Her Life and Art*
(1971). James Schroeter's *Willa Cather and Her Critics* (1967) brings
together many evaluations of her work. Indispensable for an understanding of the backgrounds of Willa Cather's work are Mildred R.
Bennett's *The World of Willa Cather* (1951, revised 1961) and *Willa
Cather: A Pictorial Memoir* (1973), with text by Bernice Slote and
photographs by Lucia Woods and others.

HART CRANE (1899-1932) has attracted many interpreters because of
the complexity and experimental form of his epic verse. Brom Weber
surveys this scholarship in an essay for *Sixteen Modern American
Authors*. Weber wrote also *Hart Crane: A Biographical and Critical
Study* (1948) that has been supplemented but not supplanted by
John Unterecker's *Voyager: A Life of Hart Crane* (1969). Donald
Pease's article draws principally on the picture that the highly self-
conscious poet presented of himself through *The Letters of Hart
Crane, 1916-1932*, edited by Brom Weber (1952). Vincent Quinn's
Hart Crane (1963) provides a useful introduction to the poet; but L.
S. Dembo's *Hart Crane's Sanskrit Charge* (1960) and R. W. B.
Lewis's *The Poetry of Hart Crane: A Critical Study* (1967) provide
less adequate overviews than R. W. Butterfield's *The Broken Arc: A
Study of Hart Crane's Poetry* (1969). A recent study of Crane's

major work is Sherman Paul's *Hart's Bridge* (1972).

E[dward] E[stlin] CUMMINGS (1894-1963), though most often recalled as a poet, won also distinction as a novelist (*The Enormous Room*) and painter. His first book-length interpreter was Charles Norman in *The Magic-Maker, E. E. Cummings* (1958), but in the 1960s Cummings became almost the private preserve of Norman Friedman, who published two studies — *E. E. Cummings: The Growth of a Writer* (1964) and *E. E. Cummings: The Art of His Poetry* (1967) — which have eclipsed Barry Alan Marks's *E. E. Cummings* (1964) and a scattering of uneven explicatory articles. Bethany K. Dumas, who summarizes in this book Cummings' activities in the 1920s, provides through her *E. E. Cummings: A Remembrance of Miracles* (1974), an occasion for the reconsideration of this often unjustly overlooked poet.

JOHN DOS PASSOS (1896-1970), long out of favor because of his tendency towards conservative polemics after completing *U.S.A.* in the 1930s, has only since his death begun to receive some of the attention showered upon his contemporary "debunkers." Melvin Landsberg's *Dos Passos' Path to U.S.A.: A Political Biography, 1912-1936* (1973) was prepared with the author's assistance, but is limited to his "years of grace" and contains little literary criticism. Also useful biographically in Townsend Ludington's *The Fourteenth Chronicle: Letters and Diaries of John Dos Passos* (1973). The earliest book about the writer is John H. Wrenn's *John Dos Passos* (1962). It is supplemented by the essays collected in *Dos Passos, the Critics, and the Writer's Intention*, edited by Allen Belkind (1971).

THEODORE DREISER (1871-1945) has become the subject of renewed interest since the celebration of the centennial of his birth. The standard biographical account is W. A. Swanberg's massive and detailed, but pedestrian *Dreiser* (1965). Pleasanter reading but more limited in its scope is Ellen Moers's *The Two Dreisers* (1969). The most esteemed study of Dreiser is Robert H. Elias's *Theodore Dreiser: Apostle of Nature*, originally published in 1949 but revised in 1970. The later edition includes also the review-essay on Dreiser scholarship that Elias contributed to *Sixteen Modern American Authors*. Still valuable is F. O. Matthiessen's *Theodore Dreiser* (1951), and important later critical studies include Charles Shapiro's *Theodore Dreiser; Our Bitter Patriot* (1962), Philip Gerber's *Theodore Dreiser* (1964) and Richard Lehan's *Theodore Dreiser: His World and His Novels* (1969). Essays about Dreiser and his work are collected in *The Stature of Theodore Dreiser*, edited by Charles Shapiro and Alfred Kazin (1955) and Jack Salzman has assembled in *The Merrill Studies in "An American Tragedy"* (1971) reviews and discussions of Dreiser's great novel of the 1920s.

T[homas] S[tearns] ELIOT (1888-1965), whose major creation, *The Waste Land* (1922), provides the focus for this book, is surely the most often studied poet of the twentieth century, though there is no standard biography — nor did Eliot wish one. Bernard Bergonzi's *T. S. Eliot* (1971) is principally a critical study that relies on the public record. Robert Sencourt's unfinished *T. S. Eliot: A Memoir* (1971) is an unauthorized account that must be viewed with caution. Eliot rarely wrote about himself except in the obscure "American Literature and the American Language" (Washington University Studies, No. 23, 1953). Eliot's varied writings are chronicled in Donald Gallup's *T. S. Eliot: A Bibliography* (Revised edition, 1969), and the profusion of writings about him is ably summarized by Richard M. Ludwig in *Sixteen Modern American Authors*. The fiftieth anniversary of the publication of *The Waste Land* was celebrated by the publication of *Eliot in His Time: Essays on the Occasion of the Fiftieth Anniversary of "The Waste Land,"* edited by Walton A. Litz (1973), but by far the most significant souvenir of this momentous occasion was Valerie Eliot's edition of *The Waste Land: A Facsimile and Transcript of the Original Drafts,* making public at last Ezra Pound's and Eliot's first wife's suggestions about the fragments that eventually became the poem. This publication has launched probably a half-century of new activity. Most notable among the initial responses are Lyndall Gordon's *"The Waste Land Manuscript"* (*American Literature*, January, 1974, pp. 557-70), M. C. Braybrooke's *T. W. Eliot: The Making of "The Waste Land"* (1972) and Grover Smith's crotchety review in the Fall, 1972 issue of *Mosaic,* which celebrates the fiftieth anniversaries of the publication of both James Joyce's *Ulysses* and *The Waste Land* with essays by a number of renowned scholars.

WILLIAM FAULKNER (1897-1962) has become the most written about of twentieth-century American novelists, as his remarkable Yoknapatawpha Saga of his native Mississippi continues to yield endless new insights to perceptive scholars. The authorized account of his life is Joseph Blotner's two-volume, nearly one million word *Faulkner: A Biography* (1974). The classic criticism of his major fiction is Cleanth Brooks's *William Faulkner: The Yoknapatawpha Country* (1963). The many other accounts of his work are reviewed by James B. Meriwether, also the principal Faulkner bibliographer, in *Sixteen Modern American Authors.* Of particular biographical significance are two volumes of reminiscences by Faulkner's brothers, John Faulkner's *My Brother Bill* (1963) and Murry C. Falkner's *The Falkners of Mississippi* (1967) [William and in his wake John added — or restored — the "u" to the family name], and also *William Faulkner of Oxford*, edited by James W. Webb and A. Wigfall Green (1965), a collection of reminiscences by fellow townsmen. Martin J. Dain's *Faulkner's Country: Yoknapatawpha* (1964) illustrates quotations from his works with splendid photographs of his native region. Still useful is the first book-length study of Faulkner, Harry M. Campbell and Ruel E. Foster's *William Faulkner* (1951). The major comprehensive analyses of his work are Olga Vickery's *The Novels of William Faulkner* (1964) and Michael Millgate's *The Achievement of William Faulkner* (1966). Much of the best criticism of Faulkner's works is collected in *William Faulkner: Three Decades of Criticism*, edited by Frederick J. Hoffman and Olga W. Vickery (1960).

F[rancis] SCOTT [Key] FITZGERALD (1896-1940) has proved a magnet to biographers since the extraordinary popular success of Arthur Mizener's *The Far Side of Paradise* (1951, revised edition 1965), *The Crack-up*, Fitzgerald's uncollected papers edited by Edmund Wilson (1956), and Sheilah Graham's soul-baring *Beloved Infidel: The Education of a Woman* (1958), which discusses her relationship with Fitzgerald during his final years in Hollywood. More searching and balanced than these is Andrew Turnbull's *Scott Fitzgerald* (1962). Turnbull also edited *The Letters of F. Scott Fitzgerald* (1963) and *Scott Fitzgerald: Letters to His Daughter* (1965, with an introduction by the daughter, Frances Fitzgerald Lanahan). Although Alfred Kazin edited *F. Scott Fitzgerald: The Man and His Works*, a collection of assessments by various critics as early as 1951, there was no full-length critical study of the writer until James E. Miller, Jr.'s *The Fictional Technique of Scott Fitzgerald* appeared in 1957. Miller has since revised this keystone study as *F. Scott Fitzgerald: His Art and His Technique* (1964). Valuable as well are Kenneth Eble's *F. Scott Fitzgerald* (1963), Henry Dan Piper's *F. Scott Fitzgerald: A Critical Portrait* (1965), and Richard Lehan's *F. Scott Fitzgerald and the Craft of Fiction*. Uniquely useful is Jackson R. Bryer's *The Critical Reputation of F. Scott Fitzgerald: A Bibliographical Study* (1967), which lists 2,100 items — many from difficult-to-locate sources — and annotates all of them to provide a running history of Fitzgerald's reception.

ROBERT FROST (1874-1963), the only twentieth-century American poet to win the highest acclaim from both literary critics and the general public for his lucid, acerb portrayals of human frustration, was for two decades before his death the most popular lecturer-reader on the American college circuit. Recent studies — epitomized by Lawrance Thompson's two-volume biography, *Robert Frost: The Early Years, 1874-1915* (1966) and *Robert Frost: The Years of Triumph, 1915-1938* (1970) — have maliciously and quite unnecessarily devoted themselves to tearing down the image of the "good, gray poet." Excellent guidance to these studies and other criticisms of Frost is provided by Reginald L. Cook's mellow review in *Sixteen Modern American Authors*. Cook calls attention particularly to three collections of essays about Frost — *Recognition of Robert Frost*, edited by Richard Thornton; *Robert Frost: An Introduction*, edited by Robert A. Greenberg, and *Robert Frost: A Collection of Critical Essays*, edited by James M. Cox. Reginald L. Cook's own *The Dimensions of Robert Frost* is one of a half dozen studies defending Frost's art; notable among the others are Reuben Brower's *The Poetry of Robert Frost: Constellations of Intention* (1963) and Elizabeth Isaacs's *An Introduction to Robert Frost* (1962).

ERNEST HEMINGWAY (1899-1961) — Melvin J. Friedman's supplement carries Frederick J. Hoffman's article surveying Hemingway studies in *Sixteen Modern American Authors* to 1972. A *Fitzgerald/Hemingway Annual*, edited by Matthew Bruccoli, began publication in 1969; and a special Hemingway number of *Modern Fiction Studies*, containing an extensive checklist of criticism of individual stories, appeared in Autumn, 1968. The standard account of the novelist's life and work is Carlos Baker's *Ernest Hemingway: A Life Story* (1969). Baker's *Hemingway: The Writer and Artist* and Philip Young's *Ernest Hemingway*, both of which first appeared in 1952 and have since been revised, remain the respected starting points for understanding of the fiction. Young also provided a useful short introduction, *Ernest Hemingway* (University of Minnesota Pamphlets on American Writers No. 1, 1959). A new approach to the study of the artist is *Hemingway's Craft* (1973) by Sheldon Norman Grebstein, who contributed articles on Hemingway to *The Thirties* and *The Fifties*.

LANGSTON HUGHES (1902-1967) — This most intelligent and artful of our black writers has not benefitted as much as might be anticipated from the growth of interest in Black American literature perhaps because, as Blyden Jackson implies, his work is too "cool" to be drawn into the heated orbit of passing fashions. Donald C. Dickinson has produced *A Bio-Bibliography of Langston Hughes, 1902-1967*

(1967), James A. Emanuel encompasses Langston Hughes (also 1967) in the ubiquitous Twayne United States Authors Series, and Therman B. O'Daniel edits a book with the frenetic title, *Langston Hughes, Black Genius: A Critical Evaluation* (1971), which calls attention to his "Simple" stories in particular; but to get anything like close to Hughes, one must — as also in dealing with Thornton Wilder and Gertrude Stein — turn to his own works, his songs and stories and *I Wonder as I Wander: An Autobiographical Journey* (1958).

ROBINSON JEFFERS (1887-1962), the only great primitive epic poet of the Western hemisphere (except for Kazantzakis, the only one of the twentieth century) has always proved too much for the fidgety-stomached American bourgeois to swallow. His self-built Tor House, which could have been appropriately preserved with the money poured into the absurd Eisenhower Museum, has even revengefully become the site of a subdivision. Two early books by friends are helpful: George Sterling, California novelist, wrote *Robinson Jeffers: The Man and the Artist* (1926) and that unparalleled librarian-conservator Lawrence Clark Powell contributed *Robinson Jeffers: The Man and His Work* (1934). Since those days, Jeffers has met his match only in Frederic Ives Carpenter, whose *Robinson Jeffers* (1962) offers extraordinary insights into a unique man's involvement with a now-vanished milieu.

RING LARDNER (1885-1933), one of America's great short story writers, is beginning at last to receive the attention he deserves. A new collection of *Best Short Stories of Ring Lardner* (1974) is the occasion for a complete reassessment by fellow writer Joel Sayre in *Village Voice* (June 27, 1974, pp. 29-30). Sayre laments the neglect of Donald Elder's sympathetic *Ring Lardner: A Biography* (1956), but fails to note three later studies that have done much to promote Lardner's reputation — Walter R. Patrick's *Ring Lardner* (1963), Maxwell Geismar's *Ring Lardner and the Portrait of Folly* (1972), and *Ring Around Max: The Correspondence of Ring Lardner and Max Perkins,* edited by Clifford M. Caruthers (1972), which discloses the famous editor's efforts to get Lardner to collect his stories and write a novel. One article indispensable to an understanding of the disillusionment behind Lardner's changing attitude towards professional sports and the culture they characterized is Leverett T. Smith, Jr.'s "The Diameter of Frank Chance's Diamond" (*Journal of Popular Culture* 6:133-56, 1972).

SINCLAIR LEWIS (1885-1951), in 1930 the first American writer to win the Nobel Prize for literature, declined in critical esteem during the four decades following this happenstance award because of the undeniable decline in the quality of the fictions he produced during the final twenty years of his life. His reputation was not really enhanced by the sensational publicity attending the publication of Mark Schorer's *Sinclair Lewis: An American Life* (1961), a voluminous, officially commissioned biography that unfortunately set a style that reached its *reductio ad absurdum* in Joseph Blotner's marathon two volumes on Faulkner. More useful to the general reader is Sheldon Grebstein's thoughtfully appreciative *Sinclair Lewis* (1962). The golden anniversaries of Lewis's four triumphs — *Main Street, Babbitt, Arrowsmith, Dodsworth* — are evoking understanding analyses of Lewis's creating as well as reflecting American history; and readers can turn from David Pugh's introduction for further provocative ideas to James Lundquist's *Sinclair Lewis* (1973) and James Lea's "Sinclair Lewis and the Implied America" (*Clio: An Interdisciplinary Journal*, 3:21-34).

DON MARQUIS (1878-1937), although a hero to many avid fans has gone — as fan Jaffe notes with exasperation — almost unnoticed by American critics, despite his introducing the love songs of Archy the cockroach to the world and writing a popular raffish play, *The Old Soak*. There is an idyllically sympathetic biography, Edward Anthony's *O rare Don Marquis* (1962). Admirers of Marquis also are usually enthusiasts of the surrealistic work of George Herriman, whose inimitable *Krazy Kat* requires recognition here as the only truly "Waste Land" comic strip.

EUGENE O'NEILL (1888-1953) remains America's greatest playwright. The basic study of his career is Arthur and Barbara Gelb's mammoth *O'Neill* (1962), an undocumented book that contains little critical discussion of his plays. The most valuable studies of these are Frederic I. Carpenter's *Eugene O'Neill* (1964), John Henry Raleigh's *The Plays of Eugene O'Neill* (1965), and Travis Bogard's *Contour in Time: The Plays of Eugene O'Neill* (1972), all curiously studies of this New England playwright by scholars associated with the University of California at Berkeley. The studies of O'Neill are reviewed by Professor Raleigh in the only essay about a dramatist in *Sixteen Modern American Authors*. The most complete critical bibliography is Jordan Y. Miller's *Eugene O'Neill and the American Critic*, (1962, revised edition, 1974).

EZRA POUND (1885-1972), with his inimitable flair for the grandiose gesture, died during the fiftieth anniversary year of the epic poem that he helped to shape, just after the publication of the massive tribute, Hugh Kenner's *The Pound Era,* that attempts to refurbish a reputation tarnished by political antics in Mussolini's Italy, the obscurity of the *Cantos* to which he dedicated much of his life, and an almost uniquely irascible temper. Pound is one of those writers whose posturings are probably more important than their writings, and a really perceptive biography is a formidable task for some unemerged critic. In the meantime Noel Stock's *The Life of Ezra Pound* (1970) is one of those voluminously detailed treatises that have proved the weighty specialty of the humorless third quarter of this century. Out of tune with the times, John Espey renders a brief, brisk account in *Sixteen Modern American Authors* of Pound criticism that expresses little enthusiasm for anything but Hugh Kenner's *The Poetry of Ezra Pound* (1951).

ELMER RICE (1892-1967) has, in view of his many and varied contributions to the American theatre, received surprisingly little critical attention, although he tells the story of his own life in *Minority Report: An Autobiography* (1963). Two critical studies — Robert Hogan's *The Independence of Elmer Rice* (1965) and Frank Durham's *Elmer Rice* (1970) — serve to launch study of one of our few underexploited writers. More on the Expressionistic techniques of *The Adding Machine* may be found in Mardi Valgemae's *Accelerated Grimace: Expressionism in the American Drama of the 1920s* (1972).

GERTRUDE STEIN (1874-1946) remains an enigma a century after her birth. Study may begin with Elizabeth Sprigge's *Gertrude Stein: Her Life and Work* (1957) and a delicately appreciative critical biography John Malcolm Brinnin's *The Third Rose: Gertrude Stein and Her World* (1959); but ultimately for any approach to an understanding of this endlessly fascinating, isolated woman one must turn to her own books, especially *The Autobiography of Alice B. Toklas* (1933), *Everybody's Autobiography* (1937), *Wars I Have Seen* (1945), although everything that she wrote was in some measure autobiographical because it is a part of the experiment that was her life. Donald Sutherland provides in *Gertrude Stein, A Biography of Her Work* (1951), an approach to the complicated canon. Only a few people know how to write about Gertrude Stein, who was always her own best subject — exemplary, however, of the enthusiastic approach is Allegra Stewart's *Gertrude Stein and the Present* (1967); about the only one to find a middle-of-the-road approach was Frederick J. Hoffman in his much too brief pamphlet *Gertrude Stein* (1961). Miss Stein also had more detractors than any of her contemporaries; their position is suggested by Benjamin L. Reid's *Art by Subtraction: A Dissenting Opinion of Gertrude Stein* (1958).

JOHN STEINBECK (1902-1968) published only his relatively obscure first novel, *Cup of Gold* — the subject of Richard Astro's essay — during the 1920s; but his early work receives attention in the major critical studies of his work — Peter Lisca's *The Wide World of John Steinbeck* (1958), Warren French's *John Steinbeck* (1961, revised edition, 1974), Joseph Fontenrose's *John Steinbeck: An Introduction and Interpretation* (1963), Richard Astro's *John Steinbeck and Edward F. Ricketts: The Shaping of a Novelist* (1973) and Howard Levant's *The Novels of John Steinbeck* (1974). Warren French reviews other writings about Steinbeck in an article for *Sixteen Modern American Authors*. Other useful reviews of Steinbeck criticism are Peter Lisca's "A Survey of Steinbeck Criticism to 1971" in *Steinbeck's Literary Dimension* (1972) and *Steinbeck Criticism: A Review of Book-Length Studies (1939-1973)* (1974), both edited by Tetsumaro Hayashi, who edits also *Steinbeck Quarterly*, an invaluable repository of information about the novelist.

JEAN TOOMER (1894-1967) — Despite the tremendous recent revival of interest in Toomer, especially his perplexing *Cane,* there is no full-length study yet of his life and work. Since the collaborative article by Blyden Jackson and the editor is devoted to reviewing studies of Toomer, these will not be listed again here, but attention should be called to *Studies in "Cane,"* edited by Frank Durham (1971), which collects a number of articles by various critics.

B. TRAVEN (pseudonym of Traven Torsvan, 1890-1960), most mysterious of modern novelists, was the subject of a great many nonsensical speculations during his long years of seclusion in Mexico from the 1920s to the 1950s. There is still no book-length biographical and critical study of Traven, but Charles Miller sets the record straight on the facts of the novelist's life in the Introduction to *The Night Visitors and Other Stories* (1966). So much effort has gone into attempting to ferret out the secrets of Traven's life that, except for Neville Braybrook's "The Hero Without a Name" (*Queen's Quarterly* 76:312-18, 1969), Philip Melling's essay is about the first to suggest the importance of Traven's novel *Death Ship* as a kind of prose "Waste Land."

GLENWAY WESCOTT (1901-) is just beginning to receive the attention lavished upon such other 1920s expatriates as Fitzgerald,

Hemingway, and Gertrude Stein. The only book-length studies of his work are William H. Rueckert's *Glenway Wescott* (1965) and Ira D. Johnson's *Glenway Wescott: The Paradox of Voice* (1971). Sy Kahn has earlier prepared a bibliography of his work (*Bulletin of Biography* 22 (1958): 156-60 and contributed an article about him to *Papers in English Language and Literature* (1965).

EDITH WHARTON (1862-1937) is the major subject of James W. Tuttleton's *The Novel of Manners in America* (1972). Tuttleton has also, through a series of articles, emerged as her principal interpreter, and he has contributed a long essay reviewing writings about her to *Resources for American Literary Study* (1973). Mrs. Wharton told the story of her own life in *A Backward Glance* (1934). She is also the subject of a number of biographical and critical books including Percy Lubbock's *Portrait of Edith Wharton* (1947) and Millicent Bell's *Edith Wharton and Henry James* (1965). Her principal recent admirer, society novelist Louis Auchincloss, has written a short critical study of her work *Edith Wharton* (1961) and discusses her among others in *Pioneers and Caretakers: A Study of Nine American Women Novelists* (1965).

WILLIAM CARLOS WILLIAMS (1883-1963) — Linda W. Wagner emerged with her *The Poems of William Carlos Williams: A Critical Study* (1964) as the principal interpreter of this doctor-poet whose reputation continues to grow as those of some of his contemporaries decline. Mrs. Wagner also contributed the invaluable essay on Williams to *Sixteen Modern American Authors.* Though not entirely reliable factually, Williams's *Autobiography* (1964) remains the best account of his busy life. Emily Mitchell Wallace's *A Bibliography of William Carlos Williams* (1968) is a useful guide to his work, most of which remains in print in editions from New Directions (Norwalk, Conn.).

Contributors

RICHARD ASTRO (Hemingway and Steinbeck), Associate Professor of English and Assistant to the Vice-President for Research, Oregon State University, is an American Council on Education Administrative Fellow for 1974-75, following the publication of his book, *John Steinbeck and Edward F. Ricketts; The Shaping of a Novelist* (1973). He has also edited *Steinbeck: The Man and His Work* (1971), with Tetsumaro Hayashi, and *Hemingway In Our Time*, with Jackson Benson (1974). Both books collect papers presented at national conferences that Professor Astro has hosted at Oregon State; the most recent of these gatherings in May 1974 climaxed a year-long, University-wide interdisciplinary study of "The West as Myth." He has also served on the editorial boards of the *Steinbeck Quarterly* and *Western American Literature* and contributed essays to these journals as well as to *Twentieth Century Views: Malamud*, edited by Leslie and Joyce Field (1974).

EILEEN BALDESHWILER (Sherwood Anderson) is a Professor of English at Loyola University, Chicago. A specialist in twentieth century British and American fiction, she has written essays on Katherine Anne Porter and Graham Greene, served on the review board for *Studies in Short Fiction*, and translated two theological treatises from French during the 1960s. She has been an American Association of University Women post-doctoral fellow and a Danforth fellow. In addition to her teaching and writing, she does volunteer work with visually-handicapped elderly persons. Her essay on Anderson's lyric story is one of two in this collection to be reprinted from *The Twenties: Poetry and Prose* (1966).

C. W. E. BIGSBY (Hemingway), Senior Lecturer in American Literature at the University of East Anglia, is one of the most prolific Americanists in Great Britain. Since receiving his Ph.D. in American Studies from the University of Nottingham, he has also taught at the University College of Wales (Aberystwyth) and on visits to the United States at the University of Missouri-Kansas City and Indiana

University (Indianapolis). He has published besides numerous articles and contributions to other symposia (including *The Forties* and *The Fifties*), *Confrontation and Commitment: A Study of Contemporary American Drama; Albee,* and *Dada and Surrealism.* He has edited *The Black American Writer* and *Superculture: American Popular Culture and Europe,* and has written a television play, *The Games of Academe,* for the British Broadcasting Company.

ROBERT DeMOTT (Robinson Jeffers) is an Associate Professor of English at Ohio University (Athens), who summers at a hideout he has built in southwestern Vermont. Although he wrote his doctoral dissertation on Thoreau and has served as guest editor of the *Thoreau Journal,* most of his writing and teaching has dealt with twentieth-century American literature. He has published essays on John Steinbeck in the *University of Windsor Review* and elsewhere and has served on the editorial board of the *Steinbeck Quarterly.* His essay on Robinson Jeffers is a reflection of his principal interest in the contemporary long poem — an interest evidenced also by his assisting in compiling *A Concordance to the Poems of Hart Crane* (1973).

MAURICE DUKE (James Branch Cabell) is an Associate Professor of English at Virginia Commonwealth University, Richmond. A graduate of William and Mary College, he has always been specially interested in the history and literature of Richmond, and Cabell was the subject of his M.A. and Ph.D. theses at the University of Iowa. He is one of the founders and a continuing editor of *Resources for American Literary Study.* Author of some twenty articles on American literature, he is also Book Editor and weekly book columnist for the Richmond *Times-Dispatch.* With Jackson Bryer and Thomas Inge, he is currently at work editing a four-volume bibliographical study of Black American writers. Away from school, he is a licensed sports car racer.

BETHANY K. DUMAS (e. e. cummings) is an Associate Professor of English at the University of Tennessee-Knoxville. She is interested not only in twentieth-century American poetry and fiction, but also British and American dialectology, sociolinguistics, and the history of the English language. Her doctoral dissertation at the University of Arkansas, however, was on Cummings, on whose poetry, she writes, she "was thoroughly hooked" by the time she was a college sophomore. "My developing interest in linguistics provided me with insights into the reasons for my admiration," she adds. She has published a book-length study, *E. E. Cummings: A Remembrance of*

Miracles (London, 1974), besides several papers on his work as well as on dialect study and elicitation techniques in investigating language variation.

KENNETH FRIELING (Gertrude Stein) mingles his interests in art and nature by operating a greenhouse while completing his graduate work at Ohio University (Athens). He is also a painter, musician, and designer, who is devoting more and more of his time to one of his principal enthusiasms, film study. He contributed the article on Flannery O'Connor to *The Fifties*, and he has been assembling materials for a collection of essays on the literature of the 1960s.

LOIS GORDON (Faulkner's *The Sound and the Fury*) is Associate Professor of English at Fairleigh-Dickinson University. She is the author of *Strategems to Uncover Nakedness* (1968), a book-length study of Harold Pinter's plays, as well as a number of articles about Pinter's work. Although she has written and taped lectures principally about contemporary drama, she is equally interested in modern fiction and poetry. With her husband Alan, a psychiatrist, she has prepared a study of Randall Jarrell, and she has earlier contributed to *The Forties* and *The Fifties* essays on Arthur Miller and Richard Eberhart. She is currently engaged in preparing a vast project on the problem of Freudian determinism and existential freedom in twentieth-century literature.

MAX HALPEREN (Ezra Pound) teaches modern literature at North Carolina State University. His essay is one of the two in this collection reprinted from *The Twenties: Poetry and Prose,* edited by Richard E. Langford and William E. Taylor. Professor Halperen also wrote about Pound for *The Thirties*. He has also published articles on Dylan Thomas and contributed his own work to poetry magazines. He frequently reviews new books for the Raleigh newspapers.

CAROL CLANCEY HARTER (Theodore Dreiser) is University Ombudsman and Assistant Professor of English at Ohio University (Athens), where she has taught since receiving her Ph.D. from the State University of New York. She has published papers on Faulkner in the *Journal of Modern Literature* and on Emerson in the *Emerson Society Quarterly*. She is currently studying the fiction of Joyce Carol Oates, whose "consumer garden" image, Professor Harter calls "another metaphoric delineation of the wasteland." She adds that she sees this wasteland image as not only a focal point of literature in the 1920s — as presented in this book — but "as perhaps the most

predominant image in literature during the entire 20th. century."
Professor Harter won in 1974 a graduate teaching award in English.

FORREST L. INGRAM (Ring Lardner) is Chairman of the English
Department at Moorhead State College, Minnesota. He is primarily
interested in the literary genre that he names and discusses in his
major book, *Representative Short Story Cycles of the Twentieth
Century* (1971). He has long been interested in Ring Lardner and has
earlier written about the short story "Champion" in *Enjoying
American Stories* (1970), which he edited for use in schools in the
Netherlands. He has published also in the Netherlands two
textbooks built around his own original works of fiction, *The Thin
Blue Line* (1970) and *Sugar Sadface and the Windmills* (1972). He
has also co-edited with Lucien Roy *Step Beyond Impasse* (1969) and
translated from the Dutch, *Fifty Psalms* (1968) and J. de Fraine's
Women of the Old Testament (1969). He has published many
articles and reviews and served between 1970 and 1973 as Fiction
Editor and Editor in Chief of the *New Orleans Review.* He has
completed editing a book of articles by a number of critics devoted
to American short-story cycles, and he is readying books on British
and continental cycles.

BLYDEN JACKSON (Langston Hughes, Jean Toomer) is Professor of
English and Associate Dean of the Graduate School at the University
of North Carolina at Chapel Hill. Earlier he was Chairman of the
Department of English and Dean of the Graduate School at
Southern University. He has headed the College Section of the
National Council of Teachers of English and served as a delegate to
the Modern Language Association's Delegate Assembly. Among the
many public service groups with which he has been associated are
the Commission for Academic Affairs of the American Council on
Education, the Post-Secondary Task Force of the Corporation for
Public Broadcasting and the NCTE Research Foundation. Besides
writing many articles on black American literature, he has co-edited
with Louis D. Rubin, Jr., *Black Poetry in America* (1974). He has
also served the College Language Association as Vice President
(1955-57) and President (1957-59) and the Southern Association of
Land-Grant Colleges and State Universities as Vice President
(1968-69).

DAN JAFFE (Don Marquis) is a poet and teacher of creative writing and
modern literature at the University of Missouri-Kansas City. Besides
many poems in national magazines, he has published *Dan Freeman*
(Nebraska, 1967), a poetic biography of the man honored as the first

to file under the Homestead Act in 1867, and *The First Tuesday in November*, a brilliant collage of poems and pictures from the BookMark Press of the Johnson County (Kansas) Library, which he directs. He has also written a play, *Some Ticket Holder Has Your Seat*; a "jazz opera," *All Cats Turn Gray When the Sun Goes Down* (with Kansas City musician Herb Six), and *Nothing Matters But the Mind*, a musical adaptation of Aristophanes' *The Clouds*. He has contributed essays on Archibald MacLeish, the poetry of World War II, and Theodore Roethke to earlier volumes in this "decades" series. He is also the subject of a short film, *Are Poets People?* by Warren French and H. Wayne Schuth, which won a CINE Eagle Award in 1969.

KENNETH JOHNSON (William Carlos Williams) is a Professor of English at Suffolk University, Boston. Since receiving his Ph.D. from the University of Denver, he has also taught at DePauw and the University of Bridgeport and has served as a Danforth Associate. He has also published more than seventy poems in many national magazines, along with book reviews and film reviews. He is particularly interested in teaching and writing about modern poetry and motion pictures. He has contributed to *The Forties* and *The Fifties* essays on Robert Lowell and Richard Wilbur. He is particularly interested in W. C. Williams, whose poetry he feels is still underrated, since "his admirers don't claim enough on his behalf," because his best poems "and the world view that is their source — could be of great value to people today."

SY KAHN (Glenway Wescott) is a fantastically energetic person who has achieved outstanding success as a literary critic, theatrical director, and poet. He is Chairman of the Drama Department at the University of the Pacific, Stockton, California; Director of the school's Pacific Playhouse, and Director of the Summer Repertory residence Theatre, Fallon House Theatre, Columbia State Historic Park, California. Besides supervising two annual theatrical seasons, he has for several years taken his players on European tours during the New Year season. He has also held three Fulbright visiting professorships — at the University of Salonika (Greece, 1958-59), the University of Warsaw (1966-67), and the University of Vienna (1970-71). He has published nearly twenty articles on modern literature, including all four of the previous "decades" books (the only essayist to be so represented). He is co-editing with Professor Martha Raetz a book on twenty years of American Studies at the Vienna University Institute of Translation. His books of poetry include *Our Separate Darkness* (1963), *Triptych* (1964), *A Later*

Sun and *The Fight is with Phantoms* (both 1966) and *Another Time* (1968). He has given approximately two-hundred poetry readings and lectures at colleges in the United States and abroad, and he has appeared often on educational radio and television programs.

A. S. KNOWLES, JR. (John Dos Passos) is a Professor of English at North Carolina State University, specializing in twentieth century literature. He earlier contributed an essay on Carson McCullers to *The Forties*; and he has also written about fiction for *Modern Fiction Studies, Southern Review*, and *Quick Springs of Sense* (1974).

PHILIP MELLING (B. Traven), after receiving his Ph.D. in American Studies with first class honours from the University of Manchester in 1973, became a lecturer in American literature at England's recently founded University of Keele. The article on Traven is his first published critical essay, but he is preparing others on American popular culture in the 1930s. With the assistance of a Fulbright grant, he studied for a year and a half in the United States and taught at Indiana University-Purdue University at Indianapolis. He considers Traven's *Death Ship* an important contribution to anti-war literature and an example of the work of those who while "within the ambience of Marxism, fell outside its orbit and the neat classifications made by *New Masses* entrepreneurs." Away from his American studies, he enjoys fishing and playing rugby.

JAMES E. MILLER, JR. (Fitzgerald, Faulkner's *Sanctuary*), one of the most eminent critics of American literature, was from 1960 to 1966 editor of *College English* and in 1970, President of the National Council of Teachers of English. He is now a member of the editorial board of *PMLA*. After receiving his Ph.D. from the University of Chicago in 1949, he taught at the Universities of Michigan and Nebraska, becoming Professor and Chairman of the Department of English at Nebraska in 1956 and Charles J. Mach Regents Professor of English in 1961. In 1962 he accepted his present position as Professor of English at the University of Chicago, and since then he has been a visiting professor in summer sessions at Northwestern University and the University of Hawaii and a Fulbright lecturer in Japan in 1968. Earlier he was a Fulbright lecturer in Naples and Rome (1958-59). The first of his numerous books, *The Fictional Technique of Scott Fitzgerald* (1957) was subsequently revised as *F. Scott Fitzgerlad: His Art and His Technique* (1964) and provided the background for his contribution to this collection. Subsequently he published *A Critical Guide to "Leaves of Grass"* (1957), which won the Walt Whitman Award of the Poetry Society of America in 1958; *Start with the Sun* (1958, in collaboration with Bernice Slote and Karl Shapiro); *Walt Whitman* (1962), *Reader's Guide to Herman Melville* (1962); *J. D. Salinger* (1965); *Quests Surd and Absurd: Essays in American Literature* (1967); and *Word, Self, Reality: The Rhetoric of Imagination* and *Theory of Fiction: Henry James* (both 1972). He has edited another dozen books, contributed many articles to scholarly journals and encyclopedias and served on many educational boards and commissions.

JORDAN Y. MILLER (Expressionism, Eugene O'Neill) is Professor and Chairman of the Department of English at the University of Rhode Island. He had previously taught at Kansas State University, after receiving his B.A. from Yale and his Ph.D. from Columbia with a dissertation on O'Neill. He has had a life-long interest in theatre and has acted in community theatres and taught courses in drama throughout his career. His bibliographical study of *Eugene O'Neill and the American Critic*, originally published in 1962 appeared in a revised edition in 1974. He has also edited *Playwright's Progress: O'Neill and the Critics* (1965) and *Twentieth Century Interpretations of "A Streetcar Named Desire"* (1971), as well as the standard textbook, *American Dramatic Literature* (1961). He has contributed essays on American drama to the previous volumes in this series and has devoted much of his time to campus film programs and activities of the American Association of University Professors. He has served also as a visiting Fulbright professor at the University of Bombay.

GUY OWEN (Robert Frost) is Professor of English at North Carolina State University, Raleigh, and founder and editor since 1964 of *Southern Poetry Review* which developed from his earlier publication *Impetus*, 1958-1964. He is best known, however, as the author of a group of outstanding lyric novels with North Carolina settings — *Season of Fear* (1960), *The Ballad of the Flim-Flam Man* (1965), *A Journey for Joedel* (1970), and *The Flim-Flam Man and the Apprentice Grifter* (1972). He has also published several books of poetry and over a dozen short stories and served as contributing editor to a number of publications. Besides contributing articles and reviews to many national and regional magazines, he has edited *Modern American Poetry: Essays in Criticism* (1972), a collection of appraisals of the most significant twentieth-century poets. He has served as writer-in-residence at the University of North Carolina at Greensboro and Appalachian State University, and he has given poetry readings and lectures at many colleges in North Carolina and elsewhere. Among other honors he has held a Breadloaf scholarship and a Yaddo fellowship. *Journey for Joedel* received the Sir Walter Raleigh Award for fiction in 1970 and was nominated for a Pulitzer Prize. In 1972 Professor Owen received the North Carolina Award for literature.

DONALD PEASE (Hart Crane) is an Assistant Professor of English at Dartmouth College, specializing in modern American literature. He contributed an essay on James Purdy to *The Fifties* and a study of the relationship of Milton, Blake, Walt Whitman, and Hart Crane to a seminar on "Blake and the Modens" at the 1974 MLA meeting; and he has taped several lectures on Norman Mailer, Kurt Vonnegut, Jr., Edward Albee, and other recent apocalyptic writers for the "Cassette Curriculum." He has also written two plays, *The Confession*, produced at the University of Missouri-Kansas City, and *It*, printed in the *Harrison Street Review*.

DAVID G. PUGH (Sinclair Lewis) is an Associate Professor of English at Western Michigan University, where he has taught since 1955, following graduate work at the Universities of Chicago and Iowa and a brief teaching stint in Faulkner country at the University of Mississippi. He has contributed essays to the earlier "decades" books on Proletarian fiction (*The Thirties*), best-sellers (*The Forties*) and Elizabeth Spencer and the Mississippi Mystique (*The Fifties*). Concerning his interest in Sinclair Lewis, the subject of increasing numbers of sympathetic reappraisals, Professor Pugh writes, "I've always been interested in how the cues in print evoke a variety of responses in the reader, and how much variation occurs because the reader's own experiences resonate differently as he fills in or supplies meanings to what he reads."

GENE W. RUOFF (Faulkner) is Associate Professor and Director of Undergraduate Studies in the Department of English, University of Illinois at Chicago Circle. Since receiving his Ph.D. from the University of Wisconsin, he has specialized in modern fiction and British Romantic poetry, contributing articles on Wordsworth's language and imagination to *Modern Language Quarterly, Studies in Romanticism*, and *The Wordsworth Circle*. He has also contributed to *The Thirties, The Forties*, and *The Fifties*, essays on the New Criticism, Truman Capote, and James Agee, reflecting the interest in Southern literature that grows out of his background as a native Kentuckian.

BERNICE SLOTE (Willa Cather), Professor of English at the University
of Nebraska and Editor of the distinguished literary journal *Prairie
Schooner*, has been the guiding spirit behind recent activities
culminating in the International Seminar on "The Art of Willa
Cather" at Lincoln, Nebraska, October 25-28, 1973, celebrating the
centennial of the novelist's birth in Virginia. Professor Slote is
editing the proceedings of this gathering of scholars from all over the
world for publication as *The Art of Willa Cather*. Earlier she has
edited with introductory essays themselves book length, *The
Kingdom of Art: Willa Cather's First Principles and Critical
Statements 1893-1896* (1966), a two-volume gathering of the
novelist's writings while a student at the University of Nebraska, as
well as *April Twilights* (Willa Cather's early poetry) and *Uncle
Valentine and Other Stories*, bringing together uncollected works.
She also provided the text for *Willa Cather: A Pictorial Memoir*
(1973) and wrote the survey of Cather scholarship for *Sixteen
Modern American Authors*. Despite her preoccupation with Willa
Cather, Professor Slote has also published, besides numerous articles,
Keats and the Dramatic Principle, Start with the Sun (with James E.
Miller, Jr., and Karl Shapiro) and for several years contributed the
essay on "Whitman and Dickinson" to *American Literary Scholar-
ship*. Her extraordinary labors have been honored by the awarding of
an honorary degree of Doctor of Letters from Nebraska Wesleyan
University.

JONAS SPATZ (Ring Lardner) is an Associate Professor, who teaches
principally nineteenth-century English literature at the University of
Missouri-Kansas City. A native of Brooklyn, he completed his Ph.D.
at Indiana University. He has published *Hollywood in Fiction: Some
Versions of The American Myth* (1969) and contributed articles to
The Thirties and *The Forties* on Fitzgerald and Dreiser. He has also
contributed "Love and Death in Tennyson's *Maud*" to *Texas Studies
in Language and Literature* and "The Mystery of Eros: Sexual
Initiation in Coleridge's *Christabel*" to *PMLA*.

ELEANOR RACKOW WIDMER (Edith Wharton) is a writer and lecturer
on modern literature at the University of California, San Diego. She
has published a novella, *Mister Jack*, and has completed another
novel, *The Trouble with Diogenes*. She has also written for the
previous books in this series about John Dos Passos's women,
Malcolm Lowry's *Under the Volcano*, and Mary McCarthy. Her essay
on Edith Wharton is part of her continuing interest in female writers
of the nineteenth and twentieth centuries. She has edited anthologies on literary censorship and *Freedom and Culture* and

contributed reviews to *Arts in Society* and the *Village Voice*. She also paints.

KINGSLEY WIDMER (The American Breakdown) is a prolific critic of the American scene and professor of literature at San Diego State University. Since receiving his Ph.D. from the University of Washington, he has taught also at California-Berkeley, Tel Aviv, Simon Fraser, Nice, Reed College, and the State University of New York at Buffalo. His books include *The Art of Perversity: D. H. Lawrence* (1962), *Henry Miller* (1963), *The Literary Rebel* (1965), *The Ways of Nihilism: Melville's Short Novels* (1970), and *The End of Culture: Essays on Sensibility in Contemporary Society* (1974). Besides contributing to the earlier books in this series key essays on Nathanael West, the Atom bomb and literature, and the Beat Generation, he has published a hundred-odd articles, essays and anthology pieces on, as he puts it, "literature from Milton to Mailer and social and cultural criticism from an anarchist point of view." He has also contributed light verse to various small magazines and pieces of "new journalism" to the *Village Voice* and other outlets. His efforts have won him a Ford Foundation Internship in Humanities, the *New Republic* Young Critics Award, and an Outstanding Educator Award from the American Education Association.

Index

Ackley, Donald G., 326.
Adams, Henry, 437, 470.
Adams, Richard P., *Faulkner: Myth and Motion*, 242, 244-45.
American Dream, 200-204.
Anderson, Sherwood, 65-74, 323; "Adventure," 70-71; "Death in the Woods," 65, 68; "Hands," 69-70; "Sophistication," 71-72; "The Thinker," 72-73; *Triumph of the Egg*, 65; *Winesburg, Ohio*, 65-74, 317, 485.
Aristotle, 159.
Arizona, 14.
Armstrong, Louis, 309.
Auden, W. H., 147, 361.
Austin, Allen, 95.

Baker, Carlos, *Hemingway: The Writer as Artist*, 225.
Baker, George Pierce, 455.
Baker, Sheridan, 227.
Baldwin, James, *Go Tell It on the Mountain*, 312.
Barth, John, *Lost in the Funhouse*, 317.
Baudelaire, Charles, 99, 358, 476, 479.
Beckett, Samuel, 163.
Belasco, David, 452.
Bell, Bernard, 321.
Berry, Wendell, 421.
Blackmur, R. P., 477, 494.
Black Voices (1968), 320.
Blake, William, 294, 402, 479.
Blitzstein, Marc, *The Cradle Will Rock*, 453.
Bone, Robert, *The Negro Novel in America*, 320-21, 325.
Bontemps, Arna, 318.
Brace, Marjorie, 178.
Bradbrook, M. C., *T. S. Eliot*, 5.
Bradbury, Malcolm, *The American Novel in the Nineteen Twenties*, 208.
Breslin, James E., *William Carlos Williams: An American Artist*, 384.

Cummings, E. E., 125, 149; 365-75; 482, 494; *The Enormous Room*, 143, 150, 367-68; *Him*, 373-74; "How I Do Not Love Italy," 372; "An Imaginary Dialogue....," 372-73; *is 5*, 370-72; "Poem," 370; *Tulips and Chimneys*, 369; "Why I Like America," 371-72

Dadaism, 482.
Daley, Mayor Richard, 92.
Dante, *Inferno*, 54-56, 92, 316, 476.
Dark Symphony (1968), 320.
Darwin, Charles, 206.
Davis, Robert Gorham, 66.
de la Mare, Walter, 356.
Delauney, Robert, 168-69.
Dial, The, 39, 371.
Dickens, Charles, 479; *Bleak House*, 30; *Our Mutual Friend*, 3, 25.
Dixon, Melvin, 322.
Doerflinger, William, 143.
Don Quixote, 87.
Dooley, D. J., 90.
Dos Passos, John, 123-37, 224, 368, 483-84; *Manhattan Transfer*, 132-37, 484; *One Man's Initiation*, 127-28, 131; *A Pushcart at the Curb*, 131-32, *Rosinante to the Road Again*, 132-33; *Streets of Night*, 124-26, 131, 484; *Three Soldiers*, 127-31, 483; *U.S.A.*, 124, 130, 132, 134, 136-38, 484.
Douglass, Frederick, 305, 307, 311.
Doyle, John Robert, *The Poetry of Robert Frost*, 355.
Dreiser, Theodore, 24, 51-64; *An American Tragedy*, 51-64.
DuBois, W. E. B., 319.
Duncan, Bowie, 328, 333.
Dunne, Finley Peter, 92.
Durrell, Lawrence, 367.

Edison, Thomas, 86.
Eliot, T. S., 1-26, 29, 32, 75, 87, 92, 96, 106, 125, 133, 178-79, 182-91, 231, 244-45, 335, 369, 387, 398-99, 402, 407, 408-09, 412, 415-16, 420, 425, 454, 469, 473, 475-96; "American Literature and Language," 354; *Ara Vus Prec*, 6; "Ash-Wednesday," 16-18, 25, 232; "Aunt Helen," 5; *The Cocktail Party*, 22; "East Coker," 21; *For Lancelot Andrewes*, 14; *Four Quartets*, 18-19, 22, 152, 296,300, 386; "Gerontion," 6, 8, 9, 12-13, 15, 19, 20, 98, 103, 218, 222; 379-82, 400; "Hamlet and His Problems," 184; "The Hollow Men," 15-17, 203, 218, 227, 263, 487; "Love Song of J. Alfred Prufrock," 5, 85-86, 102-03, 125, 401, 477; "Portrait of a Lady," 5; "Preludes,"